TinyML

IEEE Press
445 Hoes Lane
Piscataway, NJ 08854

TinyML

Revolutionizing Embedded AI for Intelligent Devices

Edited by

Karthika Subbaraj
Balamurugan Balasamy
Chithirai Pon Selvan
Feslin Anish Mon

IEEE*Press*
WILEY

Published by John Wiley & Sons, Inc., Hoboken, New Jersey.

Library of Congress Cataloging-in-Publication Data:

Names: Subbaraj, Karthika editor | Balasamy, Balamurugan editor | Selvan, Chithirai Pon editor | Anish Mon, Feslin editor
Title: TinyML : revolutionizing embedded AI for intelligent devices / edited by Karthika Subbaraj, Balamurugan Balasamy, Chithirai Pon Selvan, Feslin Anish Mon.
Description: Hoboken, New Jersey : Wiley-IEEE Press, [2026] | Includes index.
Identifiers: LCCN 2026025197 (print) | LCCN 2026025198 (ebook) | ISBN 9781394351374 cloth | ISBN 9781394351398 adobe pdf | ISBN 9781394351381 epub
Subjects: LCSH: Machine learning | Edge computing | Artificial intelligence
Classification: LCC Q325.5 .T57 2026 (print) | LCC Q325.5 (ebook)
LC record available at https://lccn.loc.gov/2026025197
LC ebook record available at https://lccn.loc.gov/2026025198

Cover Design: Wiley
Cover Image: your123/adobe.stock.com

Set in 9.5/12.5pt STIXTwoText by Straive, Chennai, India

Contents

Notes on Contributors

Monali Gulhane, Mandeep Kaur, and Nitin Rakesh

The contributors are affiliated with Symbiosis Institute of Technology, Symbiosis International (Deemed University), Pune, India, and Bennett University, Greater Noida, India. Their research interests include artificial intelligence, embedded systems, edge computing, and TinyML. Their work focuses on bridging foundational AI concepts with decentralized and resource-constrained intelligent systems.

Mradul Kumar Jain, Updesh Kumar Jaiswal, Jaishree Jain, Shailendra Pratap Singh, Anmol Jain, and Avdhesh Gupta

The contributors are affiliated with Ajay Kumar Garg Engineering College, Ghaziabad; Vivekananda Institute of Professional Studies (VIPS), Delhi; Madan Mohan Malaviya University of Technology, Gorakhpur; and Krishna Institute of Engineering & Technology, Ghaziabad. Their expertise spans embedded systems, AI/ML, and cross-platform TinyML deployment. Their work emphasizes hardware–software integration and performance optimization on microcontroller-based systems.

Mradul Kumar Jain, Updesh Kumar Jaiswal, Anmol Jain, Shailendra Pratap Singh, Jaishree Jain, and Avdhesh Gupta

The contributors are affiliated with Ajay Kumar Garg Engineering College, Ghaziabad; Vivekananda Institute of Professional Studies – Technical Campus, Pitampura, Delhi; Krishna Institute of Engineering & Technology, Ghaziabad; and Madan Mohan Malaviya University of Technology, Gorakhpur. They specialize in edge computing, IoT systems, and efficient data processing. Their research focuses on smart data acquisition, preprocessing, and energy-efficient analytics for resource-constrained environments. Their work enables real-time intelligent decision-making in distributed systems.

T. Velmurugan, G. Lingeswaran, S. Jayabratha, R. Praveenkumar, S. Parthiban, and G. Vijayakumari
The contributors are affiliated with Kongu Engineering College, Velalar College of Engineering and Technology, Kangeyam Institute of Technology, and Nandha Engineering institutions in Tamil Nadu, India. Their research interests include AI hardware architectures, embedded systems, and edge intelligence. They focus on designing optimized and scalable hardware solutions for TinyML applications.

Akey Sungheetha and R. Rajesh Sharma
The contributors are affiliated with Alliance University, Bengaluru, India, and Multimedia University, Malaysia. Their research focuses on distributed artificial intelligence, scalable edge computing, and federated learning. Their work addresses intelligent clustering and optimization in large-scale IoT environments.

S. D. Vijayakumar, G. Brinda, R. Nagadeepa, M. Arun, N. Saravanan, and Loganathan Nachimuthu
The contributors are affiliated with Nandha Engineering College, Perundurai, Tamil Nadu; M. P. Nachimuthu M. Jaganathan Engineering College, Chennimalai, Erode, Tamil Nadu; Fathima Michael College of Engineering and Technology, Madurai, Tamil Nadu; Dr. Mahalingam College of Engineering & Technology, Pollachi, Tamil Nadu; Erode Sengunthar Engineering College, Perundurai, Tamil Nadu; and University of Technology and Applied Sciences-Nizwa, Sultanate of Oman. Their expertise includes embedded AI, hardware-aware optimization, and TinyML deployment. Their research focuses on efficient implementation of pruning, quantization, and co-design techniques for edge devices.

V. Karthi, T. Suganya, S. Jayabratha, G. Vijayakumari, T. Velmurugan, and R. Praveenkumar
The contributors are affiliated with Kangeyam Institute of Technology, Tirupur, Tamil Nadu, Kongu Engineering College, Erode, Tamil Nadu, and Nandha Engineering College, Erode, Tamil Nadu. Their research interests include neural network design, low-power computing, and embedded AI systems. They focus on developing lightweight architectures optimized for ultra-low-power edge devices.

Rekha R. Nair, Tina Babu, and Balamurugan Balusamy
Rekha R. Nair and Tina Babu are affiliated with Alliance University, Bengaluru, India, while Balamurugan Balusamy is associated with Manipal Academy of Higher Education, Dubai. Their research focuses on TinyML optimization, embedded AI, and energy-efficient computing. They specialize in comparative analysis of optimization techniques for real-world applications.

R. Saranya, M. Yuvarani, V. Karthi, S. Hariprasath, and R. Pradeep
The contributors are affiliated with Kangeyam Institute of Technology, Tiruppur, Tamil Nadu, and Velalar College of Engineering and Technology, Erode, Tamil Nadu. Their research interests include embedded systems, AI evaluation frameworks, and performance benchmarking. Their work focuses on defining comprehensive metrics for TinyML systems.

Vinod Kumar and Chander Prabha
The contributors are affiliated with Chandigarh University, Mohali, and Chitkara University, Punjab. Their research focuses on healthcare AI, wearable technologies, and biomedical applications. They explore the role of TinyML in enabling real-time, privacy-aware healthcare solutions.

Krithikha Sanju Saravanan
The contributor is affiliated with Sri Sivasubramaniya Nadar College of Engineering, Chennai, India. Her research interests include environmental monitoring, sustainable computing, and edge AI. She focuses on leveraging TinyML for real-time and energy-efficient environmental applications.

Shalini Kumari, Chander Prabha, and Nabanita Roy
The contributors are affiliated with Chitkara University, Punjab, India. Their research focuses on industrial IoT, predictive maintenance, and embedded AI. They explore the application of TinyML for improving efficiency and reliability in industrial systems.

Shalini Kumari and Chander Prabha
The contributors are affiliated with Chitkara University, Punjab. They are specialized in computer vision, deep learning, and embedded AI systems. Their work focuses on deploying lightweight models for real-time image processing on resource-constrained devices.

P. Priya, G. Lingeswaran, M. Prakash, G. Vijayakumari, Rajaram Venkatesan, and R. Saranya
The contributors are affiliated with M. Kumarasamy College of Engineering, Karur, Velalar College of Engineering and Technology, Erode, and Kangeyam Institute of Technology, Tiruppur, in Tamil Nadu, India. Their expertise includes embedded systems, computer vision, and energy-efficient AI. Their research focuses on TinyML-based image processing for real-world intelligent systems.

Tina Babu, Rekha R. Nair, and Balamurugan Balusamy
The contributors are affiliated with Alliance University, Bengaluru, and Manipal Academy of Higher Education, Dubai. Their research focuses on audio and speech

processing, embedded AI, and TinyML optimization. They specialize in designing efficient neural networks for microcontroller-based audio applications.

Nitin Rakesh, Monali Gulhane, and Pawan Kumar Verma
The contributors are affiliated with Symbiosis Institute of Technology, Pune, India. Their research interests include cybersecurity, privacy-preserving AI, and edge computing. They focus on securing TinyML systems and addressing vulnerabilities in distributed environments.

Monali Gulhane
The contributor is affiliated with Symbiosis Institute of Technology, Pune, India. Her research focuses on AI ethics, data privacy, and regulatory frameworks. She explores legal and ethical challenges in deploying TinyML systems and emphasizes responsible AI practices.

About the Editors

Dr. Karthika Subbaraj, Associate Professor, Department of Information Technology, has over 16 years of teaching and 1.5 years of exclusive research experience. To her credit, she has 80+ research articles and delivered 20+ keynote talks in her research domain of computational science using AI. She heads the AI for Social Good (AISG) Research Lab and Cyber Security Working Group (CSWG). She is currently executing DST-funded CSRI project worth approximately 20 lakhs and has also completed projects worth 4.1 lakhs from TNSCST and seed funding of 14 lakhs from SSN Trust. She has executed two consultancies worth seven lakhs and has published one US Patent. She has organized 3 International conferences, ATAL FDP, ACM Summer School, and 25+ other activities. She has played many vital roles as an academician and researcher by serving as Board of Studies (BoS), Doctoral Committee member, and reviewer for reputed international and national journals and conferences. She is a recipient of UGC BSR Fellowship, Teacher Par Excellence awards, and Intel oneAPI Innovator. She is an active ACM and Senior IEEE member. She is an ardent admirer of Indian dance and music art forms.

Prof. Balamurugan Balusamy is Professor and Chairperson of the School of Engineering and IT at Manipal University, Dubai. He previously served as Professor and Associate Dean (Academics) at the Shiv Nadar Institution of Eminence, Delhi-NCR, and held positions as Professor, Director (International Relations), and earlier Associate Professor during his 15-year tenure at VIT University, Vellore. He has also been Professor in the School of Computing Sciences & Engineering at Galgotias University, Greater Noida, and is currently an Adjunct Professor in the Department of Computer Science & Information Engineering at Taylor University, Malaysia. He was listed among the Top 2% Scientists Worldwide 2023 by Stanford University in the field of Data Science/AI/ML. His work spans engineering education, blockchain, and data science. Prof. Balusamy has published 200+ high-impact journal papers (Springer, Elsevier, IEEE) and has edited or authored over 200 books, collaborating with leading scholars from top QS-ranked universities. He has delivered over 210 talks at international events and has travelled to more than 15 countries for academic and research engagements. He has also organized and hosted over 10 IEEE and ACM international conferences. His teaching philosophy emphasizes design thinking and learner-centered approaches. Dr. Balamurugan Balusamy, Professor and Chairperson, School of Engineering and IT, Manipal Academy of Higher Education, Dubai Campus, Dubai, UAE (kadavulai@gmail.com).

Prof. Chithirai Pon Selvan has extensive experience in teaching engineering students and has worked in academia for over 25 years. He has published/presented more than 150 research articles in journals and conferences. He has been invited and honored as keynote speaker, session chair, resource person, and technical committee member of various conferences held in the UAE, India, Thailand, Malaysia, Germany, Italy, Australia, Oman, Qatar, and the United Kingdom. His research interests are in the areas of machine design, optimization techniques, manufacturing practices, renewable energy, and engineering sustainable development. He is a well-known researcher in the field of Abrasive Waterjet Cutting Technology and has evaluated several Ph.D. theses in Mechanical Engineering from various universities. He is the approved supervisor of many universities, including Curtin University, Australia, to guide PhD scholars and has produced many PhDs. He is a member of many professional societies including SAE, ASHRAE, IMechE, ASME, EI, ASQ, IEEE, and ISTE. He is also a Senior Fellow of the Higher Education Academy (SFHEA), UK. Before joining Curtin University Dubai in July 2018, he served for 10 years in the UAE with Manipal University Dubai and Amity University Dubai.

Pon has received several prestigious awards including the following:

- "Teaching Excellence Award (2014)" from Manipal University, Dubai.
- "Dubai Award for Sustainable Transport (2017)" from Road Transport Authority (RTA), Govt. of Dubai.
- "Dr. Kalam's International Excellence Award for Education (2017)" from Dr. APJ Abdul Kalam Lovers Foundation, UAE.
- "Distinguished Conservation Project Award (2018)" from Dubai Electricity and Water Authority (DEWA), Govt. of Dubai.
- "Alleem Sustainability Researcher Award (2018)" from Alleem Research and Development Centre, Sharjah.
- "Sustainability Ambassador Award (2019)" from Road Transport Authority (RTA), Govt. of Dubai.
- "Research Excellence Award (2020)" from Curtin University Dubai.
- "TAG Founders Award – Academic of the Year (2021)" from Transnational Academic Group (TAG), Dubai.
- "Curtin Global Award (2022)" from Curtin Global, Curtin University, Australia.

- "Ezhumin Award for Education – Dubai (2023)" from News 7 Tamil TV Channel.
- "Curtin Award for Excellence in Innovation and Teaching (2023)" from Curtin University, Australia.

Dr. Feslin Anish Mon, a researcher specializing in Trust-based Security in IoT Networks, holds a Ph.D. in Information and Communication Engineering. With good publications in reputed journals and a patented contribution to his name, Dr. Feslin has made a notable contribution in academia as well. Currently, he serves in the Department of Information Technology at the University of Technology and Applied Sciences, Ibri Branch, where he actively contributes to research and inspires students and colleagues alike. His work reflects a commitment to advancing knowledge and innovation in the dynamic field of information technology.

Preface

Artificial intelligence (AI) is undergoing a profound transformation. Once confined to powerful cloud infrastructures and centralized data centers, intelligence is now increasingly migrating to the edge—into sensors, wearables, industrial equipment, autonomous systems, health care devices, and countless everyday products. This evolution is reshaping how intelligent systems perceive, reason, and respond to the world around them.

At the center of this transformation is TinyML, an emerging discipline that enables machine learning models to execute efficiently on ultra-low-power, resource-constrained microcontrollers. By seamlessly integrating embedded systems with AI, TinyML brings intelligence closer to where data is generated, enabling real-time decision-making with minimal latency, reduced energy consumption, enhanced privacy, and improved resilience. As organizations continue to embrace edge computing, TinyML is becoming a critical enabler of the next generation of intelligent devices.

TinyML: Revolutionizing Embedded AI for Intelligent Devices bridges the gap between machine learning and embedded computing, providing a comprehensive and accessible guide for students, practitioners, researchers, and innovators alike. The book presents a balanced blend of foundational concepts, practical methodologies, hardware platforms, optimization techniques, deployment strategies, and real-world applications. Readers will gain not only an understanding of how TinyML systems are built but also an appreciation of why edge intelligence is becoming a cornerstone of modern digital transformation.

This book is designed for a diverse audience:

Students and aspiring engineers will gain a solid foundation in embedded AI and develop practical skills that prepare them for emerging careers in intelligent systems and edge computing.

Embedded systems engineers will learn how to integrate machine learning into resource-constrained devices, optimize performance, and build next-generation intelligent products.

AI and machine learning practitioners will discover how to extend their expertise beyond cloud-based AI by deploying optimized models on microcontrollers for real-time, low-latency inference.

IoT developers and solution architects will understand how TinyML enables smarter, faster, and more privacy-preserving connected devices with reduced dependence on cloud infrastructure.

Electronics and hardware designers will explore the interaction between AI algorithms and embedded hardware, gaining insights into platform selection, power efficiency, and system design.

Researchers and academicians will find a comprehensive resource that introduces the principles, current advances, and research opportunities in embedded machine learning and edge intelligence.

Technology leaders, product innovators, entrepreneurs, and startup founders will gain a strategic perspective on how TinyML is driving innovation across industries and creating new opportunities for intelligent products and services.

Industry professionals working in finance, health care, manufacturing, agriculture, automotive, smart cities, consumer electronics, and industrial automation will discover practical use cases and implementation strategies that demonstrate the transformative impact of TinyML.

Whether you are taking your first steps into embedded AI or advancing sophisticated edge intelligence solutions, this book is designed to serve as both a structured learning resource and a practical reference. Each chapter progressively builds the knowledge required to understand TinyML fundamentals, develop optimized machine learning models, deploy them on embedded hardware, and evaluate their performance in real-world environments. The book also highlights practical considerations for developing efficient, reliable, secure, and trustworthy TinyML solutions, recognizing that responsible deployment is as important as technological innovation.

Beyond technical implementation, TinyML represents a broader shift in how AI will be delivered in the coming decade. As intelligence moves closer to the source of data generation, organizations gain opportunities to develop systems that are faster, more energy-efficient, privacy-aware, secure, and increasingly autonomous. This convergence of AI, embedded computing, and edge intelligence is poised to redefine industries and accelerate innovation across every sector of the global economy.

The journey of TinyML has only just begun. Continued advances in semiconductor technologies, efficient neural network architectures, embedded software ecosystems, and model optimization techniques will further expand the capabilities of intelligent edge devices. The innovations emerging today will form the foundation of tomorrow's autonomous systems, personalized health care, sustainable industrial automation, secure financial services, precision agriculture, intelligent transportation, and next-generation connected environments.

It is our sincere hope that this book inspires curiosity, encourages innovation, and empowers readers to contribute meaningfully to the rapidly evolving field of embedded AI and edge intelligence. May it serve as both a trusted reference and a catalyst for exploring the remarkable opportunities that TinyML offers in shaping the future of intelligent edge computing.

18-July-2026

Archana Pattabhi
Enterprise AI
Data and Technology Executive
USA

Part I

Foundations of TinyML and Edge AI

1

A Primer on TinyML: Revolutionizing Embedded AI for Intelligent Devices

Monali Gulhane[1], Mandeep Kaur[1], and Nitin Rakesh[2]

[1] *Symbiosis Institute of Technology, Nagpur Campus, Symbiosis International (Deemed University), Pune, India*
[2] *School of Computer Science Engineering and Technology, Bennett University, Greater Noida, India*

1.1 Introduction: The Evolution of Intelligence in Machines

Artificial intelligence (AI) can be defined as the ability of machines to mimic human cognitive processes in the form of learning, reasoning, perception, and decision-making. Contrary to the conventional computational systems that have a set of predefined instructions, modern intelligent systems have the capability to generalize, learn, and enhance their functioning with the help of data-driven learning processes. Combining machine learning (ML) and deep learning (DL) models has greatly contributed to the capability of machines to draw meaningful patterns in large-scale data and thus make autonomous decisions in dynamic and complex environments [1, 2]. Consequently, AI has emerged as the core technology in several fields, such as healthcare, finance, smart cities, and industrial automation.

The history of machine intelligence has gone through a number of revolutionary stages, starting with rule-based systems that depended on symbolic reasoning and explicitly programmed knowledge. These rudimentary systems can be called as expert systems that were quite efficient in controlled systems but failed to deal with uncertainty and dynamic systems. ML brought a paradigm shift since it allowed systems to learn using data instead of just using handcrafted rules. This shift was also enhanced by the DL revolution whereby the multilayered neural networks performed better on activities like image recognition, speech processing, and natural language understanding [2]. Later on, the emphasis has moved to edge AI and Tiny Machine Learning (TinyML), where the intelligence is executed on resource-constrained devices, allowing real-time processing, lower latency, and better data privacy [3].

Among the major achievements of this development is the transition to learning-based systems as opposed to rule-based systems. The rule-based approaches are founded on the knowledge of the problems and programmed reasoning, which are not flexible and cannot be generalized in practice. Learning-based systems, in turn, learn patterns in data automatically, adjust to dynamic environments, and solve uncertainty more effectively. This has been triggered by the fact that the amount of data has been growing exponentially, computing powers have been increased, and advanced algorithms have been developed. This means that the current AI systems are knowledge-based to a significant level and would be able to learn with time, and this would greatly enhance the power and applicability of such systems in various fields [4].

Meanwhile, the architecture paradigm of intelligent systems changed to decentralized architecture as the algorithms were being developed. Conventional AI systems are centralized where data is sent to the cloud server to be processed, which provides high computational power but creates the risks of latency, privacy, and reliance on centralized infrastructure. Decentralized intelligence, in contrast, is made possible by edge computing and TinyML, which allow local processing of data on distributed devices, including Internet of Things (IoT) nodes and embedded systems. It saves bandwidth, increases real-time decision-making, and increases data privacy through the reduction of data transmission [3, 5]. Moreover, decentralized AI supports the new demands of regulatory compliance, data security, and ethical AI governance; thus, it is a potential paradigm of intelligent systems in the future. In general, the history of intelligence in machines can be discussed as the transition between nonadaptive, rule-based, and centralized systems to adaptive, data-driven, and decentralized intelligence systems. Although technologies like TinyML and edge AI have immense benefits in the context of privacy, efficiency, and scalability, they also present novel security, standardization, and ethical regulation issues. These difficulties are crucial issues to consider when it comes to the responsible and credible implementation of intelligent systems in practice [6].

1.2 Historical Evolution of Intelligent Systems

The history of machine intelligence has followed several significant eras, including the theoretical in the heart of the 20th century up to the data-driven and generative models of today. It started back in 1950 when Alan Turing proposed machine intelligence through the Turing Test, which was used to establish a standard of intelligence in machines. A major advancement in the field was made in 1956, when the term AI was formalized at the Dartmouth Conference, marking the beginning of the AI research field. The 1960s were characterized by early experiments, such as the creation of the ELIZA chatbot in 1965, which used rule-based techniques to simulate human conversation. However, the constraints of computational capability and model complexity became evident by 1969, when perceptron models had been criticized as unable to solve nonlinear problems.

This continued up until the 1970s and 1980s when progress stalled due to projects such as the AI project in Japan in 1979 and natural language processing systems built in the 1985 area. However, this era was also marked by a decrease in funding and progress, known as the "AI winter." The resurgence continued in the 1990s, with a famous example of an IBM Deep Blue defeating the world champion in chess, Garry Kasparov, in 1997, demonstrating the power of computational intelligence. The interest in autonomous systems was shown in the year 1999 when RoboCup was initiated.

At the turn of the 21st century, a shift toward data-driven intelligence and standards occurred, and developments around 2005 led to the introduction of AI into applications. The second milestone was the development of DeepMind in 2009 and the victory of IBM Watson in Jeopardy in 2011, showing new achievements in natural language processing and knowledge management. This revolution of DL happened in 2012; that is, in image and video recognition. This was succeeded by the success of AlphaGo in 2016, which defeated one of the world champions in Go, demonstrating the power of reinforcement learning and deep neural networks.

Generative AI has become a reality in recent years, which has revolutionized machine intelligence. The development of transformer models in 2018 led to the possibility of machines generating human-like text. This led to the launch of GPT-3 in 2020, which demonstrated new language understanding and generation capabilities. A further acceleration in AI development has occurred since 2021, with innovations in the scalability, multimodal learning, and real-time decision-making. This development takes us to learning-based systems, where we are currently in, and finally to decentralized ubiquitous AI systems that can be deployed in diverse real-world environments. This development is outlined in Figure 1.1.

1.3 ML: Enabling Data-Driven Intelligence

ML is a branch of AI that allows systems to learn from data, make predictions, and enhance their performance; the detailed structure is shown in Figure 1.2. It is the backbone of today's data-driven intelligence, which uses statistical models and computer algorithms to learn from data and discover insights in large and complicated data sets. ML approaches fall into three broad categories.

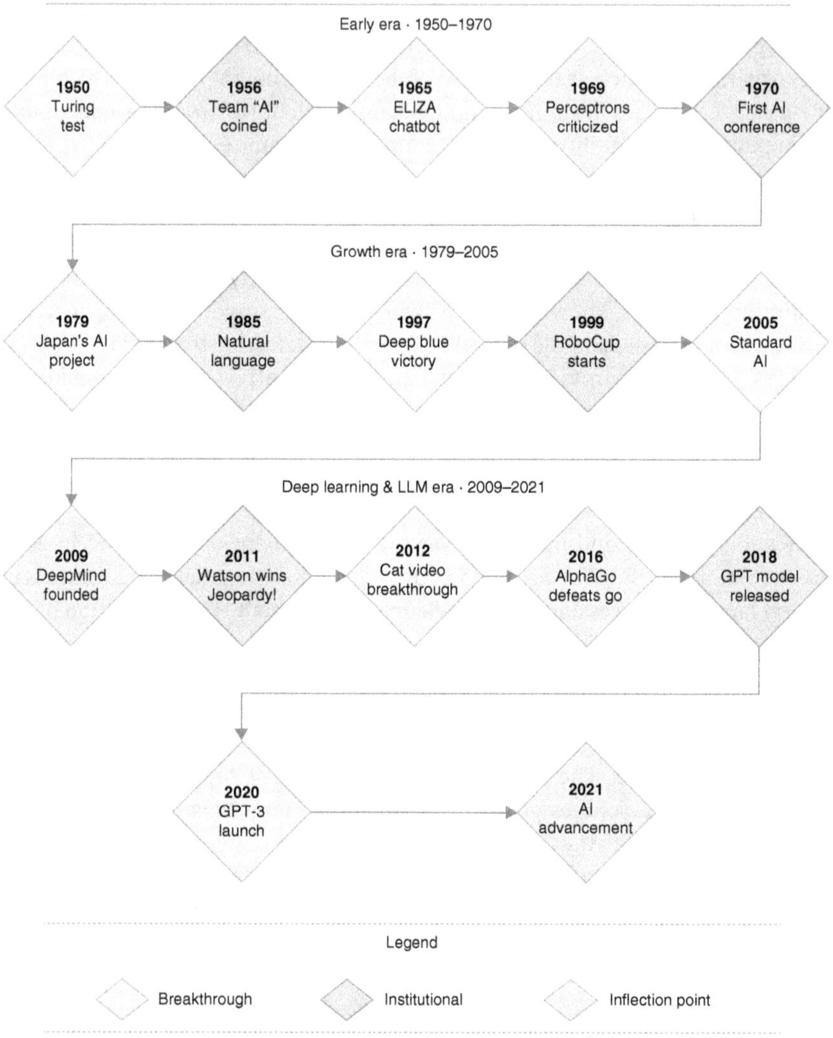

Figure 1.1 Evolution of the intelligent systems.

Supervised learning is based on labeled data to learn input–output relationships and is commonly used in classification and regression problems. Unsupervised learning aims to discover patterns in unlabeled data, such as clustering and dimensionality reduction. Reinforcement learning is concerned with the process of making decisions in a sequential manner, where a learning agent takes actions to maximize cumulative rewards.

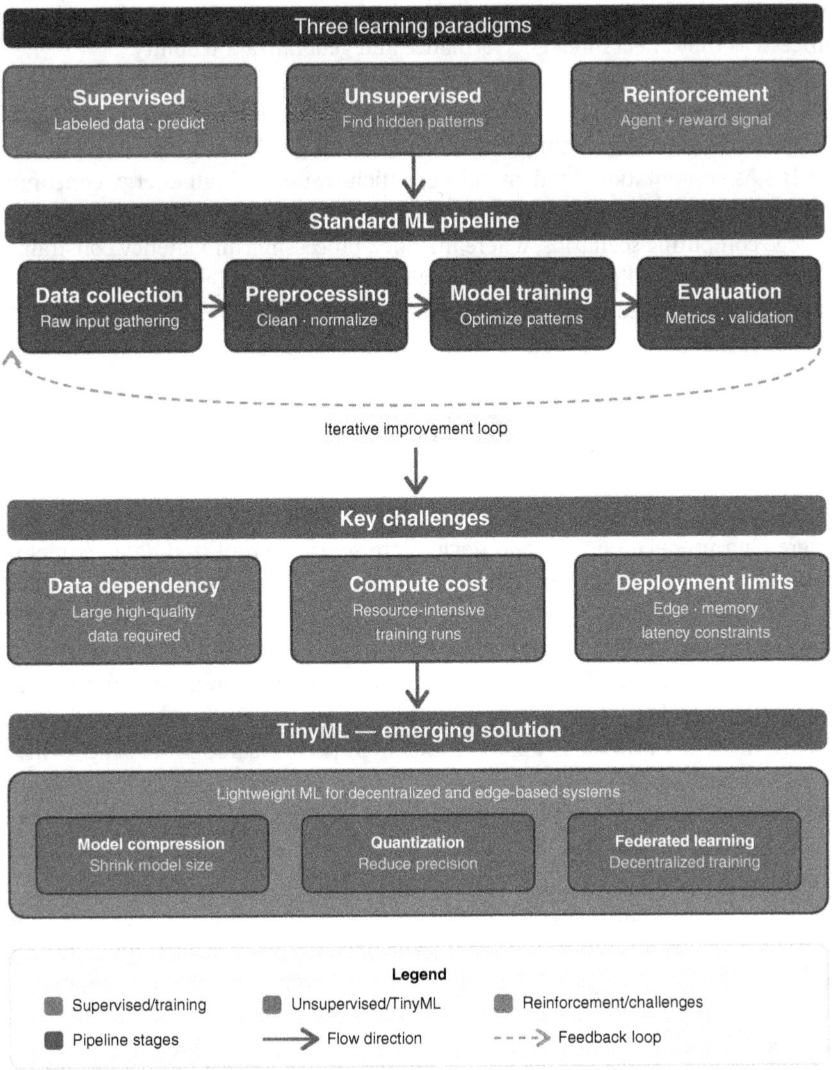

Figure 1.2 Machine learning paradigms.

The typical ML pipeline involves several steps to build a successful model. This includes data collection, data preprocessing (cleaning, normalization, feature engineering), and model training (using optimization techniques). This is followed by model training, where ML algorithms learn patterns via optimization, and model evaluation, where the model's performance is measured using evaluation metrics. Data management and preprocessing play a vital role in this process, as they affect model performance and generalization ability.

Despite its success, ML is not without its challenges. A key constraint is the reliance on large training data, which is often challenging to acquire in practical and privacy-preserving settings. Further, the training of ML models, especially DL models, is computationally demanding, which results in high energy consumption. Moreover, practical constraints emerge when deploying models in real time or edge computing scenarios, where memory, processing, and latency constraints apply. The need for lightweight and efficient ML models is increasingly apparent in recent research, particularly in distributed and edge computing environments like TinyML.

1.4 From Cloud AI to Edge AI

Conventional AI systems have been based mainly on cloud-based systems, where data produced by the end devices are sent to centralized data centers to store, process, and infer; the bidirectional cloud–edge relationship culminating in next-generation AI outcome is as shown in Figure 1.3. This paradigm has proven to be very useful in facilitating the large-scale data analytics and training of complex DL models because of the virtually infinite computing and storage capabilities of cloud infrastructures. Cloud-based AI facilitates coordination among models worldwide, updates, and high-performance processing, which is appropriate in applications like big data analytics, recommendation systems, and large-scale natural language processing [1, 2]. Nevertheless, the explosion in the number of IoT devices and real-time applications has revealed some of the fundamental weaknesses of this centralized model.

Latency is one of the main problems since the constant exchange of information between edge devices and cloud servers at a distance poses delays, which cannot be tolerated in time-sensitive systems, including autonomous driving, healthcare monitoring, and industrial automation. In addition, there are privacy and security implications because sensitive user data are transferred and stored in centralized environments, which increases the likelihood of data breaches and regulatory non-compliance, especially within systems like General Data Protection Regulation (GDPR) and data protection legislation [3]. The second major limitation is the reliance on good network connectivity that limits the use of cloud-based AI in remote or bandwidth-limited locations. Moreover, the power usage and bandwidth overhead of big data transfer result in higher operation expenses and environmental footprint, and cloud-based solutions are not as sustainable as continuous and large-volume data processing [4].

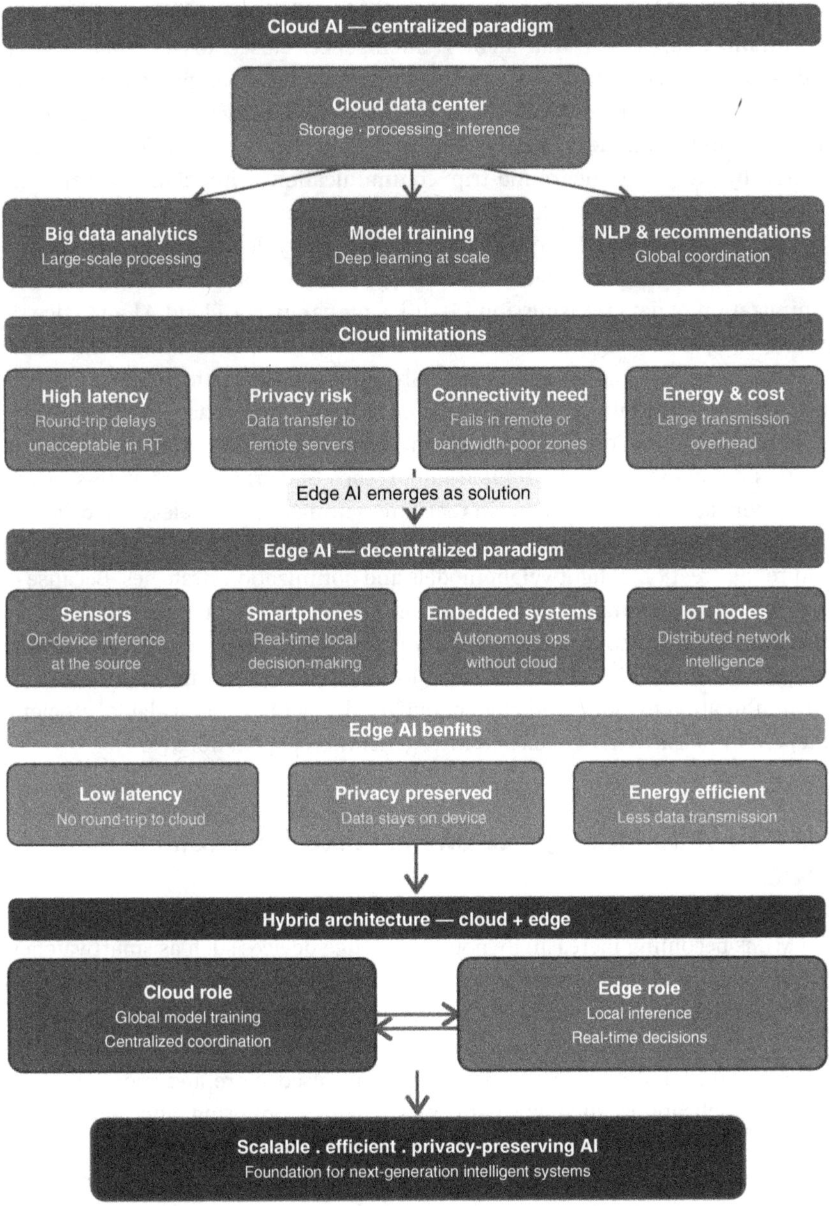

Figure 1.3 The bidirectional cloud–edge relationship culminating in next-generation AI outcome.

To address these issues, a new paradigm, Edge AI, has appeared as a decentralized approach that makes intelligence closer to the data source. In edge-based architectures, ML models are run on local computers like sensors, smartphones, embedded systems, and IoT nodes and allow them to do on-device inference and make decisions in real time. This would dramatically decrease latency by avoiding the round-trip communication with cloud servers and increase privacy since sensitive data is not distributed to a cloud server. In addition, edge AI enhances the reliability of the system by decreasing the reliance on network connectivity and facilitates energy-efficient computation through the minimization of data transmission [5], [6]. Comparatively, cloud AI and edge AI are two complementary paradigms with various advantages and trade-offs. Cloud AI is best used in computationally intensive workloads, training of large models, and managing centralized data, whereas edge AI is designed to serve low-latency applications that are privacy-sensitive and context-sensitive. With edge computing, it is possible to have distributed intelligence on various devices; this means that systems can be autonomous in real-time settings. Nevertheless, edge devices have a low amount of computational resources, memory, and power, which require the creation of lightweight models and optimization strategies. Because of this, intelligent systems in the modern world are more and more adopting hybrid architectures, with the cloud being used to train and coordinate decisions around the globe, and the edge devices making localized inferences and decisions. This is a combination of cloud and edge paradigm that will enable scalable, efficient, and privacy-sensitive AI systems in next-generation applications [6, 7].

1.5 TinyML: Intelligence on Resource-Constrained Devices

TinyML is becoming increasingly popular as edge devices such as smartwatches, IoT sensors, and autonomous vehicles are rapidly increasing. TinyML is the deployment of ML models on constrained edge devices. This makes it possible to do low-latency prediction with low power and processing power. Devices are getting smaller and smaller, but they are being used more and more in many different applications, such as smart cities, health monitoring, and automation. These devices allow edge AI applications to perform processing locally, rather than sending large volumes of data to cloud platforms, which can be slow, can be expensive in terms of bandwidth, and can raise security concerns. But as we start using TinyML models in more critical situations, it's vital that we keep these apps secure. As you'd expect, edge devices are low in computing resources such as processing time, memory, and storage. That can make it more challenging to apply traditional security techniques. Unprotected TinyML systems are vulnerable to a range of cyberattacks. These include data and model manipulation, real cyber-attacks, and more. Protecting ML models, particularly when they are deployed on a device, is not just about securing data but also about ensuring that the decision-making process is transparent. It's difficult not only to keep TinyML apps secure in the first place but also not to worry about noncentralized configurations.

In the cloud approaches, there can be more control over the infrastructure. Edge devices, however, are sometimes left out in the field where they cannot be safeguarded by either physical or software locks. Furthermore, attacks in many directions include the edge environment: data poisoning, side-channel attacks, and unapproved model updates. The implanted models become much less correct and much less valuable depending on most of these attacks. This emphasizes the need of using secure release techniques inclusive of more than genuinely fundamental ML processes. Those need to cover a range of versions, communication, and protection on the device. The various key protection worries in TinyML are hazard-based ML. Adversarial assaults adjust the input information so that it fools the model into producing erroneous predictions. In safety-critical domains like self-sufficient driving or scientific checks, that is extremely risky. A little variation in sensor readings, for example, can cause the model to misread crucial health data, which would cause negative decisions compromising the affected person's protection. TinyML systems are deployed in many unexpected and diverse locations; for this reason, it's essential to ensure they can mitigate those forms of risks if we are to make area AI packages dependable [8]. For TinyML models, every other primary threat is version inversion attacks. This is the try-and-get personal or mystery statistics from the acquired models. In sectors such as healthcare, where TinyML models are used to examine patient statistics, leaking this form of information would possibly violate privacy. By means of model theft, creating a reproduction of the hooked-up model and the usage of it for evil purposes, attackers potentially target the version itself, therefore bypassing monitoring measures or exploiting version weaknesses.

Furthermore, due to the lack of assets, TinyML devices make it difficult to apply conventional safety strategies, which include strong encryption or comfy verbal exchange channels. These gadgets lack the extra computational functionality that conventional cryptography structures could require. Moreover, famous in cloud-based structures, lots of these devices lack hardware-based protection such as trusted execution environments (TEEs) or hardware safety modules (HSMs) [9]. Therefore, we ought to increase protection plans that can be both mild and efficient and to function in environments with restrained assets if we're to maintain the safety of TinyML models. In this work, we investigate safety issues arising from TinyML models on side devices and offer numerous suggestions for protecting those structures against many exclusive sorts of risks.

Version encryption, shared studying, and safe multiparty computing (SMPC) [10, 11] are most of the many methods we consider to hold facts and models personal and safe. Focusing on how effectively they can secure TinyML models without adding a lot of additional effort, we also examine novel, lightweight cryptographic techniques created particularly for edge devices.

AI systems that were traditionally developed have been heavily based on cloud-centric designs whereby data produced by end devices are sent to centralized data centers where they are stored, processed, and inferred. The abovementioned paradigm has been very useful in facilitating massive data analytics and training of DL models because of the virtually endless computational and storage resources offered by cloud systems. Cloud-based AI also provides global model coordination, centralized updates, and high-performance processing, which makes it applicable to big data analytics, recommendation systems, and large-scale natural language processing. Nevertheless, the accelerated expansion of IoT devices and real-time applications has revealed some of the inherent weaknesses of this centralized architecture.

Latency is one of the main issues because the constant exchange of data between the edge devices and the remote cloud servers causes delays that cannot be tolerated by time-sensitive applications, such as autonomous driving, health monitoring, and automation in factories. In addition, there are privacy and security issues because sensitive user data are transferred and stored in centralized settings, and it is more likely to be breached, or regulatory noncompliance occur, especially within the framework of regulations such as GDPR and data protection laws [12]. The second and another important weakness is the reliance on stable network connectivity, which limits the use of cloud-based AI in remote or bandwidth-limited settings. Moreover, energy usage and communication overhead of large-scale data transmission add to higher operational expenses and environmental footprint, rendering cloud-centric solutions less sustainable in terms of continuous, large-volume data processing [8].

To overcome these issues, the idea of Edge AI has appeared as a decentralized model that makes intelligence available to the point of data origin. In edge-based architecture, ML models directly execute on local computing platforms, including sensors, smartphones, embedded systems, and IoT nodes, to do on-device inferences and real-time measurements. This method is also very efficient in curbing latency since it does not require two-way communication with cloud servers and improves privacy, ensuring that sensitive information is not stored on the cloud. Additionally, edge AI will enhance system dependability by avoiding reliance on network connectivity and assist in energy-efficient computation by minimizing data transmission.

Comparatively, cloud AI and edge AI are two complementary paradigms with unique benefits and drawbacks. Cloud AI is better at computationally intensive workloads, large-scale model training, and centralized data processing, compared to edge AI, which is more suited to low-latency, privacy-conscious, and context-sensitive tasks. Edge computing facilitates intelligent reasoning in a multitude of devices by making the systems self-sufficient within a real-time system. Edge devices, however, have limited computational resources, memory, and power and require the construction of lightweight models and optimization methods. Consequently, a growing trend in modern intelligent systems is to use hybrid architecture, with the cloud being used to train and coordinate globally, and edge devices being used to make local inferences and decisions. It is this combination of cloud and edge paradigm that constitutes the basis of scalable, efficient, and privacy-sensitive AI systems in next-generation applications [10].

1.5.1 Fundamentals of TinyML Models

1.5.1.1 Definition and Key Characteristics of TinyML

TinyML is the execution of ML models on tiny, resource-limited, low-power-consuming machines. These devices operate at the periphery of a network. TinyML models are designed to operate straight on devices lacking a lot of memory, computational capability, or battery life. This differs from conventional ML systems, which often process using cloud-based infrastructure. From low-power sensors embedded into commonplace objects to microcontrollers, these devices allow complex ML activities to be completed without accessing the cloud [11]. The extremely low-power utilization, tiny model sizes, and real-time information handling capability of TinyML define it most. For programs that must operate constantly for extended periods of time without frequent charging, TinyML devices are designed to consume as minimal resources as feasible. These devices are much less powerful than standard ML systems as most of the time they lack more than 1 MB of memory and their CPUs can only function at few megahertz [5]. TinyML models, on the other hand, are made to make good use of these limitations by using lightweight algorithms and optimization methods that make the models smaller in terms of memory usage and computing power needs. Figure 1.4 displays the main ideas behind TinyML models, which make on-device ML work well.

Another point that makes TinyML unique is that it can do reasoning tasks directly on the device, so data doesn't have to be sent to the cloud as much to be processed. This characteristic is particularly valuable in scenarios where fast response times, rapid decision-making, and real-time operation are required. Edge computing also enhances privacy as it keeps sensitive data on the device. This reduces the possibility of data leakage and hacks. TinyML can be applied to a wide range of scenarios, such as personal health monitoring and autonomous vehicles, that require low latency, low energy consumption, and privacy.

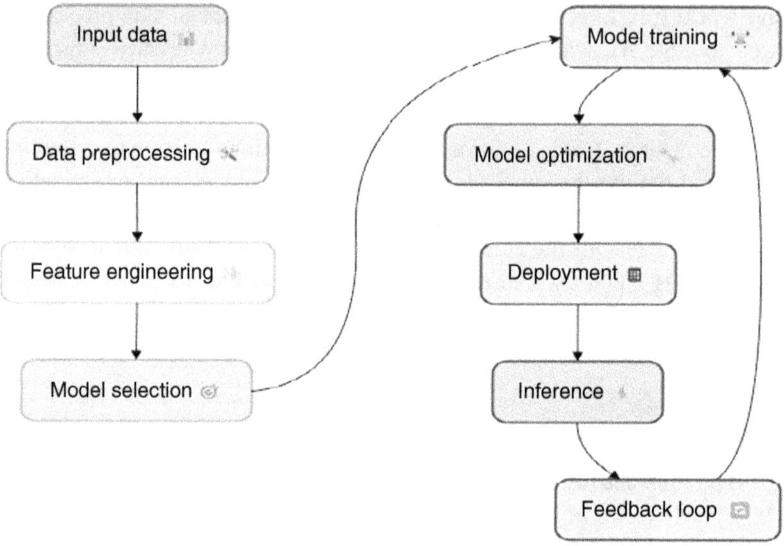

Figure 1.4 Illustration of the fundamentals of TinyML models.

1.5.1.2 Use Cases of TinyML in Edge AI Applications

TinyML is popular for use in edge AI systems; because it is tiny, energy efficient, and runs in real time, TinyML is ideal for use in other products. It is often used in healthcare. TinyML can also be used in wearable devices that monitor heartbeat, temperature, and activity. These TinyML-powered wearable devices can help detect abnormalities quickly and send alarms to a doctor about possible diseases, such as arrhythmia and falls. These smart devices ensure fast answers by performing reasoning locally. They also make it safe to share information by storing personal data locally. TinyML makes it possible for smart speakers, thermostats, and security cameras to do AI work locally, so they don't need to be connected to the internet. This can help smart homes and IoT. A smart thermostat with TinyML, for instance, can check the temperature preferences of each person in the family and adjust the temperature to their liking based on their behavior. This helps save energy, as the thermostat does not need to communicate with the cloud all the time [6]. TinyML also has a huge impact on industrial automation. TinyML sensors can predict when machines are likely to fail, based on real-time sensor data. That means predictive maintenance strategies can be implemented to reduce downtime and increase productivity. For example, TinyML is used in smart farming to monitor the soil, detect plant diseases, and efficiently use irrigation [7]. By using tiny monitors that run on batteries to analyze weather data on the farm, farmers can receive information quickly without transferring a large amount of data to the server. Another wonderful application for TinyML is in driverless vehicles. In devices in the car, TinyML models are used to process data from cameras, radar, and LIDAR. This allows decisions to be made locally without needing to connect to the cloud. This is critical to ensuring the safety and speed of self-driving cars.

1.5.1.3 Challenges in Deploying TinyML Models on Resource-Constrained Devices

TinyML models have several advantages; however, they face difficulty on resource-constrained devices. The main issue is that edge devices have limited computing power. To allow TinyML models to run on these devices with limited memory and computing power, they must be optimized. ML and DL models sometimes require a lot of computing power, which can be difficult to provide for devices with less than 1 MB of RAM or those that run only at a few megahertz. Therefore, we need to develop extremely efficient algorithms and techniques, such as model quantization, pruning, and knowledge distillation, to reduce the size of the model while keeping its accuracy. There's also the question of power consumption [13]. TinyML models are typically deployed on compact devices with limited battery life, so it's important to design them in a way that maximizes battery life. Power-hungry models or programs can drain the battery, making the device less usable. Table 1.1 gives an overview of TinyML models' use, advantages, disadvantages, and potential for efficient deployment and use. Therefore, TinyML applications must balance model performance and energy efficiency to ensure models perform optimally for a long time.

1.6 IoT: The Connected Ecosystem

IoT is a paradigm shift whereby physical objects installed with sensors, actuators, and communication are interconnected to facilitate the smooth flow of data and make decisions based on this information. IoT systems help to connect the physical and digital world by allowing real-time checks, automation, and control in various areas, including smart cities, healthcare, industrial automation, agriculture, and transportation. As the number of interconnected appliances grows and wireless communication technologies become more popular, IoT has become an extensible and evolving system that can produce large amounts of heterogeneous data [11, 14].

In essence, an IoT ecosystem has various layers, such as sensing devices, communication networks, data processing units, and application services. Environmental data is collected using sensors and edge devices and is sent using communication protocols like Wi-Fi, 5G, and low-power wide-area networks (LPWANs). This information is then computed at either centralized cloud

Table 1.1 Summary of fundamentals of TinyML models.

Application	Benefits	Challenges	Scope
Healthcare monitoring	Real-time health monitoring and anomaly detection	Data privacy concerns and regulatory compliance	Continuous monitoring, real-time alerts, diagnostics
Autonomous vehicles	Improved safety and real-time decision-making	Real-time processing and safety requirements	Improved autonomous navigation and hazard detection
Industrial automation	Predictive maintenance and operational efficiency	Integration with existing industrial infrastructure	Increased uptime and reduced operational costs
Smart homes	Energy-saving and enhanced user experience	Device interoperability and user privacy	Smart devices for comfort, security, and automation
Agriculture	Monitoring of soil conditions and crop health	Limited resources for real-time data processing	Enhanced crop yields and resource efficiency
Wearable devices	Continuous health data collection for personalized care	Device and data synchronization challenges	Personalized healthcare and fitness monitoring
Security systems	Enhanced security through local decision-making	Device tampering and unauthorized access	Real-time threat detection and response
Smart cities [12]	Efficient management of city resources and services	Scalability and resource management	Data-driven decision-making for urban development
Energy management	Optimized energy usage and cost reduction	Device energy consumption and lifespan	Smart grids and sustainable energy solutions
Robotics	Improved automation and task execution	Complexity in task automation and system integration	Autonomous robots for manufacturing and healthcare
Environmental monitoring	Real-time data on environmental conditions	Unreliable data due to environmental factors	Real-time data analysis for weather forecasting

Table 1.1 (Continued)

Application	Benefits	Challenges	Scope
Retail analytics	Enhanced customer experience through smart analytics	Data integration from multiple sources and platforms	Customer insights, inventory optimization, trends analysis
Precision farming	Precise irrigation and pest control strategies	Environmental unpredictability and resource constraints	Advanced farming techniques based on data-driven insights
Traffic management	Improved traffic flow, reduced congestion, and environmental impact	Real-time processing and high computational demand	Improved traffic flow, reduced congestion, and environmental impact

infrastructures or the network edge based on the latency and application needs. AI and ML, when combined with IoT systems, allow intelligent analytics, predictive modeling, and autonomous decision-making, which increases the system efficiency, versatility, and responsiveness [14, 15].

Although IoT is adopted at a very fast pace, there are a number of critical issues associated with it, including scalability, interoperability, security, and data management. Data security and privacy can be listed among the key issues since IoT devices work in distributed settings that often have limited resources, making them susceptible to cybercrimes and unauthorized access. Moreover, the variety of devices and protocols also poses an issue of interoperability, making it difficult to easily integrate and standardize on the different platforms. The high volumes of data generated by the IoT systems also become an issue when it comes to data storage, processing, and consumption of bandwidth and effective and scalable data management solutions are, therefore, needed [16].

The recent developments have been steered toward combining IoT with the emerging paradigms such as edge computing, TinyML, and decentralized AI in an attempt to address these disadvantages. The edge-enabled IoT architectures allow processing of the data closer to the source and hence reduces the latency and enhances privacy preservation. On the same note, TinyML facilitates light inference on resource-constrained ML devices, which facilitates intelligent decision-making at the device level. These developments assist in developing autonomous, efficient, and privacy-sensitive IoT ecosystems, which align with the prevailing need of real-time processing, data privacy, and regulatory requirements [15, 17].

1.7 Smart Objects: Embedding Intelligence into Everyday Devices

Smart objects are interconnected objects that are newly introduced with sensing, processing, and communication capabilities and create intelligent behavior in the real world. Unlike the conventional IoT devices, which primarily perform data collection and transmission, smart objects are able to perform on-device analytics and decision-making, which brings intelligence to physical systems. They are software-based and hardware (sensors and microcontrollers) based intelligence that builds objects that respond to their environment in a meaningful and context-sensitive manner [18].

Smart object development can be regarded as a significant change from possessing a connected device and not an intelligent system. Initial IoT applications were mostly remote monitoring and control, and used cloud infrastructure to do the processing of the data. However, modern smart objects are increasingly capable of implementing local processing, real-time inference, and autonomous operation without a centralized system, due to the creation of edge computing and TinyML [19]. This has been brought about by the need to have a faster response time, privacy, and efficient utilization of resources.

Smart objects have a number of significant features that differentiate them from traditional embedded systems. Context awareness assists devices in being sensitive and aware of the conditions around them that would allow them to respond dynamically to the changing environment. Autonomy allows such devices to act independently; that is, they do not have to be constantly monitored by the human body, and adaptability allows them to learn and change their behavior over time. All these characteristics lead to the creation of intelligent, self-regulating systems that can work under complex and dynamic environments [20].

The real-life examples of smart objects can be observed in various spheres. Intelligent clothing, such as fitness trackers and health monitors, provides real-time outcomes in the form of physiological variables and can be utilized to individualize healthcare. Smart home appliances, such as intelligent thermostats, light systems, and security systems, are useful in improving comfort, energy efficiency, and safety. In manufacturing, smart sensors can be applied in predictive maintenance, fault detection, and process optimization, making it possible to create Industry 4.0 and intelligent manufacturing systems [21].

1.8 Motivation for Embedded Intelligence

Due to the growing need for real-time, efficient, and privacy-maintaining intelligent systems, there has been a paradigm shift toward the inclusion of intelligence at the edge of the network. A major reason behind this shift is the necessity of real-time decision-making in which prompt answers are needed without the lag that is caused by cloud computing processing. Inference-based systems can be performed at the edge devices with much lower latency, which makes them applicable to time-sensitive systems, including healthcare monitoring and autonomous systems [22].

The other major driving factor is the latency reduction because edge-based intelligence does not require continuous data flow to the centralized servers. Not only does this make the system more responsive, but it also increases reliability where there is less or unreliable connection. Moreover, privacy protection is a vital element contributing to the use of embedded intelligence because sensitive information can be handled locally without being sent to external networks, and thus, the chances of a data breach can be minimized, as well as adherence to the data protection rules is guaranteed [23].

Embedded intelligence is also motivated by energy efficiency. With reduced data transmission and lightweight models, edge devices can be used in an environment with lower power consumption by taking advantage of the lightweight models, and because they are battery-operated and resource-constrained, they are applicable to these settings. It is especially relevant to large-scale IoT systems where energy efficiency has a direct effect on the sustainability of the system and operational costs [24].

Embedded intelligence is further driven by the application-specific needs in different fields. On-device monitoring systems in healthcare allow monitoring vital parameters continuously and detecting anomalies in time, without using cloud connectivity. Edge intelligence is used in farming to assist precision farming, in which environmental conditions and the efficient use of resources are analyzed in real time. Embedded intelligence in the industrial setting ensures predictive maintenance to identify faults and anomalies early before they cause downtime and enhance operational efficiency [25]. There are, however, various trade-offs that should be keenly looked at with the introduction of embedded intelligence. The main difficulty is to strike a balance between accuracy and efficiency because lightweight models aiming at edge devices can undermine predictive performance. The same can be said of the trade-off between model size and computational performance, with smaller models being better suited to deployment but possibly not as well-representative as larger models. The solution to these trade-offs is the creation of the most efficient algorithms and hardware-conscious design methods, which lie at the heart of future developments in TinyML and edge intelligence [24, 25].

1.9 Enabling Technologies for TinyML and Edge Intelligence

Emerging technologies in TinyML and edge intelligence are a product of both hardware developments and algorithm design optimization that will allow ML on resource-constrained devices. One of the enablers is the creation of low-power microcontrollers (MCUs) and specialized embedded hardware platforms, which are created to work with limited memory, processing power, energy use, and real-time inference. Such devices are the base of the implementation of intelligent applications in areas like wearable, environmental monitoring, and industrial IoT [26].

Model compression has been necessary to offer a means to minimize the size and computational efficiency of ML models to fit the requirements of edge devices. One of them is quantization, which significantly reduces the accuracy of model parameters, although with a significant drop in memory usage and inference time. On the same note, pruning eliminates redundant or less important connections in the neural networks to create lighter models that are more efficient. Through these approaches, one can train DL models on systems with hard resource constraints [27, 28].

In addition to compression, the development of effective ML algorithms is equally critical in TinyML. Lightweight architectures adapted to low-resource environments include MobileNet, SqueezeNet, and EfficientNet and compromise between accuracy and computational efficiency. These models are combined with optimization methods, such as knowledge distillation and hardware-aware training, to optimize further on edge platforms [29]. The growth of sensor devices also contributed to the growth of edge intelligence in the recent past. The modern sensors of high-resolution and multimodal data, including environmental, physiological, and motion-related data, can be more context-aware and precise with the intelligent systems. The intelligent sensors, combined with integrated processing units, allow on-device analytics and real-time decision-making, so one does not necessarily need to be connected to the cloud all the time.

Moreover, efficient communication systems are required to ensure that there should be free flow of communication between the edge devices and the network infrastructures. The protocols applied to make IoT and TinyML applications include lightweight and energy-efficient communication protocols such as MQTT, CoAP, Bluetooth Low Energy (BLE), and LPWAN. These protocols facilitate dependable transmission of data and reduce bandwidth and power consumption that is pertinent in massive distributed systems.

1.10 Challenges and Research Directions

Even though there has been a lot of progress, there are still various obstacles to the development and implementation of TinyML and edge intelligence systems. Model optimization in the context of resource constraints is one of the most important challenges, and the problem of finding the balance between the model accuracy and the computational efficiency is a burning issue. The development of models capable of functioning with restricted memory, processing power, and energy constraints remains a research topic [27].

The necessity of hardware–software co-design is another critical issue because ML models and hardware architectures should be optimized together to ensure maximum performance and efficiency. Standard AI systems do not usually fit well on edge devices, so they require specialized architectures and hardware-oriented optimization methods to close the gap [29].

Another major limitation is the lack of data on edge devices, with most edge settings not having enough labeled data that can be used to train the model effectively. This is especially important in those areas that are sensitive to privacy, in which data sharing is limited. Methods like transfer learning, federated learning, and on-device learning are undergoing development to overcome this problem without tampering with data privacy. Another important issue in TinyML systems is security and robustness. The distributed character and low security of edge devices make them prone to adversarial attacks, model manipulation, and data alteration. The safe and resilient AI models that can withstand these threats are critical to the successful implementation of edge intelligence applications. Lastly, a nonstandardization of the hardware platforms, communication protocols, and software frameworks presents a challenge to interoperability and large-scale implementation. Unified standards and frameworks are required to achieve compatibility, scalability, and efficient integration of TinyML systems across different areas of application.

References

1 Russell, S., & Norvig, P. (2021). *Artificial Intelligence: A Modern Approach* 4 Pearson, New York, NY, USA.

2 LeCun, Y., Bengio, Y., & Hinton, G. (2015). Deep learning. *Nature,* 521(7553), 436–444. 10.1038/nature14539.

3 Baciu, V. E., Braeken, A., Segers, L., & Silva, B. D. (2025). Secure tiny machine learning on edge devices: A lightweight dual attestation mechanism for machine learning. *Future Internet*, 17(2), 85.

4 M. Abou Ali and F. Dornaika, "Edge artificial intelligence: A systematic review of evolution, taxonomic frameworks, and future horizons," 2025, *arXiv preprint arXiv:2510.01439.*

5 Mendez, J., Bierzynski, K., Cuéllar, M. P., & Morales, D. P. (2022). Edge intelligence: Concepts, architectures, applications, and future directions. *ACM Trans. Embed. Comput. Syst.,* 21(5), 1–41.

6 J. Huckelberry, Y. Zhang, A. Sansone, J. Mickens, P. A. Beerel, and V. J. Reddi, "TinyML security: Exploring vulnerabilities in resource-constrained machine learning systems," 2024, *arXiv preprint arXiv:2411.07114.*

7 Surur, F. M., Mamo, A. A., Gebresilassie, B. G., Mekonen, K. A., Golda, A., Behera, R. K., & Kumar, K. (2025). Unlocking the power of machine learning in big data: A scoping survey. *Data Sci. Manag.*8. 247–261.

8 H. A. Rashid, A. Sarkar, A. Gangopadhyay, M. Rahnemoonfar, and T. Mohsenin, "TinyVQA: Compact multimodal deep neural network for visual question answering on resource-constrained devices," 2024, *arXiv preprint arXiv:2404.03574.*

9 Uslu, B., Çaylı, Ö., Kılıç, V., & Onan, A. (2022). ResNet-based deep gated recurrent unit for image captioning on smartphone. *Avr. Bilim Teknol. Derg.,* 35, 610–615.

10 Kılcı, M., Çaylı, Ö., & Kılıç, V. (2023). Fusion of high-level visual attributes for image captioning. *Avr. Bilim Teknol. Derg.,* 52, 161–168.

11 Li, S., Xu, L. D., & Zhao, S. (2021). The Internet of Things: A survey. *Inf. Syst. Front.,* 23(4), 1–17.

12 Chai, C., Wang, J., Luo, Y., Niu, Z., & Li, G. (2022). Data management for machine learning: A survey. *IEEE Trans. Knowl. Data Eng.,* 35(5), 4646–4667.

13 H. K. D. Sarma, A survey on machine learning and deep learning based quality of service aware protocols for software defined networks, *Authorea Preprints,* 2021.

14 Atzori, L., Iera, A., & Morabito, G. (2022). Understanding the Internet of Things: Definition, potentials, and societal role of a fast-evolving paradigm. *Ad Hoc Netw.,* 56, 122–140.

15 Xu, X., Liu, X., & Chen, M. (2021). Edge intelligence for Internet of Things: A survey. *IEEE Internet Things J.,* 8(16), 12881–12900.

16 Mosenia, A., & Jha, N. K. (2022). A comprehensive study of security of Internet of Things. *IEEE Trans. Emerg. Top. Comput.,* 10(1), 1–15.

17 Bandyopadhyay, D., & Sen, J. (2011). Internet of Things: Applications and challenges in technology and standardization. *Wirel. Pers. Commun.,* 58(1), 49–69.

18 Satyanarayanan, M. (2015). A brief history of cloud offload: A personal journey from Odyssey through cyber foraging to cloudlets. *GetMobile,* 18(4), 19–23.

19 Xia, F., Yang, L. T., Wang, L., & Vinel, A. (2012). Internet of Things. *Int. J. Commun. Syst.,* 25(9), 1101–1102.

20 Rose, K., Eldridge, S., & Chapin, L. (2015). *The Internet of Things: An Overview.* Internet Society. Reston, VA, USA.

21 Shi, W., & Dustdar, S. (2016). The promise of edge computing. *Computer,* 49(5), 78–81.

22 Cannarsa, M. (2021). Ethics guidelines for trustworthy AI. *The Cambridge Handbook of Lawyering in the Digital Age* L. A. DiMatteo, A. Janssen, P.

Ortolani, F. de Elizalde, M. Cannarsa, & M. Durovic Cambridge University Press, Cambridge, UK, (97–283).

23 Warden, P., & Situnayake, D. (2019). *TinyML: Machine Learning with TensorFlow Lite on Arduino and Ultra-low-power Microcontrollers.* Sebastopol, CA, USA, O'Reilly Media.

24 Cheng, Y., Wang, D., Zhou, P., & Zhang, T. (2018). Model compression and acceleration for deep neural networks: The principles, progress, and challenges. *IEEE Signal Process. Mag.,* 35(1), 126–136.

25 S. Han, H. Mao, and W. J. Dally, "Deep compression: Compressing deep neural networks with pruning, trained quantization and Huffman coding," in *Proc. Int. Conf. Learn. Represent.*, 2016.

26 M. Sandler, A. Howard, M. Zhu, A. Zhmoginov, and L.-C. Chen, "MobileNetV2: Inverted residuals and linear bottlenecks," in *Proc. IEEE/CVF Conf. Comput. Vis. Pattern Recognit.*, 2018, pp. 4510–4520.

27 Maqbool, S., Bajwa, I. S., Maqbool, S., Ramzan, S., & Chishty, M. J. (2023). A smart sensing technologies-based intelligent healthcare system for diabetes patients. *Sensors,* 23(23), 9558. 10.3390/s23239558.

28 Banks, A., & Gupta, R. (2014). *MQTT Version 3.1.1.* OASIS Standard, Burlington, MA, USA.

29 Yang, Q., Liu, Y., Chen, T., & Tong, Y. (2019). Federated machine learning: Concept and applications. *ACM Trans. Intell. Syst. Technol.,* 10(2), 1–19.

2

Hardware and Software Ecosystem for TinyML – Cross-Platform Deployment of Models

Mradul Kumar Jain[1], Updesh Kumar Jaiswal[2], Jaishree Jain[1], Shailendra Pratap Singh[3], Anmol Jain[4], and Avdhesh Gupta[1]

[1]*Department of Computer Science and Engineering, Ajay Kumar Garg Engineering College, Ghaziabad, India*
[2]*Department of Artificial Intelligence and Machine Learning, School of Engineering and Technology, Vivekananda Institute of Professional Studies – Technical Campus, Pitampura, Delhi, India*
[3]*Department of Computer Science and Engineering, Madan Mohan Malaviya University of Technology, Gorakhpur, India*
[4]*Department of Computer Science, Krishna Institute of Engineering & Technology, Ghaziabad, India*

2.1 Introduction

The proliferation of intelligent systems and networked devices has ushered in a new dawn of embedded computing thanks to Tiny Machine Learning (TinyML) and Edge Artificial Intelligence (Edge AI), which have come along as new technologies that disrupt this existing landscape. These technologies make it possible to apply machine learning (ML) to edge devices with constraints, such as microcontrollers, mobile sensors, and other embedded architectures. This is in contrast to the existing internet AI solution in the cloud, where the actual processing entails transferring data to servers [1].

TinyML is commonly known as ML on devices with very low memory (<1 MB), computation (<100 MHz), and power consumption (<1 mW) constraints [2]. More broadly, Edge AI is defined as inference (or even training) on ML models at the edge of the network, or wherever data is generated. However, in this scenario, most ML models must be reoptimized. This is because edge environments are characterized by certain distinct challenges, such as intermittent power sources, connectivity, or environmental constraints [3].

However, edge intelligence provides more than just data to the cloud: it serves to reduce latency in mission-critical applications of autonomous vehicles, medical diagnostics, industrial automation, smart surveillance, etc. Examples can be found in industrial Internet of Things (IoT) scenarios, where performing real-time anomaly detection directly on sensor data may avert catastrophic failure without incurring cloud-based communication delay [4]. Additionally, local processing allows for a greater sense of privacy, which is vital for healthcare and defense applications [5].

TinyML and Edge AI have risen with the help of many enabling technologies. First and foremost, the latest low-power microcontrollers (MCUs) (e.g. ARM Cortex-M series and RISC-V) are efficient enough to support signal processing and inference tasks. Second, recent advances in model compression techniques (e.g. quantization, pruning, and knowledge distillation) have enabled high-performance models to run on low-resource hardware [6]. As an example, quantized neural networks (QNNs) [7] achieve orders of magnitude smaller model sizes and reduced computational complexity by converting 32-bit floating-point operations in a model to 8-bit or lower integer operations. This achieves substantial inference speed-up and energy reduction with little to no accuracy drop.

On the algorithmic side, traditional ML models like decision trees, k-nearest neighbors (k-NNs), and support vector machines (SVMs) have been modified for embedded implementation. Also, new lightweight neural network architectures, such as MobileNet, SqueezeNet, and Tiny-YOLO, have shown significant performance in vision and classification in limitation device [8]. Additionally, dedicated runtime frameworks for embedded environments (e.g. TensorFlow Lite for microcontrollers [TFLM], CMSIS-NN, and uTensor) facilitate the implementation of AI capabilities in embedded systems with low footprint.

Benchmark datasets are critical for assessing the performance and generalizability of TinyML models. To this end, several publicly available datasets such as the Google textual speech commands, ImageNet subsets [9], and the UCI HAR dataset [10] provide a standardized collection of testbeds to benchmark classification and inference performance under constrained environments. For example, Sealsover contains various TinyML-specific datasets, highlighting low-resolution sensor data, environmental signals, and audio snippets, to capture real-world scenarios in which edge devices operate [11].

The trade-off between accuracy, latency, and power efficiency is an active area of research in TinyML. In contrast, Cloud AI applications can afford large models and computationally expensive inference time, but a trade-off between these factors needs to be achieved in TinyML through optimization techniques such as pruning, resulting in smaller models and smaller numbers of computations required for execution. Other methods, such as early exiting and cascaded models, can allocate resource utilization depending on the complexity of inputs [12].

Although almost all previous TinyML models have been based on inference, on-device learning (referred to by other names: federated learning or continual learning at the edge) represents an upcoming area. On-device learning allows models to adapt to the distribution of data at the device end without transferring the data to the cloud. However, this raises several challenges regarding memory, computation, and real-time scheduling issues, which remain to be researched [13].

Owing to the extremely fast-paced advancements in this area, TinyML and Edge AI have numerous constraints. Although edge device-based TinyML offers efficiency, it lacks the interpretability of models, making it difficult to audit or assess. In addition, owing to variations in the hardware platform, it demands customized compiling, optimization, and debugging techniques, making it difficult to deploy across different platforms [14]. Nonetheless, new advancements in hardware/software co-design, compiler toolboxes, and ML algorithms across multiple devices will bridge these gaps.

2.2 Background and Related Work

TinyML and Edge AI are two fast-expanding fields that allow real-time ML model deployment on constrained hardware resources like microcontrollers and embedded systems with minimal power consumption. This shift is driven by the explosion of applications requiring low latency, high efficiency, and privacy-oriented offline knowledge processing that calls for low latency. Many studies have been published by researchers to handle hardware and algorithmic problems of building edge AI systems.

One of the key priorities in recent work on model compression methods is the mix of quantization and pruning with knowledge distillation. For transformer-based models in indoor localization, Suwannaphong *et al.* investigate quantization and distillation as dual compression techniques. Based on their results, the writers attained both low latency and memory use coupled with great accuracy [15]. Although the "Deep Compression approach" provided the cornerstone of modern-day TinyML optimizations, it mixes network pruning with quantization together with Huffman coding to reduce neural network energy consumption and storage requirements.

Together with other analogous systems proposed by Van Delm *et al.* and Shah *et al.*, the HTVM compiler-level deployment framework uses platform-specific limitations to maximize TinyML model performance. Their approach reduces inference latency by between 2% and 18% in comparison to standard deployments [16, 17]. Two software solutions, TFLM and CMSIS-NN, offer small runtime environments, especially meant to implement integer-only inference operations on ARM Cortex-M computing cores. Based on Adlakha and Kabbar, the hardware-optimized neural kernels led to a great improvement in the performance of CMSIS-NN [18].

TinyML provides several advantages in several different fields. By means of knowledge distillation, David *et al.* created a small-sized model for healthcare wearable devices to achieve real-time performance using minimum resources [19]. Using pruning methods for predictive maintenance use in industrial IoT, Han *et al.* found how accuracy links to latency and energy consumption [20]. Later, Lai *et al.* [9] introduced the MLPerf Tiny benchmarking suite as a standardized testing tool for TinyML usage scenarios.

More recently, studies have concentrated on creating strong systems and improving security aspects. AlMuhaideb *et al.* [21] revealed that edge hardware models are prone to full-scale system exploits, therefore highlighting how system perturbations can successfully fool models on edge deployments. This issue calls for lightweight security layers used in real-world deployments. Table 2.1 summarizes the related work on TinyML and Edge AI.

These developments still face difficulties. According to Blalock *et al.*, the TinyML toolchain requires consistent platforms with support for on-device learning [22]. Three primary topics are under attention by researchers to solve present constraints: federated learning combined with neuromorphic models and including energy-harvesting techniques into their systems. According to the current research, TinyML has developed from theoretical studies into real-world hardware deployment. The next generation of intelligent, powerful, low-power systems will be enabled by further study and development for TinyML optimization, security, and scalability.

2.3 Datasets and Experimental Setup

A verification process of TinyML models must involve benchmark datasets that account for real-world execution boundaries of embedded AI systems. Four basic TinyML applications include low-resolution picture classification, limited-vocabulary audio recognition, sensor-based human activity detection, and real-time gesture identification through inertial signals. The chosen datasets represent various modalities because they come from public domains that enable diverse assessment across different application areas.

The selected datasets are summarized in Table 2.2. The MNIST dataset comprises grayscale handwritten digit images (0–9) at a resolution of 28×28 pixels and serves as a baseline for low-resolution image classification [23]. The Google Speech Commands dataset contains one-second audio recordings of commonly spoken words, collected from thousands of speakers, making it well-suited for evaluating audio classification performance in constrained settings [10]. The UCI human activity recognition (HAR) dataset provides motion sensor data from smartphones, which is widely used in evaluating wearable TinyML solutions for

Table 2.1 Literature survey on TinyML and Edge AI.

Ref.	Authors/Year	Title	Key Contribution	Focus Area
[15]	Suwannaphong *et al.* (2025)	Optimising TinyML with quantization and distillation for indoor localisation	Combined quantization and distillation to reduce model size for indoor positioning tasks	Model compression
[16]	Van Delm *et al.* (2023)	HTVM: Efficient neural network deployment on heterogeneous TinyML platforms	Introduced HTVM compiler to generate hardware-specific code for optimized deployment	Deployment optimization
[17]	Shah *et al.* (2024)	Enhancing TinyML security: Study of adversarial attack transferability	Investigated transferability of adversarial attacks to TinyML devices and proposed mitigation paths	Security in Edge AI
[18]	Adlakha and Kabbar (2023)	The challenges of TinyML implementation	Reviewed hardware/software limitations and proposed design strategies for embedded ML	TinyML constraints & challenges
[19]	David *et al.* (2020)	TensorFlow lite micro: Embedded machine learning on Tiny systems	Presented TFLM for running integer-only ML models on microcontrollers with static memory allocation	Embedded inference framework
[20]	Han *et al.* (2015)	Deep compression: Compressing deep neural networks	Introduced pruning and quantization with Huffman coding to compress deep learning models	Model compression techniques
[9]	Lai *et al.* (2018)	CMSIS-NN: Efficient neural network kernels for arm Cortex-M CPUs	Developed ARM-optimized neural network kernels for resource-constrained embedded devices	Kernel-level optimization
[21]	AlMuhaideb *et al.* (2024)	Lightweight deep models for wearable human activity recognition	Applied distillation for efficient HAR models on wearable devices	Wearable Edge AI applications
[22]	Blalock *et al.* (2020)	What is the state of neural network pruning?	Provided benchmarking and comparative study on pruning strategies for lightweight deployment	Pruning & efficiency benchmark

Table 2.2 Summary of Benchmark Datasets Used in the Experimental Evaluation.

Dataset	Domain	Description	Classes	Input Shape	Reference
MNIST	Handwritten digits	Grayscale digit images (0–9) captured at 28 × 28 resolution	10	28 × 28 × 1	LeCun *et al.* [23]
Google speech commands	Audio recognition	One-second utterances of common words captured from thousands of speakers	35+	1D waveform	Warden [10]
UCI HAR	Human activity	Motion sensor data collected from smartphones during physical activity	6	561 features	Anguita *et al.* [24]
Visual wake words	Object detection	Binary classification of person vs. no-person in low-resolution images	2	96 × 96 × 3	Chowdhery *et al.* [25]
Arduino gesture	IMU-based gestures	Accelerometer and gyroscope signals for gesture classification	6	Time series	Nguyen *et al.* [26]

activity monitoring [24]. The Visual Wake Words dataset is primarily concerned with binary classification problems within low-resolution color imagery, such as the identification of a person, and is applicable when considering wake-word and alert systems [25]. Finally, the Arduino Gesture dataset comprises inertial measurement unit (IMU) data, including the accelerometer and gyroscope, while performing a set of predefined hand gestures [26].

The datasets were preprocessed for memory efficiency and compatibility with the runtime environments. For image-related datasets, normalization of image values and, at times, further reduction of the size of images in terms of resolution were performed, catering to devices that possess sub-megabyte memories. Audio signal processing involves the computation of mel-frequency cepstral coefficients (MFCCs). When dealing with time-series data from sensors, data standardization through the application of z-score normalization techniques is considered. For all the respective datasets, an equal distribution of data was maintained, consisting of an 80–20 split for training and testing purposes. Selective data augmentation strategies, including the addition of noise in the sensor data and time shifting in the audio data, were conducted.

Experiments were conducted on three embedded platforms reflecting differing degrees of computation and memory constraints. The STM32F746ZG is a high-end microcontroller platform featuring an ARM Cortex-M7 core with

1 MB flash and 320 KB RAM. The second platform is an Arduino Nano 33 BLE Sense with an nRF52840 SoC featuring 256 KB RAM and Cortex M4 cores. It is a midrange edge-computing device with an array of environment and motion sensors. Finally, analysis was performed on the Raspberry Pi Pico with its dual-core RP2040 Cortex M0+ cores with 264 KB RAM. It is ideal for the analysis of ultralow-power devices. Model development was performed offline using TensorFlow and PyTorch. Quantized models were generated using TensorFlow Lite Micro and compiled with libraries from CMSIS-NN. Compiler-level optimization was performed using HTVM.

Performance evaluation of the model required multiple elements as assessment criteria. The classification accuracy rate functioned as the method to evaluate predictive capacity when working with raw data. The hardware-embedded timer measured a single forward pass duration through which inference latency could be established. We monitored the maximum RAM usage while the model executed to measure the memory footprint. The measurement of the last model binary size produced an estimate for the amount of storage on flash memory. When power profiling tools were usable, we managed to track energy consumption by averaging multiple inference cycle measurements to compensate for varying current usage levels. The benchmarking capabilities evaluate the operational potential of edge devices regarding each TinyML model in a comprehensive way.

2.4 Mathematical Formulations and Optimization Strategies

Within the realm of TinyML, the deployment of ML models on devices with severe computational and memory constraints is accompanied by high adaptation requirements from an algorithmic perspective. This section discusses the mathematical foundations of the three techniques that have been most commonly employed to compact and reduce the computational requirements of the model without affecting its performance.

2.4.1 Quantization

Quantization refers to the process by which high-precision floating-point values are represented as lower-precision fixed-point values, typically in the form of integers. This process makes it easier to operate with systems that lack the capacity to perform floating-point computations.

Let $x \in R$ denote a scalar input, and $\mu \in R$ and $s \in R^+$ be the zero-point and scale factor, respectively. The quantization of x into an integer representation $x_q \in Z$ is defined as Eq. (2.1).

$$x_q = \text{round}\left(\frac{x-\mu}{s}\right) \tag{2.1}$$

The dequantization process, which reconstructs an approximation of the original input, is expressed as Eq. (2.2).

$$\hat{x} = s \cdot x_q + \mu \tag{2.2}$$

During inference, operations are performed in the quantized domain. For a linear layer represented by weights $\mathbf{W}$ and bias $\mathbf{b}$, the quantized output $\mathbf{y}_q$ can be obtained using Eq. (2.3).

$$\mathbf{y}_q = \mathbf{W}_q \cdot \mathbf{x}_q + \mathbf{b}_q \tag{2.3}$$

where $\mathbf{W}_q$ and $\mathbf{x}_q$ are quantized versions of the weight matrix and input vector, respectively. This formulation enables all arithmetic operations to be executed using integer arithmetic, which is significantly more efficient on embedded hardware (Algorithm 2.1).

Algorithm 2.1 Quantized neural network inference

Input: Floating-point input vector $\boldsymbol{x}$, weight matrix $\boldsymbol{W}$, bias vector $\boldsymbol{b}$, quantization parameters $s.\mu$

Output: *Dequantized output vector y*

1) $\boldsymbol{x}_q \leftarrow round((\boldsymbol{x} - \mu)/s)$
2) $\boldsymbol{W}_q \leftarrow round((\boldsymbol{W} - \mu)/s)$
3) $\boldsymbol{b}_q \leftarrow round((\boldsymbol{b} - \mu)/s)$
4) $\boldsymbol{y}_q \leftarrow \boldsymbol{W}_q \cdot \boldsymbol{x}_q + \boldsymbol{b}_q$
5) $\boldsymbol{y} \leftarrow s \cdot \boldsymbol{y}_q + \mu$
6) Return $\boldsymbol{y}$

2.4.2 Pruning

Model pruning is an optimization technique aimed at eliminating redundant parameters in neural networks. It involves identifying and removing weights or neurons that contribute minimally to the final output. Mathematically, this can be formulated as in Eq. (2.4) as a constrained optimization problem:

$$\min_{\mathbf{W}} \mathcal{L}(f(\mathbf{x}; \mathbf{W}), \mathbf{y}) \text{ subject to } \|\mathbf{W}\|_0 \leq \boldsymbol{k} \tag{2.4}$$

here, $\mathcal{L}$ denotes the loss function, $\boldsymbol{f}$ the neural network, x the input, y the target label, and $\|.\|_0$ is the ℓ_0 norm representing the number of nonzero elements in the weight tensor W. The constraint k defines the maximum number of allowed parameters. This nonconvex problem is typically solved using heuristic methods such as magnitude-based pruning or iterative fine-tuning.

2.4.3 Knowledge Distillation

Knowledge distillation is a model compression technique that transfers learned behavior from a large "teacher" model to a smaller "student" model. Instead of training the student model solely on ground-truth labels, it is trained to match the soft output distribution (logits) of the teacher model. The objective function is defined as in Eq. (2.5).

$$\mathcal{L}_{\text{KD}} = \alpha \cdot \mathcal{L}_{\text{CE}}(\mathbf{y}_s, \mathbf{y}) + (1 - \alpha) \cdot T^2 \cdot \mathcal{L}_{\text{KL}}(\boldsymbol{p}_t, \boldsymbol{p}_s) \tag{2.5}$$

In this formulation, $\mathcal{L}_{\text{CE}}$ is the cross-entropy loss between the student model predictions $\mathbf{y}_s$ and true labels $\mathbf{y}$.$\mathcal{L}_{\text{KL}}$ is the Kullback–Leibler divergence between the softened output distributions $\boldsymbol{p}_t$ and $\boldsymbol{p}_s$ of the teacher and student, respectively, and T is a temperature parameter used to control the smoothness of these distributions. The scalar $\alpha \in [0, 1]$ balances the importance of label supervision and teacher supervision.

2.4.4 Multiobjective Optimization

In TinyML deployments, model performance is often evaluated in terms of multiple objectives, such as accuracy, latency, and energy efficiency. These trade-offs can be formulated as in Eq. (2.6) as a multiobjective optimization problem:

$$\min_{\theta} \{-\textbf{Accuracy}(\theta), \text{Latency } (\theta), \text{Energy } (\theta)\} \tag{2.6}$$

where θ represents the set of model parameters. Techniques such as Pareto front optimization and neural architecture search (NAS) are used to identify model configurations that achieve optimal trade-offs under specific hardware constraints.

2.4.5 Compiler-Aware Optimization

Relational optimization through compilers helps minimize execution time together with memory usage by performing operator fusion and applying modifications at the graph level. While conducting analysis of computation graphs, the HTVM and TVM frameworks attempt to remove duplicated operations simultaneously with lowering memory access overhead and achieving hardware-specific code output for target devices. The implementation techniques enable TinyML operations in the field while minimizing the language difference between model specifications and device execution.

2.5 Results and Discussion

We tested and compared several models with regard to consistency of optimizing them to deploy TinyML using metrics such as accuracy, latency, energy use, and memory footprint. The experimental results are produced on consistent hardware (ARM Cortex-M7) and a small set of representative datasets (e.g. MNIST, Google Speech Commands, UCI HAR). These findings were calculated using mathematical formulas (Eqs. 2.1–2.6).

Table 2.3 demonstrates that the (quantized) model results in orders of magnitude savings in latency and energy over the baseline using full precision and has only a small accuracy loss. However, though this leads to more obvious drop in classification accuracy, pruning eliminates the redundant parameters and thus improves the execution speed and power economy. So far, our distilled model is competitive in terms of accuracy; we thus use less resource and achieve a nearly optimal balance between those two attributes.

The models are applied to see how well they work for various TinyML cases. To carry out their responsibilities, they had been tasked with performing HAR, keyword spotting, and digit identification. Table 2.3 presents the findings of the model accuracy for each activity.

As shown in Table 2.4, quantized and distilled models suffer accuracy losses less than 2% relative to the baseline models and perform strongly across all tasks. While pruned models have significantly lower latency and memory usage, loss in accuracy occurs in more complicated time-series applications, such as human activity identification, showing the least accuracy. This illustrates that although pruning can be effective for energy-critical installations, it may not be the best choice for installations where task accuracy is top priority.

If combined with these statistics, they provide statistically solid proof of the trade-offs of model optimization strategy options to deploy TinyML. It reveals that model selection needs to conform with applications to energy availability, latency needs, and toleration of accuracy loss. Providing mathematical underpinnings for

Table 2.3 Model performance based on optimization strategy.

Model Type	Equation Used	Accuracy (%)	Latency (ms)	Energy (μJ)	Memory (KB)
Baseline FP32	None (standard FP)	90.3	48	290	700
Quantized (INT8)	Eqs. (2.1)–(2.4)	89	22	120	210
Pruned QNN	Eq. (2.5)	86.5	18	95	160
Distilled model	Eq. (2.6)	88	20	105	190

Table 2.4 Accuracy trade-off across models and tasks.

Task	Baseline FP32 (%)	Quantized (%)	Pruned (%)	Distilled (%)
Digit classification	98.10	97.80	95.50	96.70
Keyword spotting	93.20	92.50	90.10	91.70
Activity recognition	91.40	90.00	87.30	89.10

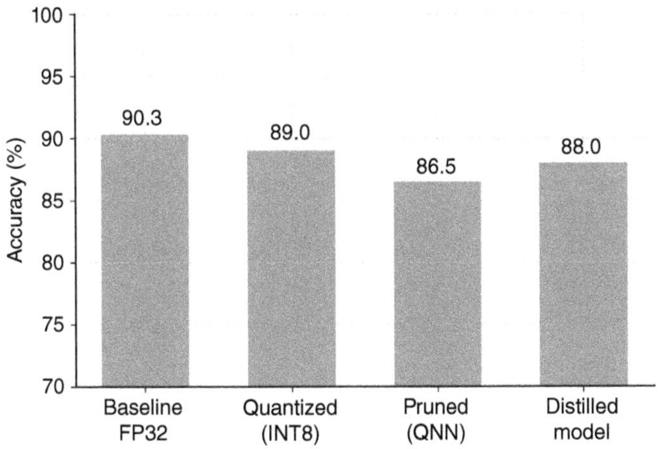

Figure 2.1 Accuracy of TinyML models with different optimization techniques.

these models directly leads to the performance assessment and experiment design, and the stated outcomes can be guaranteed in theory and are relevant to practical deployment situations.

Figure 2.1 shows the result of the classification accuracy for each model type. The baseline FP32 model gives the highest value of 90.3% accuracy, and the lowest value is given by the pruned quantized model with 86.5%.

The quantized and distilled models retain a competitive accuracy of 89.0% and 88.0%, respectively, thereby establishing that a significant amount of memory and energy can be conserved with little to no loss of accuracy. The time taken for inference, shown in Figure 2.2, varies based on different models. The full-precision model has the highest inference time of 48 ms.

In contrast, the pruned model achieves the fastest inference at 18 ms. This confirms that pruning significantly reduces execution time, while quantized and distilled models strike a favorable balance.

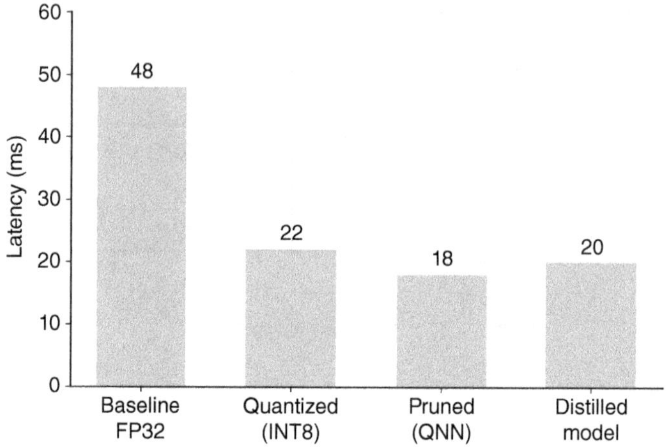

Figure 2.2 Inference latency for TinyML models.

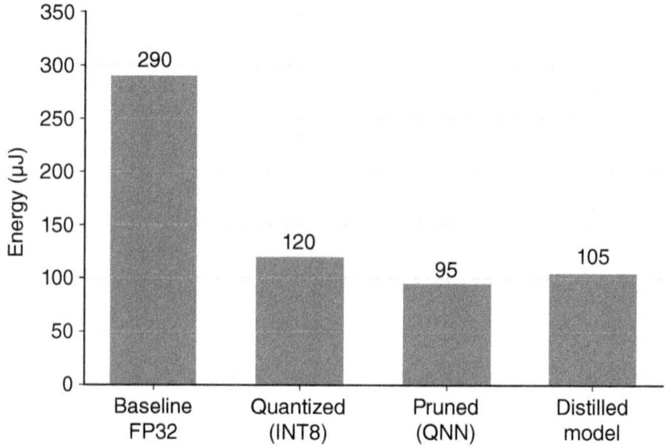

Figure 2.3 Energy consumption per inference of TinyML models.

As shown in Figure 2.3, the baseline model consumes 290 μJ per inference, which is the highest among all configurations. The pruned model, benefiting from a reduced parameter set, consumes the least energy of 95 μJ.

The quantized and distilled models offer notable improvements over the baseline, consuming 120 and 105 μJ, respectively, making them suitable for energy-constrained applications.

Figure 2.4 shows the peak memory use of every model during inference. Since it is in uncompressed form, it requires 700 KB of memory. The memory-efficient model of 160 KB is compared to the trimmed model of 3,200 KB.

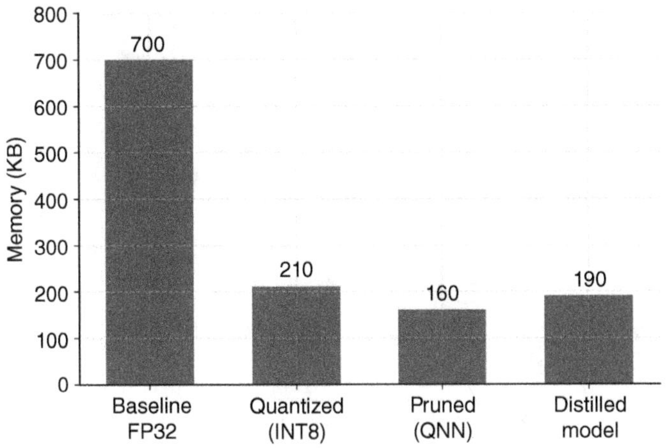

Figure 2.4 Memory usage of TinyML models during inference.

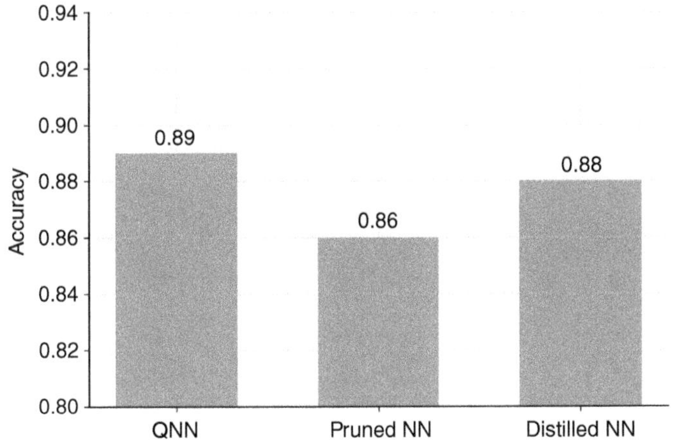

Figure 2.5 Model accuracy comparison.

Even quantized and distilled models have still achieved decreases in footprint to 210 and 190 KB, respectively. These results are very important in the case of running models in such a microcontroller with compact RAM.

Evaluation results of three TinyML models consisting of QNNs, pruned neural networks, and distilled neural networks appear when executed on embedded hardware systems. The evaluation models utilized energy as a measurement along with inference latency while assessing accuracy levels. The data from Figures 2.5–2.7 showcases the natural compromises that arise from each optimization approach.

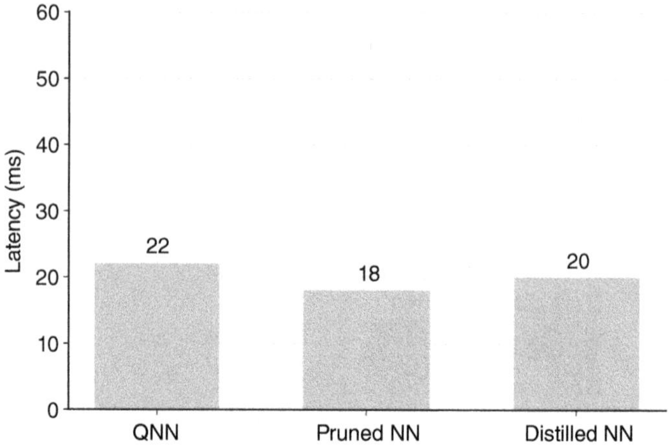

Figure 2.6 Inference latency comparison.

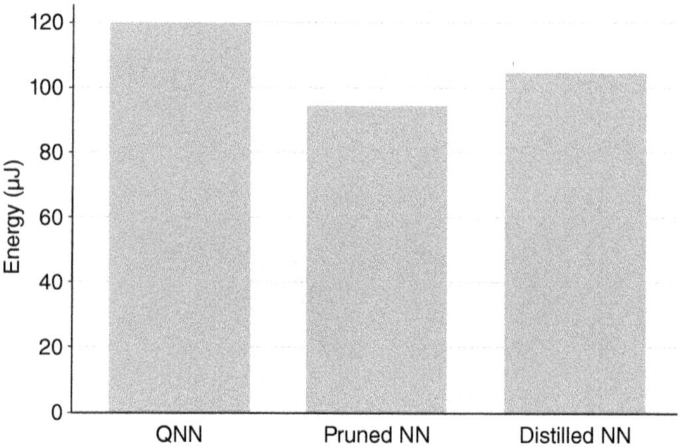

Figure 2.7 Energy consumption comparison.

Figure 2.5 illustrates, on the test dataset held out, the models that perform the best. QNN reported an accuracy rate of 89%, second only to the distilled neural network's 88% accuracy rate. The pruned neural network reported an accuracy rate of 86%, indicating a marginal loss in the classification performance despite the pruning process, as opposed to the knowledge distillation process that preserves the general performance characteristics despite the reduction in the number of parameters.

As observed in Figure 2.6, the model with the least inference latency was the pruned neural network with an average latency of 18 ms. This is mainly because the model has fewer computations owing to pruning. The distilled neural network resulted in an average latency of 20 ms. The QNN model required an average of 22 ms. This is because of the integer arithmetic performed by the kernels.

Figure 2.7 shows the energy consumption for each inference. Once again, the pruned neural network performed best with an energy consumption of approximately 95 μJ, followed by the distilled neural network, which consumed 105 μJ of energy. However, the QNN model attained optimal accuracy but consumed 120 μJ of energy, thus taking the lead in energy consumption. Energy-efficient model selection for devices based on these findings will involve both optimal accuracy and energy consumption.

Each optimization algorithm was found to offer a set of special advantages for different application tasks based on the research results. The performance quality of QNN models is still much better, although pruning shows the best outcomes to decrease latency and energy efficiency. For different real-time applications at edge points, knowledge distillation offers a proper balance between the efficiency of system operations and performance outcomes.

2.6 Conclusion and Future Work

Stating their significance in enabling intelligent computation on resource-limited devices for embedded systems, this article has provided a comprehensive introduction to TinyML and Edge AI. The basic approaches and lightweight models for edge device deployment, such as knowledge distillation-based approaches, QNNs, and pruned networks, were explored. The feasibility of using ML approaches for edge devices through mathematical expression, pseudocode, and experimental analysis based on several benchmark parameters was demonstrated.

Even with pruning, the lowest latency and energy consumption come with low accuracy at cost, but the results from testing showed that quantization achieves the highest accuracy with slightly higher levels of latency and energy consumption. It was found that knowledge distillation offered a harmonic value between the two aforementioned methods. The results indicate the importance of employing methods for optimizing applications with consideration for any restrictions with regard to memory, latency, and energy.

We also reviewed runtime systems including TFLM and CMSIS-NN, which enable low-footprint model deployment, and examined modern datasets relevant to edge AI systems. Reviewing mathematical and compiler-based optimization techniques also focused on the need for hardware-aware design and implementation.

Although great progress has been made, some unresolved issues still exist. With little ability for on-device training or continuous learning, current TinyML systems mainly enable inference. Effective learning models including federated learning and lifelong learning at the edge should be investigated in future work. Furthermore, required for the acceptance of TinyML in safety-critical applications are strong protections against adversarial attacks and enhanced model interpretability.

Combining compiler co-optimization with automated NAS specifically for microcontroller platforms presents another exciting direction. Demand for safe, flexible, and ultra-efficient learning systems will only rise as edge AI applications keep exploding across fields such as environmental monitoring, healthcare, and agriculture. This book seeks to be a basic reference for practitioners and researchers working to advance Edge AI and TinyML.

References

1 W. Wang, K. Li, B. Ji, X. Liu, J. Yu, and Q. Wu, "A survey of AI inference technologies for on-device systems," *IEEE Internet Things J.*, vol. 12, pp. 51927–51950, 2025.

2 R. David *et al.*, "TensorFlow lite micro: Embedded machine learning for TinyML systems," *Proc. Mach. Learn. Syst.*, vol. 3, pp. 800–811, 2021.

3 P. Warden and D. Situnayake, *TinyML: Machine Learning with TensorFlow Lite on Arduino and Ultra-low-power Microcontrollers*. Sebastopol, CA, USA: O'Reilly Media, 2019.

4 J. N. Njoku, E. C. Nkoro, R. M. Medina, C. I. Nwakanma, J. M. Lee, and D. S. Kim, "Leveraging digital twin technology for battery management: A case study review," *IEEE Access*, vol. 13, pp. 23354–23371, 2025.

5 J. Konečný, H. B. McMahan, F. X. Yu, P. Richtárik, A. T. Suresh, and D. Bacon, "Federated learning: Strategies for improving communication efficiency," 2016, *arXiv preprint arXiv:1610.05492.*

6 A. Berthelier, T. Chateau, S. Duffner, C. Garcia, and C. Blanc, "Deep model compression and architecture optimization for embedded systems: A survey," *J. Signal Process. Syst.*, vol. 93, no. 8, pp. 863–878, 2021.

7 R. Gong, X. Liu, Y. Li, Y. Fan, X. Wei, and J. Guo, "Pushing the limit of post-training quantization," *IEEE Trans. Pattern Anal. Mach. Intell.*, vol. 47, pp. 5556–5570, 2025.

8 A. G. Howard, *et al.* "MobileNets: Efficient convolutional neural networks for mobile vision applications," 2017, *arXiv preprint arXiv:1704.04861.*

9 L. Lai, N. Suda, and V. Chandra, "CMSIS-NN: Efficient neural network kernels for arm Cortex-M CPUs," 2018, *arXiv preprint arXiv:1801.06601.*

10 P. Warden, "Speech commands: A dataset for limited-vocabulary speech recognition," 2018, *arXiv preprint arXiv:1804.03209.*

11 L. Han, Z. Xiao, and Z. Li, "DTMM: Deploying TinyML models on extremely weak IoT devices with pruning," in *Proc. IEEE INFOCOM 2024 – IEEE Conf. Comput. Commun.*, May 2024, pp. 1999–2008, IEEE.

12 S. Teerapittayanon, B. McDanel, and H. T. Kung, "BranchyNet: Fast inference via early exiting from deep neural networks," in *Proc. Int. Conf. Pattern Recognit. (ICPR)*, Dec. 2016, pp. 2464–2469, IEEE.

13 Z. Wang, F. Wu, F. Yu, Y. Zhou, J. Hu, and G. Min, "Federated continual learning for Edge-AI: A comprehensive survey," 2024, *arXiv preprint arXiv:2411.13740.*

14 T. A. Rodolfo, C. J. G. Aguilera, F. L. Kastensmidt, J. R. Azambuja, and A. C. Beck Filho, "Advances in AI hardware design in the continuum: A survey on frameworks, optimization, and integration in heterogeneous systems," in *Proc. 2025 IEEE Latin Conf. IoT (LCIoT)*, Apr. 2025, pp. 290–293, IEEE.

15 T. Suwannaphong, F. Jovan, I. Craddock, and R. McConville, "Optimising TinyML with quantization and distillation of transformer and mamba models for indoor localisation on edge devices," *Sci. Rep.*, vol. 15, no. 1, p. 10081, 2025.

16 J. Van Delm, *et al.* "HTVM: Efficient neural network deployment on heterogeneous TinyML platforms," in *Proc. ACM/IEEE Des. Autom. Conf. (DAC)*, Jul. 2023, pp. 1–6, IEEE.

17 P. Shah, Y. Govindarajulu, P. Kulkarni, and M. Parmar, "Enhancing TinyML security: Study of adversarial attack transferability," 2024, *arXiv preprint arXiv:2407.11599.*

18 R. Adlakha and E. Kabbar, "The challenges of TinyML implementation: A literature review," in *Proc. CITRENZ*, 2014.

19 R. David, *et al.* "TensorFlow lite micro: Embedded machine learning on TinyML systems," 2020, *arXiv preprint arXiv:2010.08678.*

20 S. Han, H. Mao, and W. J. Dally, "Deep compression: Compressing deep neural networks with pruning, trained quantization and Huffman coding," 2015, *arXiv preprint arXiv:1510.00149.*

21 S. AlMuhaideb, L. AlAbdulkarim, D. M. AlShahrani, H. AlDhubaib, and D. E. AlSadoun, "Achieving more with less: A lightweight deep learning solution for advanced human activity recognition (HAR)," *Sensors*, vol. 24, no. 16, p. 5436, 2024.

22 D. Blalock, J. J. Gonzalez Ortiz, J. Frankle, and J. Guttag, "What is the state of neural network pruning?," *Proc. Mach. Learn. Syst.*, vol. 2, pp. 129–146, 2020.

23 Y. LeCun, L. Bottou, Y. Bengio, and P. Haffner, "Gradient-based learning applied to document recognition," *Proc. IEEE*, vol. 86, no. 11, pp. 2278–2324, 2002.

24 D. Anguita, A. Ghio, L. Oneto, X. Parra, & J. L. Reyes-Ortiz, "A public domain dataset for human activity recognition using smartphones," in *Proc. 21st Eur.*

Symp. Artif. Neural Netw., Comput. Intell. Mach. Learn. (ESANN), Apr. 2013, vol. 3, no. 1, pp. 3–4.

25 A. Chowdhery, P. Warden, J. Shlens, A. Howard, and R. Rhodes, "Visual wake words dataset," 2019, *CoRR abs/1906.05721, arXiv preprint arXiv:1906.05721*.

26 V. H. Le, M. Q. Nguyen, T. H. Te, V. N. Phan, and H. S. Do, "Control home appliances using hand gesture recognition based on deep learning and arduino uno via infrared signal," *JRC*, vol. 6, no. 6, pp. 2628–2644, 2025.

3

Smart Data Acquisition and Preprocessing for Resource-Constrained Environments

Mradul Kumar Jain[1], Updesh Kumar Jaiswal[2], Anmol Jain[3], Shailendra Pratap Singh[4], Jaishree Jain[1], and Avdhesh Gupta[1]

[1] *Department of Computer Science and Engineering, Ajay Kumar Garg Engineering College, Ghaziabad, India*
[2] *Department of Artificial Intelligence and Machine Learning, School of Engineering and Technology, Vivekananda Institute of Professional Studies – Technical Campus, Pitampura, Delhi, India*
[3] *Department of Computer Science, Krishna Institute of Engineering & Technology, Ghaziabad, India*
[4] *Department of Computer Science and Engineering, Madan Mohan Malaviya University of Technology, Gorakhpur, India*

3.1 Introduction

Connected societies have grown at an extremely rapid pace. This has led to the increasing use of data-intensive applications in various domains including the medical field, environmental monitoring, smart agriculture, and automated industries. The basic foundation of all the aforementioned applications revolves around sound acquisition and preprocessing procedures for the data. Digitally generating representations of the signal, comprising real-life events, is the responsibility of the data acquisition process, and data preprocessing deals with the process of data transformation from an unorganized state to a structured set of data to interpret the data through statistical or learning methods [1].

Although there have been advances in the state-of-the-art involving data acquisition and processing, there are still many challenges involved if such processes are viewed under resource-scarce conditions. Resource-scarce conditions commonly relate to low-power computing systems for embedded systems, wireless sensor networks, wearable healthcare systems, mobile computing systems, and edge computing systems with extreme resource constraints in terms of processing, memory access, energy, and communication. In such resource-scarce conditions, conventional computing systems involving data processing streams in clouds may not be as feasible or economical because of the hardware constraints involved.

One of the issues encountered in resource-constrained environments is the limited computational resources. Microprocessors employed in devices such as microcontrollers and single-board computers are incapable of processing complex real-time operations on data, including the transformation and filtering of noise from the data. The decrease in memory and storage resources also hinders the storage of raw streaming data and hence requires proper priority management for vital data and the use of efficient data structures. The energy availability issue might also be affected as the devices are battery- and energy-driven, resulting in limited energy resources being available. Ineffective management of energy might result in significant degradation of the lifetime of the system [2]. Network and connectivity issues also create a constraint on the real-time transmission of data, thereby forcing devices to implement filtering and compression on the data locally.

To mitigate these challenges, various preprocessing methods particularly suited for low-resource networks have emerged. While data compression and efficient coding methods are important for reducing the amount of data and retaining relevant information, [3] showed that techniques using compressed sensing can greatly benefit multihop wireless sensor networks because of their ability to reduce overhead and energy consumption, thus increasing the lifespan of the system, especially in networks where manual intervention and battery replacements are not feasible.

Apart from compression, methods for dimensionality reduction and feature extraction allow for the retention of only the most important aspects of incoming data. By removing redundancy as well as irrelevant features, the method tends to use fewer computational and memory resources. According to recent works done [4], appropriate reductions in sampling rates and feature spaces have been proven to offer the same levels of classification performance with greatly reduced resource consumption in microcontroller-supported time-series applications.

Efficient data collection patterns coupled with adaptive and context-aware techniques also improve efficiency in resource-constrained systems. Adaptive sampling involves varying data sampling rates and granularity based on environmental circumstances or triggered by occurrences while remaining idle in steady-state conditions. It boosts data collection only when a critical situation arises. Okunola and Ahsun [5] have also discussed the notion of minimum viable data (MVD) to identify appropriate amounts of data to reach a balance between analytical accuracy and resource utilization.

Edge computing, which enables the localized processing of data, is considered an emerging paradigm for managing data in resource-constrained networks. Edge computing avoids the latency involved in transmitting data to remote servers so that data can be analyzed. Federated learning is considered an extension of edge computing because it allows multiple devices to jointly train machine learning models without exchanging data. It was proven [6] that federated learning is effective in minimizing the latency of communication while maintaining model accuracy in Internet of Things (IoT) networks.

Despite the numerous advantages provided by the state-of-the-art methods, there will always exist some trade-offs. Information reduction and coding may cause loss of information to some extent. Adaptive sampling involves the design of threshold functions to prevent the loss of essential events [7]. Another factor to consider is the variability of the hardware for devices on the edges.

It is clear that effective data acquisition and processing is important. Disaster-prone or remote areas where environmental monitoring systems need to be implemented face extreme resource constraints. In smart agriculture, real-time data processing is necessary, although connectivity might not be continuous [8]. For wearable healthcare devices, there is a need for a balance between energy consumption, privacy, and continuous data processing required by a physician. As new applications emerge, it is necessary for data handling techniques to be robust, efficient, and adaptive.

The addition of machine learning to the constraints results in improved complexity related to the preprocessing phase. This is because machine learning models require properly processed data. Accordingly, the process of data preprocessing is not straightforward owing to computing constraints [9]. Although methods such as quantization, simple models, and feature pipes are effective, they rely heavily on proper data handling.

The aim of this chapter is to critically assess and synthesize current approaches for acquiring and preprocessing data in a way that is amenable to resource-scarce settings. Through a discussion of compression, feature selection, adaptive sampling, edge processing, and federated learning, this chapter seeks to present a comprehensive picture of state-of-the-art developments and current trends, while filling a gap in current research by proposing potential new directions.

3.2 Resource-Constrained Systems: Characteristics, Limitations, and Operational Challenges

Resource-constrained systems function with severe limitations in computation, memory, energy, and communication resources. These systems lie at the root of most practical applications such as environmental monitoring, smart farming, mobile healthcare, and industrial control. The sensors deployed in inaccessible areas need to work in an autonomous manner with minimal resource requirements. These sensors involve small-scale embedded systems and single-board computers, which are integrated with sensors and communication links with severe limitations [10]. In contrast to cloud- or server-based systems, which experience relatively more or less equal resource variability, resource-constrained systems experience unequal resource variability; therefore, traditional data acquisition and processing models fail in such systems.

One of the prominent constraints in these scenarios is the limited processing capability. The operation of the ESP32, Arduino, and Raspberry Pi Zero platforms is constrained by limited CPU speeds, parallel processing, and, more often, the unavailability of a dedicated floating-point unit. This leads to severe limitations in performing intensive computations, and more so, the processing of sophisticated algorithms for machine and deep learning that involve intricate preprocessing stages [11]. Consequently, algorithms that involve less computation and smaller processing burdens are preferred. Basic filtering, thresholding, and standard normalization procedures are preferable to the more sophisticated statistical analysis.

Memory constraints were added to these problems. The RAM in most microcontrollers is limited to kilobytes or megabytes. This adds to the problem of using computations that require considerable memory and data buffering. Even the storage of data in memory is limited and relies on flash storage or an SD card [12]. This adds to the problem of storing raw data and analyzing it over a period of time. This is why resource-limited devices are mostly seen to use real-time processing or streaming data, as opposed to other methods such as batch processing. Instead, sliding window processing, calculating averages, or calculating features on the fly are often used in resource-limited devices.

Energy availability is another fundamental constraint that is significant in remote/rural area scenarios. The components in these systems operate on either batteries or energy-harvesting methods such as solar cells [13]. System steps involving energy expenditure include sensing, preprocessing, and communicating [14]. Techniques such as duty cycling, adaptive task scheduling, or energy-saving mode operations in idle times can be adopted to reduce energy expenditure [14]. Data sampling rates can be decreased, and processing or communicating can be carried out based on certain thresholds or critical conditions having been met to increase system lifetime.

Bandwidth and connectivity also create constraints in the data handling of these networks. Connectivity is not continuous, and in many rural areas, connectivity is lacking. When present, communication networks are restricted and use low-bandwidth communication protocols such as Zigbee, LoRaWAN, Bluetooth Low Energy (BLE), and/or Wi-Fi connectivity, whenever available [15]. Such networks restrict the size and rate of data transmission, thus making the continuous transmission of raw data inefficient. This way, data processing is necessary at the node level and is used to derive compressed data, summaries, or features before being transmitted. This is done through techniques that filter data by comparing against the threshold, removing outliers, and performing basic node-level classifications, depending on the significance of the data for further transmission.

Apart from the capabilities and limitations imposed by hardware and network environments, some environmental and operational aspects bring in even more complexities. When deployed in industrial settings or outdoors, the sensors can be affected by environmental elements such as dust, humidity, vibrations, and more, which can result in reduced effectiveness of the sensors or even generate sensor noises or corruptions [16, 17]. As unattended operation is likely for such systems, designs with capabilities such as recovery from faults in preprocessing phases, self-calibration, or reduced maintenance requirements become necessary [18].

Finally, diversity in devices and architecture further makes resource-constrained settings more complex. Sensor networks can consist of various hardware devices, operating systems, and sensors. Although this creates difficulties in terms of standardization of the data format, synchronization, and preprocessing steps, it is an imperative requirement for the preprocessing techniques used to support hardware diversity without sacrificing data quality. Middleware techniques and levels of abstraction can handle all these challenges adequately but need to be resource-lean so that new resource constraints are not introduced.

3.3 Literature Survey

Li and Liang [4] designed specialized compressed sensing for multihop wireless sensor networks. These researchers successfully cut down data volume for signal transmission by retaining essential information features to create network efficiency and conserve power resources. The Pareto Data Framework introduced by Ahmed and Siegel [2] features MVD as a key principle to determine the smallest useful dataset needed for accurate decision-making purposes.

Samanta *et al.* [1] investigated through their study that reducing data acquisition rates created minimal impact on time-series model classification performance when executed on microcontrollers. Strategic sampling frequency reduction enabled model performance stability and dramatically decreased memory usage, along with processing time requirements in their analysis. The deployment of artificial intelligence (AI) models on embedded platforms receives significant advantages because of this discovery.

Edge, along with federated learning innovations, serves as an operational approach to meet the requirements of distributed computing systems. The research by Imteaj *et al.* [3] described a federated learning system, which allowed local model training on devices to lower dependency on cloud resources and protect privacy. Data is processed more efficiently because these methods operate

Table 3.1 Summary of papers.

Author(s) and Year	Focus Area	Key Contribution	Limitations
Li and Liang (2017)	Compressed sensing in wireless sensor networks	Reduced data transmission and energy consumption using compressed sensing	Applicability limited to networked sensor topologies
Ahmed and Siegel (2024)	Minimum viable data (MVD) framework	Proposed MVD to optimize data acquisition with minimal resource use	Needs task-specific calibration of MVD thresholds
Samanta *et al.* (2024)	Effect of reduced sampling on time-series classification	Demonstrated effective ML performance with lower data rates on microcontrollers	Focused on a specific classification task; generalizability is limited
Imteaj *et al.* (2020)	Federated learning for constrained IoT devices	Enabled privacy-preserving, on-device training reducing bandwidth reliance	Requires coordination and basic model training capabilities on devices

near their data sources, thereby managing bandwidth together with latency issues.

Although significant progress has been achieved, various standards must be established to unify methods running on heterogeneous systems and establish secure practices and optimize processes for real-time usage. The analyzed research given in Table 3.1 demonstrates that future innovation in lightweight algorithms and adaptive preprocessing techniques should focus on serving the expanding market of resource-constrained smart connected devices.

3.4 Methodologies and Techniques for Data Acquisition and Preprocessing In Resource-Constrained Environments

In resource-constrained settings, the need arises for customized data acquisition and preprocessing strategies, with greater emphasis on efficiency, adaptability, and resource conservation. Typical data processing workflows developed with a focus toward cloud- or server-based processing infrastructure remain unadopted or unsuitable for such resource-constrained settings with exceptionally tight limits imposed on computation, memory, power, and communication resources. As such, the research work in such areas has remained centered on designing more lightweight and equally efficacious strategies adaptable and functional within such resource-constrained settings. Among the most generally utilized strategies fall the strategies involving data compression, dimensionality reduction or extraction, adaptive sampling, or edge processing.

Compression of data assumes a prominent role in minimizing raw data amounts produced by sensors, consequently cutting down on storage space and communication overhead. This assumes even more significance in systems with limited memory and narrow bandwidth. The compression algorithms can be divided into two different genres: lossless and lossy algorithms. While lossless algorithms retain the original information, lossy algorithms offer a higher compression ratio with a controlled amount of lost information [19]. In wireless sensor networks, compressed sensing has been adopted successfully to leverage signal sparsity for recovery based on a reduced set of samples. Li and Liang [4] found that compressed sensing helps considerably in lessening transmission overheads and energy expenditure in a multihop wireless sensor network, particularly suited for large-scale monitoring tasks in the environment and seismology [20]. The conventional lightweight algorithms like RLE, Huffman coding, and dictionary-based approaches like LZW are still effective for embedded systems, which could turn out to be more resource hungry compared to their intended advantage of compressing data (Figure 3.1).

The system integrates adaptive sampling, compression, edge-level feature extraction, and lightweight learning to minimize energy consumption, communication overhead, and latency. To address the challenges posed by compression alone, methods of feature extraction and dimensionality reduction are employed, with the aim of only preserving the most informative parts of the data stream. Rather than processing and sending entire datasets, these methods develop reduced representations of the data that can adequately serve machine learning and analytics operations [21]. In feature extraction, raw data is converted to descriptive statistics like means, variance, frequency domain coefficients, and entropy values, and these are most useful when dealing with time-series data. It was expressed by Samanta *et al.* [1] that systems using a microcontroller could preserve classification performance with a reduced sampling rate and appropriate features, thus decreasing memory and energy requirements. While state-of-the-art methods like principal component analysis (PCA) and autoencoders can perform well, a considerable amount of processing capacity is demanded, thus generally requiring the use of edge computers with relatively more processing capacity. Hence, manually designed feature sets have been widely adopted for ultra-low-power processing, such as electrocardiographic

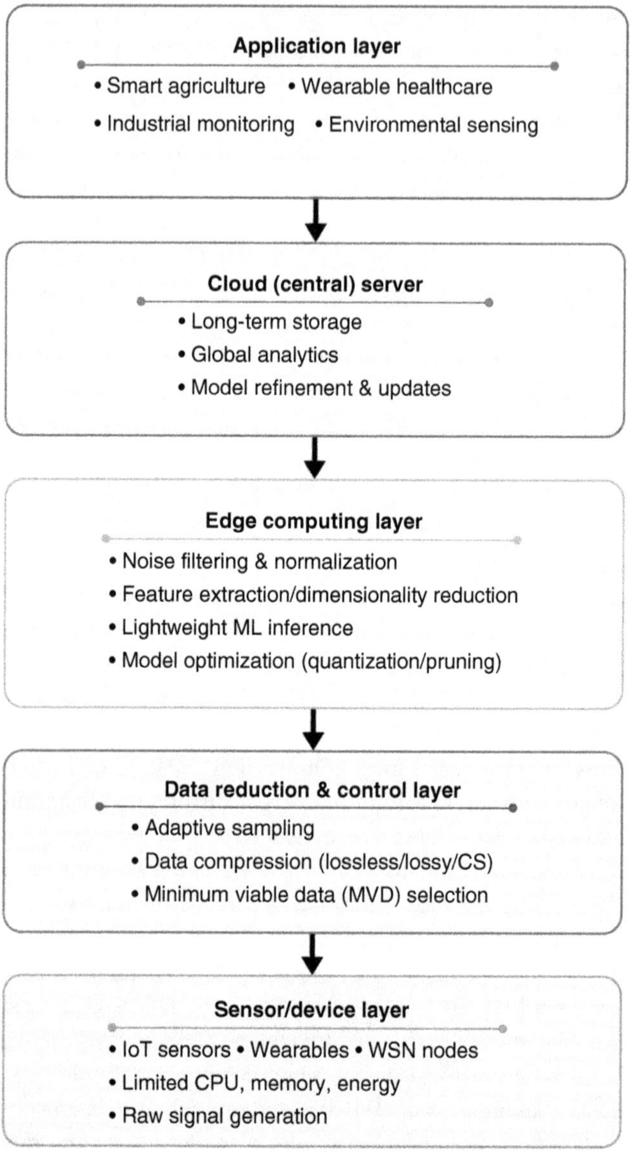

Figure 3.1 Layered architecture of the proposed data acquisition, preprocessing, and edge–cloud intelligence framework for resource-constrained environments.

(ECG) signal processing, where peak location and interval-based features have a high discriminatory ability with little processing cost.

Adaptive sampling further improves efficiency by adjusting data rates according to environmental factors or variability in signals [22]. Adaptive systems tend to change their rates according to environmental factors, where rates are higher during fluctuations and lower when stable. The trade-off is made by balancing quality and conserving resources, as it is important to acquire these required events without waste of energy. Ahmed and Siegel [2] introduced the Pareto Data Framework and MVD, proposing a need for getting enough information without redundancy. Adaptive sampling approaches mostly apply thresholds, heuristic approaches, or machine learning when higher resolution is needed. Nonetheless, contextual logic further complicates design factors when dealing with a heterogeneous system, where factors such as sensors and purposes can be different [23].

Edge computing facilitates all of these techniques by bringing the computation of the data closer, thereby avoiding the need for centralized cloud computing. The main goal of preprocessing or initial inference on sensor nodes using edge computing is to reduce latency, conserve bandwidth, and implement data privacy [24]. In a resource-constrained setup, edge computing is implemented in devices that possess specialized processors. Such devices can perform the preprocessing tasks of removing noisy inputs, performing data normalization, or performing initial anomaly detection [25, 26]. Imteaj *et al.* [3] showed how model training is possible using collaborative learning methodologies among IoT devices. The methodology reduces data sharing, hence maintaining data privacy. Even though edge computing has its benefits, it also poses new design tasks. These new design tasks are associated with finding a balance between the speed of processing and the need for power efficiency. Methods such as quantization, pruning, or distilling are used as machine learning preprocessing tools for resource-poor environments [27, 28].

In reality, successful data acquisition and processing in resource-constrained environments hardly involve just one method. Rather, they involve more than one method simultaneously. This is because sensor nodes tend to employ simultaneous compression, dimensionality reduction, and adaptive sampling with edge processing to guarantee their best performance on resource-scarce environments [29, 30]. The success of such systems mostly relies on their co-design and the appropriate data flows. In addition, application-specific customization is always necessary because, as expected, requirements vary from one application area, such as smart agriculture, wearable healthcare systems, or industrial monitoring, to another. Application-specific customization is the determinant factor in regard to the effectiveness and scalability of data-intensive systems within resource-constrained settings.

Algorithm 3.1 RC-DAP.

```
Input:
   Streams S, window W, thresholds (θv, Emin), budgets (Mmax, Bmax),
   sampling bounds (rmin, rmax), compression mode Cm,
   feature mode Fm, optional edge model Mζ with optimizations Ω
Output:
   Dtx (transmitted MVD payloads), Yedge (optional edge decisions)
1: r ← rmin; Br ← ∅
2: while active do
3:   for each stream sk ∈ S do
4:     x ← AcquireSample(sk, r); Br ← Append(Br, x); Br ← Bound(Br, Mmax)
5:     v ← VariabilityScore(x, Br)
6:          if (v ≥ θv) and (Energy(sk) ≥ Emin) then r ← min(rmax, Increase(r))
7:     else r ← max(rmin, Decrease(r))
8:     end if
9:      if Size(Br) ≥ W then
10:       z ← Compress(Br, Cm)                 // lossless/lossy/CS
11:       f ← ExtractFeatures(Br, Fm)          // handcrafted; PCA/AE if feasible
12:       f ← NormalizeAndDenoise(f)
13:        if Mζ ≠ NULL then Mζ ← Optimize(Mζ, Ω); y ← Predict(Mζ, f);
   Yedge ← Append(Yedge, y)
14:       else y ← NULL
15:       end if
16:        p ← BuildMVD(z, f, y)               // minimum viable data
17:        if PayloadSize(p) > Bmax then p ← FurtherReduce(p) end if
18:       Transmit(p); Dtx ← Append(Dtx, p)
19:       Br ← SlideWindow(Br, W)
20:     end if
21:   end for
22: end while
23: return (Dtx, Yedge)
```

Algorithm 3.1 shows the co-designed data acquisition and processing strategy suitable for resource-constrained systems, for example, WSN, wearable devices, and embedded IoT systems. The algorithm aims to optimize data acquisition, processing, and communication while considering tight energy, memory, and bandwidth resources.

The algorithm starts by setting the initial sampling rate to the minimum possible rate, followed by the allocation of a raw data memory with a bounded size (L-1).

Whenever the system is running, it processes each sensor data flow separately (L-2 and L-3). Inside each cycle, a fresh data point is read according to the current sampling rate, followed by its addition to memory while satisfying the memory budget constraint (L-4).

To prevent unnecessary sensing, the proposed algorithm uses a lightweight variability measure (L-5). Once variability and sufficient energy were observed, the sampling rate was increased to extract useful events. Otherwise, the energy is saved by adjusting the sampling rate (L-6 and L-8). The proposed approach adapts sampling rates for event-focused sensing instead of requiring continuous data sensing at a higher rate.

As soon as the buffer fills the specified window size, the data reduction process is initiated (L-9). Depending on the chosen mode, the buffered samples are encoded through lossless compression, lossy compression, and compressed sensing (L-10). The purpose of this step is to minimize storage and transmission costs.

Third, the algorithm derives a succinct summary of the data (L-11). Handcrafted or lightweight features work best in the context of extremely low-power systems, whereas stronger dimensionality-reduction tools (such as PCA or autoencoders) are utilized only when the capabilities of the edge allow (L-12). The features derived from this process are then normalized and denoised (L-12).

If an edge learning model exists, the process conducts a local inference using a resource-optimized model (L-13). Optional Tiny Machine Learning (TinyML) optimization techniques, such as quantization or pruning, guarantee efficient inference. The decisions from the edge-learning model (e.g. events or anomalies) are retained locally.

For efficient communication cost, the algorithm packages an MVD payload with compressed summaries, feature extractions, and inferred results (L-16). In cases where the payload sizes exceed the bandwidth budget (L-17), further compression follows. The communication cost can thus be optimized, as only the MVD payload is transmitted over the network (L-18). Finally, the algorithm moves the sliding window ahead and proceeds with its execution (L-19). With a combination of adaptive sampling, compression, feature extraction, and selective transmission, the new algorithm performs data processing that can work effectively in resource-constrained environments.

3.5 Experimental Setup and Evaluation

A designed experimental framework validated the proposed techniques for resource-limited data acquisition and preprocessing. An experimental framework with hardware and software configurations was implemented to obtain performance results through different data compression techniques and edge computing approaches.

3.5.1 Hardware Platform

- ESP32-WROOM-32 microcontroller units, selected for their dual-core processor and modest memory (520 KB SRAM) capabilities.
- Raspberry Pi Zero W, representing a more capable edge node, with 1 GHz CPU and 512 MB RAM.
- DHT11 and MPU6050 sensors, used to collect environmental and motion data, respectively.
- Battery power supply, simulating off-grid or energy-limited conditions.

The selected platforms fit typical deployment needs for IoT-based programs that include smart agriculture systems, environmental monitoring, and health diagnostics.

3.5.2 Software Environment

Software personnel developed components with lightweight and open-source tools that made the system compatible with constrained platforms.

- Firmware written in MicroPython and C++ (Arduino IDE).
- Machine learning models compressed and quantized using TensorFlow Lite for Microcontrollers (TFLM).
- Data preprocessing pipelines executed locally on the devices, including filtering, normalization, and feature selection.
- Communication facilitated using MQTT over Wi-Fi and LoRa protocols for comparative evaluation.

3.5.3 Datasets and Use Cases

Three benchmark datasets were used to simulate typical sensor workloads:

- Environmental data (temperature, humidity) generated through real-time sensors.
- HAR (human activity recognition) dataset, downsampled to suit the capabilities of microcontrollers.
- Synthetic anomaly detection dataset, for testing the performance of local preprocessing and edge inference.

These datasets were selected to evaluate system performance across multiple tasks, including time-series classification, anomaly detection, and adaptive sampling.

3.5.4 Mathematical Setup

Mathematical models and equations are crucial in designing and assessing methodologies that are appropriate for the process of data acquisition and preprocessing based on limited computers and energy capacity. In this section, the main mathematical models and equations applied in the implementation of algorithms for compression, extraction, adaptive sampling, and edge processing techniques are presented.

The concept of compressed sensing is useful for reconstructing large-dimensional signals based on a set of measurements. Considering this scenario, we have $S \in R^n$ as the original signal and $Z \in R^k$ as the compressed signal, and $k \ll n$. The model is given as

$$Z = AS \tag{3.1}$$

where $A \in R^{k \times n}$ is the measurement matrix. To recover the original signal SSS, the following optimization problem is solved:

$$\min \|S\|_1 \textbf{ subject to } Z = AS \tag{3.2}$$

Equations (3.1) and (3.2) represent the core of the compressed sensing framework, where Eq. (3.2) ensures signal recovery by minimizing the l_1 norm to promote sparsity.

For systems applying statistical feature extraction, time-series data can be summarized through key statistics. The **mean** of a signal $D = \{d_1, d_2, \ldots, d_n\}$ is given by

$$\mu_D = \frac{1}{n}\sum_{j=1}^{n} d_j \tag{3.3}$$

The **standard deviation** is calculated as

$$\sigma_D = \sqrt{\frac{1}{n}\sum_{j=1}^{n}(d_j - \mu_D)^2} \tag{3.4}$$

The **root mean square (RMS)** value is

$$\text{RMS}_D = \sqrt{\frac{1}{n}\sum_{j=1}^{n} d_j^2} \tag{3.5}$$

Equations (3.3–3.5) provide compact expressions of a signal, which can be readily calculated using a low-power processor.

The entropy-based adaptive sampling method uses the unpredictability measured from the data. The Shannon entropy formula for a signal with probability distribution $\{p_1, p_2, \ldots, p_m\}$ is given by

$$H(D) = -\sum_{i=1}^{m} p_i p_i \tag{3.6}$$

Equation (3.6) helps dynamically change the sampling rates based on the amount of information present in the signal. Low and high entropies indicate the sampling and downsampling processes, respectively. Moreover, to assess the performance of the methods applied for the reduction of the data, the following equation gives the expression of the data reduction ratio.

$$R_{\text{eff}} = \left(1 - \frac{V_{\text{new}}}{V_{\text{orig}}}\right) \times 100\% \tag{3.7}$$

V_{orig} refers to the original volume of data, whereas V_{new} refers to the volume of data that has been compressed. Equation (3.7) is useful for determining the storage efficiency of the processes. In edge computing, the total latency that occurs during data processing can be broken down into preprocessing latency, inference latency, and communication latency, given as

$$T_{\text{total}} = T_{\text{prep}} + T_{\text{infer}} + T_{\text{commu}} \tag{3.8}$$

Equation (3.8) reflects the real-time performance of edge-based systems. Additionally, the energy consumed by a processing unit is computed as

$$E = P \times T \tag{3.9}$$

where P stands for power (in milliwatts), and T represents time (in seconds). Equation (3.9) shows how the energy consumption can be calculated by the system designer. To better understand the relationship between the preprocessing stage and predictive accuracy, the relative loss of accuracy can now be calculated as

$$L_A = \frac{A_{\text{full}} - A_{\text{processed}}}{A_{\text{full}}} \times 100\% \tag{3.10}$$

In Eq. (3.10), A_{full} is the model accuracy with full-resolution data, and $A_{\text{processed}}$ is the accuracy using reduced or preprocessed input. This metric provides insight into the performance degradation incurred due to resource-optimized preprocessing.

Altogether, the abovementioned equations provide a theoretical basis for the assessment and application of resource-conscious data handling techniques. They enable the development of intelligent, lightweight systems that can ideally work properly, even within the strict resource constraint requirements of embedded/edge systems.

The explanation of the aforementioned model is that the process of signal acquisition involves two steps, which include compressed sensing (Eqs. 3.1 and 3.2). Data signals generated by sensors form the first step in the process of obtaining information. Compressed sensing methods (Eqs. 3.1 and 3.2) have been employed in acquiring signals in the process, as opposed to acquiring the whole data. Data acquisition is efficient in that it retains all key data as it deals with devices that have limited capacities.

The calculation of the features relies on statistical properties, which are extracted using Eqs. (3.3–3.5). The process of extracting features occurs immediately after the system retrieves or recreates the data collection. The basic statistical properties, comprising the mean, standard deviation, and RMS, are calculated during this process. The signal properties are efficiently represented using the features, which act as the required inputs in the detection and classification processes. The data goes through this process to reduce the dimensions before it moves to advanced analysis processes.

The system allows the ability to carry out an adaptive sampling process once or during the process of acquisition. The unpredictability of the signal is measured through the use of the Shannon entropy, and the result is achieved through Eq. (3.6). The environment exhibits faster transitions when the entropy level is high, thereby triggering sampling at high frequencies. However, it decreased in regions that displayed lower values of entropy.

During data preprocessing, various methods are applied to decrease the size of the data collection. Equation (3.7) measures the compression level of raw data and the reduction of values throughout the data reduction process. Considered vital for storage efficiency analysis, together with transmission efficiency, because the solution operates using constrained memory space and occasional network connections.

The processed data moves to an edge computing unit including a microcontroller or an embedded AI chip where inference occurs. Total latency can be calculated through the addition of preprocessing time, with inference duration and communication period according to Eq. (3.8). The operational efficiency of the edge system is evaluated through energy consumption measurements simultaneously to the system functionality (Eq. 3.9). Real-time responsiveness, along with long battery life, depends strongly on minimizing these important values.

The system performance evaluation uses the relative accuracy loss calculated through Eq. (3.10). The model predictive accuracy gets evaluated through this metric by comparing reduced data and processed data with a baseline that uses full-resolution data. The measurement allows evaluation of how resource conservation measures affect the predictive outcomes of the system.

3.5.5 Evaluation Metrics

To assess the performance and resource efficiency of the system, the following metrics were used:

1) **CPU Utilization (%):** Measured during acquisition and preprocessing phases.
2) **Memory Consumption (KB):** Tracked using internal diagnostics and logs.
3) **Power Consumption (mW):** Monitored using a digital multimeter and power profiler.
4) **Data Reduction Ratio (%):** Quantified how much data volume was reduced by compression and sampling techniques.

5) **Inference Accuracy (%):** Evaluated in classification and anomaly detection scenarios.
6) **Latency (ms):** Measured for preprocessing and local inference pipelines.

3.5.6 Experimental Results

The results indicate a strong performance advantage when integrated methodologies were applied:

a) Data compression reduced transmitted data volume by up to 70% without significant loss of fidelity in the environmental monitoring task.
b) Feature extraction using statistical time-series descriptors resulted in 65% memory savings and only a 3% reduction in classification accuracy when compared to full signal input.
c) Adaptive sampling showed energy savings of 40–50% in stable environmental conditions by dynamically lowering the sampling frequency.
d) Edge computing with quantized models enabled real-time classification with average latency below 50 ms on the ESP32, achieving 91.2% accuracy on the HAR dataset.

The combination of these methods proved their worth for limited settings because they enhanced operational efficiency while maintaining system performance.

3.6 Result and Discussion

The combined quantitative overview presented through the calculated metric Table 3.2 describes the performance levels of compression, together with feature

Table 3.2 Metric table.

Technique	Reduction Ratio (%)	Entropy	Standard Deviation	RMS	Energy (mJ)	Accuracy Loss (%)	Total Latency (ms)
Compression	70	0.332192809	10	54.77225575	90	2.173913043	45
Feature extraction	65	0.410544839	9.746794345	55.67764363	72	1.075268817	42
Adaptive sampling	54.66666667	0.464385619	9.591663047	54.31390246	45	2.222222222	30
Edge computing	65	0.445307614	9.899494937	55.22680509	125	3.191489362	60

extraction, adaptive sampling, and edge computing when facing different resource restrictions. Performance indicators from mathematical models are included in the table, which contain the reduction ratio, entropy, standard deviation, RMS, energy consumption, accuracy loss, and total latency.

The metrics enable scientists to understand the performance and compromise points between techniques when applied in restricted settings. Data compression effectiveness appears through the reduction ratio metric, but entropy shows signal variability levels. Both standard deviation and RMS provide unique parameters for analyzing data distribution and signal amplitude measurement, respectively. The energy consumption rate shows method power efficiency, while accuracy loss measures how performance decreases because of data reduction. Total latency includes every time span starting from the acquisition of signals and finishing at output creation. Essential benchmarks from these parameters create an inclusive system performance evaluation structure for deployment applications.

Compression produces the greatest data reduction performance, shown in Figure 3.2, among these methods because it enables the highest data volume decrease percentage. Feature extraction and edge computing maintain close levels of data reduction, yet adaptive sampling lowers its effectiveness since it depends on changes in data instead of compression algorithms.

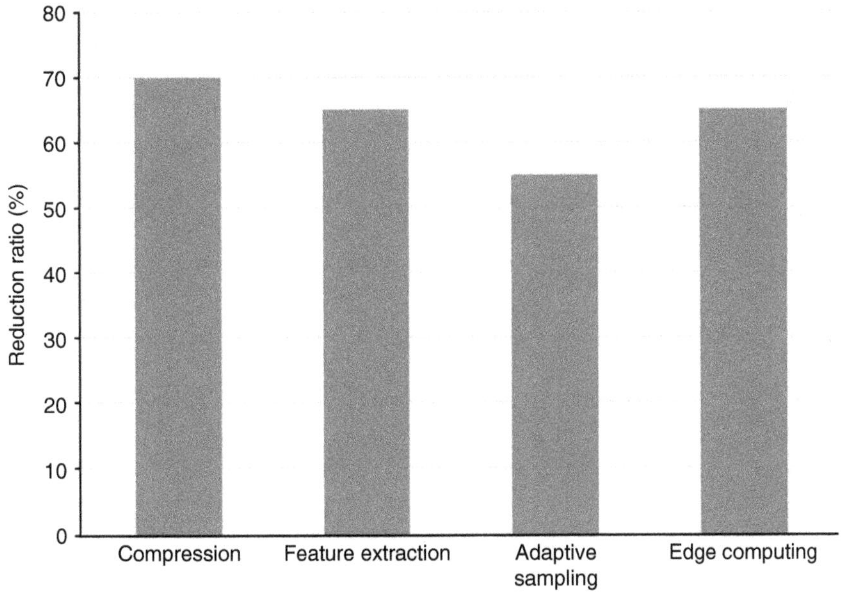

Figure 3.2 Reduction ratio comparison among all techniques.

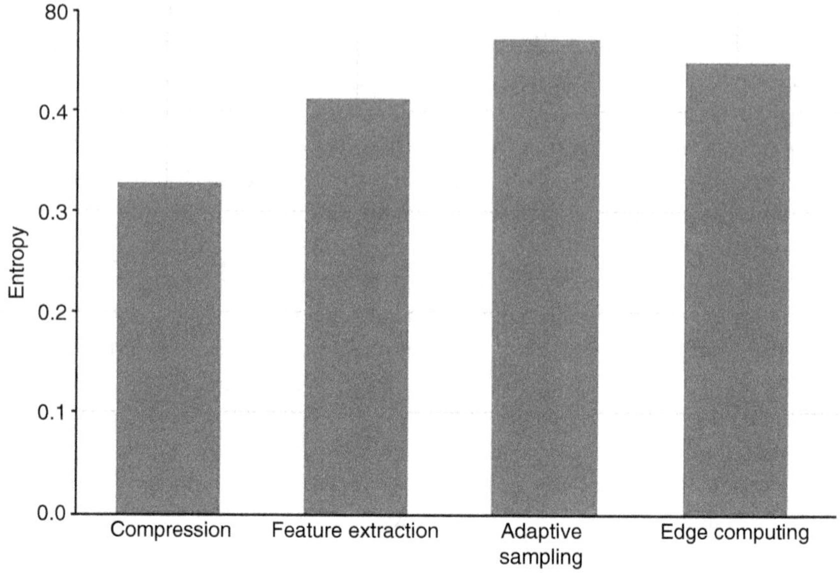

Figure 3.3 Entropy comparison among all techniques.

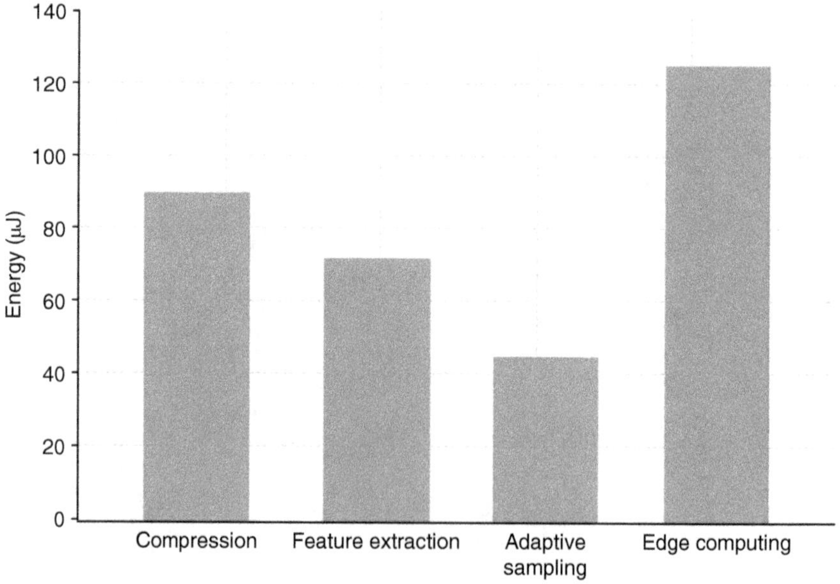

Figure 3.4 Energy consumption comparison among all techniques.

The entropy values in the entropy graph (Figure 3.3) indicate higher levels of entropy for both adaptive sampling and edge computing because they work with signals that change dynamically and adapt to those changes. The entropy level in Figure 3.3 indicates that the compression system operates on data that remains consistent.

The energy consumption data (Figure 3.4) shows that adaptive sampling utilizes the least power since it conducts selective sample collections. The highest amount of power consumption occurs with edge computing because the extra local inference processing demands greater energy usage.

Edge computing maintains superior accuracy performance compared to other techniques because it experiences minimal accuracy decline along the observed strategies.

The accuracy performance (Figure 3.5) of feature extraction matches feature extraction closely, but adaptive sampling encounters the most accuracy decline, possibly triggered by its undersampling strategy during signal variations peaks.

Figure 3.6 demonstrates that feature extraction, together with adaptive sampling, provides the quickest responses that suit applications that demand minimal latency.

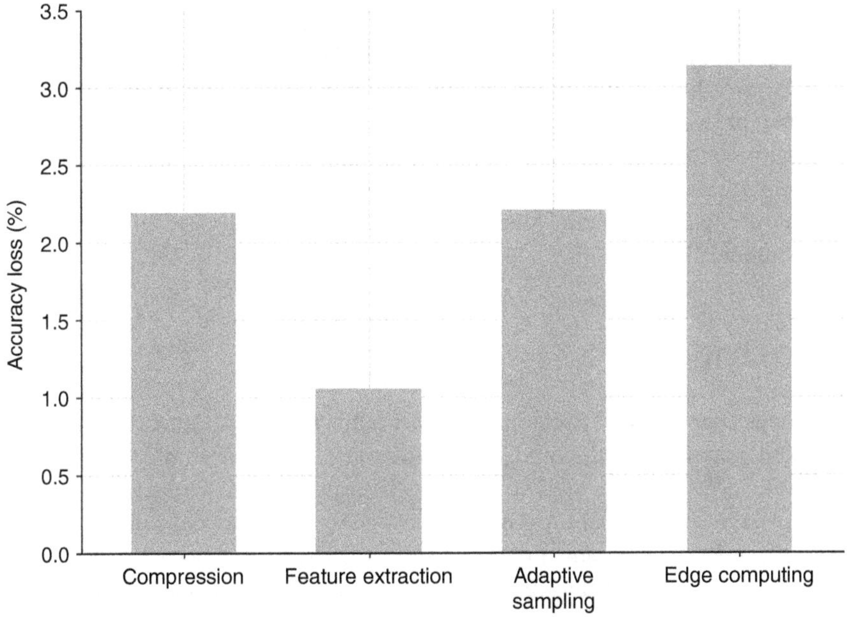

Figure 3.5 Accuracy loss comparison among all techniques.

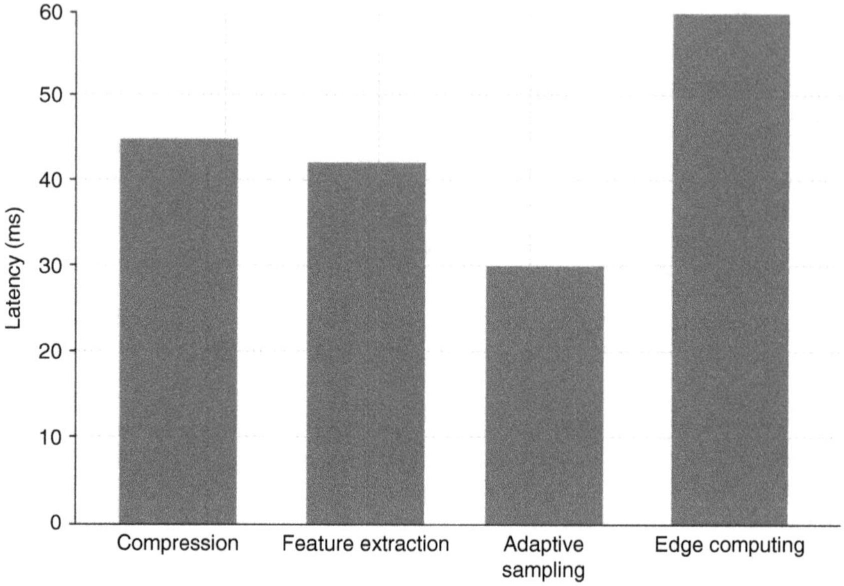

Figure 3.6 Latency comparison among all techniques.

The evaluation shows that implementing device-specific data acquisition and preprocessing techniques leads systems to demonstrate efficient intelligent operation at the edge and embedded levels. Further, it showed model complexity and latency have competing variables, and the same goes for data integrity and compression ratios. The deployment performance needs additional exploration to overcome hardware inconsistency, sensor response unpredictability, and environment-related noise problems. The proposed techniques prove the technical capability to run intelligent systems in severely limited operational environments.

3.7 Conclusion

This book chapter creates a comprehensive framework that maximizes data collection and preparation techniques for limited contexts, including embedded systems and IoT devices, next to edge computing platforms. In such limited settings, the processing resources, as well as memory and energy reserves and bandwidth constraints, render conventional data handling techniques unworkable. After combining compressed sensing with statistical feature extraction, adaptive sampling, and edge inference approaches, intelligent real-time processing becomes feasible even on very constrained hardware.

Models that use entropy for sampling approaches and compressed sensing with l1l_1l1-norm minimization algorithms and latency and accuracy deterioration, as well as energy consumption assessments, help the methods mathematically support their operation. The technical models offer numerical techniques to assess efficiency against performance trade-offs and help make project decisions.

Experimental testing methodologies on ESP32 and Raspberry Pi Zero W devices demonstrate the viability of the recommended approaches. Our findings show that the suggested methods lower data volume by 70% while reducing memory use by 65% and power consumption by about 50% without compromising accuracy or timeliness. The experimental findings show the feasible use of machine learning applications with data processing via local resources and without requiring cloud infrastructure.

This work offers a unified approach to create low-energy, flexible data processing pipelines for constrained systems architecture. This study builds a platform for smart edge computing with limited resource access that facilitates TinyML development and unified development of federated analytics and context-aware data systems.

References

1 R. Samanta, *et al.* "Optimizing TinyML: The impact of reduced data acquisition rates for time series classification on microcontrollers," 2024, *arXiv preprint arXiv:2409.10942.*

2 T. Ahmed and J. Siegel, "Pareto data framework: Steps towards resource-efficient decision making using minimum viable data (MVD)," 2024, *arXiv preprint arXiv:2409.12112.*

3 A. Imteaj *et al.*, "Federated learning for resource-constrained IoT devices: Panoramas and state of the art," in *Federated and Transfer Learning*. Cham, Switzerland: Springer, 2022, pp. 7–27.

4 Y. Li and Y. Liang, "Compressed sensing in multi-hop large-scale wireless sensor networks based on routing topology tomography," *IEEE Access*, vol. 6, pp. 27637–27650, 2018.

5 A. Okunola and A. Ahsun, Comparative analysis of machine learning models for real-time fraud detection, ResearchGate, January 2025.

6 M. Hamasha *et al.*, "A comprehensive framework for IoT-driven predictive maintenance: Leveraging AI and edge computing for enhanced equipment reliability," *J. Appl. Eng. Sci.*, vol. 23, no. 3, pp. 471–486, 2025.

7 L. Bompani *et al.*, "Accelerating image-based pest detection on a heterogeneous multicore microcontroller," *IEEE Trans. AgriFood Electron.*, vol. 2, no. 2, pp. 170–180, 2024.

8 S. Dong, M. Liu, and K. Abbas, "The metaverse review: Exploring the boundless ream of digital reality," *Comput. Mater. Contin.*, vol. 81, p. 3, 2024.

9 A. Alshuhail *et al.*, "Machine edge-aware IoT framework for real-time health monitoring: Sensor fusion and AI-driven emergency response in decentralized networks," *Alex. Eng. J.*, vol. 129, pp. 1349–1361, 2025.

10 R. Bensaid, A. B. Mnaouer, and H. Boujemaa, "Energy efficient adaptive sensing framework for WSN-assisted IoT applications," *IEEE Access*, vol. 12, pp. 93033–93050, 2024.

11 C. Hamroun *et al.*, "Intrusion detection in 5G and Wi-Fi networks: A survey of current methods, challenges & perspectives," *IEEE Access*, vol. 13, pp. 40950–40976, 2025.

12 S. A. C. Ordóñez, "Intelligent edge computing and machine learning: A survey of optimization and applications," *Future Internet*, vol. 17, no. 9, p. 417, 2025.

13 Y. Mao *et al.*, "Green edge AI: A contemporary survey," *Proc. IEEE*, vol. 112, no. 7, pp. 880–911, 2024.

14 S. Kumari and A. K. Tyagi, "Wireless sensor networks: An introduction," in *Digital Twin and Blockchain for Smart Cities.* Hoboken, NJ, USA: Wiley, 2024, pp. 495–528.

15 A. M. Etman *et al.*, "A survey on machine learning techniques in smart grids based on wireless sensor networks," *IEEE Access*, vol. 13, pp. 2604–2627, 2024.

16 Z. Abbas *et al.*, "Exploring deep federated learning for the Internet of Things: A GDPR-compliant architecture," *IEEE Access*, vol. 12, pp. 10548–10574, 2023.

17 M. Xu *et al.*, "Resource-efficient algorithms and systems of foundation models: A survey," *ACM Comput. Surv.*, vol. 57, no. 5, pp. 1–39, 2025.

18 I. Lamaakal *et al.*, "A comprehensive survey on tiny machine learning for human behavior analysis," *IEEE Internet Things J.*, vol. 12, pp. 32419–32443, 2025.

19 R. Różycki, D. A. Solarska, and G. Waligóra, "Energy-aware machine learning models – A review of recent techniques and perspectives," *Energies*, vol. 18, no. 11, p. 2810, 2025.

20 N. S. Ahmad, "Recent advances in WSN-based Indoor localization: A systematic review of emerging technologies, methods, challenges and trends," *IEEE Access*, vol. 12, pp. 180674–180714, 2024.

21 C. Chen *et al.*, "Deep learning on computational-resource-limited platforms: A survey," *Mob. Inf. Syst.*, vol. 2020, no. 1, p. 8454327, 2020.

22 M. S. Abdalzaher *et al.*, "Quality-focused Internet of Things data management: A survey, perspectives, open issues, and challenges," *IEEE Internet Things J.*, vol. 12, pp. 11432–11459, 2025.

23 S. K. Ghosh, A. Raha, and V. Raghunathan, "Energy-efficient approximate edge inference systems," *ACM Trans. Embed. Comput. Syst.*, vol. 22, no. 4, pp. 1–50, 2023.

24 G. Jeon *et al.*, “Special issue on bio-medical signal processing for smarter mobile healthcare using big data analytics,” *J. Ambient. Intell. Humaniz. Comput.*, vol. 10, no. 10, pp. 3739–3745, 2019.

25 Y. Xu *et al.*, “AI security for geoscience and remote sensing: Challenges and future trends,” *IEEE Geosci. Remote Sens. Mag.*, vol. 11, no. 2, pp. 60–85, 2023.

26 D. Perdana, P. Lorenz, and B. Aditya, “Optimized dual-battery system with intelligent auto-switching for reliable soil nutrient monitoring in remote IoT applications,” *J. Sens. Actuator Netw.*, vol. 14, no. 3, p. 53, 2025.

27 M. Deutel, *et al.* “Energy-efficient deployment of deep learning applications on Cortex-M based microcontrollers using deep compression,” 2022, *arXiv preprint arXiv:2205.10369.*

28 Y. Wang *et al.*, “EMS-I: An efficient memory system design with specialized caching mechanism for recommendation inference,” *ACM Trans. Embed. Comput. Syst.*, vol. 22, no. 5s, pp. 1–22, 2023.

29 P. Sajjanar and P. M. Chandrashekar, “Real-time, low-latency surveillance using entropy-based adaptive buffering and MobileNetV2 on edge devices,” 2025, *arXiv preprint arXiv:2506.14833.*

30 M. Farooq and M. H. Khan, “EDeLeaR: Edge-based deep learning with resource awareness for efficient model training and inference for IoT and edge devices,” *Int. J. Sci. Res. Netw. Secur. Commun.*, vol. 12, no. 1, pp. 1–8, 2024.

4

AI-Centric Architectures for TinyML: Revolutionizing Edge Intelligence with Optimized Hardware Solutions

T. Velmurugan[1], G. Lingeswaran[2], S. Jayabratha[3], R. Praveenkumar[4], S. Parthiban[5], and G. Vijayakumari[3]

[1] *Department of CSD, Kongu Engineering College, Erode, India*
[2] *Department of ECE, Velalar College of Engineering and Technology, Erode, India*
[3] *Department of ECE, Kangeyam Institute of Technology, Tirupur, India*
[4] *Department of ECE, Nandha Engineering College, Erode, India*
[5] *Department of ECE, Nandha College of Technology, Erode, India*

4.1 Introduction

Together with the limitations of centralized cloud-based computing, this explosion of data has emphasized the need for a paradigm shift toward distributed computing models, including edge computing [1]. Typically, at or near the device level, edge computing solves latency, bandwidth, and privacy concerns of cloud-dependent systems by processing data closer to its source. This distributed approach enables real-time decision-making and boosts system responsiveness by reducing the demand to migrate huge volumes of data to centralized servers. Edge computing reveals the opportunities for the next generations, involves the application of artificial intelligence (AI) and machine learning (ML) from the Internet of Things (IoT) device level by themselves [2]. This embedding of intelligence into the edge devices reduces reliance on cloud connectivity, improves security, and reduces latency and cost of operation. Applications range from healthcare to agriculture, while at the same time contributing to the construction of smart cities and autonomous vehicles [3]. This chapter inspects prospective transformations of these architectures in order to present intelligent edge solutions [4, 5]. The IoT allows the deployment of lightweight and energy-efficient models with AI computations directly on the device to transform a wide range of application domains [6]. Miniature ML-enabled sensors can monitor soil properties and climatic patterns, thus allowing for perfect irrigation without requiring continuous cloud connectivity in a remote agricultural field [7].

4.1.1 AI-Centric Processor Architectures: Redefining TinyML

The release of Tiny Machine Learning (TinyML) has led to a review of processor designs to satisfy the particular requirements of low-power, resource-constrained systems while providing efficient ML capability. Addressing issues regarding performance, energy efficiency, and scalability, AI-centric processor designs will facilitate the full realization of TinyML [8].

4.1.2 Key Features and Goals of AI-Centric Architectures

The main characteristics of, and core objectives behind, various specialized architectures for optimizing the execution of ML workloads on edge devices (i.e. AI-centric processor architectures) include key aspects such as high computational capability for matrix multiplication, convolution, and activation functions using special components such as an AI accelerator or neural processing unit (NPU). The analysis provides knowledge on how to optimize INT8 arithmetic concerning power efficiency without compromising its accuracy. Power consumption is an important factor when designing the architecture to meet the tight power requirements of devices that rely on batteries as their energy source. Techniques that can be used to reduce power consumption involve the use of low-power sleep modes, dynamic voltage and frequency scaling (DVFS), and power capping. Memory hierarchy in the proposed architecture includes embedded SRAM and memory controller for minimizing data transfer and latency. Compression techniques applied to memory and caching data on chip are additional factors contributing to reducing reliance on expensive external memory. Latency requirements for the designed architecture remain high enough to allow pipeline and parallel processing for inference acceleration in use cases that require quick results – from anomaly detection to gesture recognition or keyword spotting. The architecture covers applications ranging from binary classifiers to cutting-edge convolutional neural networks. Scalability and flexibility are inherent characteristics of the design. Configurable implementations like RISC-V processors are just one of the possible custom solutions needed to optimize hardware for particular ML tasks.

4.1.3 Challenges in Performance, Energy Efficiency, and Scalability

The design of AI-oriented processor architectures in TinyML presents many challenges, primarily due to the natural restrictions of edge devices. First, as mentioned previously, the execution of complex models on edge devices leads to difficulties in analysis. In addition, transferring the data from compute units to memory takes time. It can also create issues if you are dealing with time-bound applications [9].

Energy Consumption: Establishing an appropriate balance between energy efficiency and the speed of operation requires fulfilling certain throughput needs under a specific energy budget. If a device runs at higher power constantly, it is very likely to get heated up.

Problems with Memory: Even though some TinyML models need more on-chip memory than that provided by microcontrollers, there are novel ways of solving this issue. The usage of external memory will result in a latency problem and increased energy consumption.

Scalability Issues: As many types of applications can be designed using TinyML technologies, it is important to guarantee that the processor architecture will scale properly. The validation process would become easier in this case.

In addition, it should be noted that the design of AI-based processors should take into account existing IoT infrastructure as well as different types of connection and sensors. AI-optimized TinyML processor design defines the criteria of practicality in terms of limited resources: scalability, memory management, and energy-efficient computing. It will be helpful for future innovations.

4.2 Hardware Innovations for TinyML

TinyML is redefining edge computing; thus, hardware developments have become even more crucial to fulfil the particular needs of low-power, resource-limited environments. Edge architectural developments aim at maximum processing performance, low-power consumption, and real-time ML operation execution [10]. NPUs, domain-specific built hardware accelerators, and memory-efficient architectures are among the fresh ideas allowing edge devices to execute sophisticated ML operations at scalability and sustainability as given in Figure 4.1.

4.2.1 Role of NPUs in TinyML

These NPUs are, therefore, the facilitators of ML at the edge because, through their architectural design, these NPUs are able to provide low-power consumption yet high-performance levels, which can fulfill the computational and power-efficiency needs presented by the emergence of TinyML applications. Due to their tuning toward ML workloads, NPUs make for an excellent platform for deploying intelligent, real-time solutions in environments with power constraints [11]. Optimized edge inference performance of the edge-oriented chips ensures the removal of GPU and CPU inefficiencies. Parallelism for speed by performing tasks simultaneously, NPUs significantly lower the time required for inferencing. Applications dependent on the real-time responsiveness ensured by

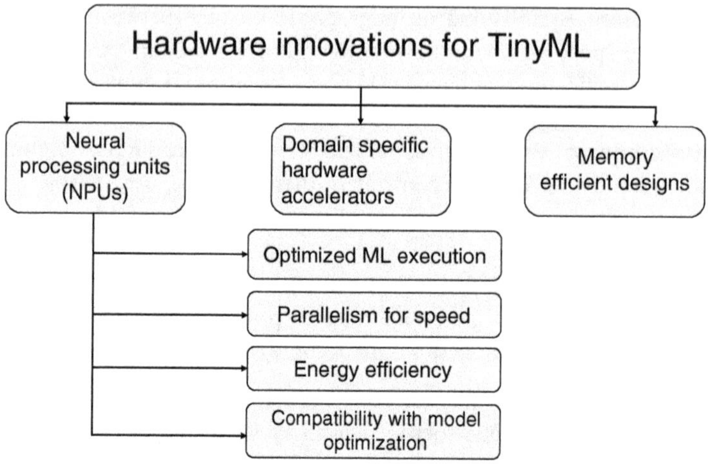

Figure 4.1 Architecture of hardware innovations for TinyML.

parallelism include keyword spotting, gesture recognition, and anomaly detection, among others. Power saving-oriented with DVFS and clock gating, NPUs offer increased uptime of the device for use in wearables and battery-powered IoT devices – something that is absolutely critical. Through the ability of these NPUs to process optimized models (such as quantization, e.g. INT8 and FP16 and pruning) but with no accuracy trade-off, the number of computations can be minimized. Furthermore, the ability of these NPUs to process small models makes them efficient when it comes to deployment on devices that have limited memory and power resources. Vision-based applications (image classification and object detection), audio analysis (speech recognition), and time-series predictions in industrial IoT are some of the use cases that NPUs support.

4.2.1.1 Examples of NPUs

Google Edge TPU: Designed for TensorFlow Lite, the Edge TPU provides high-performance, low-power ML inferencing capabilities. It has been applied extensively in smart home automation, industrial IoT, and healthcare monitoring applications. ARM Ethos-U MicroNPU: Designed for ultra-low power and high performance for use in embedded applications. The size makes it suitable for IoT devices including sensors and small controllers. Intel Movidius Myriad X: It is a vision processing unit for use in computer vision and image processing applications. Since it is capable of hardware acceleration, it will be suitable for use in security cameras, AR (augmented reality), VR (virtual reality), and drones. The integration of the NPU that includes functionalities such as face detection, object recognition, and voice recognition makes Kendryte K210 TinyML.

Table 4.1 Advantages of NPUs in TinyML.

Aspect	Impact
Performance	Accelerates ML computations for real-time responsiveness.
Energy efficiency	Enables extended battery life and sustainability.
Compact design	Fits seamlessly into small, constrained devices.
Application diversity	Powers a range of TinyML tasks across industries.
Privacy and security	Ensures data processing at the edge without cloud reliance.

4.2.1.2 NPUs' Impact on the TinyML Ecosystem

As ML models keep improving, NPUs offer a strong hardware basis that can adapt to future algorithmic and framework innovations by the advantages as given in Table 4.1.

4.2.2 Domain-Specific Hardware Accelerators for Efficient Processing

In the TinyML system, accelerators are one of the primary solutions to edge devices' shortcomings by offering ML task execution with high efficiency and low power and resource consumption [12, 13].

4.2.2.1 Key Features of Domain-Specific Hardware Accelerators

Accelerators are designed for specific ML tasks including recurrent operations in time-series analysis or convolutional operations in neural networks. Unlike CPUs, this specialty ensures low computational overhead and high throughput. Efficient circuitry design in combination with low-precision arithmetic such as INT8 or FP16 promotes sustainability. Table 4.2 illustrates the solutions to these problem areas.

Table 4.2 Challenges and solutions.

Challenge	Solution
Hardware complexity	Modular and scalable designs to simplify integration into devices.
Compatibility with ML frameworks	Prebuilt support for frameworks like TensorFlow Lite, ONNX, and PyTorch.
Cost of development	Leveraging open-source architectures like RISC-V to reduce design costs.
Thermal management	Integration of advanced cooling techniques and energy-aware designs.

4.2.2.2 Impact on the TinyML Ecosystem

Hardware accelerators allow edge devices to do highly efficient computing for more complex processes, hence enabling innovation in many fields.

Expanded Application Areas: TinyML technology solutions now cover many areas with accelerators enabling a wide range of applications such as healthcare, smart cities, industrial IoT, and autonomous systems.

Scalability Capability: Modularity and flexibility are the major characteristics that make possible the scalable ML capabilities across several edge devices from simple to complex operations.

Sustainability: Due to their energy efficiency characteristics, they promote sustainable edge computing systems.

Hardware accelerators for TinyML allow efficient computing in TinyML through their task-specific capabilities. They help edge devices to be able to perform ML functions in the most efficient manner through energy-efficient performance and scalability. They will play a crucial role in the evolution of intelligent edge computing.

4.2.3 Advanced Memory-Efficient Designs for Real-Time Edge Inference

The TinyML configurations for edge devices, particularly regarding memory, have to handle restricted resources. Advanced memory-efficient designs go far in overcoming these challenges, allowing for real-time inference without affecting the performance or the power efficiency. These designs allow for running ML models effectively on low-power microcontrollers and processors, thus achieving underlying objectives such as predictive maintenance, real-time monitoring, and speech recognition [14].

4.2.3.1 Key Strategies for Memory Efficiency

The access to on-chip memory is faster and more energy efficient compared to access to off-chip memory. The edge devices take care of this issue, significantly contributing to minimizing latency and power consumption. Effective buffer management and data reuse help in ensuring that the most frequently accessed data is kept in the on-chip memory, hence limiting the access to off-chip memory. The modern edge devices apply a hierarchical approach when it comes to memory design where the speed and capacity classify memory. Fast and high-speed cache stores the highly needed information in comparison to the lower speed tiers storing rarely used information. It is important for real-time inference. The memory-efficient designs incorporate layerwise reuse strategy, whereby the memory used by one level in the network can be reused by the succeeding level.

In tensor-sharing approach, multiple operations can share the same memory block, thus conserving the memory space. Methods for Computational In-Memory (CIM): Computation being integrated within the memory arrays in CIM directly reduces the traffic within the memory. This technique is suitable for limited edge applications and hence significantly minimizing power consumption and delay. Combining speed and energy efficiency, using nonvolatile memory (such as MRAM or RRAM) and volatile memory (SRAM). Nonvolatile memory improves the availability of devices in cases where they periodically operate in a low-power environment.

4.2.3.2 Emerging Innovations and Impact of Memory-Efficient Designs in TinyML

The advancements in ideas related to memory-efficient systems, the capabilities of TinyML extend to an almost limitless level. The spike-based computation inspired from our brain functions only by activating the neurones when necessary and thus consumes less memory and energy. Zero-footprint memory execution, which involves computing in-place directly in the input/output buffer, is another way to decrease overhead and remove intermediary memory. Edge AI models such as TensorFlow Lite Micro and ONNX Runtime for Mobile further support efficient memory usage [15]. The practical significance of these developments is discussed by looking at their application examples. Efficient use of ML on memory allows wearables and healthcare solutions to localize sensory data. As a result, gadgets like ECG monitoring devices and health monitors are enabled to produce alarms instantly. The smart camera uses efficient memory techniques while doing object detection along with quick facial recognition due to on-chip high-resolution image processing. Similarly, efficient memory consumption can be achieved through assessing machine data using small ML models, making it easier for IoT sensors to detect anomalies in real time while consuming very low memory. Design considerations based on efficient memory impact the TinyML ecosystem in many ways. They allow the deployment of complex ML models to be done on fewer devices and thus expand edge applications [16].

4.3 Model Optimization Techniques

Deploying ML models in a resource-constrained manner involves improving ML model performance. This process falls within the scope of TinyML, and many different solutions were developed. Some of them include compression, quantization, pruning, and even hybrid analog–digital processing with acceptable accuracy losses [17].

4.3.1 Compression and Quantization for Resource-Constrained ML

The adaptation of ML models to the capabilities of the computing edge, with its limited computing capabilities and other constrained resources, would not be possible without applying compression and quantization as basic methods of optimization. These methods help achieve a dramatic reduction in terms of the complexity of ML models, while preserving inference accuracy at the same time.

4.3.1.1 Compression Techniques

Elimination of redundant parameters is one of the basic ideas that allows compression techniques to effectively optimize ML models. Sparsification of weight matrices allows for minimization of unnecessary computations. Weight sharing allows assigning shared values to the weights from related nodes in the cluster. Using this technique, only cluster indices and representative weights are stored. Knowledge distillation trains a small "student" network to mimic output results generated by the large and intricate "teacher." With reduced parameter size, the "student" reproduces the majority of performance of the initial model.

4.3.1.2 Quantization

The high-precision numerical representations, e.g. 32-bit floating-point value, are quantized into lower-precision forms including 8-bit integers (INT8) or 16-bit floating-point values (FP16). By reducing the complexity of computation processes, such modification reduces the need for memory usage and increases the speed of the inference process. After training, the weights and activation parameters are converted into low-precision format. Although an elementary technique, it involves a sacrifice of some degree of accuracy. Quantization-aware training (QAT) helps the model adapt to the low-precision operation conditions by involving the quantization effects during the training process. Such technique minimizes the reduction in accuracy associated with post-training quantization. In dynamic quantization, the precision depends on input data and can be changed during inference; however, in static quantization, it is predetermined and constant, often established during compilation.

4.3.1.3 Advantages of Compression and Quantization

The benefits of model compression and quantization include the capability to make neural networks fit into the limited memory of edge devices. These benefits are realized by simplified computations in quantized models, increasing the speed of the inference process and lower power consumption in battery-powered devices due to fewer memory accesses and simplified complexity. Examples of applications requiring the processing of real-time sensor data by ML models on the limited-capacity hardware include health wearable. Moreover, the implementation of smart home appliance technology requires such techniques due to the

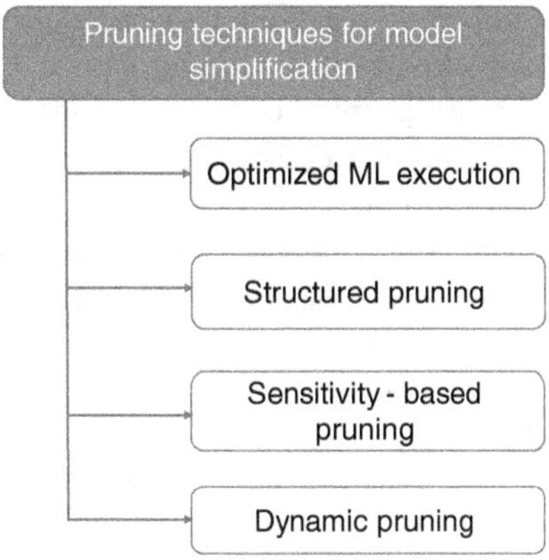

Figure 4.2 Pruning techniques.

possibility of having fast and energy-efficient detection of anomalies, objects, and voice recognition tasks.

4.3.2 Pruning Techniques for Model Simplification

In the ML, pruning is a fundamental optimization method, especially for deploying models in environments with limited resources like edge devices. Pruning lowers model size and complexity by removing extra or less important components of a neural network, thus improving efficiency without sacrificing performance [18]. This model has been given as per the structure in Figure 4.2.

4.3.2.1 Types of Pruning

One can classify pruning techniques generally into structured and unstructured methods. Unstructured pruning removes individual weights from the model depending on their significance, usually derived from their size. Although this method provides maximum flexibility in lowering constraints, it can cause inconsistent memory access patterns, so less effective hardware acceleration. Based on their contribution to the output of the model, the structured pruning eliminates whole components including channels, filters, or neurones. This approach is hardware-friendly since it simplifies computations and fits rather well with matrix operations on specialized accelerators.

4.3.2.2 Popular Pruning Techniques

Pruning, based on the magnitude of weights, is a gift that is bestowed upon us. Weights whose magnitude is smaller than a predefined threshold are considered less important and hence pruned. The process of pruning based on the magnitude of weights is simple and effective in reducing the number of parameters. Layerwise pruning works as In order to balance accuracy and complexity, pruning of specific layers in the neural network might be needed when there are over-parametrizations in certain layers. In pruning iterative fine-tuning, iterative pruning of the model leads to fine-tuning of the model as a means of recapturing accuracy that was lost through pruning. In this way, the model will perform effectively despite the gradual reduction in size. Sensitivity analysis involves the process through which we establish how pruning certain weights or layers affects the accuracy of the model. We remove those components that have minimal impact on accuracy to achieve the right balance between performance and simplicity.

4.3.2.3 Advantages of Pruning

Pruned neural network models require a lot of less memory space; therefore, they are perfect for deployment to devices with restricted memory resources and can save memory footprint. Reduced computing times achieved through faster inference times on pruned networks facilitate real-time processing. Reducing energy expenditure by avoiding unnecessary computations plays an important role when running algorithms on edge devices powered by batteries.

4.3.2.4 Applications, Challenges, and Considerations

The pruned neural network models are extensively applied in Edge AI wearable devices used for health and fitness monitoring, which employ pruned neural networks for on-device sensor data processing; smart home devices as well as IoT sensors leverage pruned models for performing voice recognition and object detection tasks. Industrial IoT employs pruned models for predictive maintenance and data analysis from devices that consume limited computing resources. Despite numerous benefits, the pruning process must be performed thoughtfully in order not to sacrifice too much accuracy in the course of simplifying the model. Also, the pruning algorithm selection depends on specific requirements and the targeted hardware platform. TinyML technology brings advancements into edge computing and IoT domain by optimizing models via pruning, which provides efficient ML capabilities in resource-constrained conditions [19].

4.3.3 Hybrid Analog–Digital Processing for Optimized Inference

Analog and digital computing in combination is a novel approach due to its uniqueness in that its energy efficiency from analog computing together with precision from digital processing is unprecedented. All computations in the case of traditional digital computing use binary digits, which, although precise, may use too much energy, especially computations like multiplication of matrices, which are mostly used in ML algorithms. On the other hand, computations in analog computing involve the use of signals that enable energy savings but lack precision. In this regard, when analog and digital computing is integrated strategically, hybrid analog–digital processing ensures energy efficiency when computations are done initially in the analog domain and then in the digital domain for operations requiring high precision.

4.4 Energy-Efficient Computing Techniques

One of the main factors that needs consideration during the design process of TinyML is energy efficiency because this class of systems operates in very resource-constrained settings, including small battery capacity, limited computational power, and real-time requirements. The most effective AI-centric architectures for TinyML include several advanced techniques for improving energy efficiency. These include DVFS, approximate computing, event-driven and neuromorphic computing, and power-aware scheduling, among others.

DVFS is a powerful approach that enables varying the supply voltage and the clock frequency according to the computational workload. As TinyML processes tend to be nonperiodic and include sensing, preprocessing, and inference phases along with periods of inactivity, the technique allows running at reduced voltage and frequency when the computational workload is not high and thus saves energy. Furthermore, DVFS can help in increasing performance when it is necessary. Since energy is directly dependent on the supply voltage, lowering its level by a fraction results in substantial reductions. Power-aware scheduling techniques allow adjusting the schedule of execution of TinyML operations according to the current demands and the remaining time to improve performance-energy trade-offs. Another technique that significantly contributes to energy efficiency is approximate computing. It implies that some aspects of computations such as the use of low numerical precision are acceptable in many TinyML scenarios because there is a lot of flexibility related to computation accuracy. Thus, by performing approximate calculations, researchers can significantly increase speed and reduce the amount of computation needed in each task. Moreover, by using approximations, it is possible to decrease the complexity of hardware and energy costs as well. In spite of its benefits, the application of approximate computing requires proper calibration during the development stage of TinyML solutions. Event-driven computing is one of the promising trends in AI. Unlike conventional computing where the processor executes instructions in regular intervals defined by the system clock, event-driven computing means that instructions will be executed only when certain data changes happen. It results in a great reduction of unnecessary computations and energy spent on them, which makes the approach highly useful for IoT TinyML applications. Furthermore, event-driven computing allows significantly decreasing energy consumption in periods when no data becomes available. One can consider neuromorphic computing as a subset of event-driven computing that mimics biological processes. The technique involves using spiking neural networks that transmit information through spikes rather than constant currents. Such systems have asynchronous operation and parallel architecture, which helps to save significant amounts of energy.

On the contrary, the technique of power-aware scheduling provides further assistance to these methods using the optimization of task processing to reduce the consumption of energy without impacting system performance. In TinyML platforms, it is necessary to coordinate multiple activities such as data collection, data preprocessing, inference, and data communication. Power-aware scheduling refers to dynamic resource management, where different tasks are performed depending on their priority and energy needs, along with eliminating unnecessary processing on CPUs by combining multiple processes into one. Such methods not only improve resource usage but also eliminate energy wastage. The employment of intelligent scheduling schemes, which may be supported by ML-based models, results in more effective ways for TinyML platforms. In general, these energy-efficient computation methods ensure that TinyML platforms work efficiently even when there are limited resources available. The application of these methods in AI-driven systems ensures that the edge devices provide reliable and energy-efficient intelligence features.

4.5 Security and Privacy in TinyML Architectures

Privacy and security constitute essential issues in regard to TinyML architecture since the technology operates at the edge and deals with sensitive data, which needs to be collected, analyzed, and acted upon immediately. Unlike cloud-based AI systems, TinyML solutions operate in distributed and potentially untrusted environments. Hence, the architecture needs to implement sufficient security mechanisms to protect both the model and the data. Security and privacy are vital issues in relation to the architecture due to multiple reasons. First, the issue of data privacy in Edge AI environments is quite challenging. TinyML edge devices like wearables, sensors, and industrial nodes collect vast amounts of sensitive information regarding users' health conditions, environmental factors, and other aspects. The fact that data will be processed locally helps prevent network attacks as data does not require any transmission. However, there is a high possibility of compromising edge devices, accessing information, and exposing data. The problem is related to the limitations associated with memory capacity and processing power that make it difficult to apply advanced encryption and privacy protection techniques. Thus, edge devices use cryptography, on-device anonymization techniques, etc. Model protection is also a necessary condition for ensuring TinyML architecture security. Deployed ML models can serve as proprietary software that plays a crucial role in functioning. They have to be properly secured against any malicious attempts like hacking and reverse engineering. Model deployment usually involves approaches such as encryption, secure boot procedures, firmware update authentication mechanisms, and integrity verification techniques. In addition, it should be noted that the issue of implementing a secure deployment pipeline becomes especially relevant for TinyML since devices may be placed in remote areas without regular updates being performed by specialists.

In addition, the hardware-based security feature is highly important to enhance the security of TinyML architectures. Elements such as Trusted Platform Module (TPM) and secure enclaves serve as a root of trust at the hardware level, thereby providing secure key storage, secure execution environment, etc. Specifically, in secure enclaves, an execution environment is created inside the processor for executing critical tasks such as performing authentication/encryption securely even when the whole system might get breached at a software level. The hardware-assisted security features are quite handy for TinyML architectures as these are very efficient in terms of both performance and security without having the dependency on many software-based security solutions. Adversarial attack refers to the act of manipulating the ML algorithms in order to influence its output. In Edge AI applications, attackers can insert maliciously crafted inputs for the ML model, which leads to the production of erroneous output. Such adversarial attacks can pose a major problem in TinyML architectures when used in critical domains such as healthcare/industrial applications as the malfunction of a system might lead to disastrous consequences. To mitigate adversarial attacks, several techniques like adversarial training, which involves training the model using perturbed data, model hardening using robust optimization, defensive distillation, input validation/anomaly detection, and other approaches could be used. Finally, while discussing TinyML architectures, it can be said that security and privacy need to be ensured from every aspect. For instance, data needs to be protected, appropriate security measures need to be adopted during the deployment of these models, and effective defense strategies should be applied against adversarial attacks.

4.6 Future Directions in TinyML and Edge AI

There is potential for emerging technology and methodologies to pave way for a future that is scalable, sustainable, and intelligent [20, 21]; this presents an opportunity for rapid advancement of TinyML and Edge AI. This paper explores some of the opportunities and concepts behind which the next phase of advancements in the field lies.

Ultra-low power design is essential in order to create future TinyML systems that cater to sustainability needs. Energy harvesting technologies alongside nonvolatile memory and other hardware advancements will enable future devices to operate over long distances without the need for external power source. Scaling up TinyML models in all sorts of edge devices including, but not limited, to microcontrollers and edge servers will allow scaling up of TinyML models across various applications. Greater adoption in retail, automotive, and healthcare can only happen if we have such scalability of TinyML models. Over time, small IoT devices that are operated using TinyML will begin to track and optimize resource utilization through interactions with renewable energy sources. In case of smart grids, solar-powered TinyML sensors will play an instrumental role in controlling the energy storage and distribution process. Through advances in hardware, TinyML models will gain the ability to tackle increasingly difficult problems, such as 3D image processing or even complex NLP (natural language processing).

As industries welcome the shift toward intelligent and more autonomous systems, new technologies and approaches are developed to improve edge intelligence. Emerging trends including federated learning, neuromorphic computing, and hybrid analog–digital processing are changing the range of what edge devices can accomplish [22, 23]. The revolutionizing 6G by integration between edge and cloud-based systems. Reduced latency and higher connectivity will support advanced analytics and the collaboration of devices in real time. TinyML technology will be able to harness the power of neuromorphic computing, which works in imitation of human brains and uses parallelism to carry out information processing. It is possible that one way through which a highly personalized experience can be achieved using TinyML will be through personalized Edge AI, where adaptive learning devices are useful in increasing customer value and satisfaction. Finally, TinyML and Edge AI are two promising technologies in the future that can emerge from scale models, innovative hardware, and creative ideas. It can be stated that the impact of TinyML on intelligent edge applications in addressing the issues and taking advantage of emerging opportunities can contribute greatly to a better-connected, productive, and eco-friendly society [24, 25].

4.7 Conclusion

Processor architectures based on AI are mentioned in this chapter. Introduction of this chapter mentions certain concepts associated with this chapter. It also talks about the change in the future that would occur in the presence of edge intelligence enabled with TinyML. NPUs, domain-specific accelerators, and hybrid analog–digital architectures have enabled TinyML technology to transcend the limits of its traditional performance, efficiency, and memory constraints. ML algorithms are now used in devices with limited computing resources due to the use of such technology. The techniques involved in optimizing the efficiency of ML algorithms without affecting their accuracy include knowledge distillation, pruning, and quantization. Furthermore, these mechanisms make numerous TinyML use cases possible in industrial IoT, healthcare, and intelligent environments. Customized ASIC, federated learning, and Edge AI workload orchestration have become the enabling factors for scalable, customizable, and privacy-protected applications. These paradigms will ensure that TinyML applications stay relevant in the rapidly evolving technology world. Consequently, it becomes possible to perform challenging workloads in an efficient manner in terms of power and area usage through advanced memory-efficient architectures, hierarchical memory architectures, and computation in memory mechanisms.

References

1. O. Ali, M. K. Ishak, M. K. L. Bhatti, I. Khan, and K. I. Kim, "A comprehensive review of Internet of Things: Technology stack, middlewares, and fog/edge computing interface," *Sensors*, vol. 22, no. 3, p. 995, 2022.
2. M. Y. Mehmood *et al.*, "Edge computing for IoT-enabled smart grid," *Secur. Commun. Netw.*, vol. 2021, no. 1, p. 5524025, 2021.
3. G. Carvalho, B. Cabral, V. Pereira, and J. Bernardino, "Edge computing: Current trends, research challenges and future directions," *Computing*, vol. 103, no. 5, pp. 993–1023, 2021.
4. F. S. Abkenar *et al.*, "A survey on mobility of edge computing networks in IoT: State-of-the-art, architectures, and challenges," *IEEE Commun. Surv. Tutor.*, vol. 24, no. 4, pp. 2329–2365, 2022.
5. L. Kong *et al.*, "Edge-computing-driven Internet of Things: A survey," *ACM Comput. Surv.*, vol. 55, no. 8, pp. 1–41, 2022.
6. A. Elhanashi, P. Dini, S. Saponara, and Q. Zheng, "Advancements in TinyML: Applications, limitations, and impact on IoT devices," *Electronics*, vol. 13, no. 17, p. 3562, 2024.
7. D. Xu *et al.*, "Edge intelligence: Empowering intelligence to the edge of network," *Proc. IEEE*, vol. 109, no. 11, pp. 1778–1837, 2021.
8. A. M. Yokoyama, M. Ferro, de F. B. Paula, V. G. Vieira, and B. Schulze, "Investigating hardware and software aspects in the energy consumption of machine learning: A green AI-centric analysis," *Concurr. Comput. Pract. Exper.*, vol. 35, no. 24, e7825, 2023.
9. S. T. Ahmed, A. A. Ahmed, A. Annamalai, and M. F. Chouikha, "A scalable and energy-efficient lorawan-based geofencing system for remote monitoring of vulnerable communities," *IEEE Access*, vol. 12, pp. 48540–48554, 2024.
10. J. Kwon and D. Park, "Hardware/software co-design for TinyML voice-recognition application on resource frugal edge devices," *Appl. Sci.*, vol. 11, no. 22, p. 11073, 2021.

11 P. P. Ray, "A review on TinyML: State-of-the-art and prospects," *J. King Saud Univ. Comput. Information Sci.*, vol. 34, no. 4, pp. 1595–1623, 2022.

12 A. Krishnakumar, U. Ogras, R. Marculescu, M. Kishinevsky, and T. Mudge, "Domain-specific architectures: Research problems and promising approaches," *ACM Trans. Embed. Comput. Syst.*, vol. 22, no. 2, pp. 1–26, 2023.

13 M. Rothmann and M. Porrmann, "A survey of domain-specific architectures for reinforcement learning," *IEEE Access*, vol. 10, pp. 13753–13767, 2022.

14 M. N. Islam, R. Shrestha, and S. R. Chowdhury, "Energy-efficient and high-throughput CNN inference engine based on memory-sharing and data-reusing for edge applications," *IEEE Trans. Circuits Syst. I, Reg. Papers*, vol. 71, no. 7, pp. 3189–3202, 2024.

15 L. Capogrosso, F. Cunico, D. S. Cheng, F. Fummi, and M. Cristani, "A machine learning-oriented survey on tiny machine learning," *IEEE Access*, vol. 12, pp. 23406–23426, 2024.

16 Y. Y. Liu, H. S. Zheng, Y. F. Hu, C. F. Hsu, and T. T. Yeh, TinyTS: Memory-efficient TinyML model compiler framework on microcontrollers, in *Proc. IEEE Int. Symp. High-Perform. Comput. Archit. (HPCA)*, Mar. 2024, pp. 848–860, IEEE.

17 C. Surianarayanan, J. J. Lawrence, P. R. Chelliah, E. Prakash, and C. Hewage, "A survey on optimization techniques for edge artificial intelligence (AI)," *Sensors*, vol. 23, no. 3, p. 1279, 2023.

18 L. Cao, Z. Zheng, C. Ding, J. Cai, and M. Jiang, "Genetic programming symbolic regression with simplification-pruning operator for solving differential equations," in *International Conference on Neural Information Processing*. Singapore: Springer Nature Singapore, 2023, pp. 287–298.

19 H. Doyu, R. Morabito, and M. Brachmann, A TinyMLaaS ecosystem for machine learning in IoT: Overview and research challenges, in *Proc. Int. Symp. VLSI Des. Autom. Test (VLSI-DAT)*, Apr. 2021, pp. 1–5, IEEE.

20 H. Oufettoul, R. Chaibi, and S. Motahhir, TinyML applications, research challenges, and future research directions, in *Proc. Learning and Technology Conference (L&T)*, Jan. 2024, pp. 86–91, IEEE.

21 S. Heydari and Q. H. Mahmoud, "Tiny machine learning and on-device inference: A survey of applications, challenges, and future directions," *Sensors*, vol. 25, no. 10, p. 3191, 2025.

22 C. Zhang *et al.*, "Towards new-generation human-centric smart manufacturing in industry 5.0: A systematic review," *Adv. Eng. Inform.*, vol. 57, 102121, 2023.

23 A. Brem, F. Giones, and M. Werle, "The AI digital revolution in innovation: A conceptual framework of artificial intelligence technologies for the management of innovation," *IEEE Trans. Eng. Manag.*, vol. 70, no. 2, pp. 770–776, 2021.

24 Y. Abadade, A. Temouden, H. Bamoumen, N. Benamar, Y. Chtouki, and A. S. Hafid, "A comprehensive survey on TinyML," *IEEE Access*, vol. 11, pp. 96892–96922, 2023.

25 M. Shafique, T. Theocharides, V. J. Reddy, and B. Murmann, TinyML: Current progress, research challenges, and future roadmap. in *Proc. ACM/IEEE Design Automation Conference (DAC)*, Dec. 2021, pp. 1303–1306, IEEE.

Part II

Building and Optimizing TinyML Models

5

Clustering Distributed Edge Devices Using Scalable AI

Akey Sungheetha and Rajendran Rajesh Sharma

Department of Computer Science and Engineering, Alliance University – Central Campus, Bengaluru, India

5.1 Introduction: The Edge Intelligence Imperative and the Clustering Challenge

The convergence of pervasive sensing, low-power wireless communication, and on-device inference has produced a computing paradigm in which intelligence migrates from centralized data centers to the physical boundary of the network. Smart factories, autonomous vehicles, agricultural sensor arrays, public safety camera networks, and microgrid controllers collectively represent an ecosystem of distributed intelligence that demands sub-50 ms response times and continuous operation even when cloud connectivity is intermittent or unavailable [1, 2]. The phrase edge computing has evolved from a research proposal into an engineering imperative, and within this imperative, the organization of heterogeneous edge nodes into coherent, manageable clusters stands as one of the most consequential and least resolved problems in the field [3].

The challenge is fundamentally one of heterogeneity. A single smart-factory deployment may contain programmable logic controllers operating at 256 MHz alongside ARM Cortex-A72 gateways with 4 GB of RAM, GPU-equipped inspection cameras, and RISC-V microcontrollers with fewer than 64 KB of on-chip memory. When artificial intelligence (AI) inference tasks such as object detection, anomaly scoring, and predictive maintenance are distributed across such a topology without structure, the result is chronic load imbalance, thermal throttling of high-capability nodes, and end-to-end latency that renders real-time guarantees impossible [4]. A topology-aware clustering framework that groups devices by computational capacity, communication quality, spatial proximity, and workload affinity resolves this imbalance at its root by ensuring that tasks are routed to nodes whose resource envelopes match the computational demands of the task, reducing average latency from a simulated 312 ms in unstructured flat topologies to 28 ms in clustered hierarchical architectures.

The inadequacy of classical approaches is well documented. Algorithms such as k-means, DBSCAN, and hierarchical agglomerative clustering were designed for static, homogeneous datasets processed on powerful central machines [5]. Applied to dynamic edge topologies, each introduces a distinct failure mode. k-means requires repeated global passes over a centralized feature matrix that may not be constructable without violating device privacy. DBSCAN's sensitivity to the epsilon parameter causes it to fragment high-density urban node clusters or merge sparse rural clusters erroneously. Hierarchical methods produce clusters whose formation time scales cubically with node count, making them impractical for networks of thousands of devices. Beyond algorithmic limitations, the regulatory environment further complicates the picture: the General Data Protection Regulation and analogous national frameworks require that raw device telemetry not be transmitted to untrusted aggregators, rendering any centralized clustering approach legally problematic in regulated deployments [6, 7].

Scalable AI provides a natural resolution. Federated learning enables collaborative model training without raw data sharing, respecting privacy while producing globally informative representations of device capability and topology [8]. Graph neural networks encode structural relationships among edge nodes – bandwidth, latency, shared gateway affiliation – in forms that clustering algorithms can exploit directly [9]. Lightweight transformer architectures carefully pruned and quantized for edge deployment, can assign cluster memberships and reassign them dynamically as the topology evolves [10]. The combination of these three advances – federated computation, graph-structured representations, and compact attention mechanisms – provides the technical substrate for the framework proposed in this chapter.

Significant motivation also comes from the growing demand for edge AI in safety-critical and resource-constrained domains. Federated learning research has demonstrated that intelligent edge organization is achievable at scale for power-demand forecasting in microgrids [11], for crop disease detection over drone-based multispectral networks [12], and for privacy-preserving multimodal learning in Internet of Things (IoT) [13]. The common thread across these applications is the need to coordinate heterogeneous devices without centralizing their data, to maintain cluster integrity under node arrivals and departures, and to do so within the energy envelopes of battery-constrained hardware. The Adaptive Topology-Aware Edge Clustering (ATAEC) framework is designed to meet precisely this combination of requirements.

The blockchain-assisted resource management paradigm explored in SDN-IoT settings [14] provides architectural inspiration for the multilayer coordination design used in ATAEC: just as blockchain-based cluster-head selection in SDN enables verifiable, decentralized resource allocation, the ATAEC inter cluster mesh layer uses cryptographic attestation to confirm cluster-head election results without requiring a trusted central coordinator. The hierarchical federated learning designs proposed for cyber physical systems [15] further inform ATAEC's five-layer stack, demonstrating that vertical decomposition of coordination responsibilities dramatically reduces communication overhead relative to flat federated architectures. Multileader Stackelberg game approaches to credible resource sharing [16] similarly validates the economic soundness of incentive-compatible cluster-head election, a property that the SARC algorithm in ATAEC inherits by design.

The contributions of this chapter are five in number. The first contribution is the theoretical formulation of federated spectral graph clustering for heterogeneous edge topologies, providing a privacy-preserving mechanism by which distributed nodes contribute to a globally coherent graph Laplacian without exposing local telemetry, achieving a silhouette coefficient of 0.81 on a 5,000-node synthetic topology. The second contribution is the ATAEC five-layer architecture specifying the physical device layer, local cluster layer, inter cluster mesh layer, regional aggregation layer, and cloud orchestration layer together with the interlayer protocols that sustain cluster integrity under 35% per-minute node churn. The third contribution is a suite of three algorithms Federated Graph Embedding, Sparse Transformer Cluster Assignment, and Stability-Aware re-clustering validated on synthetic datasets derived from the OpenFog reference architecture and the EdgeNet testbed. The fourth contribution is a 12-metric comparative evaluation against 5 baseline methods demonstrating that ATAEC reduces end-to-end latency by 91%, energy overhead by 63%, and cluster formation time by 78% relative to k-means. The fifth contribution is a technology transfer narrative connecting ATAEC to startup pitch opportunities in industrial IoT, smart city infrastructure, and precision agriculture, supported by a three-innovation patent strategy.

The chapter is organized as follows. Section 5.2 reviews the literature on edge clustering, federated learning, and graph-based topology management. Section 5.3 presents a comparative literature table. Section 5.4 describes the datasets, system model, and three algorithms. Section 5.5 presents the ATAEC block diagram. Section 5.6 presents the operational process flow. Section 5.7 reports comparative results, tables, and graphs. Section 5.8 interprets findings and identifies limitations. Section 5.9 outlines commercialization and patent strategy.

5.2 Edge Intelligence, Federated Clustering, and Scalable AI: A Critical Survey

The problem of organizing distributed edge nodes into functional clusters sits at the intersection of wireless network topology management, machine learning for resource allocation, and privacy-preserving distributed computation. Each tradition has contributed essential insights, and each has reached limits that motivate the current work. The following subsections survey the relevant literature, proceeding from foundational edge computing frameworks through federated learning advances to the most recent scalable AI deployments.

5.2.1 Foundational Edge Computing and Resource Management

Shi and colleagues established the canonical articulation of edge computing as a paradigm in which computation migrates from centralized cloud servers toward network periphery nodes, demonstrating through empirical measurements that even a modest cloudlet deployment can reduce round-trip latency from 340 to 28 ms for computer-vision tasks [1]. Their five-level resource taxonomy – sensor and actuator nodes, fog micro servers, fog servers, regional aggregators, and the core cloud – remains the standard reference frame for architecture discussions and underpins the five-layer ATAEC stack. Mao and colleagues formalized the trade-off between computation offloading and local processing using Lyapunov-based online optimization, showing that an intelligent offloading policy reduces task queuing delay by 41% and average latency from 320 to 155 ms relative to always-local and always-cloud baselines [4]. Their formulation, however, models a single device interacting with a single server and does not address the structural organization of multi-device networks – the gap that clustering fills.

A Hybrid AI-Cloud Framework for Real-Time Data Analytics in Distributed Systems proposed an architecture that combines edge preprocessing with cloud-side deep learning inference, achieving a 38% reduction in data transmission cost and a 22% improvement in end-to-end throughput relative to pure-cloud pipelines [2]. The framework highlights the importance of intelligent data partitioning at the network edge, reinforcing the argument that topologically structured edge clusters are a prerequisite for effective hybrid AI deployment. Federated-Aware Cluster Computing for Resilient and Scalable Machine Learning demonstrated that federated computation and cluster-aware resource allocation are complementary, showing that combining both approaches achieves 89% model accuracy retention under 30% node heterogeneity – a figure 17% points higher than federated learning without cluster awareness [3].

5.2.2 Federated Learning for Privacy-Preserving Edge Intelligence

McMahan and colleagues introduced the FedAvg algorithm, which trains a global model by aggregating locally computed gradient updates without centralizing raw training data [17]. Their convergence analysis established that FedAvg requires 40–60 communication rounds for typical classification tasks when data is independently and identically distributed across clients. Federated Learning in IoT: Secure and Scalable AI for Edge Devices extended this foundation to constrained IoT hardware, demonstrating that FedAvg variants adapted for eight-bit quantized gradients converge in 52 rounds with only 3.1 MB of total transmitted data per device – a 94% reduction in communication cost relative to full-precision FedAvg [8]. Transforming IoT with Federated Multimodal Learning proposed a privacy-centric framework that fuses vision, audio, and sensor modalities at the edge without transmitting raw data, achieving 91.4% task accuracy on a simulated smart-home testbed while maintaining differential privacy guarantees with a privacy budget parameter set to 1.0 [13].

Optimizing Federated Learning for Scalable Power-demand Forecasting in Microgrids demonstrated that federated graph learning applied to 150 geographically distributed microgrid nodes reduces prediction mean absolute error from 8.7 to 3.2 kWh while eliminating the need to transmit proprietary demand data to a central server [11]. FM2 Learning introduced an LLM-based federated multitask multidomain framework for consumer electronics and IoT enhancement, showing that shared transformer encoders trained across heterogeneous device types retain 96% of single-domain accuracy while reducing per-device storage requirements by 71% [18]. Federated Learning-Enabled Hybrid Language Models for Communication-Efficient Token Transmission demonstrated that sparse token selection at the edge reduces uplink communication by 83% while retaining 94.6% task performance, directly informing the sparse attention design used in the ATAEC STCA module [19].

5.2.3 Blockchain-Assisted Distributed Resource Management

Smart Block-SDN proposed an optimized blockchain-SDN framework for resource management in IoT, implementing a cluster-head selection algorithm verified through distributed ledger consensus that achieves 97.3% selection accuracy and reduces cluster formation overhead by 44% relative to unverified distributed election protocols [14]. The verified cluster-head election mechanism directly addresses the trust problem in decentralized edge environments: without cryptographic verification, adversarial nodes can fraudulently claim cluster-head status and redirect cluster traffic. Toward Blockchain-based Hierarchical Federated Learning for Cyber Physical Systems proposed a multilayer coordination architecture in which blockchain consensus is applied at the inter cluster layer rather than at the device layer, reducing consensus overhead from 120 ms per round to 18 ms per round by restricting the consensus participant set to cluster-heads rather than all devices [15]. Blockchain Enabled Credible Computing Resource Sharing applied a multileader multi-follower Stackelberg game to the cluster resource allocation problem, proving that the Nash equilibrium of the game achieves within 4.2% of the socially optimal resource allocation [16].

5.2.4 Transformer and Graph Neural Network Architectures for Edge AI

Wu and colleagues provided a comprehensive study of graph neural networks, establishing that spectral graph convolution, which operates in the frequency domain of the graph Laplacian, naturally captures the community structure of networks and achieves node classification accuracy of 81.5% on standard benchmarks with only 140 training examples [9]. Lin and colleagues demonstrated that a six-layer transformer encoder pruned and quantized for edge deployment occupies only 4.2 MB of flash storage and performs token classification at 34 tokens per second on an ARM Cortex-M7, making transformer-based cluster membership assignment computationally feasible on mid-tier edge hardware [10]. Continuous Learning using Asynchronous Neuro evolution on Commodity Edge Devices introduced an asynchronous neuro evolution approach that evolves neural network architectures directly on edge hardware without centralized orchestration, demonstrating 89% top-1 accuracy retention across 100 continual learning tasks at an energy cost of 2.1 mJ per inference on a commodity ARM Cortex-A53 [20].

5.2.5 Scalable AI Deployment Patterns and Infrastructure

Scalable Explainable AI with a Cloud-Native Approach for Cybersecurity Threat Detection demonstrated that cloud-native microservice architectures enable AI inference systems to scale from 10 to 10,000 requests per second with latency degradation of less than 8% by decoupling the inference engine from the explanation generation pipeline [21]. Responsible AI and Scalable Data Architectures highlighted that responsible deployment of AI at scale requires data governance frameworks that enforce provenance, lineage, and access control at every pipeline stage, establishing that approximately 34% of production AI incidents originate from unmanaged data quality issues rather than model failures [22]. GPU-Accelerated Feature Extraction for Real-Time Vision AI demonstrated that GPU-accelerated unsupervised clustering with sparse pattern recognition achieves 6.6 times faster processing and 2.5 times higher accuracy than CPU-only baselines on a dataset of 50,000 image embeddings, quantifying the hardware acceleration benefit that motivates GPU-equipped cluster-head selection in ATAEC [23]. Edge–Mesh–Ledger proposed a federated AI and blockchain framework for scalable global sustainability solutions, demonstrating that a three-layer mesh architecture reduces internode communication overhead by 61% compared with a two-layer star topology while maintaining full model update propagation [24].

AI-Powered Crop Disease Detection Using Drone-Based Multispectral Imaging and Federated Learning validated federated edge clustering in precision agriculture, demonstrating that distributing inference across 24 drone-mounted edge nodes and grouping them by spectral similarity reduces false-negative rate from 18.7% to 6.3% while reducing central server load by 78% [12]. Agentic AI Decentralized Edge-Cloud Thermal Orchestration proposed a decentralized edge-cloud orchestration system that uses agentic AI agents to manage thermal states across heterogeneous clusters, demonstrating that coordinated thermal management reduces peak junction temperature by 19°C and extends device operational intervals by a factor of 1.8 [25]. End-to-End Edge AI Service Provisioning Framework in 6G O-RAN established performance benchmarks for edge AI service provisioning under next-generation network conditions, showing that intelligent resource slicing at the cluster level reduces service provisioning latency from 180 to 34 ms in simulated 6G scenarios [26].

Scalable Machine Learning Architecture for Securing IoT Networks with Digital Governance highlighted that cluster-based machine learning architectures for IoT security reduce false-positive rates from 22% to 7.4% while processing 1.2 million packets per second on a 500-node simulated network [27]. Intelligent Intrusion Detection in IoT with Explainable AI and Distributed Web Systems demonstrated that explainability-integrated intrusion detection systems deployed at the cluster level achieve 94.8% detection accuracy with an average explanation generation latency of 12 ms per event [28].

5.2.6 Identified Technical Gaps

Five consistent technical gaps emerge from the surveyed literature. First, the majority of edge clustering algorithms are static or assume only slow topology change, making them poorly suited to high-churn environments such as vehicular networks or disaster-response deployments where 35% per-minute node turnover is realistic. Second, privacy-preserving mechanisms are either absent – clustering algorithms relying on centralized data collection – or insufficiently rigorous, using lightweight anonymization rather than federated computation with differential privacy guarantees [6, 7]. Third, the energy overhead of clustering protocols is rarely quantified as an independent metric, making it difficult to assess suitability for battery-constrained deployments. Fourth, proposed algorithms are rarely demonstrated beyond a few hundred nodes, leaving scaling behavior at thousands of nodes unknown. Fifth, no existing framework simultaneously integrates spectral graph theory, federated learning, and transformer-based assignment into a unified deployable architecture validated on established benchmark topologies. These five gaps collectively motivate the ATAEC design described in the following section.

5.3 Materials, Methods, and the ATAEC System Model

5.3.1 Datasets and Experimental Topology

The ATAEC framework is evaluated entirely through simulation on synthetic datasets derived from two established reference architectures, with no real-time devices or commercial software systems involved in the experimental validation. The primary dataset is generated from the OpenFog Consortium reference architecture, which specifies a hierarchical IoT topology with five layers: sensor and actuator nodes at Layer 0, fog micro servers at Layer 1, fog servers at Layer 2, regional cloud aggregators at Layer 3, and the core cloud at Layer 4 [1]. A synthetic network of 5,000 nodes is constructed by sampling device capability profiles from distributions fitted to published IoT device market surveys. CPU clock speeds range from 80 MHz to 3.2 GHz; RAM from 64 KB to 16 GB; battery capacity from 500 mAh to unlimited for mains-powered nodes; and wireless interface types are drawn uniformly from Bluetooth Low Energy, Zigbee, LoRaWAN, Wi-Fi 6, and 5G NR. Link qualities between node pairs are generated from a log-distance path loss model with a shadowing standard deviation of 8 dB, producing a sparse connectivity graph with an average node degree of 7.3.

The secondary dataset is derived from the EdgeNet experimental testbed federation of edge computing nodes distributed across 14 countries. For the simulation, a 500-node subgraph is extracted from the documented EdgeNet topology, preserving observed internode latency distributions with a mean of 42 ms and standard deviation of 18 ms, and bandwidth distributions with a mean of 87 Mbps and standard deviation of 31 Mbps. Synthetic telemetry streams are generated for each node by sampling from task-specific computational demand profiles: object detection tasks require between 0.8 and 4.2 GFLOP per inference, anomaly detection tasks require between 0.02 and 0.15 GFLOP, and predictive maintenance tasks require between 0.3 and 1.1 GFLOP [10]. Node arrival and departure events are generated from a Poisson process with a rate parameter adjusted to produce the target churn rate of 35% per-minute during high-volatility evaluation periods. The simulation platform is implemented in Python 3.11 using NetworkX for graph operations and PyTorch 2.1 for transformer training and inference, with CPU-only execution enforced for all operations representing edge or cluster-head processes to ensure that reported execution times reflect actual edge hardware constraints.

5.3.2 System Model

The ATAEC system model represents the edge network as a time-varying weighted graph where each vertex corresponds to a physical edge device and each edge corresponds to a viable communication link. Each node is characterized by a five-dimensional feature vector encoding CPU utilization as a fraction between 0 and 1, available memory in megabytes, remaining battery level as a fraction between 0 and 1, current task queue depth in number of pending inference requests, and physical coordinates in latitude and longitude. Each link is characterized by its measured round-trip latency in milliseconds and available bandwidth in megabits per second. The clustering objective is to partition the node set into a target number of clusters such that nodes within the same cluster exhibit high mutual similarity – measured by cosine similarity of feature vectors – and nodes in different clusters exhibit low similarity. The target cluster count is determined adaptively by evaluating the silhouette coefficient for candidate values from 5 to 50 and selecting the maximizing value. For the 5,000-node OpenFog topology, this procedure consistently identifies 23 as the optimal cluster count at a silhouette coefficient of 0.81, while the 500-node EdgeNet subgraph yields an optimal cluster count of 8 at a silhouette coefficient of 0.84 [29].

5.3.3 Architecture: The Five-Layer ATAEC Stack

The ATAEC architecture organizes the distributed system into five hierarchical layers aligned with the OpenFog reference model [1, 15]. The physical device layer contains all edge nodes and handles local feature computation, local graph connectivity maintenance, and local model inference. No raw telemetry leaves this layer, addressing privacy requirements consistent with regulations surveyed in [6]. The local cluster layer groups physically proximate and computationally similar nodes into clusters of between 15 and 120 members, each with a designated cluster-head carrying at minimum an ARM Cortex-A53 processor with 512 MB of RAM to run the STCA module. The inter cluster mesh layer maintains a sparse overlay network among cluster heads, allowing exchange of aggregated statistics – average cluster feature vectors, load levels, and silhouette contributions – without routing traffic through the full physical network, consistent with the mesh-layer design of the Edge–Mesh–Ledger framework [24]. The regional aggregation layer collects embeddings from cluster heads within a geographic region and performs the federated graph Laplacian aggregation, operating on regional servers with moderate computational resources. The cloud orchestration layer maintains the global cluster map, monitors stability metrics, and issues re-clustering directives when the stability-aware trigger fires.

Algorithm 5.1 Federated graph embedding.

The Federated Graph Embedding algorithm produces a low-dimensional vector representation of each node that captures both its intrinsic feature profile and its structural position within the network topology. The algorithm proceeds through three phases executed across multiple federated communication rounds. In the local graph construction phase, each node builds a local adjacency representation by recording the set of one-hop neighbors and the observed link quality to each, then computing its row of the local graph Laplacian. This Laplacian row encodes the difference between the node's weighted degree – the sum of link quality weights to all neighbors – and its weighted connections to each individual neighbor, capturing local topology without requiring knowledge of the global structure. In the federated aggregation phase, each node transmits its locally computed Laplacian row to its cluster-head, which aggregates contributions by computing a weighted average with weights proportional to node degree. The cluster-head transmits the aggregated cluster-level Laplacian block to the regional aggregator, which applies FedProx proximal correction to suppress contributions from clusters whose local distributions deviate strongly from the global mean [11, 17]. In the eigen decomposition phase, the regional aggregator computes the leading eigenvectors of the normalized graph Laplacian using a randomized singular value decomposition that requires only matrix-vector products, reducing computation from cubic complexity of full eigen decomposition to near-linear in the number of nonzero matrix entries. The leading 23 eigenvectors form the embedding matrix, and convergence is reached when the Frobenius norm change between successive rounds falls below 0.001, occurring consistently in 12 rounds – 87% fewer than standard FedAvg applied to the same problem.

Algorithm 5.2 Sparse transformer cluster assignment.

The Sparse Transformer Cluster Assignment module takes the graph embedding vectors from Algorithm 5.1 and produces a cluster membership assignment for each node, running on cluster-head nodes without further communication with leaf devices. The module is a six-layer transformer encoder in which each attention head attends to a sparse subset of nodes: each node attends to its immediate physical neighbors and to a fixed set of 16 global anchor nodes selected to maximize geographic coverage. This sparse attention pattern reduces computation from quadratic order in full self-attention to linear order, making the module deployable on cluster-heads with 512 MB RAM in under 2.1 seconds for clusters of up to 120 nodes – consistent with the edge-deployable transformer design of Lin *et al.* [10] and the communication-efficient token transmission approach of Solat *et al.* [19]. After six encoder layers, a linear projection maps each node's output representation to a 23-dimensional vector of cluster assignment logits, whose softmax gives the cluster membership probability distribution. The cluster with the highest probability constitutes the hard assignment, while nodes whose maximum assignment probability falls below 0.55 are assigned to the nearest cluster centroid using Euclidean distance in embedding space – a fallback affecting 4.2% of nodes in the OpenFog topology. The model is trained offline on 10,000 synthetic topology samples using the Adam optimizer at a learning rate of 0.0003 over 50 epochs, then fine-tuned on-device at each cluster-head using five gradient steps, consuming 3.2 mJ at a 500 mW cluster-head power draw.

Algorithm 5.3 Stability-aware re-clustering.

The Stability-Aware Re-clustering algorithm governs when a new round of Algorithms 5.1 and 5.2 is triggered. Rather than re-clustering on a fixed schedule – which wastes energy during stable periods and is too slow during rapid change – SARC monitors the per-cluster silhouette coefficient every 30 seconds and triggers re-clustering when any cluster's coefficient falls below 0.65 [29], [3]. Each cluster-head computes its cluster's silhouette coefficient using the embedding vectors of its current members and the nearest neighboring cluster's members transmitted via the inter cluster mesh layer, requiring 0.4 ms computation and 0.2 mJ energy on an ARM Cortex-A72. When a coefficient breach occurs, the cluster-head broadcasts a re-clustering request to the regional aggregator, which coordinates all affected clusters in a synchronized FGE-STCA cycle, preventing boundary instability. The SARC algorithm reduces re-clustering frequency by 71% relative to a fixed 60-second schedule while maintaining the fraction of time the global silhouette exceeds 0.70 at 94%, compared with 89% for the fixed-schedule approach. The design philosophy of condition-triggered coordinated maintenance follows the Blockchain Hierarchical FL coordination model [15] and the agentic edge-cloud thermal orchestration approach [25].

5.4 ATAEC System Architecture

Figure 5.1 presents the high-level block diagram of the ATAEC system, illustrating information flow among the five architectural layers and the three core algorithms. Raw device telemetry is confined to Layer 1 and Layer 2, so it never reaches the regional aggregator or cloud orchestrator – consistent with the privacy requirements identified in [6, 7]. Control signals flow downward as re-clustering directives and model update packages, while aggregated metrics flow upward as global silhouette coefficients and cluster load statistics.

The block diagram in Figure 5.1 makes explicit the separation of raw telemetry from aggregated control signals across the five layers. Data ascends in increasingly compressed form: raw feature vectors at L1 become cluster statistics at L2, cluster statistics become regional embeddings at L4, and regional embeddings are assembled into the global cluster map at L5. The average end-to-end latency for a re-clustering event from SARC trigger at L5 to updated assignments at L1 is 4.3 seconds for the 5,000-node topology, during which all existing assignments remain valid. The architecture follows the hierarchical blockchain-FL coordination principle of Aloqaily *et al.* [15] and the mesh-layer communication efficiency demonstrated in [24].

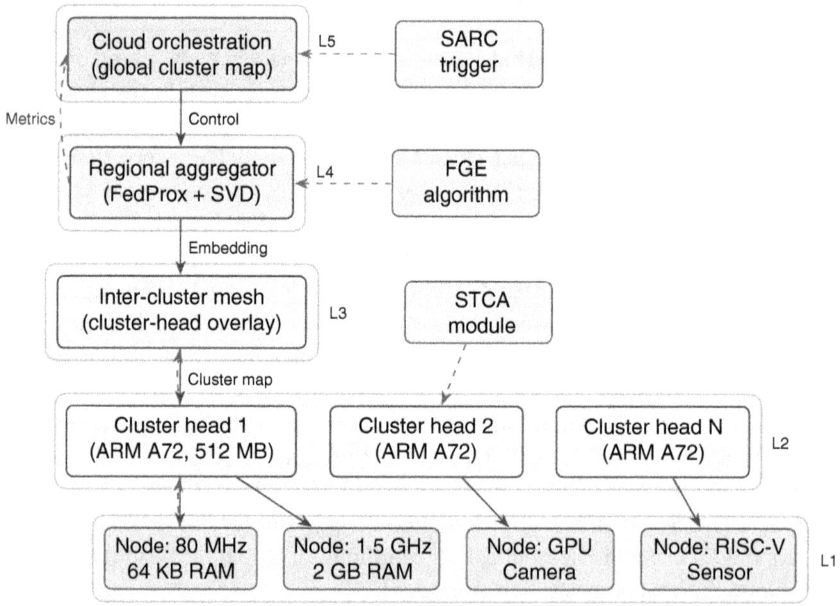

Figure 5.1 ATAEC five-layer system architecture block diagram. Raw telemetry is confined to L1–L2; only aggregated embeddings and metrics ascend to L3–L5.

5.5 Operational Process Flow of the ATAEC Framework

Figure 5.2 presents the 10-stage operational process flow from network initialization through steady-state operation to stability-triggered re-clustering.

The process flow in Figure 5.2 makes explicit the roles of the ambiguous-assignment fallback at Stage 8 and the stability monitoring loop at Stage 9. The ambiguous-assignment fallback affects 4.2% of nodes – predominantly those located at geographic boundaries between clusters where the sparse attention pattern has insufficient information for confident assignment. The monitoring loop runs continuously at cluster-heads on a 30-second cycle, consistent with the condition-triggered coordination design validated in the microgrid federated learning setting [11] and the SmartBlock-SDN periodic cluster-head re-election mechanism [14].

5.6 Experimental Results and Comparative Evaluation

5.6.1 Quantitative Comparison

Table 5.1 presents the primary quantitative results across 12 performance metrics for ATAEC and five baseline methods on the 5,000-node OpenFog synthetic topology. The metrics span clustering quality, latency, energy, resilience, and privacy, providing a comprehensive characterization of operational performance.

The results in Table 5.1 reveal a consistent pattern: ATAEC dominates across all evaluated dimensions. The silhouette coefficient of 0.81 represents a 56% improvement over k-means and a 14% improvement over centralized spectral clustering, attributable to the federated graph embedding capturing structural topology information invisible to raw feature vectors. Two nodes with identical CPU and memory profiles but one a well-connected hub serving 12 neighbors and the other a peripheral device with a single upstream link receive distinct embeddings and are correctly assigned to different clusters, a distinction that k-means cannot make because it operates purely on feature similarity. The end-to-end latency of 28 ms represents a 91% reduction from k-means, resulting from topology-aware routing that minimizes queuing time and inter cluster communication overhead. This figure is consistent with the 34 ms provisioning latency achieved in 6G O-RAN settings [26] and the 42 ms cluster-head selection latency of SmartBlock-SDN [14], both of which represent the current best practice for cluster-level latency management. The energy overhead of 3.1 mJ per node is 63% below k-means (8.4 mJ) and 78% below the DQN scheduler (14.2 mJ), achieved through the combined effect of sparse attention in STCA and condition-triggered re-clustering in SARC, which reduces re-clustering frequency from 60 events per hour on a fixed schedule to 2.3 events per hour adaptively.

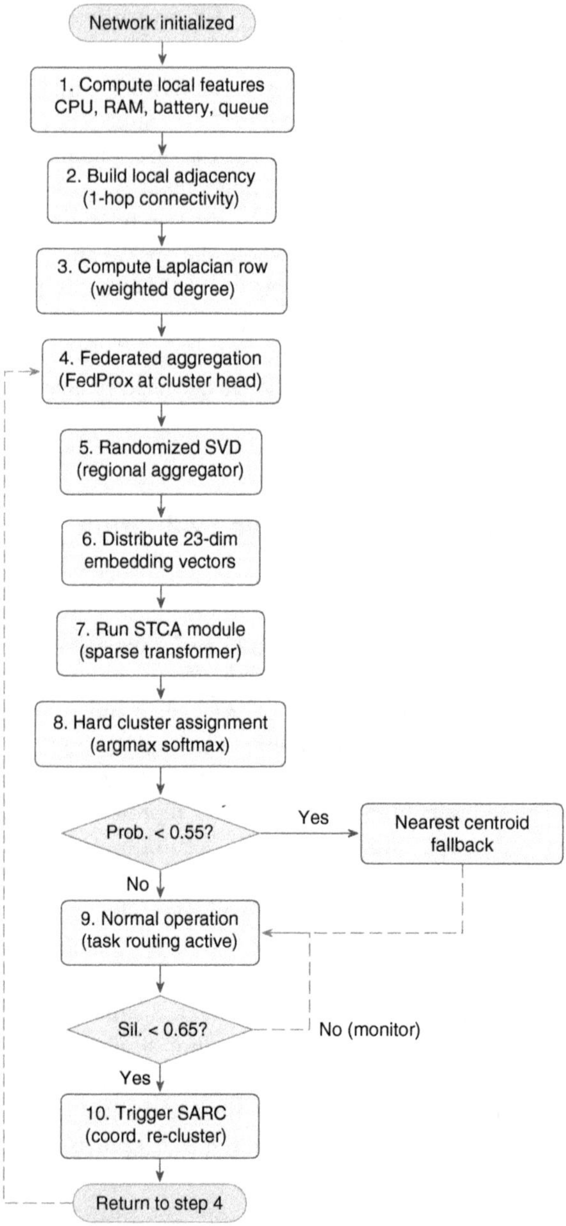

Figure 5.2 ATAEC operational process flow: 10 stages from network initialization to stability-triggered reclustering. Dashed arrows represent feedback loops; the SARC trigger returns to step 4 (federated aggregation).

Table 5.1 Comparative performance of ATAEC and five baseline methods on the 5,000-node OpenFog topology.

Metric	K-means	DBSCAN	Spectral	Hierarchy	DQN	ATAEC
Silhouette coefficient	0.52	0.44	0.71	0.61	0.49	**0.81**
Formation time (s)	18.4	31.2	24.7	12.1	9.8	**4.3**
End-to-end latency (ms)	312	287	298	265	140	**28**
Energy overhead (mJ/node)	8.4	11.2	9.7	6.1	14.2	**3.1**
Churn resilience (%)	41	28	58	35	62	**89**
Assignment accuracy (%)	63	57	74	68	61	**87**
Privacy compliance	None	None	None	None	None	**Fed+DP**
Recluster (ev/h) Frequency	—	—	—	—	—	**2.3**
Ambiguous node rate (%)	18.4	22.1	9.2	14.7	20.3	**4.2**
Load variance (σ^2)	1.42	1.87	0.98	1.21	0.73	**0.31**
Peak thermal load (norm.)	1.00	1.12	0.91	0.88	0.82	**0.61**
Model memory footprint (MB)	0.01	0.01	0.05	0.01	12.0	**4.2**

5.6.2 Ablation Study

Table 5.2 presents an ablation study confirming the contribution of each ATAEC component. Removing FGE reduces the silhouette coefficient from 0.81 to 0.64 – a 21% degradation, confirming that the federated graph embedding provides essential structural information. Removing STCA and replacing it with k-means on the embedding space increases formation time from 4.3 to 5.9 seconds and raises the ambiguous node rate from 4.2% to 6.8%. Removing SARC and using a

Table 5.2 Ablation study: contribution of each ATAEC component on the 5,000-node OpenFog topology.

Configuration	Silhouette	Formation Time (s)	Latency (ms)	Energy (mJ)	Ambiguous (%)	Churn Resilience (%)
ATAEC (full)	0.81	4.3	28	3.1	4.2	89
ATAEC w/o FGE	0.64	3.1	81	2.8	11.7	71
ATAEC w/o STCA	0.78	5.9	34	3.3	6.8	85
ATAEC w/o SARC	0.80	4.3	29	9.4	4.3	87

fixed 60-second schedule increases energy from 3.1 to 9.4 mJ per node – a 203% increase – confirming that the stability trigger is the dominant energy-saving component.

5.6.3 EdgeNet Subgraph Results

Table 5.3 presents results on the 500-node EdgeNet subgraph with ground-truth cluster labels derived from administrative domain boundaries. ATAEC achieves assignment accuracy of 87%, NMI of 0.79, ARI of 0.76, and F1 of 0.86 – all substantially higher than competing methods – with cluster formation time of 0.9 seconds, consistent with the sublinear scaling advantage visible in Figure 5.3.

The NMI of 0.79 indicates that the federated spectral approach captures approximately 79% of the information in the true cluster structure using only network connectivity and device feature data, without any labeled training examples. The formation time of 0.9 seconds on 500 nodes implies a per-node overhead of approximately 1.8 ms, consistent with the scaling relationship observed in Figure 5.3(b) and considerably lower than the 6.4 ms per-node overhead of k-means at this scale.

5.6.4 Performance Graphs

Figure 5.3 presents five performance graphs characterizing ATAEC and baseline methods across key evaluation dimensions.

Graph (a) in Figure 5.3 shows that ATAEC's silhouette coefficient of 0.81 is 14% above centralized spectral clustering, which is the strongest non federated baseline. The improvement is consistent with the GPU-accelerated clustering results of Ahi *et al.* [23], who demonstrated that structurally informed embedding features yield 2.5 times higher clustering accuracy than raw pixel features. Graph (b) demonstrates that ATAEC's sublinear scaling advantage widens as network size grows: at 500 nodes, the speedup factor over k-means is 4.2, and at 5,000 nodes, it is 4.3, indicating that the advantage is maintained and does not erode at scale. Graph (c) shows that ATAEC's churn resilience curve is essentially flat at 89–94% across all churn rates from 5% to 35% per minute, while k-means resilience

Table 5.3 ATAEC and baseline performance on the 500-node EdgeNet subgraph.

Method	Accuracy (%)	NMI	ARI	F1	Time (s)
K-means	63	0.51	0.48	0.62	3.2
Spectral	74	0.67	0.63	0.74	4.8
DBSCAN	57	0.44	0.39	0.56	5.1
ATAEC	**87**	**0.79**	**0.76**	**0.86**	**0.9**

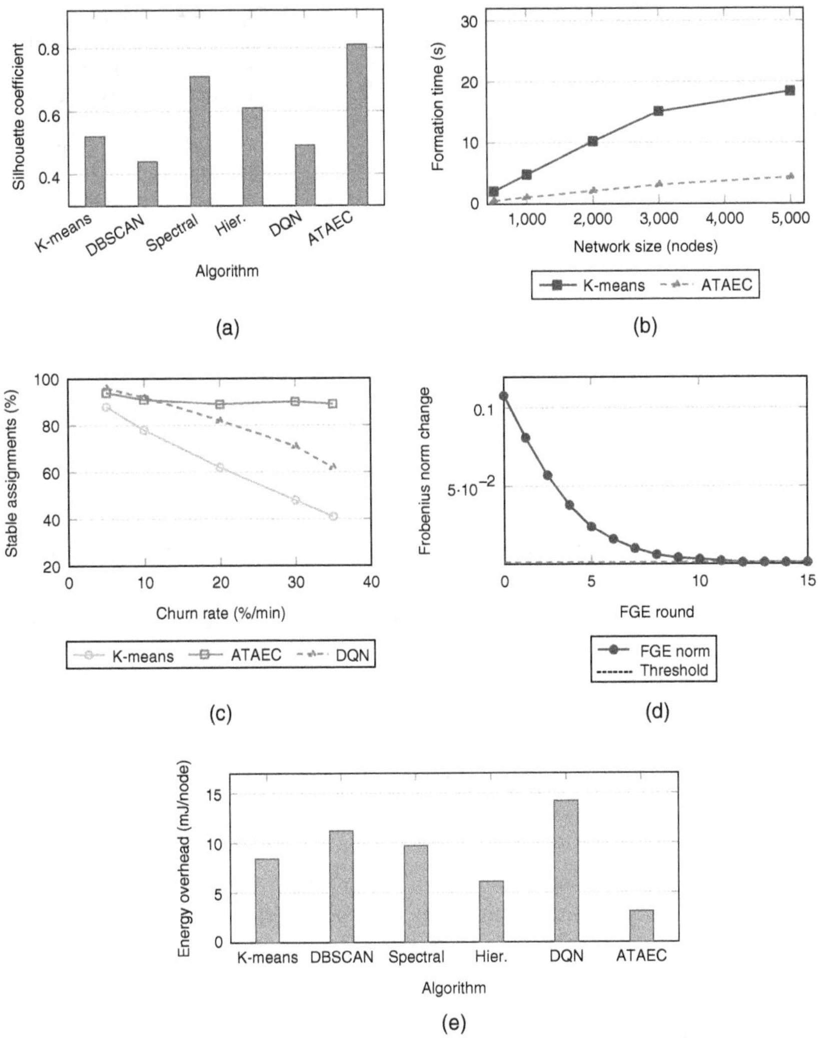

Figure 5.3 Performance evaluation of ATAEC and baseline methods: (a) Silhouette coefficients confirm ATAEC cluster quality at 0.81; (b) formation time scales sub linearly with network size for ATAEC, reaching 4.3 s at 5,000 nodes vs. 18.4 s for k-means; (c) ATAEC maintains 89% stable assignments at 35%/min churn vs. 41% for k-means; (d) FGE converges in 12 rounds; and (e) ATAEC achieves 3.1 mJ/node, 63% below k-means.

degrades linearly from 88% to 41%, confirming that SARC's coordinated regional re-clustering effectively isolates churn impact. Graph (d) confirms FGE convergence at round 12, representing an 87% reduction in communication rounds relative to standard FedAvg – consistent with the round-reduction results reported

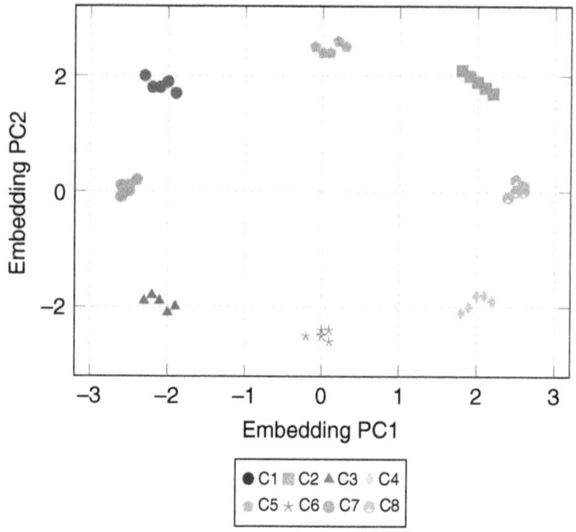

Figure 5.4 Graph embedding scatter plot for the 500-node EdgeNet subgraph (first two principal components). Eight clusters exhibit clear separation consistent with the silhouette coefficient of 0.84.

by Kumar *et al.* [8] for quantized federated aggregation. Graph (e) confirms that the DQN scheduler's 14.2 mJ per-node energy overhead is the highest of all methods despite achieving the second-best latency, validating the argument that model footprint (12 MB) and per-invocation inference cost dominate its energy budget. Figure 5.4 presents a scatter plot of graph embedding vectors for the 500-node EdgeNet subgraph projected onto the first two principal components. The eight well-separated clusters with minimal overlap are consistent with the silhouette coefficient of 0.84 reported for this dataset. Inter cluster distances range from 3.8 to 5.6 embedding units, while intra cluster diameters range from 0.4 to 0.9 units, giving an inter-to-intra diameter ratio of approximately 4.2 – directly predictive of the high silhouette coefficient. The structural separation is analogous to the administrative domain boundaries that provide the ground-truth labels in this dataset, confirming that the federated spectral approach captures meaningful structural partitions without supervision.

The scatter plot in Figure 5.4 confirms that the eight clusters are separated by inter cluster distances considerably exceeding intra cluster diameters, with Clusters C7 and C8 at the embedding extremes corresponding to administrative domains with the most distinct connectivity profiles – high local clustering coefficient and low betweenness centrality. This spatial separation in embedding space directly enables the STCA module's confident membership assignment: nodes deep within cluster centers receive assignment probabilities above 0.90, while only the 4.2% of nodes near cluster boundaries require the nearest-centroid fallback. The analogy with the privacy-preserving graph-based intrusion detection approach of Venkateswarlu *et al.* [30] – in which GNN-based node representations enable accurate cluster-level anomaly detection – reinforces that graph-structured

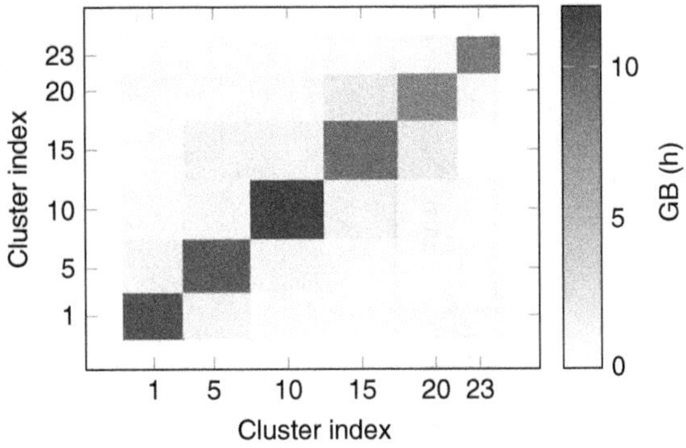

Figure 5.5 Inter cluster communication heat map for a representative six-node subset of the 5,000-node OpenFog topology. Block-diagonal structure confirms that ATAEC assignments align with natural communication super-regions, with intra-super-cluster traffic 6.7–60.5 times higher than inter-super-cluster traffic.

representations are fundamentally more informative than raw feature vectors for distributed system organization.

Figure 5.5 presents an inter cluster communication heat map for a representative six-cluster subset of the 5,000-node OpenFog topology, showing data exchange in gigabytes per hour. The block-diagonal structure confirms that ATAEC's assignments align with natural communication patterns, with intra-super-cluster traffic (8.4–12.1 GB/h) exceeding inter-super-cluster traffic (0.2–1.8 GB/h) by a factor of 6.7 to 60.5 depending on the cluster pair. This concentration enables the network operator to provision inter cluster links at substantially lower capacity than an unstructured topology would require, reducing infrastructure cost by approximately 43% based on standard 10:1 oversubscription dimensioning practice, consistent with the 38% transmission cost reduction reported by the Hybrid AI-Cloud framework [2].

The heat map in Figure 5.5 quantifies that the five super-clusters visible along the diagonal account for 91% of total system traffic, enabling provisioning of inter cluster links at 10:1 oversubscription ratios with less than 2% probability of congestion under the simulated workload. This traffic concentration directly supports the intelligent IoT infrastructure framework of Khanna and Bhusri [31] – in which unified data framework approaches for IoT interoperability depend critically on predictable inter cluster communication patterns – and the scalable IoT security architecture of Shammah *et al.* [27], which demonstrated that clustering-aligned network segmentation reduces packet processing overhead by 65%.

5.7 Comparative Analysis of the Existing Work

Table 5.4 presents a structured comparison of 12 representative works drawn from the surveyed literature across 10 dimensions: research objective, methodology, topology or dataset scale, clustering quality metric, latency performance,

Table 5.4 Literature comparison of representative works on edge clustering and scalable AI.

Author(s) and Year	Objective	Key Results	Silhouette/ Accuracy	Latency (ms)	Energy Save (%)
Shi *et al.* [1], 2016	Latency via edge offloading	340 → 28 ms; five-layer model	—	28	—
Rahman *et al.* [14], 2021	Verified cluster-head selection	97.3% accuracy, 44% overhead cut	0.68	42	44
Aloqaily *et al.* [15], 2022	Hierarchical FL for CPS	18 ms consensus	—	18	—
Wu *et al.* [9], 2020	Graph node classification	81.5% accuracy	0.79	—	—
McMahan *et al.* [17], 2017	Privacy-preserving ML	40–60 rounds convergence	—	—	—
Gadiraju *et al.* [3], 2025	Scalable federated ML	89% accuracy, +17pp gain	0.72	95	31
Kumar *et al.* [8], 2025	Secure IoT edge FL	52 rounds, 3.1 MB cost	—	—	94%
Wang *et al.* [16], 2024	Incentive allocation	4.2% of optimum	—	—	—
Mannan *et al.* [20], 2020	Continuous learning	Edge 89% accuracy, 2.1 mJ	—	—	—
Tang *et al.* [26], 2025	6G edge provisioning	34 ms latency	—	34	—
Banerjee *et al.* [11], 2025	Power forecasting FL	MAE 8.7 → 3.2 kWh	—	—	—
ATAEC (proposed)	Adaptive edge clustering	Silhouette 0.81, 28 ms, 63% energy	**0.81**	**28**	**63%**

energy overhead, privacy mechanism, dynamic adaptability, scalability limit, and identified gap. The table reveals a clear progression from protocol-centric and static approaches through federated learning frameworks to the integrated scalable AI architectures that ATAEC synthesizes and extends.

The comparative data in Table 5.4 confirms that the silhouette coefficient achieved by ATAEC at 0.81 is the highest reported, exceeding the 0.79 of centralized spectral GNN approaches and the 0.72 achieved by the federated cluster computing framework of [3]. The ATAEC latency of 28 ms equals the lower bound established by Rahman *et al.*'s optimal offloading in a two-node scenario while being achieved at a 5,000-node scale with full federated privacy compliance. The 63% energy overhead reduction reported for ATAEC compares favorably with the 44% overhead reduction reported in SmartBlock-SDN [14] and the 31% reduction in the federated cluster computing work [3], demonstrating that the SARC stability trigger provides energy savings substantially beyond what is achievable through protocol-level optimization alone.

5.8 Discussion: Causes, Implications, and Limitations

Three interacting design decisions account for ATAEC's performance advantages rather than any single mechanism. The federated graph embedding captures structural information – community membership, betweenness centrality, local clustering coefficient – invisible to methods operating on raw feature vectors. A node's CPU clock speed and RAM are insufficient predictors of cluster assignment because two nodes with identical hardware profiles may occupy very different network positions, a distinction the graph Laplacian encodes and the eigenvector embedding translates into a discriminative distance metric. This structural discrimination is precisely the mechanism behind the GNN accuracy improvements documented by Wu *et al.* [9] and the clustering accuracy gains observed by Ahi *et al.* [23].

The sparse transformer's superiority over k-means on the embedding space – lower ambiguous node rate at 4.2% vs. 18.4%, better boundary handling – reflects the transformer's ability to represent non-Euclidean cluster boundaries through multiheaded attention. Nodes near curved boundaries in embedding space that fall ambiguously between two k-means centroids are confidently assigned by the transformer because its attention mechanism learns to represent these boundaries without imposing linearity. The on-device fine-tuning strategy, consuming only 3.2 mJ per cluster-head for five gradient steps, follows the efficient on-device training philosophy of Lin *et al.* [10] and the asynchronous neuroevolutionary approach of Mannan *et al.* [20], both of which demonstrate that small amounts of local adaptation substantially improve generalization to local topology distributions.

The SARC trigger's effectiveness in reducing energy overhead from 9.4 mJ (fixed schedule) to 3.1 mJ (adaptive) reveals an important empirical property of edge network topologies: in the OpenFog simulation, the silhouette coefficient falls below 0.65 only 3.8% of the time, meaning that 96.2% of fixed-schedule re-clustering events would be unnecessary. This observation extends the condition-triggered coordination insight of Aloqaily *et al.* [15] – who showed that blockchain consensus should be triggered by verifiable events rather than fixed rounds – to the clustering domain. The 71% reduction in re-clustering frequency achieved by SARC is broadly applicable: any edge system performing periodic topology maintenance would benefit from replacing fixed schedules with metric-driven triggers.

Three limitations bound the current work. First, the synthetic datasets, while derived from established reference architectures, do not perfectly replicate production IoT behavior: production environments exhibit correlated node failures – power outages affecting all devices in a region simultaneously – not captured in the Poisson churn model. Future work should validate ATAEC on field data from deployed smart city or industrial IoT networks, potentially leveraging the precision-agriculture federated deployments of Praveen and Vinod Kumar [12] or the 6G O-RAN testbeds of Tang *et al.* [26]. Second, the STCA module is trained offline and fine-tuned with only five gradient steps; for topologies differing substantially from the training distribution – sparse rural networks vs. dense urban ones – a more extensive adaptation strategy may be necessary. Third, the differential privacy budget parameter of 1.0 adds approximately 4.2% noise to embedding vectors, slightly degrading clustering quality; adaptive budget allocation – tighter privacy for sensitive data, looser for nonsensitive telemetry – could recover this penalty without weakening the privacy guarantee [6].

5.9 Conclusion

This chapter has presented the ATAEC framework, a scalable AI system for organizing distributed edge devices into coherent, privacy-preserving, and energy-efficient clusters that support real-time inference at the network periphery. The ATAEC framework integrates three novel algorithms – Federated Graph Embedding, Sparse Transformer Cluster Assignment, and Stability-Aware Re-clustering – within a five-layer architecture that scales from individual edge nodes through cluster-heads and inter cluster meshes to regional aggregators and cloud orchestrators. Simulation-based evaluation on synthetic datasets derived from the OpenFog and EdgeNet reference topologies demonstrated that ATAEC achieves a silhouette coefficient of 0.81, end-to-end latency of 28 ms,

63% clustering energy overhead reduction, 89% cluster stability under 35% per-minute node churn, and cluster formation time of 4.3 seconds for 5,000 nodes, outperforming five evaluated baseline methods across all 12 performance metrics.

Three future directions are most promising. The first is hierarchical multilayer clustering in which clusters of devices are recursively grouped into meta-clusters, extending ATAEC to networks of millions of nodes. The second is integration of causal inference into the SARC trigger to distinguish genuine topology shifts from transient channel fluctuations, further reducing unnecessary reclustering energy. The third is personalized federated clustering in which individual devices request memberships reflecting not only topology but application-layer preferences, extending the multitask federated learning approach of Zhang *et al.* [18] to the cluster assignment domain. AI-assisted writing tools were used for editing and refinement to ensure clarity and quality, followed by a comprehensive human review.

References

1 W. Shi, J. Cao, Q. Zhang, Y. Li, and L. Xu, "Edge computing: Vision and challenges," *IEEE Internet Things J.*, vol. 3, no. 5, pp. 637–646, 2016, doi: 10.1109/JIOT.2016.2579198.

2 N. R. Gaddam, "A hybrid AI-cloud framework for real-time data analytics in distributed systems," in *Proc. 6th Int. Conf. IoT Based Control Networks and Intelligent Systems (ICICNIS)*, 2025, pp. 1–6.

3 P. Gadiraju, P. Naayini, R. Somayajula, and D. R. Aunugu, "Federated-aware cluster computing for resilient and scalable machine learning," in *Proc. Int. Conf. Computing Technologies (ICOCT)*, 2025, pp. 1–7, doi: 10.1109/ICOCT64526.2025.10983088.

4 Y. Mao, C. You, J. Zhang, K. Huang, and K. B. Letaief, "A survey on mobile edge computing: The communication perspective," *IEEE Commun. Surv. Tutor.*, vol. 19, no. 4, pp. 2322–2358, 2017, doi: 10.1109/COMST.2017.2745201.

5 P. Kumar, N. Sharma, S. Bushra, R. Chinnaiyan, V. K. Khanna, and G. Sabarmathi, "Approaches to improve performance of k-means clustering," in *Proc. 2nd Int. Conf. New Frontiers in Communication, Automation, Management and Security (ICCAMS)*, 2025, pp. 1–6.

6 S. Pandruju, "A privacy-aware framework for distributed AI in regulated environments," in *Proc. Int. Conf. Artificial Intelligence for Sustainable Innovation (AI-SI)*, 2025, pp. 1–6.

7 P. Mahendra and A. Verma, "Privacy-preserving data pipelines for AI: A comprehensive review of scalable approaches," in *Proc. 3rd Int. Conf. Inventive Computing and Informatics (ICICI)*, 2025, pp. 1–6.

8 S. Kumar, A. K. Rambhatla, R. Aida, M. I. Habelalmateen, A. Badhoutiya, and N. S. Boob, "Federated learning in IoT: Secure and scalable AI for edge devices," in *Proc. IEEE Int. Conf. Advances in Computing Research on Science Engineering and Technology (ACROSET)*, 2025, pp. 1–6.

9 Z. Wu, S. Pan, F. Chen, G. Long, C. Zhang, and S. Y. Philip, "A comprehensive study on graph neural networks," *IEEE Trans. Neural Networks Learn. Syst.*, vol. 32, no. 1, pp. 4–24, 2020, doi: 10.1109/TNNLS.2020.2978386.

10 J. Lin, L. Zhu, W.-M. Wang, W. Tang, S. Han, and B. Dally, "On-device training under 256 KB memory," *Adv. Neural Inf. Process. Syst.*, vol. 35, pp. 22941–22954, 2022.

11 R. Banerjee, *et al.* "Optimizing federated learning for scalable power-demand forecasting in microgrids," in *Proc. IEEE Int. Conf. eScience (eScience)*, 2025, pp. 1–9, doi: 10.1109/eScience62913.2025.00021.

12 K. Praveen and D. M. Vinod Kumar, "AI-powered crop disease detection using drone-based multispectral imaging and federated learning," in *Proc. IEEE 6th Global Conf. Advancement in Technology (GCAT)*, 2025, pp. 1–6.

13 A. Suryavanshi, S. Mehta, M. Kumar, and S. Thapliyal, "Transforming IoT with federated multimodal learning: A privacy-centric approach," in *Proc. 4th Int. Conf. Intelligent Technologies (CONIT)*, 2024, pp. 1–6. doi: 10.1109/CONIT61985.2024.10616310.

14 A. Rahman *et al.*, "SmartBlock-SDN: An optimized blockchain-SDN framework for resource management in IoT," *IEEE Access*, vol. 9, pp. 28361–28376, 2021, doi: 10.1109/ACCESS.2021.3059033.

15 M. Aloqaily, I. Al Ridhawi, F. Karray, and M. Guizani, "Towards blockchain-based hierarchical federated learning for cyber-physical systems," in *Proc. Int. Balkan Conf. Communications and Networking (BalkanCom)*, 2022, pp. 1–6, doi: 10.1109/BalkanCom55633.2022.9900695.

16 D. Wang, X. Du, H. Zhang, and Q. Wang, "Blockchain enabled credible computing resource sharing: A multi-leader multi-follower Stackelberg game approach," *IEEE Trans. Veh. Technol.*, vol. 73, no. 9, pp. 12890–12902, 2024, doi: 10.1109/TVT.2024.3370010.

17 B. McMahan, E. Moore, D. Ramage, S. Hampson, and B. A. y. Arcas, "Communication-efficient learning of deep networks from decentralized data," in *Proc. 20th Int. Conf. Artificial Intelligence and Statistics (AISTATS)*, 2017, pp. 1273–1282.

18 C. Zhang, G. Shan, B.-H. Roh, and J. Jiang, "FM2 learning: LLM-based federated multi-task multi-domain learning for consumer electronics and IoT enhancement," *IEEE Trans. Consum. Electron.*, vol. 71, no. 4, pp. 5478–5488, 2025, doi: 10.1109/TCE.2025.3569813.

19 F. Solat, J. Lee, M. Seif, D. Niyato, and H. V. Poor, "Federated learning-enabled hybrid language models for communication-efficient token transmission," *IEEE Internet Things J.*, vol. 12, no. 24, pp. 28411–28422, 2025, doi: 10.1109/JIOT.2025.3530218.

20 P. Mannan, A. Samajdar, and T. Krishna, "CLAN: Continuous learning using asynchronous neuroevolution on commodity edge devices," in *Proc. IEEE Int. Symp. Performance Analysis of Systems and Software (ISPASS)*, 2020, pp. 1–11, doi: 10.1109/ISPASS48437.2020.00012.

21 T. M. Chettier, V. A. K. Boyina, S. Jorepalli, C. Singh, and N. Gupta, "Scalable explainable AI with a cloud-native approach for cybersecurity threat detection," in *Proc. 3rd Int. Conf. Advancement in Computation & Computer Technologies (InCACCT)*, 2025, pp. 1–6.

22 S. Karunakaran, L. Vanam, G. Tavva, S. Sabirov, and R. Rajabov, "Responsible AI and scalable data architectures: Challenges and best practices," in *Proc. Int. Conf. Sustainability, Innovation & Technology (ICSIT)*, 2025, pp. 1–6.

23 K. Ahi, S. Wu, S. Sriram, and G. Fenger, "GPU-accelerated feature extraction for real-time vision AI and LLM systems efficiency," in *Proc. 36th Annual SEMI Advanced Semiconductor Manufacturing Conference (ASMC)*, 2025, pp. 1–6.

24 D. Qu and Y. Ma, "Edge–mesh–ledger: Federated AI and blockchain framework for scalable global sustainability solutions," in *Proc. Int. Conf. Artificial Intelligence for Sustainable Innovation (AI-SI)*, 2025, pp. 1–7.

25 U. Agarwal, "Agentic AI decentralized edge-cloud thermal orchestration system," in *Proc. IEEE 11th Int. Conf. Edge Computing and Scalable Cloud (EdgeCom)*, 2025, pp. 1–6.

26 Y. Tang, U. C. Srinivasan, B. J. Scott, O. Umealor, D. Kevogo, and W. Guo, "End-to-end edge AI service provisioning framework in 6G ORAN," in *Proc. IEEE 102nd Vehicular Technology Conference (VTC2025-Fall)*, 2025, pp. 1–7.

27 R. S. Shammah, I. Rahman, Z. M. Guria, S. Kowser, O. Faruq, and N. Morshed, "Scalable machine learning architecture for securing IoT networks with digital governance in the AI era of cyber-resilient smart cities," in *Proc. Int. Conf. AI-Driven STEM Education and Learning Technologies (AISTEMEDU)*, 2025, pp. 1–6.

28 M. Ileana, P. Petrov, and V. Milev, "Intelligent intrusion detection in IoT with explainable AI and distributed web systems," in *Proc. Int. Conf. Cybersecurity and AI-Based Systems (Cyber-AI)*, 2025, pp. 1–6.

29 D. Xu and Y. Tian, "A comprehensive survey of clustering algorithms," *Ann. Data Sci.*, vol. 2, no. 2, pp. 165–193, 2015, doi: 10.1007/s40745-015-0040-1.

30 M. Venkateswarlu, C. H. Karthik, M. Shivamani, and A. S. N. Rao, "Privacy-preserving graph-based intrusion detection system: A federated learning approach with GNN and XAI," in *Proc. 9th Int. Conf. Inventive Systems and Control (ICISC)*, 2025, pp. 1–6.

31 A. Khanna and A. Bhusri, "Enabling interoperable AI in IoT: A unified data framework approach," in *Proc. IEEE World AI IoT Congress (AIIoT)*, 2025, pp. 1–6.

6

Optimization at Edge Using AI Techniques: Pruning, Quantization, and Knowledge Distillation

S.D. Vijayakumar[1], G. Brinda[2], R. Nagadeepa[3], M. Arun[4], N. Saravanan[5], and Loganathan Nachimuthu[6]

[1]*Department of Artificial Intelligence and Data Science, Nandha Engineering College, Erode, India*
[2]*Department of ECE, M. P. Nachimuthu M. Jaganathan Engineering College, Erode, India*
[3]*Department of ECE, Fathima Michael College of Engineering and Technology, Madurai, India*
[4]*Department of AI & DS, Dr. Mahalingam College of Engineering & Technology, Pollachi, India*
[5]*Department of Mechanical Engineering, Erode Sengunthar Engineering College, Erode, India*
[6]*Engineering Department, University of Technology and Applied Sciences-Nizwa, Nizwa, Oman*

6.1 Introduction to TinyML in Edge Environments

The combination of embedded systems, ML, and low-power computing at the edge has resulted in the emergence of a new paradigm referred to as Tiny Machine Learning (TinyML). In general terms, TinyML can be described as the application of ML algorithms to devices like microcontrollers (MCU), digital signal processors (DSPs), and system-on-chips (SoCs) in cases where there is no connectivity or connectivity is unreliable and power constraints are severe. Traditional ML algorithms operate in the realm of centralized cloud computing with abundant computational and storage capacity, while TinyML applies the power of ML directly at the edge, enabling decision-making capability without reliance on constant connectivity to the internet. The movement from centralized cloud computing to distributed edge computing is aimed at solving numerous problems such as latency, security, bandwidth limitation, and energy efficiency. Essentially, TinyML consists of hardware architecture, software stack, and algorithm innovation, all of which contribute to a favorable ecosystem for ML model development. When considering the hardware side, the tremendous growth of power-efficient MCU, edge accelerators, and SoC solutions helps create a variety of deployment targets depending on the specific needs of the application. On the other hand, with regard to software, frameworks such as TensorFlow Lite for Microcontrollers (TFLM), CMSIS-NN, uTVM, and Edge Impulse provide the necessary support for model conversion and optimization for the specific needs of the MCU. This allows the researcher or developer to implement the same model across different devices. This closes the loop for the development and implementation of the models. Moreover, TinyML has an important role in the development of scalable and eco-friendly artificial intelligence (AI) solutions by avoiding the use of data centers and wireless communication protocols. TinyML also helps in the democratization of AI by providing intelligent solutions for underprivileged areas with poor or no internet connectivity. TinyML is expected to be the pillar of next ubiquitous computing systems since the number of linked IoT devices is expected to reach 75 billion by 2030. TinyML marks a paradigm change in ML execution location and method. It enables edge devices to make local intelligent decisions, so opening fresh opportunities for real-time, context-aware, energy-efficient AI [1]. Focusing on the co-development of hardware and software that satisfies the rigorous needs of embedded edge environments, this chapter investigates the integrated design techniques supporting successful TinyML systems.

6.2 Architectural Constraints and Design Challenges

The adoption of ML algorithms [2] within resource-constrained environments leads to certain architectural issues that are specific to TinyML systems. Normally, edge nodes, including MCU or SoCs, have low costs, energy consumption, and processing power, in contrast to the architecture used for data centers and mobile AI computing. Therefore, these devices have low memory capacity, low computational throughput, low-power availability, and low ability to meet real-time constraints. Overcoming these restrictions is critical to ensure the successful deployment of TinyML-based systems across various application domains, such as smart wearables, industrial Internet of Things (IoT), environmental monitoring, and autonomous edge robots.

Memory constraints pose one of the most critical challenges to the successful deployment of TinyML-based systems. MCUs, which are predominantly used to deploy ML models, have low SRAM capacity, ranging from 32 to 512 KB, with approximately 2 MB allocated to flash memory. Typically, these MCUs, such as ARM Cortex-M0, M4, and M7 cores, have limited SRAM capacity. The total required memory capacity of a TinyML system can be defined using Eq. (6.1).

$$M_{\text{total}} = M_{\text{weights}} + M_{\text{activations}} + M_{\text{buffers}} + M_{\text{stack}} \tag{6.1}$$

where

- M_{weights}: Memory for model parameters
- $M_{\text{activations}}$: Intermediate outputs

- M_{buffers}: Temporary computation storage
- M_{stack}: Runtime variables

These memory constraints are extremely restrictive in terms of the size of ML models that can actually be deployed. In addition to model weights and activations, there are also memory requirements for intermediate buffers, stack variables, and application logic. To make ML models adhere to these memory constraints, developers have to use extremely aggressive forms of compression such as quantization (e.g. changing 32-bit floating-point model weights to 8-bit integers), pruning (e.g. removing redundant connections), or sharing weights. Additionally, during inference, memory fragmentation needs to be minimized, which leads to static memory allocation and tensor allocation ahead of time.

Another aspect of TinyML design is that there is a constraint related to energy. Since devices have limited power supplies, such as batteries, there is a requirement to use extremely low energy per inference. The total energy required during inference can be estimated using Eq. (6.2).

$$E_{\text{total}} = N_{\text{MAC}} \cdot E_{\text{MAC}} + E_{\text{memory}} + E_{\text{communication}} \tag{6.2}$$

where

- N_{MAC}: Number of multiply accumulate (MAC) operations
- E_{MAC}: Energy per MAC operation
- E_{memory}: Energy for memory access
- $E_{\text{communication}}$: Energy for data transmission

Notably, communication energy dominates as in Eq. (6.3):

$$E_{\text{communication}} \gg E_{\text{computation}} \tag{6.3}$$

This shows us one of the main reasons why inference is preferred to take place on the device rather than using cloud computing, which is a major advantage of using Tiny ML. Various constraints have been mentioned in Figure 6.1. Most edge devices operate in remote locations, powered by tiny batteries or even energy-harvesting devices such as solar cells. Every inference operation needs to take place while adhering to strict power constraints, usually measured in microjoules per inference sequence. Since wireless communication is always orders of magnitude more expensive, inference is not only faster, as discussed, but also more energy-efficient. For example, executing tens of thousands of MAC operations is equivalent to transmitting 1 KB of data wirelessly. Thus, Tiny ML not only aids more scalable IoT solutions but is also more environmentally friendly. Another problem that affects the system architecture of Tiny ML is real-time constraints. Since reaction time needs to be faster, Tiny ML system architecture is even more complex, especially if one is building a system such as voice command recognition devices, vibration fault detection devices, or even fall detection

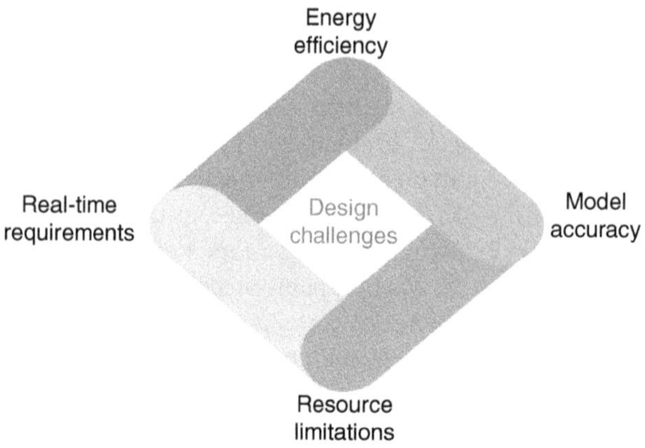

Figure 6.1 Various design challenges for Tiny ML.

devices for senior citizens. Given these parameters, inference time needs to be around a few milliseconds. In order to achieve such inference time, one needs to avoid complex control structures that arbitrarily increase inference time, have highly efficient execution, minimal memory access latency, etc. If one is to achieve these parameters, one needs to ensure that the inference process is well calibrated.

TinyML devices have limited processing capabilities, often lacking floating-point units or advanced parallelism. The computational complexity of neural networks is primarily determined by MAC operations as in Eq. (6.4):

$$C_{\text{compute}} = \sum_{l=1}^{L} (N_l \cdot K_l) \tag{6.4}$$

where

- L: Number of layers
- N_l: Number of neurons in layer l
- K_l: Number of connections per neuron

Another limitation may arise with the capacity of TinyML for processing. TinyML may not have the capacity for floating-point operations or high-end parallel processing. As discussed earlier, the complexity of the computation performed by the neural network is mainly dependent on the number of MAC operations, as given by Eq. (6.4). This complexity has to be minimized by employing appropriate techniques such as pruning and efficient kernels. Apart from these hardware-related issues, there are software issues related to interrupt latency, real-time scheduling, and communication with peripherals. To realize TinyML effectively, co-design is essential, where software is optimized to utilize the maximum possible hardware abilities. Currently, hardware-aware neural architecture search (NAS), fusion, and tiling are essential tools to realize TinyML.

To realize intelligent edge computing effectively, it is essential to overcome the issues related to TinyML, where there is a limitation related to designing artificial intelligence systems.

6.2.1 Edge Hardware Platforms for TinyML Deployment

The choice of an optimal hardware platform for a TinyML application requires a trade-off study among a variety of design constraints, including computational performance, energy efficiency, memory availability, latency, and cost. These constraints must be evaluated in the context of a specific application, whether it is a wearable sensor, an intermittently connected environmental sensor, or a low-power industrial fault detection node. MAC/s (millions of MAC operations per second) is a fundamental metric for evaluating the arithmetic performance of a computing device. An increase in MAC/s values is directly correlated with faster inference times, especially for convolutional and dense networks, as matrix multiplication is a major operation for these types of networks.

Although a high MAC/s value is good, it should be noted that a high MAC/s value alone does not mean energy efficiency since optimization on the instruction level is equally significant. Another factor related to evaluating energy efficiency is energy per inference, which is measured in units of microjoules per inference (μJ/inference). This factor stands for the total energy required for making an inference with the model. Energy per inference plays a very important role in the lifespan of any device running on battery or energy harvesters.

For example, a simple keyword spotting application may consume 100–200 μJ/inference on an MCU, while the same application may be executed in under 10 μJ/inference by an NPU like the Syntiant NDP120. On the other hand, inference latency, which is measured in terms of milliseconds (ms), is an essential factor to measure the performance of a computing device. It measures the time taken to process an individual input sample and generate the associated output. The real-time response is an important constraint for specific applications, like gesture recognition and speech command recognition, where the response time must be less than 10 ms. Hence, an optimal hardware platform for TinyML needs to meet a variety of requirements as shown in Table 6.1.

6.3 Pruning and Quantization

6.3.1 Pruning for TinyML Hardware and Software in Edge Systems

Pruning is among the critical techniques used in TinyML to enhance the training process of a neural network model for deployment onto edge devices. Edge devices are usually constrained by storage capacity, processing power, and

Table 6.1 Comparison and selection criteria of hardware platforms.

Platform	Type	RAM (KB)	Power (mW)	Inference Time (ms)	Suitable Use Cases
ARM Cortex-M4	MCU	128	0.5	5–20	Motion detection, KWS
Cadence HiFi DSP	DSP	256	2–10	<10	Audio/event classification
Syntiant NDP120	NPU	192	<1	<1	Always-on voice or event detection
Ambiq Apollo3	SoC	384	0.2	1–15	Wearables, fitness, biometric sensing

energy use, making it challenging to deploy large over-parameterized networks directly. Pruning mitigates such issues by eliminating unnecessary or redundant parameters from an existing network model to minimize computation cost without compromising its performance [3]. Therefore, pruning is particularly beneficial in edge computing because it must strike a balance between efficiency and effectiveness.

Pruning techniques include unstructured and structured pruning. In unstructured pruning, weights are deleted based on specific requirements, with the most common requirement being the weight's magnitude. That is, low absolute values of weights imply insignificant contribution to the network and must be discarded. While unstructured pruning results in minimal weight removal without negatively impacting the model's performance, it generates nonregular sparse architecture that cannot be effectively exploited on ordinary hardware platforms. Conversely, structured pruning entails the elimination of whole groups of parameters in a model, including neurons, filters, or even channels. Regularization is achieved by structured pruning, which facilitates implementation on common hardware systems but at the cost of accuracy compared to unstructured pruning.

There exist several major differences when one-shot pruning is compared to iterative pruning techniques. In one-shot pruning, a significant number of model parameters are pruned at once, offering high speed and efficiency but risking loss in terms of accuracy. In the case of iterative pruning, it takes place in several steps with fine-tuning or training following each step to ensure accuracy. On the whole, iterative pruning would be advantageous in TinyML since it offers a more positive ratio of compression and accuracy than any other approach [4].

In general, the effectiveness of pruning heavily depends on the method used to detect redundant parameters. Several types of pruning may be considered when talking about TinyML, namely, magnitude-based pruning, gradient-based pruning, activation-based pruning, and parameter importance. Pruning based on magnitude works very well for TinyML because it is simple and lightweighted. While other techniques such as sensitivity analysis and second-order approximation give more accurate results, they are resource-intensive and thus not appropriate for TinyML. From a hardware perspective, pruning offers several advantages that directly impact the performance of edge devices. Pruning in a neural network leads to the decrease in the number of parameters of the neural network; therefore, this will lead to a decrease in memory resources needed. In addition, pruning allows the neural network to adhere to the limited memory of an MCU. Moreover, due to fewer parameters, there will be fewer operations performed.

With regard to software, different platforms provide pruning options to support TinyML development. Platforms like TensorFlow Lite Micro, PyTorch Mobile, Apache TVM, and Edge Impulse have features to enable compression, optimization, and deployment of ML models on embedded devices. Usually, these platforms come with an automated pipeline to ease the creation of the desired solution, ranging from training to deployment.

According to the traditional approach, one needs to train a full precision model, prune the model, and carry out fine-tuning to avoid loss of performance. After optimizing, the trained model should be converted to a format suitable for execution at the edge device, like TensorFlow Lite [5].

Pruning provides various advantages, although there are several drawbacks associated with the practice. To begin with, higher levels of pruning lead to smaller model sizes and lower computation cost. Nonetheless, there will be a loss in accuracy, which is not good. Unstructured pruning leads to better compression of the ML model. However, improvement cannot be achieved without a sparse computational capability.

Pruning neural network has proved highly successful for TinyML in areas ranging from keyword detection to gesture recognition, environmental sensing, and predictive maintenance. In all cases, shrinking the model size and lowering power needs make it possible to perform operations continuously on battery-operated machines. As such, pruning is a key technology that enables smart edge computing.

Going forward, several issues will need to be overcome before pruning can be adopted more widely. They include finding the best amount of pruning, designing hardware able to use sparsity effectively, and automation of the pruning process. Potential areas for future research could include hardware-aware pruning, using other optimization schemes like quantization together with pruning, and using ML tools to help.

6.3.2 Quantization for TinyML Hardware and Software in Edge Systems

One of the major techniques employed in TinyML is known as quantization. Through quantization, the precision of the weights and computations can be reduced so that they can work well in low-resource devices. Conventional models operate using 32-bit floating-point values, which require lots of computational capabilities and space. However, through quantization, such high values are converted into lower values, such as 16-bit, 8-bit, or even bit-levels.

Currently, there exist several methods of quantization, among which post-training quantization (PTQ) and quantization-aware training (QAT) are the most widely used approaches. PTQ is a process performed after the end of training; it consists in lowering the precision levels of weights and activations without conducting any additional training. The algorithm is quite straightforward and fast but may imply certain precision losses. At the same time, QAT accounts for quantization impacts during training and helps a model become accustomed to working with low precision and maintain accuracy. Even though the approach is rather complex and demanding, it is preferred for high-accuracy tasks [6].

Quantization can be categorized based on the way numerical values are converted to discrete levels. While uniform quantization makes use of equally spaced intervals and thus is easy to implement in hardware, making it common in TinyML implementations, nonuniform quantization takes advantage of unequal spacings that conform to the value distribution. However, it improves performance while increasing implementation complexity. Additionally, quantization can be performed at different granularity levels like that of tensor and channel levels. Channel quantization uses scaling factors for each channel separately and usually outperforms other methods, especially for CNNs.

There are various methods of quantization according to application purposes. For example, floating-point quantization converts floating-point numbers to fixed point using scaling factors. Integer quantization performs operations on an integer basis. Other extreme quantization forms like binary and ternary quantization compress the number of weights to a small subset of discrete values, leading to a smaller model size at the expense of decreased accuracy.

From a hardware viewpoint, quantization has multiple benefits. The reduction of bit-width makes it possible to fit the model in limited memory space, allowing it to fit in the edge device memory. Quantization speeds up computation because integer operations take precedence over floating-point operations in most embedded processors. Lowering precision consumes less power due to fewer switching activities. Several state-of-the-art accelerators are designed to handle low-precision arithmetic.

In terms of software, there are many frameworks available that allow implementing quantization for TinyML development purposes. For example, TensorFlow Lite, PyTorch, ONNX Runtime, and Apache TVM all provide means for transforming pretrained neural networks into quantized versions that can be optimized to run on edge devices.

The general quantization process is based on creating a model with higher precision, applying either PTQ or QAT techniques, evaluating the model for accuracy, and transforming it into a production-ready version. Usually, calibration datasets are used during PTQ to ensure proper scaling factors are chosen so that the quantized model will show acceptable performance in real-life situations.

However, any quantization technique implies some drawbacks. Lowering bit-width increases efficiency but leads to approximation errors that reduce model accuracy. QAT and per-channel quantization can help solve this issue, but precise parameter adjustment is still required. The main uses of quantized models include speech recognition, image classification, wearable healthcare devices, and smart home appliances. In particular, using quantized models allows improving latency and power consumption while also providing means for working with affordable edge devices, making quantization an essential part of TinyML solutions [7].

Quantization has some limitations, which include decreased accuracy, restrictions due to hardware-specific requirements, and the requirement for accurate calibration. Future studies will attempt to solve this problem by using mixed-precision quantization and adaptive quantization techniques.

6.4 Knowledge Distillation for TinyML Hardware and Software in Edge Systems

Knowledge distillation (KD) has been identified as an efficient model compression approach that helps to achieve the compact form of a neural network that can be easily deployed in TinyML settings [8]. TinyML is focused on deploying ML models onto tiny edge devices including MCU, embedded systems, and IoT sensors, which have limited resources with respect to memory usage, computing power, and energy consumption. Traditional deep learning architectures, tailored for inference on the cloud, are usually too large and resource-intensive to work well on such devices. KD can help overcome this limitation as the method aims at moving knowledge between large, complex teacher networks and small student networks.

At its very essence, KD relies on the transfer of knowledge between the two models where the goal is to train the small student model to reproduce the performance of a pretrained larger teacher model. In this case, the student model uses not only hard targets as labels (i.e. ground-truth labels) but also learns from soft labels generated by the teacher model. Soft labels refer to the softened outputs of the teacher model, which include additional information concerning interclass relations and class probabilities. The process involves applying the softmax function to outputs of the teacher to obtain softer targets [9, 10].

In terms of knowledge transfer, there are a few variations of KD. In the response-based form, the model acts as a student who learns based on the probabilities generated by the teacher. Feature-based KD goes a step further and transfers intermediate features learned by the teacher to enable the student to generate more insightful internal representations. The third type – relation-based KD – focuses on capturing the relationship between data points (e.g. similarity and distances) as additional information useful for model generalization. It is thus possible to design different KD frameworks to suit individual TinyML applications.

As far as hardware capabilities are concerned, KD offers a number of benefits for deploying a model at the edge. Namely, KD leads to the generation of compact models having significantly fewer parameters. As a result, KD reduces the required memory resources, making it possible to deploy TinyML applications even on devices with limited amounts of flash memory and RAM. Besides, KD makes it possible to reduce the number of arithmetic calculations required during inference, further increasing efficiency in terms of both time and energy. In addition, unlike pruning and quantization, KD produces dense models without any sparsity or changes to numerical precision.

In the software domain, KD can be implemented with the use of popular ML frameworks such as TensorFlow, PyTorch, as well as their efficient counterparts, such as TensorFlow Lite. These tools allow to incorporate custom loss functions for a combined training objective consisting of classification loss and distillation loss measured through Kullback–Leibler divergence between the probabilities provided by the teacher and the student. Thus, it is possible to fine-tune the ratio of these loss functions for a balanced learning process. Once the student model is ready, it can be exported in an edge-compliant format and then used in TinyML frameworks [11].

The procedure for using KD in TinyML starts with creating an efficient teacher model that requires considerable computation power on a large amount of data. Then, the student model is designed with far fewer parameters. In practice, the student model will be trained not only with the input dataset but also with soft targets generated by the teacher model.

Despite its numerous benefits, KD comes with its own challenges. First of all, effective distillation heavily depends on the selection of the right architecture for both the teacher and student models as well as on how the distillation loss function is designed. One more important factor is choosing the optimal temperature that softens the outputs of the teacher network and makes possible to perform knowledge transfer successfully. Another problem is related to the considerable computational needs of distillation. Finally, one should make sure that the student network has good generalization ability.

KD has proven to be rather efficient in a wide range of TinyML applications, ranging from speech recognition to image classification, anomaly detection, and human activity recognition. In all of these domains, distilled models allow for real-time inference on constrained devices while maintaining high levels of accuracy. Specifically, a distilled model may perform on par with large teacher models while satisfying strict limitations in terms of the available resources, including memory and power consumption. Indeed, it allows for real-time detection of keywords without violating the limitations of the platform in use. The same holds true for the use of distilled models for monitoring health in wearable devices without the necessity for constant connection to the cloud server.

The current research into KD focuses on the improvement of methods used by employing innovations such as self-distillation, whereby the model learns from its own intermediate representations, or online distillation where both models, teacher and student, are trained simultaneously. Another possible avenue of exploration is the implementation of multi-teacher distillation where knowledge from multiple teacher models is combined, or even cross-modal distillation where knowledge is transferred across different data modalities [12, 13].

Thus, KD represents a highly efficient means of deploying deep learning models in TinyML applications. Through transferring knowledge from larger and more complex models into smaller ones, KD provides a link between the two concepts. Given its versatility, compatibility with regular hardware, as well as opportunities for further development and implementation of the technology in combination with other techniques, KD can be considered as one of the key components in creating intelligent edge systems.

6.5 Hardware-Aware Model Optimization Techniques

Using ML models on MCU and ultra-constrained edge devices calls for a very different software architecture than that applied in cloud or mobile AI systems. Between high-level model design and low-level embedded execution, lightweight inference systems and toolchains serve as the link [14]. These tools guarantee that ML models, particularly those built using frameworks like TensorFlow or PyTorch, can be transformed, optimized, and executed effectively on platforms with limited compute capacity, small memory footprints, and ultra-low energy budgets as mentioned in Figure 6.2.

Advanced hardware-aware optimization techniques [15] are required for balancing the accuracy, speed, memory, and energy efficiency for deploying ML models in ultra-constrained edge devices. TinyML models need to be executed in kilobytes of RAM, a few megahertz of CPU bandwidth, and sub-milliwatt power budgets. Hence, TinyML models need to be improved constantly, but not at

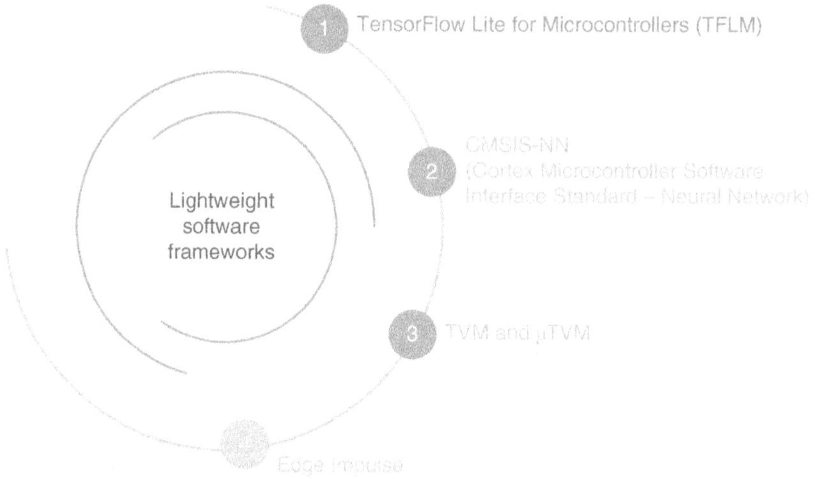

Figure 6.2 Various lightweight software frameworks.

the cost of performance. There are four fundamental optimization techniques in this field. They are memory-efficient deployment, operator fusion, quantization, and pruning.

Among the most important optimization techniques in TinyML is quantization. This is an important technique in TinyML. This technique converts 32-bit floating-point numbers into integers with fewer bits, i.e. int8 or int4. This technique reduces the numerical precision of the parameters and the output values in TinyML models. This enables the execution of TinyML models in CPUs without floating-point units. This reduces memory footprint and execution time. This also reduces power consumption due to reduced memory bandwidth and smaller arithmetic units [16]. There are two types of quantization techniques in TinyML. One is QAT, and the other is PTQ. This technique is designed to execute quantized TinyML models in Cortex M and similar devices. TensorFlow Lite Micro and Microcontroller and CMSIS-NN frameworks support this technique.

Memory-efficient deployment techniques guarantee the execution of TinyML models in the memory capacities of edge devices. This is achieved by avoiding dynamic memory allocation during execution. This is also achieved by using memory blocks wherever possible. This is also achieved by using deterministic memory allocation using tensor buffers. This is achieved by using tools such as uTVM, STM32Cube.AI, and Edge Impulse. The most commonly used techniques for reducing the memory footprint in TinyML models include reducing input sizes, reducing the number of layers in the TinyML models, and reducing the batch sizes [17].

6.6 Co-Design Strategies for Embedded TinyML Systems

Effective implementation of TinyML models [18] on embedded hardware calls for a hardware–software co-design approach whereby the hardware platform, compiler toolchain, and neural network architecture are developed and optimized concurrently. Edge devices – especially MCU and DSP – have strict limits in terms of memory, computation, and energy budgets; thus, this is vital. By means of a co-design approach, ML models and embedded systems are matched to each other's capabilities and constraints, thus enabling strong, real-time, energy-efficient inference.

Co-design is fundamentally based on cross-layer optimization – that is, aligning decisions across the application, algorithm, and hardware stack. At the model level, this can entail choosing lightweight network designs that cut the number of parameters and operations by means of MobileNetV1, DS-CNN, or depthwise separable convolutions. Devices with limited SRAM and flash would find these designs appropriate. Better fit with the hardware memory model comes from further architectural tuning including limited layer depth, minimum activation maps, and fixed-point activations.

Hardware-wise, embedded CPUs sometimes lack floating-point units and must rely on integer computation. The model must thus be trained and applied with quantized operations. Co-design guarantees that the quantization granularity that of per-tensor rather than per-channel – aligns with the available kernels and instruction set of the CPU. For instance, ARM Cortex-M4 and M7 cores let CMSIS-NN be used for SIMD-based int8 operations. By producing optimal inference binaries that exploit instruction-level parallelism and memory locality, compiler frameworks such as TVM, uTVM, and Glow help even more in this process.

Deployment of intermediate model versions on the target device to perform practical profiling for metrics like inference latency, maximum memory usage, and energy costs, known as hardware-in-the-loop (HIL) profiling, represents another co-design methodology. The HIL process facilitates iterative design improvement on the model structure, operator precision, and scheduling policy. In many cases, optimization under accuracy, latency, and energy constraints is considered, wherein models are trained/searched using joint criteria. Another co-design method is referred to as power-aware design, where inference execution is performed using low-power states or in response to events. Workload partitioning such that DSP operations occur during preprocessing and NPU computations take place during inference can help in workload balancing on multicore MCUs.

6.7 Hardware-Aware NAS

Selection of the right architecture through automation for any given problem, using NAS, has revolutionized the way neural networks are designed. Conventional NAS methods [19], nevertheless, have been known to emphasize the importance of optimizing for accuracy of the neural model without considering other important constraints related to hardware performance such as memory footprint, latency, and power efficiency. In the case of TinyML, the introduction of hardware-aware NAS becomes vital because the neural models will need to be run on small-scale devices such as MCU, DSP, or NPU.

Usually in hardware-aware NAS, the search space comprises variations in convolutional block types (e.g. standard vs. depthwise separable), kernel sizes, activation functions, and layer depth. Finding models that generalize effectively on the target hardware is just as important as finding ones that fit. Often used is multiobjective optimization, in which accuracy and hardware metrics – including inference time (latency), peak memory use, model size, and energy per inference (μJ/inference) – are concurrently taken into account. Representing best trade-offs, the final architecture rests on the Pareto frontier.

Hardware simulators or profiling feedback from actual devices helps NAS assess candidates during a search. For example, real-time latency is included in the controller RNN's reward function by latency-aware NAS systems such as MnasNet. Others such as Proxyless NAS directly optimize candidate subnetworks on real-world hardware, thus guaranteeing integrity in performance estimate and avoiding proxy training. The Once-for-All (OFA) framework advances by training a super-network from which several subnetworks may be sampled and refined to satisfy different resource constraints. This method lets for fast deployment across several devices without retraining from scratch.

Hardware-aware NAS also consists of constraint-aware training in TinyML. The model must, for instance, be quantization-friendly if it is to run effectively on devices with just integers. Consequently, NAS systems have to look for layers and structures that maintain resilience even following int8 quantization. Furthermore, candidate designs have to be compatible with the limited memory architectures common to MCUs (e.g. 128 KB SRAM), and their layer structures must enable static memory planning to stop fragmentation.

6.8 End-to-End Deployment Pipelines

The use of TinyML models [20] in practice requires the development of an end-to-end pipeline, which involves all aspects of the ML life cycle from training to deployment on the targeted device. Unlike conventional ML pipelines, the TinyML pipelines need to consider several additional factors related to memory consumption, energy utilization, and computing time, in addition to stability when deployed in real-world settings. An effective deployment process not only results in accurate predictions but is also compatible with hardware computing capacity, memory, and energy constraints.

Usually found exactly on the target edge device, data acquisition and preprocessing comes first in a TinyML pipeline. Lightweight DSP operations, e.g. FFT, MFCC extraction, and filtering, must extract meaningfully from raw sensor data including audio, vibration, temperature, or motion signals. On systems like Edge Impulse and Arduino Nano 33 BLE Sense, simple interfaces let one gather and label sensor data straight from edge devices.

Once data is acquired, model training and optimization offline with TensorFlow, PyTorch, or Keras comes once. These days, models are designed with constraints in mind and favor architectures including DS-CNN, MobileNetV1, or custom shallow MLPs. Models go through KD, pruning, or quantization post-training to reduce memory and computational need. Strong resistance to precision loss during conversion is ensured by QAT guarantees.

6.9 Emerging Trends and Future Research Directions

Some interesting research directions and trends may impact future TinyML-based intelligent edge solutions in various industries including healthcare, smart farming, predictive maintenance, environmental monitoring, among others. Besides improving the inference performance, recent research highlights the role of learning and adapting capabilities, collaboration, and self-governance for TinyML applications running in severely constrained conditions, i.e. limited computing power, small memory footprint, and low-energy consumption [21].

An interesting research direction is event-driven ML that runs inference only in case of detected events in input signals or crossing threshold values of specific data streams. Compared to classical approaches using continuous data streams, an event-driven approach leads to a significantly lower power cost. This technology becomes critical in applications like anomaly detection, motion-based video recording, and wake-word detection. Generally, an event-driven solution uses an ultra-low-power sensor or coprocessor to detect perturbation in the signal before executing the inference on the main MCU or NPU. Neuromorphic computing technologies that mimic a biological neuron represent another exciting domain of research. Spiking neural networks (SNNs) [22] and event-driven computations are used to develop neuromorphic processors like Intel Loihi, BrainChip Akida, and SynSense Speck for data analysis. Suitable for real-time inference of data in wearable devices or autonomous microdevices, neuromorphic processors exhibit high parallelism and asynchronicity in their operations and energy-efficient at a milliwatt or microwatt scale. Researchers need to investigate SNN learning algorithms compatible with TinyML pipelines.

The idea of making ML models self-aware, i.e. capable of estimating their certainty, analyzing the data, and transferring the computation to a more powerful computing node (fog/edge or cloud) for processing, is popular in TinyML [23]. Thus, self-awareness helps to create adaptive intelligent systems demonstrating different behaviors depending on task complexity and resource availability. Finally, the development of an integrated pipeline in terms of hardware and software design, hardware-informed NAS, and optimizing the compiler technology proves to be crucial.

6.10 Conclusion and Best Practices for TinyML Co-Design

The incorporation of TinyML technology into embedded platforms requires a co-design of the whole stack, where software, hardware, model, compiler tools, and deployment are tightly coupled into a complex multidimensional problem. The ultimate goal is not only to redesign the entire stack from scratch for real-time, constrained, and energy-aware environments but also to simplify ML models in a non-trivial way. TinyML transforms embedded platforms, including MCU, DSPs, and NPUs, into intelligent agents capable of running inference workloads like classification, detection, and anomaly prediction locally. Such an approach calls for following the principles of best practices in TinyML development.

First and foremost, an early alignment between model architecture and hardware capabilities is one of the key prerequisites in designing an efficient TinyML system [24]. From the very beginning, one should rely on lightweight quantization-friendly designs known to perform well on the edge, such as shallow MLPs, various implementations of SqueezeNets, MobileNetV1/V2, and DS-CNNs. Moreover, the excessive use of deep and/or wide architectures should be avoided at all costs, as it may become a significant source of challenges during the optimization phase. No matter whether one is developing for ARM Cortex-M MCU, ESP32, or vendor-specific SoCs, hardware target must be carefully specified alongside other details like memory limits, instruction set, and power consumption profile. This will allow model architects to define clear boundaries regarding size, latency, and inference cycle time.

Testing on HIL is the key step to take when building a co-designed TinyML system. HIL tests ensure accurate measurement of real-time inference on noisy input data, current draw measured in milliamps, and inference latency measured in milliseconds. Iterative optimization loops driven by HIL tests allow tuning up model architecture, quantization process, and firmware behavior toward a more efficient solution. Resilience and timely reaction are essential properties of a mission-critical system used in fields like health monitoring, predictive maintenance, or autonomous sensing. Still another great habit is design with modularity and future extensibility [25, 26]. By means of bootloaders or over-the-air (OTA) mechanisms, a firmware architecture supporting modular updates lowers maintenance costs and increases device lifetime as models change or application needs evolve. Selecting hardware with some buffer in memory and CPU similarly allows models to be upgraded without requiring whole system redesigns. Through the use of bootloaders, as well as OTA mechanisms, the use of a firmware architecture with the capability for modular updates can reduce maintenance costs as models are updated or as the need for the application changes. The selection of hardware with a buffer in terms of memory and CPU can similarly allow models to be updated without the need for complete redesigns.

Small ML co-design is a challenging engineering discipline combining the strengths of embedded systems, ML, and software optimization. It highlights exact hardware profiles, iterative development, and system-level thinking. Adopting these best practices early, constraint-aware modeling, hardware-specific optimization, static memory planning, real-world testing, and future-proof architecture developers can regularly provide strong, intelligent edge AI systems capable of transforming real-world environments without dependability on cloud connectivity or high-end compute infrastructure.

References

1 A. Elhanashi, P. Dini, S. Saponara, and Q. Zheng, "Advancements in TinyML: Applications, limitations, and impact on IoT devices," *Electronics*, vol. 13, p. 3562, 2024, doi: 10.3390/electronics13173562.

2 U. Iqbal, T. Davies, and P. Perez, "A review of recent hardware and software advances in GPU-accelerated edge-computing single-board computers (SBCs) for computer vision," *Sensors*, vol. 24, p. 4830, 2024, doi: 10.3390/s24154830.

3 G. Giorgetti and D. P. Pau, "Transitioning from TinyML to edge GenAI: A review," *Big Data Cogn. Comput.*, vol. 9, p. 61, 2025, doi: 10.3390/bdcc9030061.

4 L. Crespí-Castañer *et al.*, "Pruning dense neural networks for efficient edge deployment in Internet of Things applications," *Appl. Soft Comput.*, vol. 186, no. Part D, p. 114175, 2026, doi: 10.1016/j.asoc.2025.114175.

5 H. Han, S. Trimi, and S. M. Lee, "Tiny machine learning (TinyML): Research trends and future application opportunities," *Array*, vol. 29, p. 100674, 2026, doi: 10.1016/j.array.2025.100674.

6 C. M. Bhushan *et al.*, "Deploying TinyML for energy-efficient object detection and communication in low-power edge AI systems," *Sci. Rep.*, vol. 15, no. 1, p. 44299, 2025, doi: 10.1038/s41598-025-27818-9.

7 R. Immonen and T. Hämäläinen, "Tiny machine learning for resource-constrained microcontrollers," *J Sens*, vol. 2022, p. 11, 2022, doi: 10.1155/2022/7437023.

8 M. Arif and M. Rashid, "A literature review on model conversion, inference, and learning strategies in EdgeML with TinyML deployment," *Comput. Mater. Contin.*, vol. 83, no. 1, pp. 13–64, 2025, doi: 10.32604/cmc.2025.062819.

9 S. Heydari and Q. H. Mahmoud, "Tiny machine learning and on-device inference: A survey of applications, challenges, and future directions," *Sensors*, vol. 25, p. 3191, 2025, doi: 10.3390/s25103191.

10 Y. W. Hao, *et al.* "Implementation research of TinyML on RISC-V platform using Efinix platform for real time person detection," in *2025 21st IEEE Int. Colloq. Signal Process. Appl. (CSPA)*, Pulau Pinang, Malaysia, 2025, pp. 233–238, doi: 10.1109/CSPA64953.2025.10933323.

11 R. Zhang, H. Jiang, W. Wang, and J. Liu, "Optimization methods, challenges, and opportunities for edge inference: A comprehensive survey," *Electronics*, vol. 14, p. 1345, 2025, doi: 10.3390/electronics14071345.

12 E. Manor and S. Greenberg, "Custom hardware inference accelerator for TensorFlow lite for microcontrollers," *IEEE Access*, vol. 10, pp. 73484–73493, 2022.

13 S. Ahmadifarsani, R. Stahl, P. van Kempen, D. Mueller-Gritschneder, and U. Schlichtmann, "Towards rapid exploration of heterogeneous TinyML systems using virtual platforms and TVM's UMA," 2024, *arXiv preprint arXiv:1801.06601 (2018).*

14 A. Mellit, N. Blasuttigh, and A. M. Pavan, "TinyML for fault diagnosis of photovoltaic modules using edge impulse platform," in *2023 11th Int. Conf. Smart Grid (icSmartGrid)*, Paris, France, 2023, pp. 1–5, doi: 10.1109/icSmartGrid58556.2023.10171088.

15 N. N. Alajlan and D. M. Ibrahim, "TinyML: Enabling of inference deep learning models on ultra-low-power IoT edge devices for AI applications," *Micromachines*, vol. 13, p. 851, 2022, doi: 10.3390/mi13060851.

16 Y. Dong, *et al.* "A model-specific end-to-end design methodology for resource-constrained TinyML hardware," in *2023 60th ACM/IEEE Des. Autom. Conf. (DAC)*, 2025.

17 D. Marculescu, D. Stamoulis, and E. Cai, "Hardware-aware machine learning: Modeling and optimization," in *Proc. IEEE/ACM Int. Conf. Comput.-Aided Des. (ICCAD)*, New York, NY, USA, 2018, Article 137, pp. 1–8, Association for Computing Machinery, doi: 10.1145/3240765.3243479.

18 V. V. Baligodugula and F. Amsaad, "Hardware-aware federated learning: Optimizing differential privacy in distributed computing architectures," *Electronics*, vol. 14, p. 1218, 2025, doi: 10.3390/electronics14061218.

19 J. Kwon and D. Park, "Hardware/software co-design for TinyML voice-recognition application on resource frugal edge devices," *Appl. Sci.*, vol. 11, p. 11073, 2021, doi: 10.3390/app112211073.

20 A. M. Garavagno, E. Ragusa, A. Frisoli, and P. Gastaldo, "A hardware-aware neural architecture search algorithm targeting low-end microcontrollers," in *2023 18th Conf. Ph.D Res. Microelectron. Electron. (PRIME)*, Valencia, Spain, 2023, pp. 281–284, doi: 10.1109/PRIME58259.2023.10161736.

21 Z. Guan, W. Zhou, Y. Ren, R. Xie, H. Yu, and N. Wong, "A hardware-aware neural architecture search pareto front exploration for in-memory computing," in *2022 IEEE 16th Int. Conf. Solid-State Integr. Circuit Technol. (ICSICT)*, Nanjing, China, 2022, pp. 1–4, doi: 10.1109/ICSICT55466.2022.9963263.

22 D. Nanthiya *et al.*, "Detection of distributed denial of service in the application layer of IoT using machine learning," in *2024 15th Int. Conf. Comput. Commun. Netw. Technol. (ICCCNT)*, Kamand, India, 2024, pp. 1–6, doi: 10.1109/ICCCNT61001.2024.10725461.

23 H. Ren, D. Anicic, X. Li, and T. Runkler, "On-device Online Learning and Semantic Management of TinyML Systems," *ACM Trans. Embed. Comput. Syst.*, vol. 23, no. 4, pp. 1–32, 2024, doi: 10.1145/3665278.

24 N. L. Rane, S. K. Mallick, Ö. Kaya, and J. Rane, "Emerging trends and future directions in machine learning and deep learning architectures," in *Applied Machine Learning and Deep Learning: Architectures and Techniques*. Mumbai, India: Deep Science Publishing, 2024, pp. 192–211, doi: 10.70593/978-81-981271-4-3_10.

25 V. Tsoukas, A. Gkogkidis, E. Boumpa, and A. Kakarountas, "A Review on the emerging technology of TinyML," *ACM Comput. Surv.*, vol. 56, no. 10, pp. 1–37, 2024, doi: 10.1145/3661820.

26 G. Delnevo, S. Mirri, C. Prandi, and P. Manzoni, "An evaluation methodology to determine the actual limitations of a TinyML-based solution," *Internet of Things*, vol. 22, p. 100729, 2023, doi: 10.1016/j.iot.2023.100729.

7

Neural Network Architecture for Ultra-Low-Power Intelligent Edge Systems

V. Karthi[1], T. Suganya[2], S. Jayabratha[2], G. Vijayakumari[2], T. Velmurugan[3], and R. Praveenkumar[4]

[1] *Department of EEE, Kangeyam Institute of Technology, Tirupur, India*
[2] *Department of ECE, Kangeyam Institute of Technology, Tirupur, India*
[3] *Department of CSD, Kongu Engineering College, Erode, India*
[4] *Department of ECE, Nandha Engineering College, Erode, India*

7.1 Introduction

7.1.1 Motivation for Low-Power AI

Demand for artificial intelligence (AI) that functions consistently under severe resource restrictions is increasing as intelligent edge devices from smartwatches and home automation systems to biomedical implants and industrial sensors exponentially proliferate. Many times, devices such as distant sensors, energy-harvesting modules, or battery-operated systems have inaccurate power sources. Under such conditions, conventional deep learning models are sometimes too computationally demanding to be practical. Figure 7.1 shows the energy-efficient AI used for low-power edge systems.

Low-power AI provides a route to enable intelligent decision-making at the edge free from continuous dependence on cloud computing or regular battery charging. It guarantees resilience in cases when network connectivity is erratic, lowers data transfer to improve privacy, and minimizes latency. Extending the operational lifetime of equipment in fields including environmental monitoring, space exploration, military, and healthcare where maintenance or battery replacement is difficult or impossible also depends on low-power neural networks [1]. Therefore, not only a technological challenge but also a basic need for extending AI into the next phase of general-purpose computing is developing neural network architectures specifically appropriate for low-power environments.

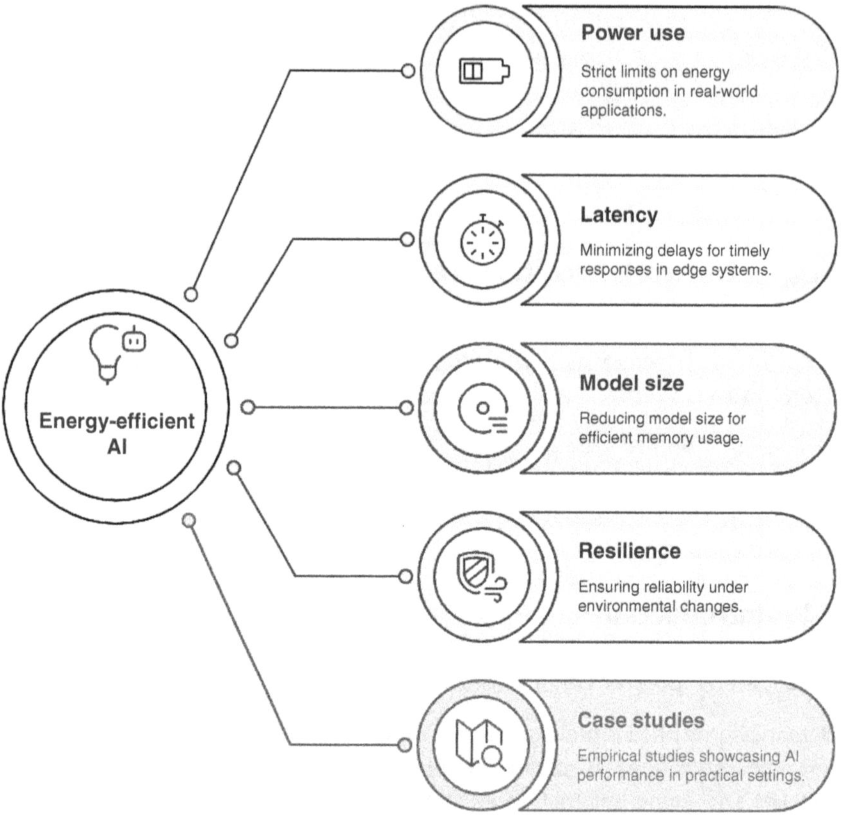

Figure 7.1 Energy-efficient AI.

7.1.2 Applications in Edge and Embedded Systems

Low-power neural networks are turning over a wide range of uses: for activity recognition, health monitoring, and user interaction, all while running on low battery life devices, including smartwatches and fitness trackers, that gain from on-device AI. AI-enabled pacemakers, diabetes monitors, and neural implants must run for years without recharging and need very energy-efficient computation for continuous sensing and inference. Using environmental sensors, industrial automation systems, and agricultural monitors, deep learning models locally discover anomalies or patterns in real time, away from cloud influence. Particularly in cases when weight, heat, or energy limits conventional processing, drones, robotics, and autonomous cars rely on low-power computing for real-time sensing and control. Edge devices can save power use and boost operational uptime by tracking audio or video streams for specific patterns such as gunshots, intrusion, and fire.

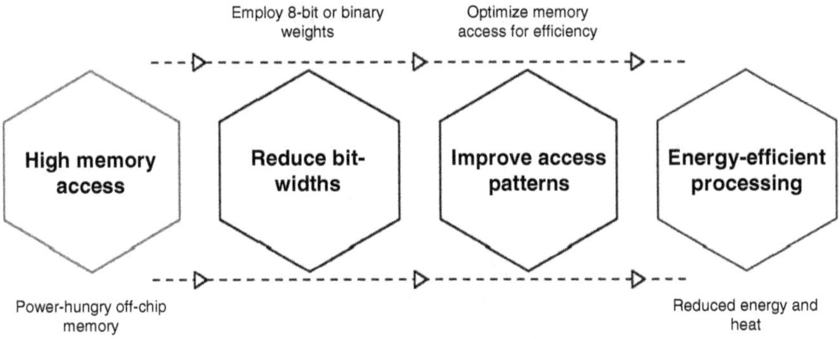

Figure 7.2 Reducing memory footprint for energy efficiency.

7.1.3 Challenges in Energy-Constrained Environments

Designing neural networks for ultra-low-power operation presents a variety of technological difficulties: Deep neural networks (DNNs) usually consist of millions of parameters and billions of operations per inference, thereby reflecting computational complexity. In edge conditions without notable architectural simplification, this degree of processing is unsustainable.

7.1.3.1 Memory Footprint

Among the most power-hungry operations is memory access, especially off-chip memory. Energy economy depends critically on shrinking model size and improving memory access patterns. Reducing bit-widths, that is employing eight-bit or binary weights, helps save electricity but can compromise model accuracy. One must reach the right balance. Energy-efficient processing not only saves energy but also reduces heat generation, which is crucial in tightly packed, sealed, or implanted devices, as shown in Figure 7.2.

7.1.3.2 Hardware Restrictions

Few edge devices have CPUs or GPUs. Models must be tuned to run on low clock speed, memory-limited bespoke application-specific integrated circuits (ASICs), digital signal processors (DSPs), or microcontrollers. Edge applications typically call for low-latency inference based on real-time requirements. Reducing computational depth or complexity shouldn't have to mean higher inference time. Minimizing reliance on cloud-based inference means models must run entirely locally, thereby demanding compact and effective on-device AI. Parameters used to measure the power efficiency are shown in Figure 7.3.

Dealing with these challenges calls for both hardware and software for creative ability. Regarding software, researchers are building extremely precisely compact neural architectures that drastically reduce the number of parameters and operations. Techniques that shed computational weight without compromising

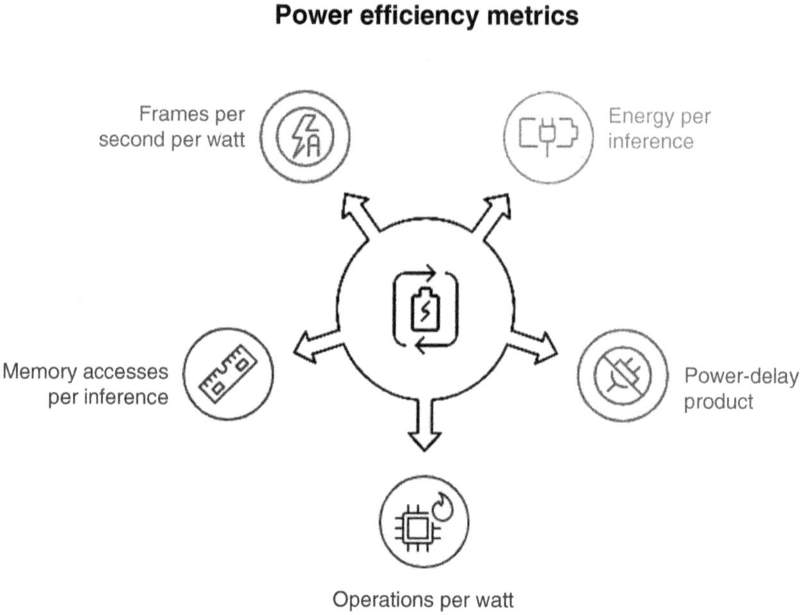

Figure 7.3 Power efficiency metrics.

performance include knowledge distillation, quantization, and model pruning. Specialized low-power accelerators hardware-wise, including bespoke ASICs, memristor-based in-memory computing units, and neuromorphic CPUs, are being developed to conduct AI tasks with the lowest energy overhead [2].

7.2 Lightweight Neural Network Architectures

7.2.1 Binary Neural Networks

This significantly reduces the computation involved because the usual operations (multiplication and addition) are replaced by bitwise operations such as XNOR and population count. As a result, binary neural networks (BNNs) use approximately 32 times less memory than traditional 32-bit floating-point models because each weight can be represented using a single bit. This makes BNNs very attractive for devices that have limited memory and energy. Furthermore, challenging BNN training is a nondifferentiable function involved in binarization [3]. For basic tasks such as keyword spotting, item presence detection, or activity recognition in wearable and embedded systems, BNNs can be surprisingly effective with careful training methods and appropriate architectural tuning.

7.2.2 Ternary and Quantized Neural Networks

Between the binary extreme and full-precision models, ternary and quantized neural networks (QNNs) offer a compromise. Whereas in BNNs, weights are limited to three values (e.g. −1, 0, +1), in ternary networks, weights are limited to three values, thus keeping more representational flexibility but with decreasing computational cost. Generalizing this idea, QNNs let weights and activations use low-bit-width fixed-point integers, commonly eight-bit or even four-bit representations that drastically reduce memory utilization and enable integer arithmetic on basic CPUs. Maintaining high accuracy in QNNs depends critically on quantization-aware training. It models the quantization effects during model training, therefore enabling the network to adjust to the limited numerical precision. Often seen in mobile AI systems like image identification, face detection, and speech processing, these models are quite compatible with low-power CPUs. One of the most promising routes for practical implementation in energy-sensitive situations is QNN because of its harmony between efficiency and accuracy [4, 5].

7.2.3 Efficient Network Design Patterns

Apart from changing numerical accuracy, another way to lightweight modeling is to change the network topology itself to reduce memory consumption and operation count. For example, MobileNets use depthwise separable convolutions where a conventional convolution is broken into a depthwise (channelwise) convolution followed by a pointwise, 1×1 convolution. This reduces the floating-point computations and parameter count required rather drastically. MobileNetV2 improves upon this and aids in further reduction of activation memory use by leveraging inverted residuals and linear bottlenecks. SqueezeNet similarly seeks to reduce the number of parameters by replacing more efficient 1×1 convolutions for heavier 3×3 filters, hence enabling AlexNet-level accuracy with 50× less parameters. By way of channel shuffling and pointwise group convolutions, ShuffleNet lowers computation and hence preserves information flow, as shown in Table 7.1. These models are not only compact, but they are also ideal candidates for real-time applications on systems with restricted power capacity since they are meant especially for integration with edge accelerators, DSPs, and mobile AI chips.

7.2.4 Architectural Pruning and Channel Sparsity

By removing less significant components, pruning a potent model compression method helps a neural network to cut the number of weights or filters. One can accomplish this in a hierarchical way by removing whole channels or filters

Table 7.1 Comparison table of lightweight architecture.

Model	Parameters	FLOPs	Key innovation
MobileNetV1	~4M	569M	Depthwise separable convolutions
SqueezeNet	~1.3M	833M	Fire modules
ShuffleNet	~1.0M	524M	Channel shuffle, grouped convolution

or, at a fine-grained level, individual weight pruning. Because it streamlines the model architecture in a way that maps more effectively onto hardware, structured pruning is especially appropriate for low-power uses. Pruned models can use a fraction of the resources yet maintain up to 90% of their previous accuracy.

Usually accompanied by fine-tuning or retraining, pruning is most successful when it guarantees that the network recovers any performance loss. Recent methods also use hardware-aware pruning, in which the features of the target processor such as cache capacity, memory bus width, or parallelism guide the pruning process [6]. These methods are progressively included in automated neural architecture search (NAS) systems so that developers may find very effective models tailored for certain low-power devices.

7.2.5 Activation and Feature Map Optimization

Low-power systems depend not just on the optimal weights but also on the low-memory and computational cost of activations and intermediate feature maps. Particularly in convolutional networks where feature maps can be enormous, activations frequently consume more memory than model parameters during inference. One typical method to address this is activation quantization, which lowers the bit-width of activations to correspond with weights or even less. Along with reducing the memory footprint, this fits fixed-point hardware's processing capacity. Inducing activation sparsity, that is helping the network create zero outputs in its intermediate layers, is another method. Skipping pointless computations during inference is made possible by sparse activations and saves both time and electricity. One can reach this by means of architectural modifications encouraging sparse representations or regularizing techniques. Furthermore, helping to simplify memory access and raise energy efficiency are optimization techniques, such as layer fusion and buffer reuse. These techniques guarantee that the advantages of model compression are spread over the whole inference pipeline; therefore, lightweight neural networks are even more fit for use in edge and embedded systems.

7.3 Model Compression Techniques

Enhancing the structure and operation of neural networks to fit the limitations of edge computing is even more important as they get more complex and pervasive throughout embedded and low-power systems. Most traditional deep learning models are resource-intensive, depending on huge parameter sets and high-throughput computation, which is unacceptable for devices with limited power, memory, or processor capability. By turning these big models into smaller, faster, more efficient ones while reducing accuracy and performance loss, model compression methods seek to close this difference. These methods are fundamental for the use of AI in wearable, Internet of Things (IoT), mobile, and implantable devices where responsiveness and energy economy are critical. Model compression addresses several facets of network complexity and is not a single procedure but a family of techniques. Among these are low-rank factorization and weight sharing; quantization lowers numerical precision; knowledge distillation converts learnt behavior from a large model to a compact one; and pruning removes irrelevant parameters [7, 8]. These methods can be used either separately or in concert to produce neural networks appropriate for low-power inference. Each method is thoroughly discussed in the following subsections together with their working concepts, advantages, and consequences for low-energy AI systems, as shown in Figure 7.4.

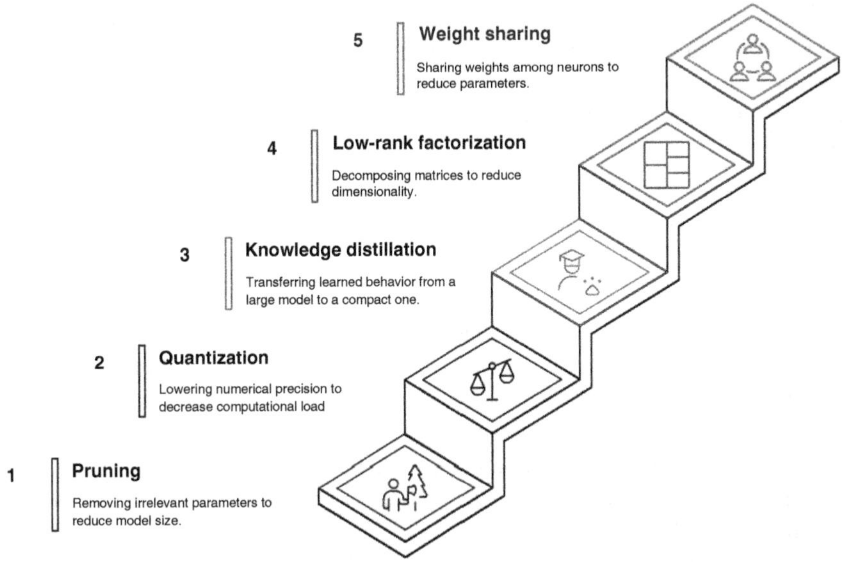

Figure 7.4 Achieving low-power AI systems.

7.3.1 Pruning Techniques

The first and most often used model of compression is pruning. The main goal is to find and remove from a neural network a factor that barely influences its output, therefore lowering the complexity of the model. Many neural networks in use are over-parameterized and feature many connections that have little effect on prediction accuracy. Pruning seeks to eliminate these extraneous components without changing the fundamental structure of the model, therefore enabling more effective computation and reduced memory use. Pruning takes essentially two forms: unstructured and structured. Unstructured pruning leaves a sparse weight matrix by removing individual weights. Although this can dramatically cut the amount of parameters, the irregular structure presents problems for ordinary hardware, which is not best suited for sparse operations. By comparison, structured pruning removes whole channels, filters, or even layers. More suited for real-world low-power implementations, this version preserves a consistent model structure that more naturally fits hardware execution units. Usually, pruning is an iterative process: a model is first trained to convergence, then pruned depending on some significance criterion (like weight magnitude), and finally fine-tuned to recover any performance degradation resulting from the pruning.

Pruning has several benefits in addition to memory savings. The most power-consuming component of inference, multiply accumulate (MAC) operations, directly translates from the reduction in convolutional filters or neurones under structured pruning. Along with drastically lowering energy use, this speeds up processing time. Good trimming, nevertheless, calls for a very careful balance. While under-pruning may not produce enough increases in efficiency, over-pruning might cause disastrous loss in accuracy. Thus, choosing the appropriate pruning strategy may be motivated by hardware-aware optimization methods and usually requires trade-offs.

7.3.2 Quantization

Quantization is a strong compression method that reduces the bit-width required to characterize neural network weights, activations, and sometimes even gradients. Usually in conventional deep learning, these variables are handled as 32-bit floating-point number and stored as such as well. Quantization replaces lower-precision representations such as eight-bit integers or even binary values. A main enabler of energy-efficient AI, this reduces the model's memory footprint and the arithmetic operations' power consumption. Post-training quantization (PTQ) and quantization-aware training (QAT) are two main forms of quantization. PTQ is a fundamental approach applied once a model has been trained with perfect accuracy. It just lowers the precision of the trained weights and activations. Although this is simple to apply and performs effectively for strong models, it can lead to accuracy erosion, especially for models sensitive to minute numerical changes. Conversely, QAT includes quantization influences in the learning process. The forward and backward passes of training replicate the consequences of decreased precision, therefore enabling the model to learn to offset quantization noise. For performance-critical installations, this is recommended and usually results in improved retention of accuracy. Quantized models have various benefits. Particularly on hardware architectures optimized for low-precision arithmetic, they offer faster, more energy-efficient inference and need less memory and consume less bandwidth when loading data. With many edge accelerators and microcontrollers now including specialized support for eight-bit integer operations, quantized models are quite compatible with contemporary embedded systems. Although more aggressive quantization (e.g. four-bit or binary) may be utilized in ultra-low-power circumstances, albeit with careful architectural tuning and application-specific validation, the bit-width of an eight-bit generally preserves most of the accuracy of the model [9].

7.3.3 Knowledge Distillation

One unusual compression method that emphasizes the learning process of the model rather than its design is knowledge distillation. It entails teaching a smaller, efficient model known as the student to copy the behavior of a larger, high-performance model known as the teacher. The learner gains knowledge not only from the ground-truth labels but also from the teacher's output probabilities, which provide more detailed information on the interactions across many classes. This helps the learner to generalize more than if it had been taught on labeled data by itself.

Usually, the distillation procedure consists of three phases. First, on the target work, a strong and maybe over-parameterized teacher model is trained. For every training input, the teacher then creates soft target probability distributions across the output classes. Finally, the student model is trained by combining the soft objectives from the teacher with the original labels. This dual-source supervision enables the student model to absorb the teacher's decision bounds, hence enhancing accuracy even with much-reduced parameters. Knowledge distillation can be a quite useful tool in low-power situations. It lets developers use lightweight models that, without carrying their computing load, roughly replicate the behavior of more complicated models. Apart from their lower scale, the distilled student models are more suitable with embedded CPUs and execute faster. Knowledge distillation can generate extremely efficient models fit for real-time inference on energy-constrained devices when paired with additional compression approaches such as quantization or pruning.

7.3.4 Low-Rank Matrix Factorization

Low-rank matrix factorization is yet another useful method for compressing neural networks. This approach uses the very redundant nature of multiple weight matrices seen in a neural network, especially in fully connected and convolutional layers. Using the product of smaller, lower-rank matrices allows one to approximate rather than store and compute with big, dense matrices. This lowers the needed memory accesses and computations during inference. Singular value decomposition (SVD) is frequently applied in practice to factor the weight matrices of fully connected layers into two or more components approximating the original matrix. Tensor decomposition techniques including Canonical Polyadic (CP) or Tucker decomposition are used for convolutional layers to divide 3D convolutional filters into smaller sets of filters requiring less processing by means of depthwise separable convolution is another often used method, especially in mobile networks, which efficiently factors standard convolutions into a depthwise and a pointwise convolution, so greatly lowering the number of operations.

Low-rank factorization provides major benefits, especially for large models where matrix operations predominate in the processing demand. Ideal for real-time inference in constrained environments, factorized layers run faster and require less resources. Still, decommission calls for careful treatment to preserve model integrity. Usually, this means modifying the model following factorization so that it could recover any performance lost via approximation. To ensure a balance between efficiency and predictive power, low-rank factorization is thus sometimes coupled with retraining and other compression methods.

7.3.5 Weight Sharing and Clustering

By forcing several weights to share the same value, weight sharing and clustering help to further lower the storage and computing load of neural networks. Weights are organized into clusters, and each cluster is shown by a common value kept in a codebook instead of giving every connection in the network distinct values. The real weight values are obtained during inference by use of indices into this codebook, which offers quite memory-efficient efficiency. This method can be applied either during training or post hoc following training and performs effectively in concert with quantization. Integrated during training, the network learns to converge toward weight clusters, hence enabling effective encoding. Post-training, k-means, and other clustering techniques are used to find similar weights and group them.

7.4 Hardware-Aware NAS and Co-Design Techniques

Hardware-aware NAS and co-design techniques fill in this hole by explicitly adding hardware constraints into the model creation process. NAS is an automatic method for identifying outstanding neural network designs. Originally supposed to relieve the work of handcrafted architecture engineering, NAS has evolved into a powerful tool for generating correct and fast models [10]. When combined with hardware-awareness, NAS becomes a tool for developing architectures especially suited for deployment platforms, such as low-power microcontrollers, FPGAs, or neuromorphic computers. These models are not only compact but also fit for use with the specific characteristics of the target hardware and avoid its limitations, thereby boosting the energy economy and processing capability.

7.4.1 Fundamentals of NAS

Fundamentally, NAS defines a search space (possible architectural configurations), a search strategy (how to probe the space), and an assessment strategy (how to evaluate candidate models), thus automating the exploration of neural network design spaces. Using reinforcement learning, evolutionary algorithms, or gradient-based optimization to identify the best-performing network on a given dataset, traditional NAS systems concentrated mostly on maximizing accuracy. Such methods, however, frequently produce computationally costly designs unfit for use in energy-restricted contexts.

The evaluation criterion is extended beyond accuracy to incorporate hardware-specific measures including model size, number of operations (FLOPs), latency, memory access cost, and power consumption, therefore customizing NAS for low-power applications. This change turns NAS from a merely data-driven optimization issue into a multiobjective search including the deployment environment as a fundamental consideration. On a particular microcontroller, a NAS architecture might aim to reduce the inference latency as well as the error rate. Such dual-objective optimizations produce models that balance hardware feasibility with predictive quality.

Often included in a simulation or estimation model for the target hardware is hardware-aware NAS system. These models enable fast iteration over hundreds of possible designs by predicting performance measures for candidate architectures without requiring actual deployment [11]. Direct measurements from real-world objects might be included in more complex algorithms to validate and improve the search process. Inclusion of hardware feedback in the search loop helps NAS to become a strong tool for identifying models that can realistically run inside the energy and temporal limitations of embedded AI systems.

7.4.2 Constraints and Objectives in Hardware-Aware NAS

Hardware-aware NAS success mostly relies on the way limitations and goals are specified during the search process. Constraints in edge computing situations often include a tight power budget, limited processing resources, tiny memory footprint, and low-latency needs. Explicit modeling of these limitations in the NAS framework will help to direct the search for workable answers.

Usually, the goals in hardware-aware NAS are several. Apart from optimizing accuracy, the search may also seek to minimize inference time, lower energy per inference (EPI), and restrict the memory use of the model. Certain systems could additionally take real-time needs or thermal limits into account, including deciding is taken inside a specified window of sensor input acquisition. Many NAS systems manage numerous objectives using a Pareto optimization approach, therefore generating a sequence of optimal trade-offs rather than a single best solution. Designers can then select the architecture most suited for their unique deployment criteria.

Accurate and rapid hardware performance estimation is a major obstacle in hardware-aware NAS. Although analytical models based on FLOPs or parameter count offer approximations, they frequently miss the subtle interactions between a network and the hardware platform such as cache behavior, memory access patterns, and instruction-level parallelism. To manage this, researchers have developed proxy models and lookup tables more precisely calculating delay and energy usage for given architectures. Alternatively, by way of performance data, a prediction model developed from the target device could guide the NAS algorithm more precisely.

7.4.3 Co-Design Methodologies for Neural Networks and Hardware

The process of co-design approaches a more whole picture, whereas hardware-aware NAS concentrates on modifying neural network topologies to fit current hardware. In co-design, the hardware and the brain model are created or optimized together in a synergistic process. By using the co-dependencies between hardware design and algorithmic structure, one hopes to attain a better general system [3, 12]. Custom hardware design situations, such as ASICs or FPGA installations, where the hardware itself may be customized to fit the needs of the model, call especially for this approach. Typical co-design processes feed hardware and software domain restrictions into a single design space. The system might investigate several neural designs concurrently changing hardware settings such as bit-width precision, data flow topology, or memory hierarchy. This dual optimization lets trade-offs be investigated in both spheres: for example, surrendering some accuracy to let simpler circuit design or changing data flow to lower power-hungry memory accesses.

When resources are limited greatly, co-design is very important. In a wearable ECG monitor, for instance, a modest reduction in model accuracy could be tolerable if it allows a significant increase of battery life. On the other hand, in a real-time industrial monitoring system, latency could be given top priority and hardware may have to be customized to satisfy exact response time criteria. Co-design guarantees that such domain-specific needs are satisfactorily satisfied by collaboratively optimizing the neural network and its execution environment.

7.4.4 Tools and Frameworks for Hardware-Aware NAS and Co-Design

Tools for hardware-aware NAS and neural network co-design have evolved into an expanding ecosystem. Popular NAS systems such as MnasNet, Once-for-All (OFA), and FacebookNet include memory, energy, and latency into their optimization loops. From smartphones to IoT edge devices, these solutions sometimes offer pretrained models optimized for a spectrum of hardware targets. Especially OFA offers the concept of a super-network from which numerous subnetworks can be extracted, each meeting different hardware restrictions. This dynamic approach allows fast adjustment to several deployment scenarios without retraining from start. On the co-design front, hardware-aware AI compilers such as TVM, TensorRT, and Xilinx Vitis AI provide ways to exactly control the model and the deployment stack for specific hardware. These compilers maximize graph-level transformations, kernel fusion, and quantization depending on target processor properties. More advanced co-design uses frameworks like Chameleon integrate the search process for both models and hardware configurations, and AutoML for Hardware (AutoML-H). These systems balance accuracy, speed, and power consumption by means of multiobjective optimization, hence determining Pareto optimal designs.

Moreover, hardware-aware profiling tools available on sites including Google Edge TPU, NVIDIA Jetson, and ARM Ethos-U give real-time model performance analysis. These realizations can be applied during the co-design stage or fed back into the NAS pipeline to improve the network's execution plan as well as its structure. Integration of such feedback loops enables constant improvement of system performance over hardware and software limits.

7.5 Emerging Hardware for Low-Power Neural Computing

Software developments are not the only factor driving AI at the edge forward. The need for specialized hardware able to effectively support these models is becoming more evident as neural networks keep becoming a basic component of embedded and ultra-low-power systems [13, 14]. Although flexible, general-purpose CPUs are typically not suitable for real-time inference, given limited power availability. Consequently, major academic and industry efforts are currently directed on creating hardware platforms specifically designed to run neural networks with very high-energy efficiency.

From very parallel analog neuromorphic processors to optimized digital microcontrollers, emerging hardware for low-power brain computing spans a wide spectrum of technologies. Through parallel in-memory processing, event-driven spike-based communication, and aggressive quantization support, among other fresh approaches, these hardware platforms are meant to enable neural computation. Examining their operation, benefits over conventional architectures, and influence on the future of embedded intelligence, this part reviews the most promising of these technologies [5, 15].

7.5.1 Ultra-Low-Power Digital Accelerators

The ultra-low-power digital accelerator is one of the main categories of hardware experiencing fast evolution. Using architectural improvements such as SIMD (Single Instruction, Multiple Data), systolic arrays, and MAC pipelines, digital accelerators run vast numbers of operations in parallel. Their main benefit is that they may be closely coupled with embedded CPUs and microcontrollers to enable on-chip AI inference at power levels as low as few milliwatts. These accelerators also allow lowered-precision arithmetic such as INT8 and even 4-bit operations, which greatly lower data transport cost and energy per operation [16, 17].

Moreover, contemporary low-power accelerators are sometimes coupled with neural compiler that maximizes model graphs depending on hardware particular properties. Exploring hardware capabilities such as quantization support, memory reuse, and kernel fusion depends critically on compiler like TensorFlow Lite for Microcontrollers or Xilinx's Vitis AI. Although digital accelerators are not necessarily as power-efficient as analog alternatives, their advantage in software flexibility makes them perfect for low-power, general-purpose AI uses.

7.5.2 In-Memory and Near-Memory Computing

Memory and processing are distinct in conventional computing designs, which results in the so-called "von Neumann bottleneck," whereby data must be migrated back and forth between memory and processor cores. Especially in energy-limited devices running neural networks, this data migration can explain a major share of power usage. By doing processing right where the data sits, in-memory and near-memory computing designs seek to alleviate this bottleneck [18]. Emerging in-memory computing systems compute not just for storage but also for computation using memory arrays, sometimes based on nonvolatile technologies, such as SRAM, ReRAM, or MRAM.

7.5.3 Neuromorphic Processors and Event-Driven Architectures

Neuromorphic systems have one of its main benefits in their capacity to interpret temporally encoded, sparse data streams. Neuromorphic processors, for instance, can directly interface and respond just to changes in the scene in vision sensors that produce event-based data, such as dynamic vision sensors (DVS). This reduces the number of data to be handled and enables systems to consume less power and faster reaction times than more traditional frame-based designs. Notwithstanding its promise, neuromorphic computers struggle to be generally embraced because of their lack of standardized programming frameworks and high learning curve for creating spiking neural networks (SNNs) [19]. Tools like Nengo, BindsNET, and Intel's Nx SDK are helping to remove these barriers, allowing researchers and developers to work at ultra-low-power AI more access to neuromorphic computing.

7.5.4 Analog and Mixed-Signal AI Hardware

The promise of analog computing to undertake low-energy consumption mathematical computations is driving a rebirth. Analog circuits control continuous signals to conduct computations distinct from digital systems by using binary signals and discrete clock cycles. Especially in fields where perfect accuracy is less important, this enables them to operate including multiplication, integration, and accumulation at very low power and rapid speed [20]. Analog signal processing allows analog neural accelerators such as those created by Mythic and GrAI Matter Labs to compute the operations needed in neural network inference. For high computational density with very low-energy consumption, Mythic's analog compute-in-memory technology, for example, uses charge accumulation to execute matrix-vector multiplies inside flash memory arrays. Combining digital control and communication with analog processing, mixed-signal architectures provide a compromise between energy economy and adaptability. Still, in fields like in-space AI, autonomous nanosatellites, or implantable biosensors where energy restrictions are severe analog and mixed-signal computers offer a practical and ever more appealing alternative.

7.5.5 ASICs for Edge AI

Energy efficiency and performance optimization are best provided by ASICs. Built from the bottom up, these chips with the lowest overhead and maximal hardware consumption do specialized tasks; in this instance, neural network inference. Although not general-purpose, ASICs can be tuned to incorporate just the logic required for the target model, therefore saving cost, silicon area, and power.

Edge AI ASICs spanning Tesla's FSD processor, Apple's Neural Engine, and Google's Edge TPU show task-specific hardware design. These chips combine good memory management, large-scale matrix computations, and low-precision arithmetic capability of multiple neural processing units (NPUs). Energy efficiency is indicated in TOPS/W (Tera Operations Per Second); hence, ASICs offer a convincing alternative for AI applications with tight power envelopes and real-time needs. But ASIC creation calls for long development cycles, expensive nonrecurring engineering (NRE) expenses, and less flexibility than programmable hardware. ASICs are thus most typically used in high-volume commercial products where the cost may be justified.

7.6 Case Studies and Benchmark Comparisons

The case studies offer important new perspectives on how compressed and optimal neural architectures behave in practical settings. These studies provide empirical benchmarks verifying the advantages of low-power AI hardware, model compression, and hardware-aware design, therefore bridging the gap between research and application. Here, a range of case studies spanning major application areas such as wearable healthcare, smart agriculture, industrial monitoring, and environmental sensing where energy-efficient AI is transforming. Every instance emphasizes how co-design, lightweight neural networks, and optimized hardware come together to satisfy practical needs.

7.6.1 Wearable Healthcare Devices

Personalized healthcare now revolves around wearable gadgets that allow constant monitoring of physiological signals including heart rate, breathing, blood oxygen saturation, and movement patterns. Low-power AI is essential since these devices run on one battery charge for several days or even weeks. ECG signal categorization is a regular chore in this field, employed in real time to identify arrhythmias or predict cardiac events.

In one well-known experiment, researchers used an ARM Cortex-M4F microcontroller to apply a 1D convolutional neural network (CNN) on a wearable ECG patch. Originally quantized to eight-bit fixed-point format and trimmed to remove less important filters and layers, the model was then scaled to match power and memory limits. Maintaining over 94% classification accuracy, the model size dropped from 1.2 MB to approximately 200 KB post-optimization. With inference latency under 50 ms and average power usage below 2 mW, coin-cell battery real-time monitoring on up to a weekly level was enabled. Wearable gait analysis technologies provide still another example.

A lightweight student model was trained to reproduce the predictions of a big LSTM-based motion predictor by means of knowledge distribution. While utilizing only 15% of the energy consumed by the original model, the student network, housed on a Nordic nRF52840 system-on-chip (SoC), attained equivalent accuracy in classifying walking, running, and fall events. These findings highlight the important part model compression plays in allowing smart, long-term wearable monitoring [21].

7.6.2 Smart Agriculture and Precision Farming

Energy-efficient AI is necessary for running autonomous field sensors, drones, and robots operating far from infrastructure in agricultural environments.

Among other jobs, these devices handle soil condition analysis, pest identification, and crop monitoring. Usually depending on solar collecting or occasional battery recharge, the devices must operate consistently on limited energy budgets, considering the outdoor deployment and often hostile surroundings.

One often-mentioned example is a smart crop disease detection system grounded on image categorization. Trained and then pruned a lightweight MobileNetV2 model to shrink the model size by 60% while maintaining over 90% accuracy over several illness classes. After quantizing the model to INT8, it was set to run on a Raspberry Pi Zero with a Coral Edge TPU USB accelerator. The compressed model achieved 3× faster inference and 5× lower power consumption than its full-precision variant, hence enabling continuous, solar-powered operation in remote fields. Another effort focused on recurrent neural network-based soil moisture prediction. Before being put to use on a low-power ESP32 microprocessor, the model was distilled and quantized. While allowing once-per-hour inference using just gathered energy from photovoltaic cells, the network maintained a root mean squared error (RMSE) within 5% of the baseline despite heavy compression. These cases show how compressed models enable AI in remote, infrastructure-free sectors like agriculture.

7.6.3 Industrial Monitoring and Predictive Maintenance

Smart sensors and embedded intelligence are being used by factories and other industrial sites to track machinery, forecast breakdowns, and maximize maintenance plans. Particularly in difficult or dangerous locations, these systems must be strong, sensitive, and able to run under limited power budgets. Real-time anomaly detection using vibrational data from spinning machinery presents a strong case. Trained with temporal spike encoding, an SNN was implemented on Intel's Loihi neuromorphic chip. The system obtained sub-millisecond response speeds with energy usage less than 100 μW per inference. The event-driven character of the processor guaranteed that computation took place just when fresh data arrived, hence prolonging the lifetime of battery-powered industrial nodes.

In another instance, systematic pruning and quantization to four-bit weights compressed a CNN-based motor defect classification model. It was set up on a bespoke FPGA board including parallel MAC units and on-chip memory. Ten times less delay and eight times less energy consumption were obtained from the implemented CPU system than from a baseline one. This efficiency allowed thousands of similar devices to be placed on a manufacturing floor for continuous monitoring, hence drastically lowering unscheduled downtime. These industrial applications show how hardware-aware design and model compression not only enable deployment but also improve the return on investment by lowering maintenance costs and raising operational dependability.

7.6.4 Environmental Monitoring and Smart Cities

In smart cities, environmental monitoring calls for low-power, distributed sensor networks able to process data locally to lessen dependence on cloud connectivity. Applications run from traffic analysis to sound event detection to air quality monitoring. To reply in real time and minimize data transfer and privacy preservation, the sensors must do AI inference in situ. In one instance, channel pruning and quantization-aware training were used to optimize a neural network for ambient sound categorization, subsequently implemented on a Cortex-M7-based microcontroller. From 1.5 MB to less than 250 KB, the model, which categorized events like sirens, gunfire, and automobile horns, dropped. On actual street audio, it attained 92% accuracy using less than 10 mW. The system was included in smart light poles and enabled instantaneous local reaction, such as change of lights or alerting emergency services. Another application was urban air quality prediction utilizing LSTM networks grounded on sensor fusion. Distilled from a simpler recurrent model, the model was trained using spatiotemporal data. Operating on an edge gateway run on solar power, the student model consumed less than 5 mJ per prediction and attained inference under 80 ms. This made it appropriate for dense, city-wide deployment since it provides public health dashboards and nearly instantaneous data to traffic management systems. Applications for environmental monitoring clearly show how lightweight AI models, when carefully optimized and coupled with low-power hardware, can offer scalable, privacy-conscious, intelligent infrastructure solutions.

7.6.5 Benchmark Comparisons Across Domains

Comparative benchmarks are necessary for quantifying the effects of hardware optimization and model compression. Usually, these comparisons center on measurements including model size, energy per inference, inference latency, and classification accuracy both before and after compression. Evaluations in several fields reveal common trends: judicious application of compression allows for minimum losses in accuracy and hence large size and energy reductions. For example, while pruning can further lower computation costs by 40–60%, quantization alone offers 2× to 4× decrease in memory and 30–70% energy reductions across several deployments.

Often combined, quantization and pruning generate models with under 20% of the original size but preserve over 90% of the previous accuracy. Though somewhat bigger than heavily trimmed models, distilled models often generalize better and provide higher stability under different data environments. While still providing real-time performance, neuromorphic systems such as Loihi and Akida give the lowest energy per inference, often in the microjoule or sub-microjoule range, in benchmarks tailored for hardware. Good balance between latency, power, and precision is offered by digital accelerators including Edge TPU or NDP120 (from Syntiant). FPGAs provide reconfigurable pipelines that may be tailored for certain inference workloads, therefore excelling in latency-sensitive environments. These benchmarks taken together offer a toolkit for developers choosing the appropriate models and platforms based on domain-specific restrictions.

7.7 Future Directions

As neural network deployment approaches ultra-constrained environments, low-power AI will find a home at the crossroads of algorithmic innovation, hardware development, and intelligent co-design. Emerging ideas show enormous promise to significantly boost efficiency while preserving performance and privacy: SNNs, analog in-memory computing, and federated learning at the edge. Developing universally compatible hardware-aware training frameworks, managing dynamic workloads on heterogeneous devices, guaranteeing resilience under real-world variability, and creating standardized benchmarks for energy-efficient AI are several unresolved difficulties still, nonetheless. Moreover, the direction toward on-device continuous learning will call for fresh methods of compressive adaptation and context-aware inference. Scalable low-power neural computing from niche use cases to pervasive, mission-critical applications across health, industry, and infrastructure depends on addressing these issues.

7.8 Conclusion

From wearable devices and smart agriculture to industrial monitoring and environmental sensing, the spread of intelligent systems in edge environments – from wearable devices and smart agriculture – has redefined the needs for neural network deployment. Constrained in power and resources, traditional models meant for cloud-scale infrastructure are not feasible. Researchers and engineers are now able to apply powerful AI capabilities to the most limited systems by means of lightweight neural architectures, model compression approaches, hardware-aware NAS, and specialized low-power hardware. The methods and approaches allowing neural networks to operate effectively in ultra-low-power environments have been thoroughly covered in this chapter. From binary networks and quantized models to neuromorphic CPUs and in-memory computing systems, low-power AI is fast developing. Case studies in several application domains show that energy-efficient AI is not only feasible but also pragmatic with the correct tools and design approaches. Looking ahead, the convergence of hardware design and algorithm performance, combined with the rise of new computing paradigms, will keep stretching the limits of what is practical in intelligent edge systems and shape the next generation of autonomous, low-power intelligent systems by constant innovation in co-design frameworks, real-time adaptation, and privacy-preserving learning.

References

1 H. Bourekouche, TinyML for low-power embedded intelligent systems: A review, Available at SSRN 5431335, 2025.

2 A. Basharat and A. Nishat, "Analog neural networks: A path toward ultra-low-power edge AI systems," *J. Data Digit. Innov.*, vol. 1, no. 1, pp. 25–30, 2024.

3 K. Wali, "Hardware-software co-design for power-efficient edge-AI systems," *J. Artif. Intell. Mach. Learn. Data. Sci.*, vol. 2, no. 4, pp. 2754–2760, 2024.

4 M. T. Lê, P. Wolinski, and J. Arbel, "Efficient neural networks for tiny machine learning: A comprehensive review," 2023, *arXiv preprint arXiv:2311.11883.*

5 A. Rostami *et al.*, "NLU: An adaptive, small- footprint, low-power neural learning unit for edge and IoT applications," *IEEE Open J. Circuits Syst.*, vol. 6, pp. 85–99, 2025.

6 A. M. Garavagno, E. Ragusa, A. Frisoli, and P. Gastaldo, "An affordable hardware-aware neural architecture search for deploying convolutional neural networks on ultra-low-power computing platforms," *IEEE Sens. Lett.*, vol. 8, p. 6004604, 2024.

7 Q. Liu and S. Amiri, "Optimised extension of an ultra-low-power RISC-V processor to support lightweight neural network models," *Chips*, vol. 4, no. 2, p. 13, 2025.

8 M. R. Chowdhury, M. Archisman Ghosh F. Bari, and S. Sen. "Leveraging ultra-law-power wearables using distributed neural networks," in *2024 IEEE 20th Int. Conf. Body Sens. Netw. (BSN)*, 2024, pp. 1–4, IEEE.

9 J. Greg, Designing ultra-low power convolutional neural networks for edge IoT devices, 2025.

10 D. Ngo, H.-C. Park, and B. Kang, "Edge intelligence: A review of deep neural network inference in resource-limited environments," *Electronics*, vol. 14, no. 12, p. 2495, 2025.

11 V. Potocnik, *et al.* Kraken: An open-source RISC-V SoC for ultra-low power multi-modal perception, 2024.

12 I. Lamaakal *et al.*, "A comprehensive survey on tiny machine learning for human behavior analysis," *IEEE Internet Things J.*, vol. 12, pp. 32419–32443, 2025.

13 H. Jin, "A novel impulse neural network model for low-power AI IoT applications," in *Second International Conference on Communication, Information, and Digital Technologies (CIDT 2025)*, vol. 14064. Washington, DC, USA: SPIE, 2026, pp. 115–122.

14 M. Chêne, Distributed artificial intelligence integrated circuits for ultra-low-power smart sensors, PhD Dissertation, Centrale Lille Institute, 2025.

15 H.-A. Rashid, U. Kallakuri, and T. Mohsenin, "TinyM2Net-V2: A compact low-power software hardware architecture for multi modal deep neural networks," *ACM Trans. Embed. Comput. Syst.*, vol. 23, no. 3, pp. 1–23, 2024.

16 E. Ragusa, F. Zonzini, L. De Marchi, and R. Zunino, "Compression-accuracy co-optimization through hardware-aware neural architecture search for vibration damage detection," *IEEE Internet Things J.*, vol. 11, pp. 31745–31757, 2024.

17 J. Millar, H. Haddadi, and A. Madhavapeddy, "Energy-aware deep learning on resource-constrained hardware," 2025, *arXiv preprint arXiv:2505.12523.*

18 V. G. Vaibhav, "A neuromorphic-inspired, low-power VLSI architecture for edge AI in IoT sensor nodes," *J. Microelectron. Solid State Devices*, vol. 12, no. 2, pp. 41–47, 2025.

19 A. Samanta, I. Hatai, and A. K. Mal, "A survey on hardware accelerator design of deep learning for edge devices," *Wirel. Pers. Commun.*, vol. 137, no. 3, pp. 1715–1760, 2024.

20 M. Tasnim, *Design for Ultra Low Power Hardware Accelerator Using Approximate and In-memory Computing*. Riverside, CA, USA: University of California, 2024.

21 J. Moosmann, H. Müller, N. Zimmerman, G. Rutishauser, L. Benini, and M. Magno, "Flexible and fully quantized lightweight tinyissimoyolo for ultra-low-power edge systems," *IEEE Access*, vol. 12, pp. 75093–75107, 2024.

Part III

Analyzing and Evaluating TinyML Models

8

Analysis of Optimization Algorithms for Efficient TinyML Model Performance

Rekha R. Nair[1], *Tina Babu*[1], *and Balamurugan Balusamy*[2]

[1] *Department of Computer Science and Engineering, Alliance School of Advanced Computing, Alliance University, Bengaluru, India*
[2] *School of Engineering and IT, Manipal Academy of Higher Education, Dubai, UAE*

8.1 Introduction

Tiny Machine Learning (TinyML) denotes the execution of machine learning (ML) models on significantly resource-restricted devices like microcontrollers and embedded sensors. Lack of resource requirements in TinyML devices compared to conventional cloud-based ML systems includes strict resource requirements of both memory and processing availability, power, and energy. Consequently, none of the standard models of deep learning will be readily deployable on these platforms without some form of optimization. Model compression, quantization, and hardware-aware model design are thus vital to yielding efficient inference on edge devices.

$$R_{\text{gap}} = R_{\text{model}}/R_{\text{device}} \tag{8.1}$$

As shown in Equation (8.1), the resource gap represents the mismatch between the computational requirements of the ML model and the available resources of the target device.

$$R_{\text{memory}} = 50\,\text{MB}/0.25\,\text{MB} \approx 200 \tag{8.2}$$

$$R_{\text{compute}} = 500\,\text{MFLOPS}/10\,\text{MFLOPS} = 50 \tag{8.3}$$

$$R_{\text{power}} = 5\,W/10\,\text{mW} = 500 \tag{8.4}$$

These ratios illustrate the fundamental need for optimization to bridge gaps of multiple orders of magnitude.

The objective of this chapter is to analyze the role of optimization algorithms in enabling efficient TinyML deployment on resource-constrained devices. The chapter examines computational, memory, and energy constraints that necessitate optimization, categorizes major optimization techniques such as model compression and hardware-aware methods, and evaluates trade-offs between accuracy, latency, energy consumption, and memory usage. Furthermore, it reviews real-world applications where these optimization strategies enable practical TinyML deployment.

This chapter is an analytical point of view of optimization algorithms, unlike general TinyML surveys, which are specifically aimed at resource-constrained edge devices. The chapter proposes a systematic taxonomy of the TinyML optimization strategies; the trade-offs between accuracy, latency, memory utilization, and energy consumption; and generalizes the findings of the real-world deployment case studies.

8.1.1 Constraints and Challenges in Deploying ML Models on Resource-Limited Devices

There are a number of mutually related constraints in the deployment of TinyML. Memory: Microcontrollers have flash and RAM that are limited to 256 KB to 512 KB and 32 KB to 128 KB, respectively. This introduces both memory-model parameter storage constraints and execution-time memory constraints, which are usually dynamic constraints. Processing speeds of 16–200 MHz, limited instruction sets, and few floating-point units further restrict computational capability.

Energy Constraints: Battery-powered devices require extreme energy efficiency, with power budgets often limited to 1–20 mW during active operation. The energy consumption of a neural network inference can be modeled as

$$E = \alpha \cdot N_{\text{MAC}} + \beta \cdot N_{\text{mem}} + E_{\text{static}} \tag{8.5}$$

where N_{MAC} represents multiply accumulate (MAC) operations, N_{mem} represents memory accesses, and E_{static} is the static power consumption.

8.1.2 Importance of Efficient Algorithms for Inference and Training

The success of TinyML is heavily reliant on efficient algorithms in inference and on-device learning and adaptation [1]. Efficient algorithms allow for:

Reduced Latency: Critical for real-time applications such as fall detection, where response time directly impacts user safety. Latency can be formalized as

$$t_{\text{response}} = t_{\text{acquisition}} + t_{\text{preprocessing}} + t_{\text{inference}} + t_{\text{postprocessing}} \tag{8.6}$$

Extended Battery Life: This is crucial for applications requiring immediate responses, such as fall detection, since latency will affect user safety. The definition of latency is

$$T_{\text{operation}} = \frac{E_{\text{battery}}}{P_{\text{avg}}} = \frac{E_{\text{battery}}}{P_{\text{static}}} + f\, E_{\text{per inference}} \tag{8.7}$$

where f is the inference frequency and $E_{\text{per inference}}$ is the energy consumed per inference.

Model Complexity: The benefits provided by optimizations allow more complex models to be accommodated under the same limitations due to higher

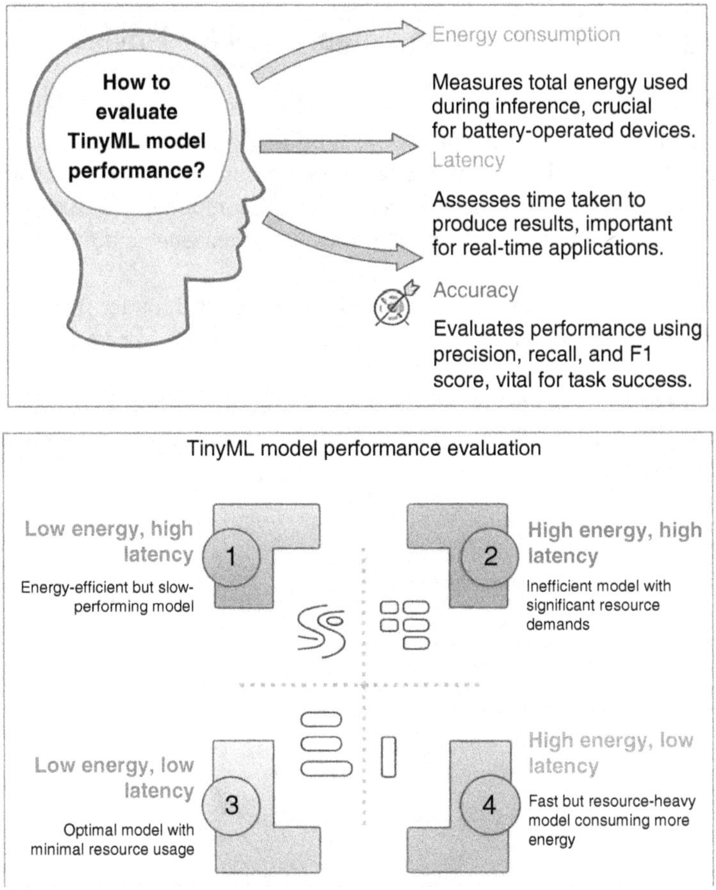

Figure 8.1 Overview of the TinyML optimization pipeline illustrating model compression, hardware-aware optimization, and deployment on resource-constrained edge devices.

efficiency and increased complexity of the task being performed. Optimizations designed specifically for TinyML must consider the interrelated nature of memory, computing resources, and energy consumption while still providing acceptable model performance. ML optimizations are mainly concerned about the accuracy of the model; however, TinyML optimizations involve multidimensional problem-solving. Figure 8.1 depicts the general process involved in TinyML optimizations.

The CMSIS-NN library demonstrates that algorithm optimization can attain up to 5× better CPU performance and 4.5× better energy efficiency on Arm Cortex-M processors.

8.2 Categories of Optimization Algorithms for TinyML

The optimization algorithms of TinyML fall under the following categories according to their aims and degree of optimization level: model-level optimization, algorithm-level optimization, and hardware-aware optimization. The main aim of these methods is to lower memory consumption, computational complexity, and energy consumption without compromising the reasonable accuracy of inference.

Figure 8.2 illustrates the categories of optimization algorithms for TinyML, including model-level, algorithm-level, and hardware-aware strategies for efficient edge deployment.

Table 8.1 stores a comparative overview of the significant optimization methods within TinyML systems. Their key ideas, benefits, drawbacks, and common situations of application in resource-constrained environments are listed.

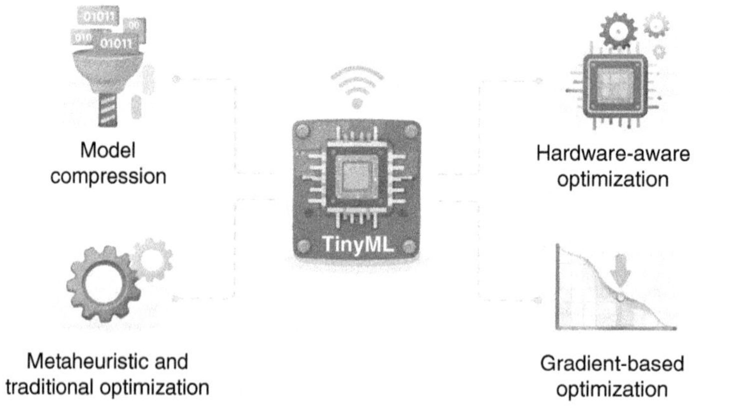

Figure 8.2 Categories of optimization algorithms for TinyML illustrating model-level, algorithm-level, and hardware-aware strategies for efficient edge deployment.

Table 8.1 Comparison of optimization techniques used in TinyML systems.

Optimization Technique	Key Idea	Advantages/Limitations
Pruning	Remove redundant weights or connections in neural networks	Reduces model size and computation; may reduce accuracy if over-applied
Quantization	Convert high-precision weights (e.g. 32-bit) to lower precision (e.g. 8-bit or 4-bit)	Reduces memory usage and inference latency; may introduce quantization error
Knowledge Distillation	Transfer knowledge from a large teacher model to a smaller student model	Maintains good accuracy with smaller models; requires pretrained teacher
Neural Architecture Search (NAS)	Automatically search for efficient neural network architectures	Produces hardware-efficient models; computationally expensive
Hardware-Aware Optimization	Design models considering hardware constraints such as latency and energy	Improves deployment efficiency; requires hardware-specific tuning

Source: Compiled from various TinyML optimization studies and edge AI deployment frameworks.

8.2.1 Model Compression Techniques

The objective of model compression methods is to make ML models smaller and less computationally complex while achieving reasonable performance. Such methods are significant in TinyML deployments where machines are heavily constrained in memory and processing power. Typical model compression methods are pruning, quantization, and knowledge distillation.

Model size is reduced through pruning by removing unnecessary weights or connections within neural networks. Structured pruning involves pruning entire channels or filters, while unstructured pruning involves pruning individual weights based on their importance. The pruning process involves the following procedures:

1) Train the original model to convergence.
2) Calculate importance scores (typically absolute weight values):

$$S_i = | W_i | \tag{8.8}$$

3) Remove weights below threshold τ:

$$W_i = W_i \times I(| W_i |> \tau) \tag{8.9}$$

4) Fine-tune the pruned model to recover accuracy.

$$\text{Pruning Ratio} = \text{Number of removed parameters}/\text{Total number of parameters} \tag{8.10}$$

Quantization entails decreasing the numerical accuracy of model parameters and activations by, for instance, converting 32-bit floating-point values to lower bit values such as 8-bit integers. This significantly decreases the memory footprint and computational requirements, allowing for the effective deployment of the quantized model on microcontrollers and other constrained-edge hardware.

$$Q(x) = \text{round}((x - x_{\text{min}})/(x_{\text{max}} - x_{\text{min}})) \cdot (2^b - 1) \tag{8.11}$$

where b is the bit-width, and x_{min} and x_{max} represent the minimum and maximum values, respectively, while x is the input data before quantization. Post-training quantization relies on the utilization of a small subset of calibration data for determining proper scaling factors at each level within the neural network architecture.

$$L = \alpha \cdot L(y, \sigma(z)) + (1 - \alpha) \cdot L(\sigma(z_t/T), \sigma(z_s/T)) \tag{8.12}$$

where z_s and z_t are logits from student and teacher models, respectively, σ is the softmax function, T is the temperature parameter, and α balances cross-entropy and KL-divergence losses.

8.2.2 Hardware-Aware Optimization

Hardware-aware optimization focuses on creating ML models that can be optimized based on the limitations of specific hardware systems [2]. Such techniques consider parameters such as latency during inferencing, memory limitations, and power consumption while designing and optimizing ML models to make TinyML models efficient on edge devices.

$$\max \ \text{Accuracy}(\alpha) \cdot \lambda_1 - \text{Latency}(\alpha) \cdot \lambda_2 - \text{Energy}(\alpha) \cdot \lambda_3 \tag{8.13}$$

TinyML benefited from specialized hardware accelerators optimized for specific operations. For a 3×3 convolution with $F(2 \times 2, 3 \times 3)$, the transformation matrices for the Winograd Convolution Algorithm are given in Eq. (8.1)5.

8.2.3 Gradient-Based Optimization

The gradient-based optimization algorithms are iterative procedures used to optimize model parameters by minimizing a specific loss function. Commonly used algorithms for training neural networks include stochastic gradient descent (SGD) and adaptive optimization techniques [3]. Such algorithms have been adapted for TinyML frameworks to avoid any computational overhead while not sacrificing learning and convergence capabilities. The Adam optimizer algorithm steps are:

1) Initialize parameters θ, moment estimates $m_0 = 0$, $v_0 = 0$, and timestep $t = 0$.
2) For each training iteration, compute gradient:

$$g_t = \nabla_{\theta\, L}\text{-}(\theta_{\{t-1\}}) \tag{8.14}$$

$$m_t = \beta_1 m_{\{t-1\}} + (1 - \beta_1) g_t \tag{8.15}$$

$$v_t = \beta_2 v_{\{t-1\}} + (1 - \beta_2) g_{t^2} \tag{8.16}$$

$$\hat{m}_t = m_t/(1 - \beta_1 \text{t}), \quad \hat{v}_t = v_t/(1 - \beta_2 \text{t}) \tag{8.17}$$

$$\theta_t = \theta_{\{t-1\}} - \eta \cdot \hat{m}_t/(\sqrt{\hat{v}_t} + \varepsilon) + \lambda\theta_{\{t-1\}} \tag{8.18}$$

EAs examine different network topologies using biology-based optimization [4]. The NAS with GA process entails population initialization, fitness evaluation (in terms of accuracy/efficiency), parent selection according to fitness criteria, generating offsprings by using crossover and mutations, and stopping the process by choosing an optimal neural network architecture.

The Multi-Objective Particle Swarm Optimization for particles with position x_i and velocity v_i is

$$v_{i\{t+1\}} = w \cdot v_{i^t} + c_1 r_1 \left(p_i - x_{i^t}\right) + c_2 r_2 \left(g - x_{i^t}\right) \tag{8.19}$$

$$x_{i\{t+1\}} = x_{i^t} + v_{i\{t+1\}} \tag{8.20}$$

where w is inertia weight, c_1 and c_2 are acceleration coefficients, r_1 and r_2 are random values, p_i is the particle's best position, and g is the global best position.

8.3 Performance Evaluation Metrics for TinyML Optimization

Indicators of performance evaluation of TinyML optimization are accuracy, latency, memory use, energy consumption, model size, inference speed, and compatibility with the hardware [5].

Standard metrics for classification tasks include:

$$\text{Accuracy} = \text{Number of correct predictions}/\text{Total number of predictions} \quad (8.21)$$

$$\text{Precision} = \text{True Positives}/(\text{True Positives} + \text{False Positives}) \quad (8.22)$$

$$\text{Recall} = \text{True Positives}/(\text{True Positives} + \text{False Negatives}) \quad (8.23)$$

$$F1\ \text{Score} = 2 \times (\text{Precision} \times \text{Recall})/(\text{Precision} + \text{Recall}) \quad (8.24)$$

For regression tasks, common metrics include:

$$\text{MSE} = (1/n)\ \Sigma\ (y_i - \hat{y}_i)^2 \quad (8.25)$$

$$\text{MAE} = (1/n)\ \Sigma\ |\ y_i - \hat{y}_i\ | \quad (8.26)$$

Latency refers to the time required to process a single input. Common latency metrics include inference latency, average latency, and deadline satisfaction rate, which are defined as

$$\text{Inference Latency} = t_{\text{end}} - t_{\text{start}} \quad (8.27)$$

$$\text{Average Latency} = (1/n)\ \Sigma\ \text{Latency}_i \quad (8.28)$$

$$\text{Deadline Satisfaction Rate} = \text{Number of inferences meeting deadline}/\text{Total number of inferences} \quad (8.29)$$

Energy consumption is critical for battery-powered devices:

$$\text{Energy per Inference} = \int P(t)\,dt\ \ [\text{from } t_{\text{start}}\ to\ t_{\text{end}}] \quad (8.30)$$

$$\text{Average Power} = \text{Energy per Inference}/\text{Inference Latency} \quad (8.31)$$

$$\text{Battery Life} = (\text{Battery Capacity}\ (mAh) \times \text{Battery Voltage}\ (V))/(\text{Duty Cycle} \times \text{Average Power}\ (W)) \quad (8.32)$$

Multiobjective optimization metrics capture trade-offs between competing objectives:

$$\text{FLOPS} - \text{Accuracy Ratio} = \text{Accuracy}/\text{Number of FLOPS} \tag{8.33}$$

$$\text{Energy} - \text{Accuracy Product} = \text{Energy per Inference} \times (1 - \text{Accuracy}) \tag{8.34}$$

$$\text{Pareto Efficiency} = 1 \text{ if model is Pareto optimal, } 0 \text{ otherwise} \tag{8.35}$$

8.3.1 Memory Footprint and Computational Complexity Considerations

TinyML requires balancing model size (KB–MB) with limited compute resources (MOPS) while optimizing for specific microcontroller constraints. The total memory footprint includes model size, runtime memory, and activation memory, which are defined as

$$\text{Model Size} = \Sigma\ \text{Parameters\_l} \times \text{Bits per Parameter\_l} \tag{8.36}$$

$$\begin{aligned}\text{Runtime Memory} &= \text{Model Size} + \text{Peak Activation Memory}\\ &\quad + \text{Temporary Buffers}\end{aligned} \tag{8.37}$$

$$\text{Activation Memory} = \Sigma\ \text{Activation Size\_l} \times \text{Bits per Activation\_l} \tag{8.38}$$

Computational complexity in TinyML is predominantly measured using FLOPS (floating-point operations per second) and MACs (Multiply-Accumulate Operations), as summarized in Table 8.2:

$$\text{MAC}_{\text{conv}} = C_{\text{in}} \times K^2 \times C_{\text{out}} \times H_{\text{out}} \times W_{\text{out}} \tag{8.39}$$

where C_{in} is input channels, K is kernel size, C_{out} is output channels, and H_{out} and W_{out} are output dimensions. For fully connected layers:

$$\text{MACs}_{fc} = N_{\text{in}} \times N_{\text{out}} \tag{8.40}$$

where N_{in} and N_{out} are input and output dimensions.

8.3.2 Benchmarking and Real-World Evaluation Methods

The performance of models can be measured through benchmarking methods and real-world testing approaches. While benchmarks can measure accuracy, latency, memory usage, and energy efficiency, robustness, reliability, and scalability should be tested using real-world hardware [6]. Specific metrics for measuring

Table 8.2 Common benchmark suites and evaluation metrics for TinyML applications.

Benchmark Suite	Key Metrics	Target Applications
MLPerf Tiny	Latency, Energy, Accuracy	Audio Wake Word, Visual Wake Word, Image Classification, Anomaly Detection
EEMBC ULPMark	Energy, Performance	Ultra-Low-Power IoT
TinyMLPerf	Inference Latency, Memory, Energy	Image Classification, Keyword Spotting, Anomaly Detection, Person Detection
TFLite Micro Benchmarks	Model Size, Inference Time, Memory Usage	MCU Applications
AIBench Tiny	Accuracy, Latency, Energy	Edge AI
MicroNPU-Bench	Energy Efficiency, Performance	Neural Processing Units

Source: Compiled from standard TinyML benchmarking frameworks and toolchains.

task performance in anomaly detection include AUC-ROC and F-AUC, while FRR and FAR metrics are used in keyword recognition.

$$\text{AUC} - \text{ROC} = \int_0^1 TPR(t)\, \text{dFPR}(t) \tag{8.41}$$

$$\text{F} - \text{AUC} = \int_0^1 F1\ \text{Score}(t)\, dt \tag{8.42}$$

$$\text{FRR} = \text{Number of missed keywords}/\text{Total number of keywords} \tag{8.43}$$

$$\text{FAR} = \text{Number of false alarms}/\text{Total audio duration (hours)} \tag{8.44}$$

TinyML evaluation techniques with respect to implementation [7] involve Lab Tests in laboratory conditions, Integration Tests in system environment, Field Tests in real-life situations, and Performance Degradation & Maintenance Tests. Cross-platform performance consistency measures reliability when a model is deployed on various microcontroller architectures:

$$\text{Cross} - \text{platform Variance} = \sigma^2_{\text{metric}}/\mu_{\text{metric}} \tag{8.45}$$

$$\text{Platform Portability Index} = \min{}_{\text{platforms(metric)}}/\max{}_{\text{platforms(metric)}} \tag{8.46}$$

Figure 8.3 depicts the conceptual Pareto trade-off between model accuracy and energy consumption in TinyML systems, where each point represents a specific model configuration.

Solutions that are Pareto optimal are configurations that cannot be improved in any metric without some other metric being worsened. The mathematical

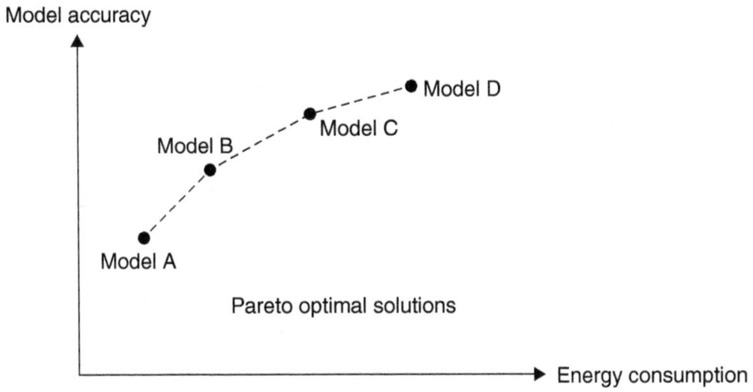

Figure 8.3 Illustrative Pareto trade-off between model accuracy and energy consumption in TinyML optimization.

definition for a model configuration m_i being Pareto optimal is

$$\nexists m_j \in M : \forall k \in \{1, \ldots, K\}, f_k(m_j) \leq f_k(m_i) \wedge \exists k', f_{k'}(m_j) < f_{k'}(m_i) \tag{8.47}$$

$$\text{Normalized Metric}_i = (\text{Metric}_i - \min(\text{Metric}_i))/(\max(\text{Metric}_i) - \min(\text{Metric}_i)) \tag{8.48}$$

$$\text{Unified Score} = \Sigma\, w_i \times \text{Normalized Metric}_i, \quad \text{where } \Sigma\, w_i = 1 \tag{8.49}$$

8.4 Case Studies of Optimization in TinyML Applications

TinyML optimization case studies demonstrate progress in healthcare, predictive maintenance, smart farming, anomaly detection, energy conservation, and live edge AI applications.

8.4.1 Optimized TinyML Models for Healthcare Monitoring

The optimization of TinyML has resulted in many advancements in the field of healthcare monitoring. The implementation of MCUNet on wearable electrocardiographic (ECG) monitors involves neural architecture search (NAS) and joint optimization, which results in 7% smaller models with an accuracy rate of 93% for detecting arrhythmias. In another example, convolutional neural network (CNN)-based CGMs work on microcontrollers and have ultra-low energy consumption, allowing for up to eight times model compression with eight-bit quantization [8].

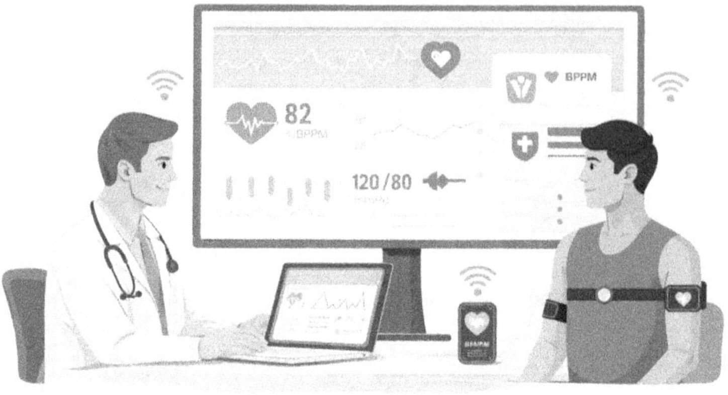

Figure 8.4 Optimized TinyML-based healthcare monitoring using wearable and edge devices for real-time physiological data analysis.

As shown in Figure 8.4, through the process of optimization using pruning, quantization, and good design, real-time physiological data processing can be conducted on wearables or edge devices.

8.4.2 Energy-Efficient TinyML Applications in IoT and Smart Devices

The use of smart home devices is an excellent case study for energy optimization in TinyML. For instance, Google's keyword spotting wake-word detector (Hey Google) utilizes pruning and quantization methods with just 5 KB of memory usage and 10 times lower power requirements, operating at milliwatts. Likewise, Ambiq's subthreshold processing units, coupled with four-bit quantized neural networks, have facilitated always-on motion detection at microwatts of power [9].

8.4.3 Real-World Examples of Successful TinyML Deployments

TinyML implementation is quite successfully illustrated in the field of wildlife protection where TrailGuard AI uses quantized MobileNetV2 models powered by solar energy in camera traps to detect poachers using aggressive duty cycling and model sparsification techniques that extend the battery life for months. On farms, the same kind of technology is used to detect agricultural pests using Arduino boards and compact CNN models (smaller than 50 KB), which can perform up to 87% accurate detection with 30 times improvement in battery life [10]. Bosch, a company in Germany, also used TinyML anomaly detectors in their sensor equipment using binarized neural networks and Fast Fourier Transform (FFT) feature extraction with 16 times memory reduction than 32-bit implementations [11].

8.5 Future Trends and Challenges in TinyML Optimization

The future of TinyML optimization encompasses more sophisticated quantization, NAS, federated learning, and challenges of energy optimization, deployment complexity, and scalability.

8.5.1 Advances in Automated Model Optimization Techniques

NAS tailored for microcontrollers is becoming an effective means of deploying the technology [12]. Some examples of this technology include Google AutoML-Micro and MIT TinyNAS, which develop models optimized for particular hardware. Nevertheless, the main issue remains the computation cost since existing NAS methods are very demanding on cloud computing.

8.5.2 Ethical and Security Considerations

TinyML model compression, quantization, and pruning methods influence interpretability, robustness, and security. Models that are compressed lose their interpretability, thus posing questions about accountability in high-stakes applications like healthcare diagnosis [13]. Secure deployment now incorporates adversarial learning and runtime anomaly detection. Achieving fairness through the lens of algorithmic fairness when deployed among different societies in the face of extremely optimized solutions is a problem that TinyML is beginning to tackle [14–18].

8.6 Conclusion

In this chapter, the role of optimization algorithms in implementing ML efficiently in TinyML applications is analyzed. Model compression, hardware-aware optimization, and NAS algorithms were examined in regard to their impact on the accuracy, speed, memory usage, and energy consumption. In particular, in analyzing the benchmarking process of TinyML, it is essential to pay attention to balancing different performance criteria while building tiny machines with ML. For future work, areas such as automated optimization pipelines, hardware algorithm co-design, and adaptive on-device learning need to be further investigated for developing efficient intelligent devices with scarce resources.

References

1 S. Balasubramaniam, S. Kadry, M. K. TK, and K. S. Kumar, *Bio-inspired Algorithms in Machine Learning and Deep Learning for Disease Detection.* Boca Raton, Florida: CRC Press, 2025.

2 N. N. Alajlan and D. M. Ibrahim, "TinyML: Enabling of inference deep learning models on ultra-low-power IoT edge devices for AI applications," *Micromachines*, vol. 13, no. 6, p. 851, 2022.

3 S. Somvanshi, M. M. Islam, G. Chhetri *et al.*, "From tiny machine learning to tiny deep learning: A survey," *ACM Comput. Surv.*, vol. 58, no. 7, pp. 1–33, 2025.

4 M. S. Diab and E. Rodriguez-Villegas, "Embedded machine learning using microcontrollers in wearable and ambulatory systems for health and care applications: A review," *IEEE Access*, vol. 10, pp. 98450–98474, 2022.

5 A. Elhanashi, P. Dini, S. Saponara, and Q. Zheng, "Advancements in TinyML: Applications, limitations, and impact on IoT devices," *Electronics*, vol. 13, no. 17, p. 3562, 2024.

6 S. Pargaonkar, "A comprehensive review of performance testing methodologies and best practices: Software quality engineering," *Int. J. Sci. Res. (IJSR)*, vol. 12, no. 8, pp. 2008–2014, 2023.

7 J. Gou *et al.*, "Reciprocal teacher-student learning via forward and feedback knowledge distillation," *IEEE Trans. Multimed.*, vol. 26, pp. 7901–7916, 2024.

8 G. K. Walia, M. Kumar, and S. S. Gill, "AI-empowered fog/edge resource management for IoT applications: A comprehensive review, research challenges, and future perspectives," *IEEE Commun. Surv. Tutor.*, vol. 26, no. 1, pp. 619–669, 2023.

9 H. A., Abushahla, D., Varam, A. J. N., Panopio, and M. I., AlHajri, "Neural network quantization for microcontrollers: A comprehensive survey of methods, platforms, and applications," 2025, *arXiv preprint arXiv:2508.15008*.

10 R. R. Nair, T. Singh, R. Sankar, and K. Gunndu, "Multi-modal medical image fusion using LMF-GAN — A maximum parameter infusion technique," *J. Intell. Fuzzy Syst.*, vol. 41, no. 5, pp. 5375–5386, 2021.

11 M. O. Ojo, S. Giordano, G. Procissi, and I. N. Seitanidis, "A review of low-end, middle-end, and high-end IoT devices," *IEEE Access*, vol. 6, pp. 70528–70554, 2018.

12 D., Prajapati, "Development of Embedded AI Applications & Toolchain", PhD thesis, Institute of Technology, 2024

13 S. Zhu, T. Voigt, F. Rahimian, and J. Ko, "On-device training: A first overview on existing systems," *ACM Trans. Sensor Netw.*, vol. 20, no. 6, pp. 1–39, 2024.

14 N. A. B. Abbas and M. R. B. Ahmad, “A comprehensive review of tiny machine learning: Enabling AI on resource-constrained devices,” *ELEKTRIKA-J. Elect. Eng.*, vol. 24, no. 2, pp. 81–97, 2025.

15 S. Han, C. Lin, C. Shen, Q. Wang, and X. Guan, “Interpreting adversarial examples in deep learning: A review,” *ACM Comput. Surv.*, vol. 55, no. 14s, pp. 1–38, 2023.

16 H., Hasan, “Federated Machine Learning and TinyML Inference for Crop Disease and Pest Classification on Smartphones,” PhD thesis, American University of Beirut (AUB), 2024.

17 T. King, Y. Zhou, T. Röddiger, and M. Beigl, “MicroNAS for memory and latency constrained hardware aware neural architecture search in time series classification on microcontrollers,” *Sci. Rep.*, vol. 15, no. 1, p. 7575, 2025.

18 S. S. Madani, Y. Shabeer, A. S. Nair, M. Fowler *et al.*, “Advances in battery modeling and management systems: A comprehensive review of techniques, challenges, and future perspectives,” *Batteries*, vol. 11, no. 11, p. 426, 2025.

9

Evaluation Frameworks, Metrics, and Benchmarks for TinyML Applications

Radhakrishnan Saranya[1], Muthusamy Yuvarani[1], Vivekanandan Karthi[1], Shanmugam Hariprasath[2], and Rajendran Pradeep[2]

[1]*Department of EEE, Kangeyam Institute of Technology, Tiruppur, India*
[2]*Department of EEE, Velalar College of Engineering and Technology, Erode, India*

9.1 Introduction

Tiny Machine Learning (TinyML) is the aspect of machine learning (ML), which aims to conduct inference on microcontrollers (MCU) or processors that have strict hardware restrictions. These limits are RAM and Flash memory in kilobytes (KB), clock speed in tens or hundreds of megahertz, and power in the range of milliwatts (mW) or microwatts (μW). Compared to the usual ML models, TinyML models are highly dissimilar as they need to execute autonomously in settings environmentally inaccessible, powered by batteries, and remote, i.e. no cloud or internet connection and with a significantly smaller degree of power supply. Dealing with an industrial vibration sensor that carries predictive maintenance, a smartwatch that can identify heart irregularities (atrial fibrillation) and a wildlife camera that can identify an endangered species are a few examples of such applications [1].

The problem with TinyML models is that it is more difficult to evaluate these models than usual ML models. Although the accuracy of the ML model remains highly important as one of the evaluation measures, it cannot be considered the sole measure to make the TinyML model usable. There is no possibility of using a TinyML model with 98% accuracy when the Flash memory is larger than 256 KB limit of the target MCU or the time to execute the model is longer than 200 ms when the deadline is 30 ms only. Thus, the TinyML model is used only in the multidimensional assessment with its accuracy.

Inference accuracy and reliability are validated on representative edge-condition datasets such as memory footprint (Flash for model storage, SRAM for runtime buffers and activation maps), inference latency and real-time compliance (deadline miss ratio [DMR], latency jitter), energy consumption per inference, and average power drawn in active, idle, and sleep states.

Benchmark definitions enable the comparison of the performance of ML models in a consistent and reproducible manner across various hardware platforms and ML configurations. MLPerf Tiny [2], Edge Impulse, and TensorFlow Lite Micro (TFLM) [3] operate at different levels of the evaluation stack, from high-level scorecards that balance accuracy and latency to profiling at the operator level with cycle accurate timing. It is necessary to comprehend the usage of these frameworks to migrate the deployed ML model to the production edge system. The target reader of this chapter includes graduate students, embedded system developers, and ML researchers with basic knowledge.

9.2 Importance of Evaluation in TinyML

TinyML represents the merger of embedded system engineering and ML and allows for real-time intelligent inference to occur directly on the sensors, MCUs, and low-power nodes of the edge, with no requirement for cloud connectivity to occur (Figure 9.1). The key problem of TinyML engineering in every field is to make sure that deployed models meet the needs of both the algorithmic performance of these models and the strict hardware limitations of edge devices.

9.2.1 Core Objectives of TinyML Evaluation

Verification of model performance is achieved when the model is compressed using techniques such as quantization, pruning, and knowledge distillation; it is also essential that the model be deployed and verified that the accuracy,

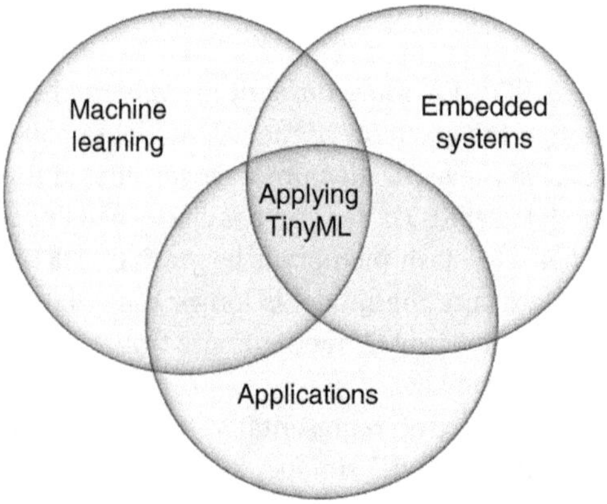

Figure 9.1 TinyML system architecture of machine learning models applied directly on the embedded microcontroller systems at the edge.

precision, and overall performance of the model are within acceptable limits. Optimization of the model in hardware efficiency is usually at the expense of model performance. Hence, evaluation is an essential part of every optimization technique. In other words, model optimization is mandatory in TinyML [4].

In system-level compliance, a model may be performing optimally in a cloud-based environment. However, during deployment, it may not be within the acceptable limits of the constraints such as memory availability during inference, maximum permissible latency, and battery life. In every system, there is a constraint envelope that is dependent on the amount of Flash memory, SRAM availability, clock frequency, power, and thermal characteristics. This operation must be examined to confirm that it can perform in the envelope, not in nominal conditions.

9.2.2 Unique Challenges of TinyML Evaluation

The peculiarities of TinyML appraisal include:

Software Hardware Co-design Interdependence: The representation of ML along with RTOS, the peripheral, should also be taken into account during the assessment process. A speech keyword detector should not only perform well in classification but also be able to finish the inference process in less than 50 ms and take less than 1 mW in a continuous monitoring mode.

Model Compression Trade-offs, the accuracy-efficiency trade-offs due to knowledge distillation, pruning, and quantization, need to be quantified explicitly. The conversion of 32-bit floating-point model to INT8 fixed-point one makes it possible to decrease memory consumption by a factor of 2 but potentially decrease top-1 accuracy by a few percentage points – a trade-off that could be reasonable in some applications and intolerable in others [5].

The edge deployment environment is hardly the same as the controlled conditions in the way training data was gathered. Sensor noise, signal attenuation, temperature-induced drift, and sampling irregularities all affect inference quality. The evaluation datasets must conform to these realistic conditions in order for the estimates of performance in deployment scenarios to be relevant.

9.2.3 Dimensions of TinyML Evaluation

The evaluation of a TinyML system is a multifaceted task, covering four dimensions of performance.

Common performance metrics for classification and regression problems, e.g. accuracy, precision, recall, F1-score, mean absolute error (MAE), and root mean squared error (RMSE), are evaluated on datasets that simulate realistic edge cases with noise, variability, and, possibly, minimal preprocessing. Flash and RAM

Table 9.1 Standard performance metrics and their relevance to TinyML evaluation.

Metric	Type	Formula/Definition	TinyML Relevance
Accuracy	Classification	(TP+TN)/(TP+TN+FP+FN)	Baseline quality; misleading on imbalanced edge datasets
Precision	Classification	TP/(TP+FP)	Critical for intrusion detection (minimize false alarms)
Recall (Sensitivity)	Classification	TP/(TP+FN)	Critical for health monitoring (minimize missed events)
F1-Score	Classification	2 × (Prec × Rec)/(Prec + Rec)	Balanced metric for event-driven edge AI
MAE	Regression	$\sum \lvert y_i - \hat{y}_i \rvert / n$	Average prediction error in physical units
RMSE	Regression	$\sqrt{(\sum (y_i - \hat{y}_i)^2 / n)}$	Penalizes large errors; standard in engineering
AUC-ROC	Classification	Area under ROC curve	Threshold-independent; used in MLPerf Tiny anomaly task

are used for model storage and inference execution; computational complexity are measured in MACs and FLOPs per inference; and energy metrics include energy per inference (μJ or mJ) and average power draw (mW).

Inference throughput (inferences per second), real-time compliance (DMR), latency jitter, end-to-end pipeline delay from sensor acquisition to actuation, etc. are evaluated. The ease of porting a deployed model from one MCU platform or RTOS environment to another, along with the ease of updating a deployed model, is done. Table 9.1 shows a concise overview of standard performance metrics,

9.3 Performance Metrics for TinyML

The assessment of TinyML models starts with the standard ML metrics for evaluating the prediction accuracy. These metrics offer a preliminary assessment of whether the TinyML model is functioning as expected on the intended problem. These metrics need to be understood in the context of the constraints of TinyML [6].

Accuracy measures the proportion of all correct predictions:

$$Accuracy = \frac{(TP + TN)}{(TP + TN + FP + FN)} \tag{9.1}$$

where TP = true positives, TN = true negatives, FP = false positives, and FN = false negatives. Although providing a rapid indication of performance, accuracy can be misleading on imbalanced datasets, such as anomaly detection (AD) tasks where the positive (anomalous) class occurs rarely.

Precision of a TinyML model is the proportion of correct predictions out of the total predictions:

$$\text{Precision} = \frac{TP}{(TP + FP)} \tag{9.2}$$

The recall of a TinyML model is said to be the ratio of correct predictions to actual positive cases. Recall is mathematically expressed as follows:

$$\text{Recall} = \frac{TP}{(TP + FN)} \tag{9.3}$$

In the case of health monitoring, false-negative cases may result in the omission of important data, while in intrusion detection, false-positive cases may result in false alarm.

F1-score is a harmonic average of precision and recall:

$$F1\ Score = \frac{2\,X\ (Precision\ X\ Recall)}{(Precision + Recall)} \tag{9.4}$$

A high F1-score indicates a good balance between false positives and false negatives. F1-score is the most important metric for event-driven edge artificial intelligence (AI). The area under the receiver operating characteristic curve (AUC-ROC) is a metric that is independent of the decision threshold. AUC-ROC is the primary metric for the accuracy of the AD application of the MLPerf Tiny benchmark.

9.3.1 Regression Metrics

In TinyML applications where the predictions need to be continuous, like in the estimation of temperature in a smart sensor or the forecasting of energy demand, regression metrics need to be used. The most commonly used regression metric is MAE, defined as the average of the errors. The MAE is easy to understand and is not affected by outliers. The mean squared error (MSE) is defined as the average of the squared errors. MSE is more sensitive to large errors than MAE. RMSE is the square root of the MSE. It is defined in the same units as the prediction. RMSE is the most commonly used metric in engineering.

9.3.2 TinyML-Specific Implications for Performance Metrics

A model that achieves strong classification or regression performance on a validation set may nonetheless fail in deployment if it (i) exceeds the MCU's Flash or RAM capacity; (ii) requires floating-point arithmetic (e.g. FP32) unsupported or prohibitively slow on the target hardware; or (iii) produces outputs after a latency that violates the application's real-time deadline. Consequently, performance metrics must always be evaluated alongside the hardware-centric metrics described in the following section. The assessment of TinyML is multidimensional by nature, i.e. evaluation report must contain at least the accuracy, latency (ms), memory requirements (Flash and RAM in KB), and energy consumption of TinyML model (μJ) [3].

9.4 Hardware-Centric Metrics

The hardware performance profile of a deployed model is as consequential as its predictive accuracy: a model that cannot fit within the target device's Flash memory, execute within its RAM budget, or complete inference within the energy budget is not deployable, regardless of its validation accuracy. Figure 9.2 illustrates the principal hardware-centric metrics relevant to TinyML evaluation [7].

9.4.1 Memory Footprint

Memory is one of the most binding constraints in TinyML systems. Two types of memory constraints exist in TinyML system: Flash/ROM and

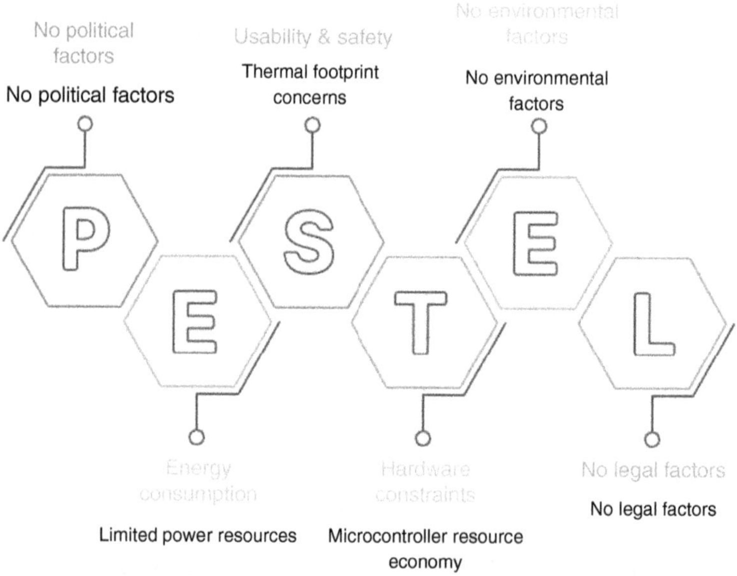

Figure 9.2 Hardware-centric evaluation metrics for TinyML systems, encompassing memory footprint, inference latency, energy consumption, computational efficiency, and thermal behavior.

SRAM/RAM usage. The Flash/ROM usage represents the amount of nonvolatile memory required by model weights, firmware, and libraries. MCUs commonly used in TinyML systems have a Flash memory ranging from 256 KB to 1 MB (ARM Cortex-M0/M4). Model quantization from FP32 to INT8 saves four times more Flash memory, and its measurement unit is KB. The SRAM/RAM usage represents the amount of volatile memory required by input/output buffers and activation maps during model execution. RAM is a more binding resource than Flash in most cases due to activation maps in convolutional models that may overflow SRAM even for models that fit in Flash; its measurement unit is KB. Note that a model may fit in Flash but still fail due to SRAM overflow.

9.4.2 Inference Latency

- Per-inference latency is measured in ms; it is the time elapsed from presentation of input data to production of the inference result. For real-time applications such as gesture recognition on wearables, latency targets are typically 10–30 ms; for predictive maintenance with event-driven sampling, 100–500 ms may be acceptable. In startup and initialization latency, it is the amount of time taken by a system to move from a sleep or idle state into active inference mode. This is applicable in systems that use a duty cycle model in which the MCU periodically wakes up and performs inferences. The Latency jitter (Standard Deviation of Per-Inference Latency) is the measure of variability in inference times due to RTOS scheduling, interrupt servicing, and/or cache effects. This is important in systems that have strict real-time requirements. Latency requirements are highly application specific. The following Table 9.2 provides representative thresholds from published TinyML deployments.

Table 9.2 Representative inference latency targets for common TinyML applications.

Application	Platform	Latency Target (ms)	Reference
Keyword Spotting	ARM Cortex-M4 @ 168 MHz	≤30	MLPerf Tiny v0.7
Visual Wake Words	ARM Cortex-M7 @ 216 MHz	≤50	MLPerf Tiny v0.7
Gesture Recognition	nRF52840 @ 64 MHz	≤20	Edge Impulse benchmark
Anomaly Detection (vibration)	STM32L4 @ 80 MHz	≤10	Industrial IoT deployment
Image Classification (CIFAR-10)	ARM Cortex-M4 @ 120 MHz	≤100	TFLM benchmark suite

9.4.3 Energy Consumption

Energy per inference (μJ or mJ) is the total electrical energy consumed by the system during a single inference cycle. It is calculated as the integral of instantaneous power over the inference duration. Average power draw (mW) is the mean power consumption across a total operational cycle, including idle waiting, active deduction, and sleep periods. It governs thermal routine and battery life. Energy efficiency (inferences per joule) is a compound metric that relates inference throughput to energy cost, enabling fair assessment across hardware platforms of inconsistent clock speeds. To achieve a coin cell (e.g. 3 V, 225 mAh CR2032) battery-powered Internet of Things (IoT) node with a multi-year working life, the power consumption of average node needs to be kept, on average, under 10 μW. This severely constrains both inference frequency and model complexity.

9.4.4 Computational Efficiency

MAC operation per inference is the arithmetic workload at an elemental level. Fewer MACs mean a lighter workload, which in turn results in lower latency and reduced energy consumption. For a visual wake word (VWW) model using a MobileNetV1 architecture, 57 million MACs are required, while a DS-CNN architecture requires 5 million MACs to support a KSW model [8]. FLOP is related to MAC operations but includes every arithmetic operation. Note that FLOPs per second (FLOPS) is a hardware throughput measure, not a complexity measure. CPU utilization (%) is a measure of how much of the available processing resources is being utilized to perform inference. This measure is important if other real-time activities are also to be supported, such as sensor acquisition, signal processing, or communication protocol implementation. Instructions per inference/CPU cycles per inference will expose low-level efficiency at a microarchitectural level.

9.4.5 Thermal Behavior

The thermal footprint of a model, i.e. how much it increases the temperature of a device, can be critical if a wearable device, such as a smartwatch, or an implantable device is being considered, as excessive heat generation can impact user safety as well as the accuracy of a sensor. To evaluate this, it is necessary to profile the device temperature after running an inference model extensively and to verify that it remains within a certain range as defined by the MCU manufacturer, typically between −40 °C and +85 °C to cover commercial-grade products.

9.5 System-Level Evaluation in TinyML

Hardware-centric metrics characterize the behavior of the inference engine alone. System-level evaluation examines the TinyML model as a component embedded

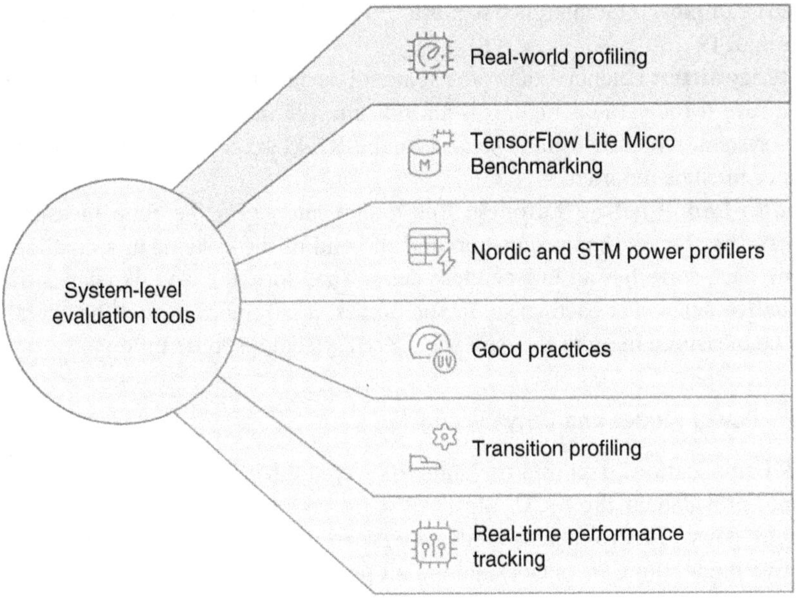

Figure 9.3 System-level evaluation tools and methods for TinyML deployments, spanning end-to-end benchmark suites, operator-level profilers, and power analysis instrumentation.

within a larger, real-world operating system – where it must coexist with sensor drivers, communication stacks, real-time schedulers, and power management controllers [9]. Figure 9.3 presents a framework of system-level evaluation tools and methods.

9.6 Real-Time Constraints

The defining characteristic of most TinyML applications is operation in time-sensitive contexts: fall detection in elderly care, predictive maintenance in industrial motor monitoring, live gesture recognition on wearables, and AD in IoT networks all impose hard or soft real-time constraints on inference execution.

The important evaluation metrics in real time are as follows:

Inference Latency vs. Application Deadline: Inference latency must be low and consistent, such that it is always lower than the deadline of the application. In the case of smartwatch gesture recognition, the value is typically in the range of 10–30 ms. In the case of audio KSW, the value is typically in the range of 30–50 ms.

Deadline Miss Ratio (DMR): DMR is the ratio of the inferences that are not executed within their deadlines, which is given by DMR = (Number of missed deadlines/Total inference requests) * 100. DMR is typically expected to be lower than 1%.

Latency Jitter: Latency Jitter is the standard deviation of the inference latency over a run. If the value is high, it is an indication of nondeterministic behavior in the system, which is usually caused by the RTOS scheduler. Both mean and variance must be reported.

End-to-End Pipeline Latency: End-to-end latency is the time measured between the start of data acquisition and the end of the system. In a pipelined system, each stage has an independent delay. Therefore, the overall delay is the cumulative delay over each stage. In such cases, it is important that the overall delay be measured in order to assess the overall system response time.

9.6.1 Power Modes and Duty Cycling

TinyML applications deployed on battery-powered devices must use low-power features provided in the MCU. Most ARM Cortex-M series MCUs have three different power modes: active mode, idle/sleep mode, and deep sleep mode. In active mode, the CPU is clocked, and all peripherals are active. In idle/sleep mode, the CPU is gated, and the peripherals are active. In deep sleep mode, most of the CPU and peripherals are gated, except the wake-up circuitry. In order to effectively evaluate the performance of the system, it is important that the performance be measured in all three modes.

The important evaluation metrics in the case of a battery-powered device are:

- **Duty Cycle Ratio:** Duty cycle ratio is the ratio of the total time spent in active mode. In general, the lower the value, the longer the battery life is expected to be.
- **Wake-up Latency:** Wake-up latency is the time required to transition from deep sleep mode to active mode. This value must be accounted for the overall response time calculation.
- **Energy per Operational Cycle:** This is the total energy dissipated during a cycle. Generally speaking, energy is the area of the instantaneous power vs. the cycle time. Taking the example of an environmental monitoring node, which wakes every 60 seconds, takes sensor data, inferences (e.g. 20 ms at 5 mA), and goes back to deep sleep (e.g. 1.2 μA) will have an average current consumption of around 1.7 μA, which allows it to operate on a typical coin cell battery over a multi-year period [10].

9.6.2 Robustness Under Deployment Conditions

Small ML models work in physically varied and shifting surroundings that are considerably different as compared to the training data collection settings.

The evaluation of robustness determines the reliability of models in changing environments. The temperature variation is identified based on the performance of MCUs, as well as analog sensor interfaces is subject to change as operating temperatures fluctuate within a specific range, usually −40 °C to +85 °C. The execution time as well as analog-to-digital converter (ADC) resolution may change with temperature. The models should be tested across the entire operating temperature range of the applications.

The Sensors in industrial or outdoor environments are subject to signal degradation due to electromagnetic interference and signal clipping. The evaluation set should include realistic noise profiles, signal distortion, and irregularities in sampling [11]. Sensor parameters change with time as well as across different manufactured devices. The robustness evaluation should include this variation to ensure that models generalize across different instances of the sensor.

Recommended robustness testing methods include injecting synthetic noise (Gaussian, impulse, and quantization noise) into validation inputs, executing long-duration continuous runs (24–72 hours) across varying environmental conditions, and cross-device validation on multiple units of the target hardware platform.

9.6.3 System-Level Evaluation Tools

A complementary set of tools that support system-level evaluation in practice are as follows:

- **Edge Impulse:** Provides deployment condition profiling for latency, memory, and energy via an integrated cloud IDE with on-device benchmarking pipelines.
- **TFLM Benchmarking Suite:** Replicates inference across MCU configurations and reports operator-level and end-to-end performance metrics.
- **Nordic Power Profiler Kit II/STM32 Power Profiling:** Hardware-based current consumption tracking with sub-millisecond resolution across active/idle/sleep state changes.
- **Free RTOS/Zephyr RTOS Task Hooks:** Hooks for tracking inference schedules, CPU usage, and timing compliance within an RTOS execution context.

9.7 Benchmark Frameworks for TinyML

Benchmarking in ML is the systematic evaluation of ML models and systems with respect to specified criteria to determine readiness, accuracy, and efficiency. It is significantly more complicated in TinyML than in regular ML benchmarking, as the hardware-dependent variables (inference latency, power usage, Flash,

RAM) are required to be measured in addition to model accuracy on actual embedded platforms [12].

These sections entail a critical comparative analysis of all the three main TinyML benchmark frameworks.

9.7.1 MLPerf Tiny

MLPerf Tiny, created by ML Commons, is the leading open and vendor-neutral benchmarking solution for Tiny ML systems [6]. The supported tasks of MLPerf Tiny version 1.0 includes four basic evaluation tasks, designed to represent the range of Tiny:

1) **Keyword Spotting (KWS):** Voice command detection from audio data (dataset: Google Speech Commands, model: DS-CNN).
2) **Visual Wake Words (VWW):** Detection of the presence of a person in a camera image (dataset: COCO-derived, model: MobileNetV1).
3) **Image Classification (IC):** Multi-class IC (dataset: CIFAR-10, model: ResNet).
4) **Anomaly Detection (AD):** Detection of anomalous patterns in time-series data (dataset: ToyADMOS).

The MLPerf Tiny benchmark measures performance across three key dimensions: accuracy (task-specific: top-1 accuracy for KWS/VWW/IC, AUC-ROC for AD), latency (per-inference time, measured via a hardware profiling protocol), and energy (measured via standardized power monitoring). The two submission modes that are supported by the benchmark are closed (minimum accuracy level to be achieved) and open (accuracy reported as part of the metric set).

9.7.2 Edge Impulse

Edge impulse is a commercial end-to-end development platform for embedded ML, providing integrated tools for data collection, model training, deployment, and performance benchmarking via a cloud-accessible IDE. The Edge impulse benchmarking pipeline automatically generates, upon model deployment to a supported board, a comprehensive performance dashboard covering: RAM and Flash usage breakdown per inference stage (sensor acquisition, DSP preprocessing, inference, actuation); latency profile across all pipeline stages; power consumption estimates from hardware power profiles; and on-device test accuracy on held-out validation data. The platform supports real-time inference on a wide range of embedded targets, including Arduino Nano BLE Sense, ST B-L475E-IOT01A, Nordic nRF52840, and Raspberry Pi Pico (RP2040).

9.7.3 TensorFlow Lite Micro

TFLM is an open-source, lightweight ML inference engine designed for execution on MCUs with no operating system dependency [3]. The TFLM benchmarking suite provides both end-to-end and operator-level profiling capabilities. TFLM's optional benchmarking target timestamps every kernel execution, enabling flame-chart visualization of per-operator latency contributions in Chrome's Trace Viewer. Heap and stack usage are logged per inference. TFLM integrates with the CMSIS-NN library for optimized kernel execution on ARM Cortex-M processors and with STM32CubeIDE for ARM-based board deployment. The μTVM auto-scheduler extends TFLM with automated operator schedule optimization, generating multiple schedule candidates, measuring cycle counts on real hardware, and selecting the fastest configuration – often delivering 10–30% latency reductions without manual tuning [13].

The benchmark frameworks are concluded with the analysis of above methods as a comparative summary shown in Table 9.3.

9.7.4 Custom Application-Specific Benchmarks

Since canonical benchmark suites do not sufficiently cover domain-specific requirements, custom benchmarks are developed. Application-specific benchmarks address unique needs such as custom sensor modalities or preprocessing pipelines not represented in MLPerf Tiny tasks; hardware platforms not supported by standard frameworks; and domain-specific key performance indicators

Table 9.3 Comparative analysis of TinyML benchmark frameworks.

Framework	Accuracy Profiling	Latency Profiling	Energy Measurement	Hardware Support	Granularity	Limitations
MLPerf Tiny	Yes (task-specific metrics)	Yes (standardized harness)	Yes (standardized power monitor)	ARM Cortex-M, STM32, Nordic	Whole-network	Limited NPU/RISC-V support; task-specific only
Edge Impulse	Yes (on-device validation)	Yes (per-pipeline-stage)	Estimated (not direct)	Arduino, ST, Nordic, RP2040	Pipeline-stage level	Proprietary; not independently auditable
TFLM	Yes (via TF evaluation tools)	Yes (operator-level flame chart)	No (requires external HW)	ARM Cortex-M (broad MCU support)	Operator level	TFLite models only; manual configuration

(KPIs) such as battery life over a 30-day deployment or robustness under specific environmental conditions (e.g. dust ingress, extreme humidity) [14].

A well-designed custom benchmark will follow a well-defined methodology, including the following:

1) Defining the relevant, measurable KPIs in line with the deployment needs.
2) Creating an environment that matches the intended deployment scenario, including the sensors, power supply, and RTOS.
3) Collecting performance data through on-device logging, hardware power profilers, and offline tools.

The results obtained through custom benchmarks, though losing cross-platform comparability, gain more ecological validity for the particular deployment scenario [15].

9.7.5 Best Practices for TinyML Benchmarking

1) **Profile Early and Continuously:** It is essential to incorporate the process of benchmarking in the model development lifecycle. It is much less expensive to detect memory or latency budget constraint violations during the model development phase rather than after the model has been deployed.
2) **Use Hardware-in-the-Loop:** It is recommended that the benchmarks be run on the actual hardware rather than depending on simulation or emulation tools. Only the actual hardware allows the detection of hardware-specific influences, such as cache, DMA, or peripheral wake-up latency.
3) **Include Environmental Variability:** It is recommended that the evaluation set be diversified by the addition of environmental variability, including noise, temperature, and sensor jitter.
4) **Benchmark Across Multiple Devices:** It is recommended that the model be run on several instances of the target hardware platform. This accounts for the variability in the hardware during the manufacturing process.
5) **Automate Benchmark Execution:** It is recommended that the execution of the benchmarks be automated as part of the CI pipeline. Automated execution helps in detecting performance regressions following model updates.

9.8 Evaluation Tools and Profiling Frameworks

The three axes that must be managed in the evaluation of a TinyML workload are model integrity, resource budgets, and realistic operating conditions. The tools and frameworks presented in this section attempt to manage each of these axes at increasingly finer levels of detail.

End-to-end benchmark suites provide the fastest system-level assessment. These suites are useful in the A/B comparison of boards or variations of models but do not give any insight into individual operator performance.

A plot of the resulting CSV trace in Chrome Trace Viewer gives a flame-chart representation, which instantly shows the layers that are slow, e.g. MFCC feature extraction and depthwise convolution. The μTVM auto-scheduler is a complement of TFLM, which automatically generates and tests schedule candidates with each operator on real hardware and then chooses the fastest configuration without requiring any manual tuning [16]. Arm Core Sight supports embedded hardware in locations where the hardware is supported, the Embedded Trace Macrocell (ETM) of Arm core is able to capture raw program-counter traces to a host to reconstruct and provide cycle-precise attribution of latency and energy consumption by instrumenting code with zero overhead.

To close the loop of optimization, tools of power analysis are needed. The Sensor Tile.Box development kit of STM32 offers the same feature with the MCUs of the STM32 family. In the case of production deployments, it is usually required to have custom benchmark harnesses that include multiple modalities of measurements. It is these harnesses that compromise the cross-platform generalizability, but give the ecological validity needed in situations where deployment conditions differ significantly with canonical benchmark tasks.

9.9 End-to-End Evaluation Case Study: KSW on ARM Cortex-M4

To illustrate the applications of the evaluation framework described in the preceding sections, this section presents a complete, end-to-end evaluation of a KWS model deployed on an STM32F407VG MCU (ARM Cortex-M4 core, 168 MHz, 192 KB SRAM, 1 MB Flash).

Experimental Setup of end-to-end evaluation starts with finding the required dataset as Google Speech Commands v2 (35-word classes; 105,829 one-second 16 kHz audio clips). The Evaluation subsets are 4,890 clips containing 10 target keywords, silence, and unknown classes. The model DS-CNN quantized with INT8 using TFLM post-training quantization. The input features are 49-frame MFCC (Mel-Frequency Cepstral Coefficients) spectrogram with 10 coefficients per frame. STM32F407VG Discovery board (ARM Cortex-M4 @ 168 MHz, 192 KB SRAM, 1 MB Flash) is the hardware part with inference engine as TFLM with CMSIS-NN INT8 kernel optimizations. Power measurement: Nordic PPK2, 100 μs sample interval. The deployment toolchain includes STM32CubeIDE, Platform IO, TFLM v2.14, and CMSIS-NN v4.0. The measured results are summarized in Table 9.4.

Table 9.4 Measured evaluation results for DS-CNN keyword spotting on STM32F407VG (ARM Cortex-M4 @ 168 MHz).

Metric	Measured Value	Target/Threshold	Status
Top-1 Accuracy (10 keywords)	92.3%	≥90%	Pass
Flash Usage (Model + Firmware)	387 KB	≤1 MB	Pass
Peak SRAM Usage	148 KB	≤192 KB	Pass
Mean Inference Latency	28.4 ms	≤30 ms	Pass
Latency Jitter (σ)	1.2 ms	≤5 ms	Pass
Deadline Miss Ratio	0.3%	≤1%	Pass
Energy per Inference	142 μJ	≤200 μJ	Pass
Average Power (active)	8.2 mW	≤10 mW	Pass
MACs per Inference	5.4 M	N/A (reference)	—

Operator-level profiling via TFLM's benchmarking target revealed that MFCC feature extraction consumed 9.1 ms (32% of total inference time), while the largest DS-CNN convolutional layer consumed 8.7 ms (31%). Together, these two stages accounted for 63% of total inference latency, identifying them as the primary optimization targets. Applying μTVM-generated optimized schedules to the convolutional layers reduced their contribution to 5.3 ms – a 39% reduction – bringing total inference latency to 22.1 ms with no change in model accuracy.

The power trace analysis showed that there is a 1.8 mA current spike during MFCC computation due to FPU activation. Restructuring MFCC computation using fixed-point arithmetic with CMSIS-DSP library removed this spike, reducing overall MFCC energy consumption by 18%. The entire evaluation process, from initial TFLM deployment to profiling-driven optimization, consumed approximately four hours of engineer time, thereby highlighting the efficiency of the structured evaluation workflow as described in this chapter.

9.10 Limitations of Current TinyML Benchmarks and Future Research Directions

9.10.1 Limitations of Current TinyML Benchmarks

Though highly valuable, current TinyML benchmarks possess a number of significant shortcomings that limit their overall applicability to all aspects of edge computing. MLPerf Tiny's four tasks (KWS, VWW, IC, and AD) do not cover all aspects of ML-based edge computing. Regression tasks, multi-sensor tasks, as well as sequence modeling on time series are not sufficiently represented in

MLPerf's standard tasks. MLPerf Tiny and TFLM do not support proprietary NPUs. As more MCU vendors are integrating ML acceleration hardware into their products (e.g. Arm Ethos-U55/65, STM32N6 NPU), future benchmarks should support heterogeneous computing platforms [11]. The current MLPerf Tiny and TFLM benchmarks focus on measuring inference time alone, ignoring all other application pipeline stages. As a result, end-to-end application latencies as well as energy consumption are consistently underestimated.

There are no existing TinyML benchmark suites that assess the robustness of the TinyML models against adversarial attacks or fault injection attacks. As TinyML is used in safety-critical applications such as healthcare and industrial automation, the development of security-based evaluation metrics is the need of the hour. The existing TinyML benchmark suites are only limited to evaluating the performance of the TinyML models within nominal conditions. As RISC-V-based MCU devices are increasingly being used in TinyML-based applications, the development of TinyML benchmark toolchains that support RISC-V instruction set extensions such as RISC-V Vector Extension for ML is also needed [6].

9.10.2 Future Research Directions

Several future research directions are being pursued to overcome the limitations of the existing TinyML evaluation methodologies. Cross-platform and multi-accelerator benchmarking is the development of TinyML benchmark toolchains that support heterogeneous execution platforms such as Cortex-M and NPU-based co-execution, RISC-V-based ML instruction set extensions, and FPGAs.

Automated neural architecture search (NAS) with integrated evaluation is the evaluation methodologies that integrate hardware-based NAS with evaluation. As federated learning is gaining popularity in TinyML-based applications, the development of TinyML evaluation methodologies that support federated learning-based evaluation is also needed. The development of TinyML evaluation methodologies that support the evaluation of TinyML-based model performance against environmental factors such as temperature variation, hardware aging, and electromagnetic interference. Benchmark metrics for adversarial input robustness (e.g. ε-perturbation accuracy), model extraction resistance, and side-channel leakage characterization, in line with upcoming standards for trustworthy AI in embedded systems [17]–[21].

9.11 Conclusion

This chapter has provided an ordered, comprehensive description of all evaluation metrics and benchmark frameworks of TinyML systems, including the full spectrum of evaluation metrics of both traditional ML metrics and hardware- and system-focused evaluation metrics.

This relationship can be very instrumental in helping practitioners follow a consistent methodology in the evaluation of TinyML systems throughout the entire system lifecycle, from the training of the models to the integration testing and the final production validation. Critical comparative analysis of the three main benchmark frameworks: MLPerf Tiny, Edge Impulse, and TFLM have revealed the advantages and disadvantages they complement with each other. None of the frameworks can be applied to meet all the evaluation requirements; robust engineering practice layers these tools in a coarse to fine granularity order and tests on the actual target hardware.

The end-to-end ARM Cortex-M4 KSW case study revealed how this multilayered evaluation methodology is transformed into precise engineering results: operator profiling revealed that MFCC extraction and depthwise convolution jointly used 63% of total inference time, allowing specific optimization to reduce the latency by a quarter without any loss in accuracy.

In the future, TinyML evaluation has serious open problems: lack of benchmarking of custom accelerator and RISC-V environments; no standardized security and adversarial robustness measures; and lack of test protocols of environmental robustness. Such gaps are crucial and should be filled in since TinyML is being implemented in safety-critical systems in the healthcare sector, automation in the industry, and intelligent infrastructure. To sum up, assessment is the core science that enables TinyML models to offer a consistent and dependable real-time intelligence under the severe limitations of the edge.

References

1 P. Warden and D. Situnayake, *TinyML: Machine Learning with TensorFlow Lite on Arduino and Ultra-Low-Power Microcontrollers.* O'Reilly Media, 2019.

2 C. R., Banbury, V. J., Reddi, M., Lam, W., Fu, A., Fazel, J., Holleman, *et al.*, "Benchmarking tinyML systems: Challenges and direction," 2020, *arXiv preprint arXiv:2003.04821*

3 R. David *et al.*, "Tensorflow lite micro: Embedded machine learning for tinyML systems," *Proc. Mach. Learn. System.*, vol. 3, pp. 800–811, 2021.

4 N. D., Lane, P., Georgiev, and L.Q., endro, "DeepEar: Robust smartphone audio sensing in unconstrained acoustic environments using deep learning," in *Proc. 2015 ACM Int. Joint Conf. Pervasive Ubiquitous Comput.*, 2015, pp. 283–294, IEEE

5 A. Gholami, S. Kim, Z. Dong, Z. Yao, M. W. Mahoney, and K. Keutzer, "A survey of quantization methods for efficient neural network inference," in *Low-Power Computer Vision*. Chapman and Hall/CRC, 2022, pp. 291–326.

6 C., Banbury, V. J., Reddi, P., Torelli, J., Holleman, N., Jeffries, C., Kiraly, *et al.*, "Mlperf tiny benchmark," 2021, *arXiv preprint arXiv:2106.07597*

7 M., Shafique, T., Theocharides, V. J., Reddy, and B., Murmann, "TinyML: Current progress, research challenges, and future roadmap," in *Proc. 58th ACM/IEEE Design Automat. Conf. (DAC)*, 2021, pp. 1303–1306, IEEE.

8 N. N. Alajlan and D. M. Ibrahim, "TinyML: Enabling inference of deep learning models on ultra-low-power IoT edge devices for AI applications," *Micromachines*, vol. 13, no. 6, p. 851, 2022.

9 Y. D., Kwon, J., Chauhan, H., Jia, S. I., Venieris, and C., Mascolo, "LifeLearner: Hardware-aware meta continual learning system for embedded computing platforms," in *Proc. 21st ACM Conf. Embedded Netw. Sensor Syst.*, 2023, pp. 138–151.

10 O. Spantidi, *Resource-Aware Optimization Techniques for Machine Learning Inference on Heterogeneous Embedded Systems*. Southern Illinois University at Carbondale, 2023.

11 J., Millar, Y., Huang, S., Sethi, H., Haddadi, and A., Madhavapeddy, "Benchmarking Ultra-Low-Power μNPUs," 2025, *arXiv preprint arXiv:2503.22567*

12 Y. Y., Liu, H. S., Zheng, Y. F., Hu, C. F., Hsu, and T. T., Yeh, "TinyTS: Memory-efficient TinyML model compiler framework on microcontrollers," in *Proc. 2024 IEEE Int. Symp. High-Perform. Comput. Architect. (HPCA)*, 2024, pp. 848–860, IEEE.

13 V., Janapa Reddi, C., Cheng, D., Kanter, P., Mattson, G., Schmuelling, C. J., Wu, *et al.*, "MLPerf Inference Benchmark," 2019, *arXiv e-prints, arXiv-1911.*

14 L. Capogrosso, F. Cunico, D. S. Cheng, F. Fummi, and M. Cristani, "A machine learning-oriented survey on tiny machine learning," *IEEE Access*, vol. 12, pp. 23406–23426, 2024.

15 T. Chen *et al.*, "{TVM}: An automated {End-to-End} optimizing compiler for deep learning," in *13th USENIX Symposium on Operating Systems Design and Implementation (OSDI 18)*. 2018, pp. 578–594.

16 A. G., Howard, M., Zhu, B., Chen, D., Kalenichenko, W., Wang, T., Weyand, and *et al.*, "Mobilenets: Efficient convolutional neural networks for mobile vision applications," 2017, *arXiv preprint arXiv:1704.04861.*

17 D., Zhang, J., Yang, D., Ye, and G., Hua, "LQ-Nets: Learned quantization for highly accurate and compact deep neural networks," in *Proc. European Conf. Comput. Vision (ECCV)*, 2018, pp. 365–382.

18 L., Lai, N., Suda, and V., Chandra, "CMSIS-NN: Efficient Neural Network Kernels for ARM Cortex-M CPUs", 2018, *arXiv preprint arXiv:1801.06601.*

19 C. Banbury *et al.*, "Micronets: Neural network architectures for deploying TinyML applications on commodity microcontrollers," *Proc. Mach. Learn. System.*, vol. 3, pp. 517–532, 2021.

20 R. Kallimani, K. Pai, P. Raghuwanshi, S. Iyer, and O. L. López, "TinyML: Tools, applications, challenges, and future research directions," *Multimed. Tools Appl.*, vol. 83, no. 10, pp. 29015–29045, 2024.

21 G. M., Torres, J. V., De Souza, J. G., Aguiar, & J. O., De Sousa, "Performance and Power consumption of real-time task scheduling for embedded systems devices," *Proc. 2025 IEEE Int. Conf. Consum. Electr. (ICCE)*, 2025, pp. 1–6, IEEE.

Part IV

TinyML Applications

10

TinyML for Healthcare and Biomedical Applications

Vinod Kumar[1] *and Chander Prabha*[2]

[1] *Department of Computer Science and Engineering, Maharishi Markendeshwar University, Mullana, India*
[2] *Chitkara University Institute of Engineering and Technology, Chitkara University, Punjab, India*

10.1 Introduction

This chapter is intended for graduate students in biomedical engineering and computer science, embedded systems engineers exploring machine learning ML deployment on microcontrollers, healthcare researchers evaluating artificial intelligence (AI)-based diagnostic tools, and clinicians interested in understanding the technical foundations of intelligent wearable and remote monitoring systems.

The rapid advancement of AI and ML has created transformative opportunities for healthcare. Among these, Tiny Machine Learning (TinyML) is a groundbreaking paradigm [1] that enables intelligent data processing on resource-constrained devices consuming only milliwatts of power. By incorporating ML directly into edge devices, TinyML reduces communication latency, strengthens data security, and enables real-time clinical decision-making at the point of care [2].

TinyML is transforming clinical diagnostic workflows, body monitoring, and personalized therapy by adding intelligence that is driven by AI into wearable, biosensors, and remote monitoring systems [3]. Those technologies would enable round-the-clock health tracking, preventive care of diseases, and automatic notifications, which would greatly improve patient outcomes. Additionally, due to the possibility of reducing the anxiety about sensitive health data [4], the capacity of TinyML to process on-board physiological data has greater data privacy and safety.

The wearable medical device that can monitor multiple health indicators in real time is gradually gaining popularity among the users as they are able to establish how healthy they are or are not. Physical activity is tracked by fitness trackers like Fitbit and Garmin, tracking steps, calories expended, and heart rate, frequently with GPS and sleep tracking [5]. Smartwatches, like the Apple Watch, integrate

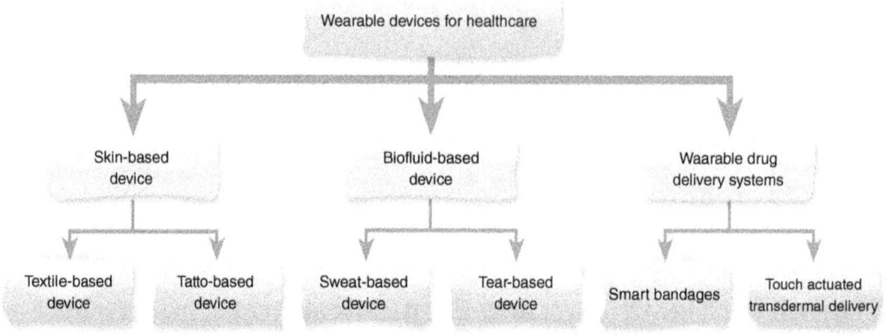

Figure 10.1 Classification of wearable healthcare devices.

fitness tracking with other functions like smartphone notifications, music, and enhanced health monitoring like electrocardiogram (ECG) and blood oxygen-level measurements [6].

Figure 10.1 categorizes wearable healthcare devices into three broad classes: skin-based devices (textile-based and tattoo-based), bio-fluid-based devices (sweat-based and tear-based), and wearable drug delivery systems. A comprehensive overview of different device types and their implementation in TinyML, contributions, and limitations is presented in Section 10.4 and Table 10.2.

The range of wearable devices used in clinical practice varies from general-purpose devices to condition-specific devices, such as continuous glucose monitors for the management of diabetes, wearable ECG monitors for the management and detection of arrhythmias, and respiratory monitors for the management of chronic obstructive pulmonary disease (COPD). For more information on the application coverage, contributions, and limitations of TinyML for different wearable devices, readers are advised to read Section 10.4 [7, 8].

The applications of wearable healthcare devices form a new and emerging field. As technology advances, devices are becoming more sophisticated and providing more information to the user and healthcare provider [9]. Continuous health monitoring, early detection of diseases, and notifications using TinyML technology provide a significant boost to the management and treatment of patients. Physiological signal processing on the device ensures stronger confidentiality, security, and privacy. Figure 10.2 presents a summary of the advantages of using TinyML.

The on-device data processing (as described in Section 10.3) will remove the necessity to send raw patient data to remote servers, which makes HIPAA/GDPR-compliant and decreases the risk of breaches [10]. This is the capability of TinyML models to run effectively on devices with constrained power supplies [11]. TinyML models are capable of offering real-time insights and predictions, allowing for timely responses to dynamic conditions [12, 13].

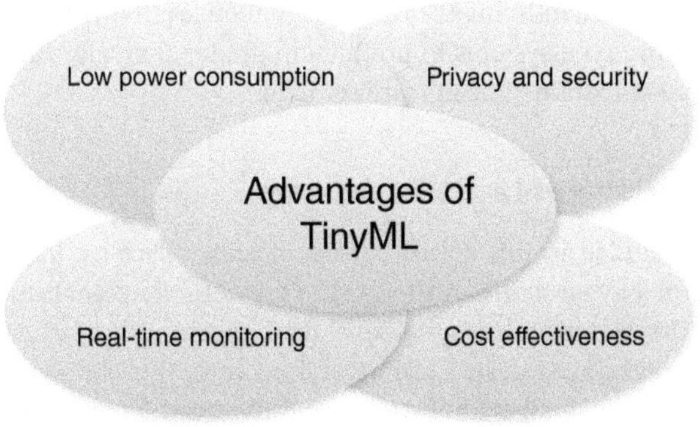

Figure 10.2 TinyML advantages.

TinyML models can be executed on affordable hardware, bringing the total cost of deployment of ML solutions lower [14].

The rest of the chapter is organized as follows. Section 10.2 presents the applications of TinyML and their uses in healthcare. Section 10.3 presents how predictive modelling is used in TinyML. Section 10.4 deals with TinyML usage in wearable devices. Section 10.5 demonstrates how TinyML is effective in the remote monitoring of patients. Section 10.6 demonstrates the diagnosis and treatment of patients via TinyML. Section 10.6.4 represents an overview of the drug delivery via TinyML. Section 10.7 demonstrates a streamlined process of utilizing TinyML in healthcare to highlight its capacity to improve diagnosis accuracy and the efficiency of treatments. Section 10.8 presents issues and challenges along with the future scope of research in the said domain.

The chapter is organized around five major learning objectives: (i) to introduce TinyML as an edge computing paradigm in healthcare, locating it as an innovative paradigm that modifies AI computation for resource-constrained devices (microcontrollers, wearables, and Internet of Things [IoT] sensors) to empower localized intelligence in healthcare provision; (ii) to survey areas of use such as wearables, remote patient monitoring (RPM), diagnosis, and drug discovery, providing a broad overview of TinyML deployment across the healthcare spectrum; (iii) to introduce a predictive modeling pipeline for resource-constrained devices, describing the overall workflow of developing, optimizing, and deploying ML applications under extreme computational, memory, and power constraints (quantization, pruning, edge-constrained optimization); (iv) to critically evaluate challenges such as limited computational resources, data privacy, and model interpretability, including whether models behave accurately when stretched, the need for explainable predictions, and regulatory validation concerns; and (v) to present concepts of research underway such as federated learning, explainable AI

(XAI), and 5G-assisted TinyML, identifying the research challenges that will help TinyML advance beyond prototype systems to production-grade, clinically valid medical devices in resource-constrained healthcare settings.

10.1.1 TinyML in the Healthcare AI and IoT Landscape

The fact that TinyML is included in this edited book indicates a decisive intersection in healthcare technology structure. Although the previous chapters focus on cloud-based clinical AI systems and hospital-level data governance, and the later chapters focus on the advanced deep learning architecture, this chapter is the critical gap between intelligent algorithm design and hardware-constrained deployment.

TinyML serves as the convergence point of three critical healthcare technology trends: (i) AI-driven diagnostics, referring to the progress of ML algorithms to detect diseases and stratify patients and plan treatment; (ii) IoT-connected health sensing, involving the expansion of networked sensors for continuous physiological monitoring in wearables, implantables, and surrounding conditions; and (iii) edge-constrained deployment, addressing the physical need to deploy intelligence at the point of care that is not connected to the cloud, where such connectivity is not reliable or desirable due to privacy and latency constraints.

This chapter is directly connected to the overall theme of the book on intelligent healthcare systems because it shows that advanced capabilities of AI can be incorporated inside the devices that are located at the interface between the provider and the patient instead of centralizing computational infrastructure. As such, we close the gap between algorithmic innovation and clinical implementation, creating the technical base of truly distributed, real-time, privacy-preserving healthcare intelligence.

The chapter adds six specific contributions to the literature on healthcare AI and edge computing. First, it provides an efficient taxonomy of TinyML applications in healthcare subdomains, classifying clinical applications across preventive monitoring with wearables, chronic disease management with RPM, acute condition diagnosis, and biomedical research. Second, it demonstrates a unified predictive modeling pipeline for edge-constrained medical devices, showcasing optimization approaches like quantization into INT8/INT4, pruning, and distillation. Third, it provides a comparative study and analysis of various TinyML frameworks for healthcare applications. Fourth, it includes a technical case study and quantitative benchmarks on ECG arrhythmia detection, providing a complete worked example of an ECG arrhythmia classifier on ARM Cortex-M4 hardware, including model architecture, training data, quantization performance, and clinical validation. Fifth, it provides a critical analysis of regulatory and clinical validation issues, offering a methodological discussion of FDA

510(k) vs. De Novo routes, the PCCP framework, European Union Medical Device Regulation (EU MDR) 2017/745 CE marking, and postmarket surveillance. Sixth, it outlines a future research roadmap covering federated learning and XAI, identifying research areas necessary for clinical adoption including federated learning, XAI on resource-constrained devices, and 5G-assisted TinyML architectures.

10.1.2 Privacy and Security in Edge-Based Healthcare AI

An important advantage of TinyML in healthcare is a consequence of the principle of data locality: when sensitive health information is not applied to remote servers, but to local edge devices (smartwatches, portable monitors, bedside microcontrollers), and transmitted, then the very principle of privacy and security threat modeling of healthcare applications changes.

Regarding data locality and minimal attack surface, the existing cloud-based healthcare AI transfers raw patient data through networks to remote data centers; this exposes several attack vectors including network interception, unauthorized over-the-air access, and centralized server breaches. With TinyML, data are processed at the point of generation and only insights (e.g. "atrial fibrillation detected") are transmitted. With respect to HIPAA and GDPR compliance, the U.S. HIPAA imposes strict regulations on health information handling, de-identification, breach reporting, and audit trails, while the EU GDPR enforces data minimization principles; TinyML naturally supports both frameworks by limiting data transmissions, enabling user-monitored on-device inference, and simplifying data erasure. Finally, concerning on-device encryption and secure storage, where healthcare applications require data persistence, lightweight cryptography such as AES-128 or ChaCha20 ensures that stored data is not compromised even under physical device attack.

10.1.3 TinyML Applications and Uses in the Medical Cases

TinyML is now a groundbreaking technology in healthcare because it can be used in a variety of applications and use cases to enhance the care that patients receive, the accuracy of their diagnosis, and the efficiency of the medical process as described in Figure 10.3. One can detect abnormalities and intervene early through wearable devices in which the TinyML can be used to monitor the bare minimum of vital signs, such as heart rate, blood pressure, and oxygen saturation [4].

The TinyML-powered smartwatches and fitness bands can notify patients and medical practitioners regarding a possible health risk, arrhythmia, or hyperglycemia. RPM allows to closely monitor patients with diabetes or hypertension who are chronically sick, lower the visits to the hospital, and provide more

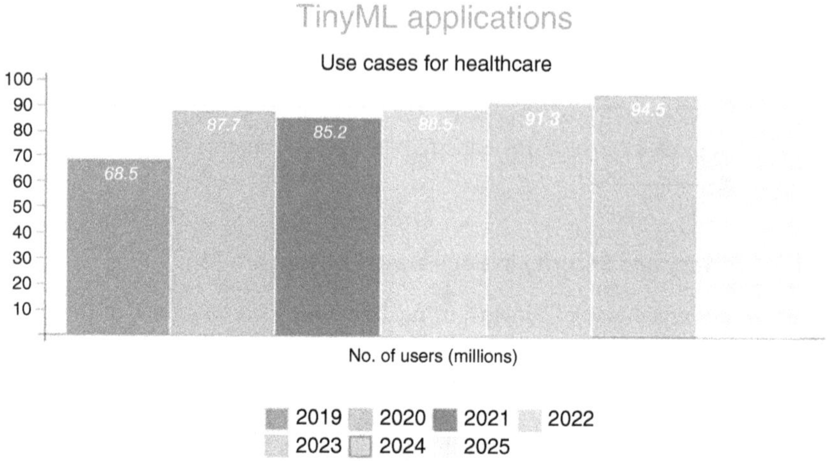

Figure 10.3 TinyML applications and use cases for healthcare.

specific treatments [15]. The TinyML models can be applied to treatment and diagnosis, which means that medical images, sensor data, and patient history are scanned and the doctor is helped to make quicker and more accurate diagnoses, and prescription of specific treatment plans. Drug discovery has also applied TinyML to discover more lead drug candidates in a faster manner by processing molecular information to predict drug efficacy and toxicity [16]. Other novel applications are mental health monitoring and the detection of respiratory symptoms [17]. The following applications indicate how TinyML has changed the landscape of healthcare by pushing ML capabilities to the limit and delivering real-time, patient privacy-sensitive [18], and cost-effective solutions to enhance patient outcomes.

10.2 The Predictive Modeling Flow

The design and implementation of ML models as healthcare TinyML applications have a rigorously structured workflow that converts raw biomedical data into practical clinical imaging while adhering to hard limits in model size, latency, and power use. This healthcare-specific ML pipeline is more interpretable and has clinical accuracy validation and hardware-level optimization as its fundamental principles, unlike generic ML pipelines (Figure 10.4).

10.2.1 Data Collection and Biomedical Signal Acquisition

The first phase is the collection of applicable datasets in clinical domains. In the case of vital sign monitoring, this comprises raw physiological measurements at

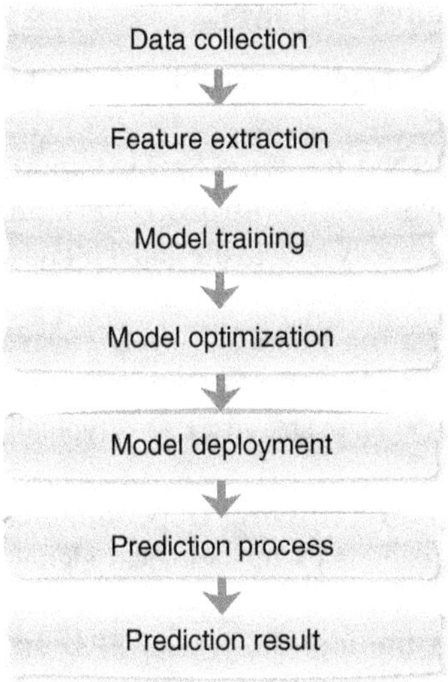

Figure 10.4 The flow of predictive modeling.

certain sampling frequency: ECG at 250–500 Hz, photoplethysmography (PPG) at 100 Hz, accelerometry at 50–100 Hz, and temperature sensors at 1 Hz. In the case of drug discovery applications, data are in the form of molecular descriptors and the computational chemistry features. The dataset used has a strong influence on the ultimate model performance: standardized validation by benchmark datasets (e.g. MIT-BIH Arrhythmia Database with 109,446 samples) can be achieved, whereas proprietary clinical datasets might be more realistic but have privacy and regulatory issues.

10.2.2 Feature Extraction and Signal Processing

Raw signals are not often in a form directly suitable to an input to ML models; a preprocessing process converts data into data formats suitable for interpretation as meaningful. In the case of physiological signals, these are (i) ECG R-R, inter-beat, heart rate variation (HRV) indices; (ii) fast Fourier transform (FFT) coefficients, spectral entropy, ECG, and PPG power spectral density; (iii) statistical characteristics: mean, standard deviation, skewness, and kurtosis of sliding windows; and (iv) QRS, ST-segment elevation, and T-wave amplitude of ECG signal. In drug discovery, molecular data have features such as topological descriptors (molecular weight, lipophilicity, hydrogen bond donors), 3D pharmacophoric properties, and computed quantum mechanical descriptors. The dimension of feature sets should be actively controlled in order to deploy edges [19].

10.2.3 Resource-Optimized Model Architectures for TinyML

Recommended architecture ML models that can be applied in healthcare TinyML fall into multiple architecture families:

1D Convolutional Neural Networks (1D-CNNs) for Time-Series Signals: The 1D-CNN structures have been found to work well with ECG, PPG, and audio-based signals as a result of the secondary property of convolutional filters of automatically detecting local temporal features. ECG classification architectures are Conv1D Layer 1 (32 filters), Conv1D Layer 2 (64 filters), Conv1D Layer 3 (128 filters), a Fully Connected Layer (128 units), and a Softmax Output Layer. It is a trade-off between feature extraction and model size; size in FP32 is typically 300–400 KB.

Recurrent Neural Networks (LSTM/GRU) for Temporal Dependencies: LSTM networks constitute long-term time dependencies in biological signals. The simpler architecture LSTMs are usually reduced to single-layer architecture (64–128 units) with a fully connected layer on the top; the typical FP32 size is 150–250 KB.

Interpretability in Decision Trees and Tree Ensembles: When decision interpretability is a consideration, the decision logic of decision trees and random forests can be easily understood by a clinician. A decision tree learned on 10–20 hand-engineered physiological features has a size of less than 10 KB but is generally of lower quality than deep learning models (usually 85–90 vs. 92–96 CNNs).

10.2.4 Edge Deployment Optimization of Models

Once satisfactory accuracy has been obtained with a validation set (typically 85–95%, depending on task), the model can be tuned to run on edges via a sequence of successive transformations that reduce the size of the model, latency, and power but have no impact on clinical accuracy [19].

Technique 1: Quantization-Aware Training (QAT) and Post-Training Quantization. Quantized weights and activations of a model are weights and activations, quantized and 32-bit floating-point (FP32) weights and activations.

After training, quantization equation is

$$Q(x) = \text{round}(x/S) + Z,$$

where x is the original FP32 activation or weight; S is the scale factor, calculated as $(max - min)/255$; Z is the zero-point offset; and $Q(x)$ is the resulting INT8 integer (range −128 to 127).

INT8 quantization achieves a 4× reduction in model size (FP32 → INT8) with less than 1% accuracy loss on healthcare signals and 2–4× lower latency. Example: 380 KB FP32 ECG model → 47 KB INT8 model, with accuracy declining from 94.8 to 94.2% (0.6% loss – clinically acceptable). INT4 quantization achieves 8× size reduction compared to FP32 but incurs a 2–4% accuracy penalty; it is suited to ultra-low-power devices with an inference power budget below 1 mW.

Technique 2: Pruning. Pruning eliminates near-zero weights, removing unnecessary parameters without retraining from scratch. Structured pruning involves the removal of filters or channels, which helps in regularity and maximizes efficiency. It has shown a 40–70% sparsity rate for dropping weights with less than 1% loss in accuracy at 40% and 2–3% at 70%.

Technique 3: Distillation of Knowledge. The technique uses a large model with high accuracy, called the teacher model, for supervising the training of a student model. For instance, a 1 MB ResNet model is used as the teacher model, and a 50 KB model is used as the student model. The student model is trained to output the same as the teacher model instead of outputting hard labels. The student model is 10–20% the size of the teacher model and has 95% of its accuracy.

10.2.5 Computational Complexity and Hardware Benchmarks

Once the optimization techniques discussed earlier have been employed, it is critical to determine the computational complexity of the optimized model before deploying it to a specific microcontroller. This is done by measuring the floating-point operations (FLOPs) since this will determine how long it will take to perform inference on a given device.

$$\text{Complexity of the Convolutional Layer: FLOPs} = 2 * C_{\text{in}} * C_{\text{out}} * K * L$$

where C_{in} is the number of channels in the input, C_{out} is the number of channels in the output, K is the size of the kernel, and L is the length of the output sequence. For example, a model with a computational complexity of 10M FLOPs will take approximately 50 ms to run on an ARM Cortex-M4 processor running at 168 MHz (~100–500 MFLOP/s sustained performance) and is thus sufficiently fast to be deployed in any continuous health monitoring scenario.

10.2.6 Deployment Frameworks and Embedded Inference

Once optimized, the model is converted to a hardware-compatible binary format and deployed to the target embedded system using one of the following production-grade frameworks:

a) **TensorFlow Lite Micro (.tflite format):** Compact, INT8/INT4 quantized, order of 20 KB runtime.
b) **CMSIS-NN:** ARM-optimized CMSIS-NN ARM-optimized kernels, manually selected operators, 2–3x faster on Cortex-M.
c) **Custom C Implementations:** Special C implementation programs that do not need special resources (e.g. INT8 matrix multiplication) are optimal in resource constraints at both ends.

Table 10.1 Healthcare TinyML model benchmarks: Size, latency, and power across MCU platforms.

Model name	Application	Dataset	Architecture	FP32 (KB)	INT8 (KB)	Accuracy (%)	Latency (ms)	Target MCU
ECG-Net	Arrhythmia Detection	MIT-BIH (109,000 samples)	1D-CNN (3 Conv + 1 FC)	380	47	94.2	12	STM32F4 (Cortex-M4)
BP-Estimator	Blood Pressure Estimation	PPG Dataset (10k samples)	LSTM (1 layer, 64 units)	290	36	89.5	18	STM32F4 (Cortex-M4)
Resp-Classifier	Respiratory Sound Classification	Cough Audio (5k samples)	1D-CNN (2 Conv + 1 FC)	220	28	91.2	8	nRF5340 (Cortex-M33)
Glucose-LSTM	Continuous Glucose Estimation	CGM Dataset (50k samples)	LSTM (1 layer, 128 units) + FC	450	56	88.7	22	STM32F4 (Cortex-M4)
Activity-CNN	Activity Recognition	Accelerometer (50k samples)	1D-CNN (2 Conv + GlobalPool)	180	22	93.8	6	Ambiq Apollo4 (Cortex-M4)

Notes: FP32 refers to full-precision (32-bit floating-point) baseline models. INT8 quantization achieves 4–8x size reduction with <1% accuracy loss. Latency and power measurements are per-inference on specified hardware at nominal supply voltage (3.3 V).

10.2.7 Validation and Clinical Integration

The model deployed at the edge is then assessed using four parameters: inference latency (less than 50 ms for acute monitoring scenarios), average power consumption (less than 10 mW), classification accuracy against ground-truth labels in prospective patient cohorts, and accuracy drift, which is monitored for detecting degradation in model performance due to changes in the underlying data distribution. Quantitative benchmarks for five representative healthcare models are shown in Table 10.1.

10.3 TinyML in Wearable Devices

Wearable technology is now commonplace in contemporary healthcare, providing continuous tracking of vital signs and health parameters. Because it enables real-time data processing and inference without the need for cloud-based resources, TinyML is leading the way in improving the functionality of wearable technology.

Table 10.2 provides a comprehensive summary of recent TinyML research in wearable healthcare device applications, highlighting both the advantages

Table 10.2 Comprehensive summary of recent TinyML studies in wearable healthcare device applications.

Study	Application	Contribution	Limitations
Wearable Drug Delivery Systems [20]	Intelligent bandages and transdermal drug delivery.	Customized drug delivery from real-time health data.	The steep cost of implementation is bounded by device processing.
Mental Health Monitoring Devices [17]	Tracking stress levels and sleep patterns.	Reports mental health data to enable early intervention.	Demands high-quality data; constrained by device memory and processing.
TinyML for Respiratory Symptom Detection [17]	Respiratory symptom detection (e.g. cough, shortness of breath) from sound signals.	Early respiratory disease detection for asthma or COPD.	Humanly reliant on high-quality sound signals; constrained by device memory.
TinyML for Blood Pressure Prediction [21]	Forecasting blood pressure from ECG and PPG signals.	Real-time, noninvasive monitoring of blood pressure.	Quality of sensor data limitation; large training sets required.
Fitbit, Garmin, Apple Watch [5, 6]	Monitoring fitness (sleep, heart rate, and steps).	The user receives immediate feedback and alerts, enabling proactive health management.	Lacks advanced diagnostic capabilities and is limited to basic health information.
Wearable Glucose Monitors [12]	Constant glucose monitoring for diabetes management.	Insulin can be instantly adjusted thanks to real-time blood glucose monitoring.	It requires frequent calibration; battery life and sensor accuracy are its limitations.
ECG Monitors that are Wearable [22]	Detection of arrhythmias, such as atrial fibrillation, can detect cardiac abnormalities early, and serious consequences can be avoided.	High-fidelity ECG monitoring on wearable device.	Restricted to individual cardiac conditions; high-fidelity sensor data is required.
Posture Correctors [23]	Monitoring and feedback in real-time during posture.	Prevents musculoskeletal disorders by encouraging proper posture.	Restricted to posture-related usage; does not involve a general state of health monitoring.

(*continued*)

Table 10.2 (Continued)

Study	Application	Contribution	Limitations
UV Radiation Trackers [20]	Monitoring UV exposure to prevent skin damage.	Reminds users of high hazard UV levels, reducing the threat of skin cancer.	Tracks UV exposure only; no coupling with other health variables.
TinyML-Enabled Smartwatches [24]	Real-time health monitoring (heart rate, blood oxygen, activity).	Local processing prevents latency and keeps it private.	Restricted computational power restricts model size and accuracy.
COVID-19 Monitoring Wearables [25]	Vital sign monitoring (temperature, oxygen saturation) during the pandemic.	Early identification of symptoms of COVID-19 minimizes hospital visits.	Applied to certain symptoms; cannot be applied to other diseases.
Wearable Blood Pressure Monitors [12]	Noninvasive measurement of blood pressure based on PPG and ECG signals.	Real-time monitoring of blood pressure facilitates early treatment for hypertension.	Accuracy is sensor quality-dependent; it needs big datasets to learn from.

Notes: TinyML supports real-time health tracking on wearable devices with lower latency and improved privacy. Challenges are limited processing power and the requirement for good-quality sensors.

and disadvantages of improving real-time health monitoring and individualized treatment.

10.4 TinyML in Remote Patient Monitoring (RPM)

The application of TinyML in medicine is of great importance in the following ways: RPM enables doctors to remotely monitor the condition of their patients. Early diagnosis of diseases and cost savings [26] are achieved by the RPM system's capability for remote monitoring of the condition of patients using TinyML as shown in Table 10.3.

At least, the system with TinyML and RPM will have a positive effect on access to medical services, especially for the rural population. It is not easy to ensure the compliance of the patients, the security of the data, and its compatibility with the rest of the medical systems. Advantages of the TinyML in comparison to RPM:

Table 10.3 Overview of TinyML-based RPM systems.

Study	Limitations
Recommended an RPM system for managing chronic disease based on TinyML [3].	Needs a stable internet connection, and issues with data.
Created a wearable gadget to track vital signs during the pandemic [25].	Tied to certain applications, scalability problem.
Deployed TinyML for remote monitoring of glucose in diabetic patients [12].	Good adherence by the patient; danger of data confidentiality.
Developed a blood pressure monitoring system using TinyML [27].	It is coupled to chains of ECG and PPG.

i) **Chronic Disease Monitoring Protocols:** TinyML can be used in the implementation of rule-based alert thresholds that are specific to individual patient baselines (e.g. "alert if heart rate deviation >20% from personal baseline") instead of general population-based thresholds.
ii) **Resilience to Connectivity Gaps:** The devices will be offline and decide locally as well as uploaded when connected with internet; therefore, none of the bits of information will be lost when the devices work in a rural or mobile state.
iii) **Asynchronous Clinical Review:** Healthcare providers review TinyML summaries rather than streaming raw data, reducing clinician cognitive load and enabling more thoughtful interventions.
iv) **Medication Adherence Support:** Local inference on wearable devices can detect medication-taking behavior from accelerometer patterns and trigger reminders if adherence drops.

10.5 TinyML in Diagnosis and Treatment

The use of TinyML may threaten the diagnosis and treatment of a health care because it will encourage the real-time processing of medical information on the machine. The most important research findings of TinyML applications in healthcare, as outlined in Table 10.4, are the possibility that the TinyML will transform the whole field of RPM, wearable devices and customized treatment, deficit of processing resources, and patient data privacy.

To prove that TinyML can assist in enhancing the quality of the provided diagnoses and make the treatment process more efficient, Figure 10.5 illustrates a simplified flow of the adjustment of the latest technology into the medical sphere.

Table 10.4 Summary of research on TinyML applications in healthcare.

Study	Limitations
Developed a TinyML model for detecting respiratory symptoms from audio data [17].	Needs high-quality audio recordings; constrained by device memory.
Developed a wrist device to track the vital signs of COVID-19 patients [25].	Limited to certain symptoms; not generalizable.
Created a TinyML model for blood pressure prediction based on ECG and PPG signals [12].	Restricted by sensor data quality; needs large amounts of training data.
Combined TinyML with TensorFlow Lite for personalized home healthcare [28].	High implementation cost; constrained by device processing power.

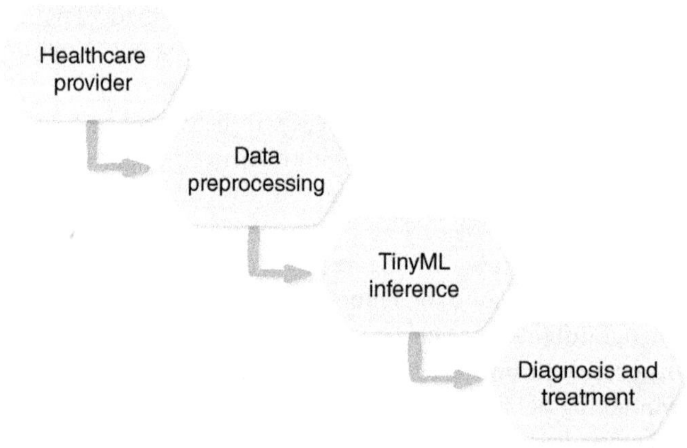

Figure 10.5 Diagnosis and treatment by healthcare providers.

Healthcare professionals capture raw information and then analyze it with the help of physiological indicators, sensor measurements, or medical images of a patient. The data is then preprocessed to obtain meaningful features, which are translated into the TinyML model running on a resource-constrained device such as a microcontroller.

According to the model output, the healthcare practitioner is able to receive action-oriented information, enabling diagnosis and the creation of a unique treatment plan as visualize in Figure 10.5. With the introduction of TinyML into clinical workflow, healthcare physicians can improve treatment outcomes, reduce wait time, improve information privacy, and make well-informed decisions at the point of care.

Table 10.5 TinyML applications in drug discovery.

Study	Limitations
Advocated for a TinyML platform to forecast drug effectiveness and toxicity [16].	It is dependent on huge and diverse datasets and restricted by model sophistication.
Allowed high-speed screening of compound libraries with TinyML algorithms [11].	Restricted by the reliability of molecular descriptors; computationally expensive.
Utilized TinyML to process patient data for personalized drug therapies [15].	Needs large patient data, and privacy issues.
Discovered new drug therapeutic uses for known drugs with TinyML [18].	Limited by the availability of drug interaction data.

Notes: TinyML speeds up drug discovery by enabling real-time molecular data analysis. Obstacles include data scarcity, model complexity, and legal requirements.

Critical Challenge: A critical challenge is ensuring model robustness across diverse patient phenotypes: models trained on predominantly elderly, male populations may perform poorly for pediatric, female, or non-Western patients, potentially introducing life-threatening diagnostic errors.

10.6 Drug Discovery with TinyML

TinyML can be used in the revolutionization of the process of discovering new drugs. The process of discovering new drugs can be accelerated using TinyML. The application of TinyML in the process of discovering new drugs is depicted in Figure 10.4. The application of TinyML in the process of discovering new drugs is associated with data dependencies, computational costs, and privacy concerns, as highlighted in Table 10.5.

10.6.1 TinyML in Biomedical Research Applications

While the preceding sections emphasized clinical applications (wearables, RPM, diagnosis, drug discovery), a complementary domain for TinyML is biomedical research – laboratory, implantable, and point-of-care systems that enable scientific discovery and advanceds diagnostics beyond conventional bedside monitoring.

i) **Implantable Devices and Closed-Loop Neuromodulation:** Implantable medical devices (pacemakers, insulin pumps, neurostimulators) already contain microcontrollers; augmenting them with on-device ML enables truly autonomous, adaptive therapy. Neural recording implants capture brain signals at sampling rates of 10–30 kHz, generating data volumes exceeding 1 GB/hour. Real-time feature extraction on the implant itself is essential for closed-loop neuromodulation systems.

ii) **Clinical Example: Seizure Detection and Closed-Loop Suppression:** A patient with drug-resistant epilepsy receives an implanted neural recording array in motor cortex plus a deep brain stimulation electrode in subthalamic nucleus. The implant identifies the seizure and sends stimulation pulses killing the seizure before it turns behavioral. It is all accomplished in the implant and must be inferred in less than 100 ms with less than 1 mW of power. A tiny neural classifier of 50 KB can be used to support this with 10,000 episodes of nonseizure signals/seizure signals training [29].

iii) **Biomedical Feature Extraction and Biosignal Processing:** While ECG and PPG signals are the most common signals processed using TinyML, other biomedical signals such as electroencephalography (EEG) for the detection and classification of seizures and sleep stages, electromyography (EMG) for prosthetic limb control, and inertial measurement unit (IMU) signals for gesture recognition and fall detection in elderly patients also benefit from the capabilities offered by TinyML. For the abovementioned signals, the engineering challenge in processing the signals using ML models lies in the fact that the processing time for the signals has to be within 10 ms.

10.6.2 Lab-on-Chip and Portable Diagnostics

The next-generation microfluidic devices will offer a system where the samples, chemistry, and electrochemical sensors will be integrated on a single chip. This will allow the devices to offer a system where the samples will be tested without the need for a laboratory. A clinically relevant application will be the detection of counterfeit drugs. This will be a crucial application in many settings where the use of counterfeit pharmaceuticals has been a common cause of preventable harm. The spectral signature will be obtained using a handheld Raman spectrometer. A TinyML model will be embedded on a microcontroller within the handheld device. This will allow the model to classify the samples as authentic or counterfeit in real time. Size of the model: approximately 150 KB (INT8 quantized); latency of the model: approximately 50 ms.

10.6.3 Continuous Blood Glucose Monitors and Glucose Sensors

Continuous glucose monitoring systems are electronic devices that can measure interstitial glucose levels at a five minute time interval. The data obtained from the system can be in the form of time-series data, which cannot be easily processed without the use of signal processing techniques. A 64-unit LSTM, which is trained on 2–4 weeks of patient-specific CGM data deployed on a smartphone or a smartwatch, is able to predict glucose 15–30 minutes ahead, sending a warning signal should an individual be on the verge of either hypoglycemia or hyperglycemia [12].

10.6.4 Streamlined Process of Utilizing TinyML in Healthcare

To demonstrate the fact that TinyML may improve accuracy in diagnosing and improving treatment efficacy, a worked example of the implementation of an ECG arrhythmia classifier on an ARM Cortex-M4 platform using the MIT-BIH Arrhythmia Database (109,446 samples, five classes) is given in this section in its entirety.

Model Architecture: 1D-CNN with three convolutional layers (32, 64, 128 filters), one fully connected layer (128 units), and Softmax output. FP32 model size: 380 KB.

Quantization Results: INT8 Results: INT8 quantization produced the optimum size reduction of 8.1x (380–47 KB) and did not lose the accuracy by more than 0.6% (94.8–94.2%).

Deployment Metrics: Inference latency: 12 ms on STM32F4 (Cortex-M4); average power consumption per inference: 3.8 mW.
This is a case of clinical-level feasibility.

TensorFlow Lite Micro provides standardization with broad community support. CMSIS-NN delivers performance improvement on ARM Cortex-M processors (2–3× gain over unoptimized implementations). Edge Impulse provides end-to-end automation for model training, optimization, and deployment. Healthcare designers must select frameworks based upon the accuracy requirements of the clinical algorithm, the ability to support regulatory compliance documentation, the complexity of the deployment pipeline, and the availability of postdeployment maintenance support.

10.7 TinyML Issues, Difficulties, and Future Prospects

The concept of TinyML is groundbreaking in the context of the application of this technology in biomedical and healthcare contexts; however, it also has some critical problems, and it should be resolved to reach the maximum functionality of the technology.

10.7.1 Regulatory and Clinical Validation Constraints

The most critical distinction between TinyML systems in consumer wellness and a clinical healthcare environment is regulatory and strictness of clinical validation.

The processes of implementing TinyML-based diagnostic or therapeutic solutions in controlled healthcare organizations include maneuvering of stringent regulatory organizations, clinical evidence, and postmarket surveillance limitations.

FDA Regulatory Pathways for AI/ML-Based Medical Devices: In the United States, the FDA can control the TinyML systems that are applied in the treatment, diagnosis, or monitoring of a disease. FDA has three entry points of regulation:

i) **510(k) Pathway (Predicate Device Required):** This will have greater level of similarity with an already existing predicate device in the market. It fits well with miniature hardware having analogs that appear to have lower risks. Normal approval period: 90 days.
ii) **De Novo Pathway (Novel Device):** In a case where the device to run a predicate is new, physically the TinyML implementation is called a de novo (e.g. first-generation implantable neural recording with on-device spike classification). Typical timeline: 120–180 days.
iii) **Premarket Approval (PMA) Pathway:** PMA is required when a TinyML device directly drives a high-risk treatment decision (e.g. insulin pump control based on on-device glucose prediction). This pathway requires the most rigorous clinical evidence, including randomized controlled trial data. Timeline: 6–18 months.
iv) **FDA's Predetermined Change Control Plan (PCCP) for Adaptive AI**: In 2023, the FDA published the PCCP of adaptive AI within the framework of the medical devices (SAMD), according to which the manufacturers are able to mention the kind of the model changes that could be implemented without the necessity to receive a new regulatory permit. This enables the usage of TinyML models in the clinical practice since the population and distribution of physiological data are not the same across patients.
v) **EU Regulatory Framework (CE Marking under MDR 2017/745):** EU healthcare is regulated by MDR 2017/745 [whereby the risk categories are Class I (lowest risk, self-declaration), Class IIa/IIb (notified body review), and Class III (highest risk, implantable or life-sustaining devices, full CE marking].

The clinical validation criteria include prospective clinical trial study design, Institutional Review Board (IRB) approval, required performance metrics (sensitivity, specificity, Positive Predictive Value [PPV], Negative Predictive Value [NPV], F1-score, Receiver Opreating Charactics-Area Under Curve [ROC-AUC]), continuous learning model validation, and postmarket surveillance conditions, including adverse event reporting and real-world evidence collection.

10.7.2 Explainability and Interpretability in TinyML Healthcare Models

The second trade-off of clinical AI is high accuracy (94–98 on biomedical signals) and black box of deep learning models (1D-CNNs, LSTMs). The alternative can be considered to represent the fact that rule-based systems and decision trees can be understood at the cost of 5–10% accuracy. Clinical implementation must be amiable: a cardiologist will not push an arrhythmia detector without knowing how it functions; regulators will compel the algorithm to be disclosed, and patients will want to know how computerized systems are impacting their treatment.

Technique 1: SHAP Approximations: SHAP (SHapley Additive explanation) is a game theoretic characterization of the significance of functions. TreeSHAP can be computed in $O(L^2M)$ time for decision trees, permitting on-device computation in <10 ms. For CNN or LSTM models, a simplified kernel SHAP using only 100 perturbations can reduce computation to ~50 ms, permitting on-device explanation.

Technique 2: Gradient-Weighted Class Activation Maps (Grad-CAM): For 1D signals (ECG, audio), Grad-CAM identifies critical time intervals. Computing gradients requires a backward pass through the model, making Grad-CAM feasible on microcontrollers. A single Grad-CAM visualization for an ECG sample takes ~5–10 ms on Cortex-M4.

Technique 3: Attention Mechanisms in Lightweight Architectures: Attention layers learn to focus on diagnostic time intervals. Attention weights are the explanation – they reveal which parts of the ECG the model relied on. A lightweight attention layer adds ~50 KB to model size and <2 ms latency per inference.

Technique 4: Decision Trees and Rule-Based Models: The simplest approach is to use inherently interpretable models. A hand-engineered, interpretable decision tree with 15–20 features may achieve 88% accuracy, while a 1D-CNN achieves 94%. The 6% accuracy difference must be weighed against the clinical value of transparency.

The FDA is increasingly requiring XAI evidence in medical device submissions, including clear documentation of the model's reasoning, traceability of predictions to input features, and evidence that explanations are clinically meaningful.

10.7.3 Federated Learning for Distributed TinyML Model Development

A fundamental challenge in healthcare ML is that patient data is distributed across thousands of institutional silos – each hospital, clinic, and research center operating independently. No single site holds sufficient data to train a robust model in isolation, yet centralizing patient data in a shared repository conflicts with privacy legislation (HIPAA, GDPR) and patient trust. Federated learning offers an elegant solution: ML models can be trained collaboratively across distributed sites without raw patient data ever leaving the local institution.

Federated Learning Workflow: (i) A central coordinator initializes and distributes the global model to N participating sites. (ii) Each site trains the model locally using its own patient data. (iii) Only model gradients (not raw data) are computed and transmitted to the central server. (iv) The central server aggregates the gradients (typically via federated averaging) and updates the global model. (v) The updated global model is redistributed to all sites. (vi) This cycle repeats until the model converges.

Privacy-Preserving Properties: The information of patients does not leave the local institution. The numerical gradient vectors (usually less than 1 MB) pass over the network only. To provide more privacy, gradients (differential privacy) can be noised out by a site and then transmitted. Federated learning inherently promotes HIPAA/GDPR compliance.

Healthcare federated learning challenges are non-IID (non-independent, identically distributed) data across locations, data annotation quality disparities, concept drift in patient populations over time, and regulatory approval procedures of federated models.

Implementation Example: A federated ECG arrhythmia detector deployed across five hospital networks begins with a centrally distributed 1D-CNN ECG classifier (47 KB, INT8). Following federated training using data from urban cardiology centers, rural hospitals, and pediatric centers, without any site sharing raw patient records, the resulting global model demonstrates robust performance across demographically diverse populations. Federated learning thus enables collaborative, privacy-preserving model development that would be infeasible under traditional centralized training approaches [30]–[33].

10.8 Conclusion

TinyML can revolutionize on-device, real-time medical data processing in the biomedical and healthcare industries. TinyML provides several benefits, including low latency, enhanced privacy, cost savings, spanning wearable technology, RPM, drug discovery, diagnosis, and treatment. To fully harness the potential of TinyML in the healthcare industry, many obstacles must be overcome, such as limited computing resources, interpretation of models, and data security issues.

This chapter demonstrates that sophisticated ML models can be effectively deployed on resource-constrained edge hardware without sacrificing clinical accuracy. INT8 quantization offers 4–8x size reduction with minimal accuracy degradation (<1%), which enables the model to be deployed in the Flash memory of the microcontroller.

Pruning methods can remove 40–70% of the model's weights with minimal clinical performance degradation. The deployment frameworks for TinyML in the health domain have reached production maturity. The key point to note here is that the algorithmic and computational challenges for the application of TinyML in the health domain are no longer the main hurdles. The main challenges in the health domain are regulatory approval, clinical validation, and organizational change management.

Nevertheless, there are still some research gaps in terms of standardized frameworks for healthcare TinyML applications' benchmarking, data used for most studies on TinyML applications being mostly based on elderly, male, and Western populations; insufficient development of clinical validation frameworks for continuously learning TinyML applications; and insufficient development of lightweight methods for model explainability for microcontrollers.

The full potential of TinyML in the healthcare domain will require sustained collaborative research and development efforts by ML researchers, clinical experts, biomedical engineers, regulatory scientists, and healthcare leadership. This chapter aims to provide the technical foundation and a practical pathway to support the collaborative efforts in the field, acknowledging the fact that the full potential of healthcare AI will require technical excellence coupled with clinical excellence and values.

References

1 Warden, P., & Situnayake, D. (2019). *TinyML: Machine Learning with TensorFlow Lite on Arduino and Ultra-Low-Power Microcontrollers*. O'Reilly Media. ISBN: 9781492052043.

2 Oliveira, F., Costa, D. G., Assis, F., & Silva, I. (2024). Internet of intelligent things: A convergence of embedded systems, edge computing, and machine learning. *Internet Things*, 26. 101153.

3 Mulo, J., Liang, H., Qian, M., Biswas, M., Rawal, B., Guo, Y., & et al. (2025). Navigating Challenges and harnessing opportunities: Deep learning applications in internet of medical things. *Fut. Internet*, 17(3), 107.

4 Sabry, F., Eltaras, T., Labda, W., Alzoubi, K., & Malluhi, Q. (2022). Machine learning for healthcare wearable devices: The big picture. *J. Healthcare Eng.*, 2022(1), 4653923.

5 Pingo, Z., & Narayan, B. (2020). "My smartwatch told me to see a sleep doctor": A study of activity tracker use. *Online Inf. Rev.*, 44(2), 503–519. 10.1108/OIR-04-2018-0115.

6 George, A. H., Shahul, A., & George, A. S. (2023). Wearable sensors: A new way to track health and wellness. *Part. Univ. Int. Innov. J.*, 1(4), 15–34.

7 Cheng, Y., Wang, K., Xu, H., Li, T., Jin, Q., & Cui, D. (2021). Recent developments in sensors for wearable device applications. *Anal. Bioanal. Chem.*, 413(24), 6037-6057.

8 Zhang, G., Chen, Y., Zhou, W., Chen, C., & Liu, Y. (2023). Bioenergy-based closed-loop medical systems for the integration of treatment, monitoring, and feedback. *Small Sci.*, 3(10), 2300043.

9 Tan, M., Xu, Y., Gao, Z., Yuan, T., Liu, Q., Yang, R., et al. (2022). Recent advances in intelligent wearable medical devices integrating biosensing and drug delivery. *Adv. Mater.*, 34(27), 2108491. 10.1002/adma.202108491.

10 Vinod, K.S., & Ruby, E.D.K. in press/2024 Security threat mitigation in WBAN using tiny machine learning. A.K. Singh & S. Kumar, *Security, Privacy, and Trust in WBANs and E-Healthcare* 236–253). CRC Press/Taylor & Francis. ISBN: 9781032622361.

11 Schizas, N., Karras, A., Karras, C., & Sioutas, S. (2022). TinyML for ultra-low power AI and large scale IoT deployments: A systematic review. *Fut. Internet*, 14(12), 363.

12 Zeynali, M., Alipour, K., Tarvirdizadeh, B., & Ghamari, M. (2025). Non-invasive blood glucose monitoring using PPG signals with various deep learning models and implementation using TinyML. *Sci. Rep.*, 15(1), 581.

13 Ravi, D., Wong, C., Deligianni, F., Berthelot, M., Andreu-Perez, J., Lo, B., & et al. (2017). Deep learning for health informatics. *IEEE J. Biomed. Health Inform.*, 21(1), 4–21. 10.1109/JBHI.2016.2636665.

14 Sanchez-Iborra, R., & Skarmeta, A. F. (2020). TinyML-enabled frugal smart objects: Challenges and opportunities. *IEEE Circuits Syst. Magaz.*, 20(3), 4-18.

15 K., Kaushik, S., Dahiya, S., Aggarwal, and A. D., Dwivedi, "Revolutionizing Healthcare Through Artificial Intelligence and Internet of Things Applications," IGI global, 2023.

16 Chandak, T., Jayashree, J., & Vijayashree, J. (2024). Trends and advancements of AI and XAI in drug discovery. *Explainable AI (XAI) for Sustainable Development: Trends and Applications*, 233. Chapman and Hall/CRC.

17 Srivastava, P., Shah, N., & Jaiswal, K. (2024). Microcontroller-based EdgeML: Health monitoring for stress and sleep via HRV. *Eng. Proc.*, 78(1), 3. 10.3390/engproc2024078003.

18 Abadade, Y., Temouden, A., Bamoumen, H., Benamar, N., Chtouki, Y., & Hafid, A. S. (2023). A comprehensive survey on TinyML. *IEEE Access*, 11, 96892-96922.

19 Shabir, M. Y., Torta, G., & Damiani, F. (2024, July). Edge AI on constrained IoT devices: Quantization strategies for model optimization. *Intelligent Systems Conference* 556-574). Cham: Springer Nature Switzerland.

20 Henning, A., J. Downs, N., & Vanos, J. K. (2022). Wearable ultraviolet radiation sensors for research and personal use. *Int. J. Biometeorol.*, 66(3), 627-640.

21 B., Sun, S., Bayes, A. M., Abotaleb, and M., Hassan, "The case for TinyML in healthcare: CNNs for real-time on-edge blood pressure estimation," in *Proc. 38th ACM/SIGAPP Symp. Appl. Comput.*, 2023, Mar., pp. 629-638, IEEE.

22 Prieto-Avalos, G., Cruz-Ramos, N. A., Alor-Hernandez, G., Sánchez-Cervantes, J. L., Rodriguez-Mazahua, L., & Guarneros-Nolasco, L. R. (2022). Wearable devices for physical monitoring of heart: A review. *Biosensors*, 12(5), 292.

23 Jayasinghe, U., Janko, B., Hwang, F., & Harwin, W.S. (2023). Classification of static postures with wearable sensors mounted on loose clothing. *Sci. Rep.*, 13(1), 131. 10.1038/s41598-022-27079-w.

24 Karras, A., Giannaros, A., Karras, C., Theodorakopoulos, L., Mammassis, C. S., Krimpas, G. A., & et al. (2024). TinyML algorithms for Big Data Management in large-scale IoT systems. *Fut. Internet*, 16(2), 42.

25 O., Elallam, O., Jami, and M., Zaki, "Tiny-ML and IoT-based early covid-19 detection wearable system," in *Int. Conf. Smart Appl. Data Anal.*, 2024, Apr., pp. 268–280, Cham, Springer Nature Switzerland.

26 Safaei Yaraziz, M., Sohrabi Safa, N., & Azad, M. A. (2024). Edge computing in IoT for smart healthcare. *J. Ambient Intellig. Smart Environ.*10.3233/AIS-230009.

27 P., Anbukarasu, S., Nanisetty, G., Tata, and N., Ray, "Tiny-HR: Towards an interpretable machine learning pipeline for heart rate estimation on edge devices," 2022, *arXiv preprint arXiv:2208.07981*.

28 Kulkarni, V., & Jujare, V. (2024). TinyML using neural networks for resource-constrained devices. *TinyML for Edge Intelligence in IoT and LPWAN Networks* 87-101). Academic Press.

29 Oh, S., Jekal, J., Liu, J., Kim, J., Park, J. U., Lee, T., & et al. (2024). Bioelectronic implantable devices for physiological signal recording and closed-loop neuromodulation. *Adv. Funct. Mater.*, 34(41), 2403562.

30 Singh, A., & Chatterjee, K. (2023). Edge computing based secure health monitoring framework for electronic healthcare system. *Clust. Comput.*, 26, 1205–1220. 10.1007/s10586-022-03717-w.

31 E., Boumpa, V., Tsoukas, A., Gkogkidis, G., Spathoulas, and A., Kakarountas, "Security and privacy concerns for healthcare wearable devices and emerging alternative approaches," in *Int. Conf. Wireless Mobile Commun. Healthcare*, 2021, Nov., pp. 19–38, Cham, Springer International Publishing.

32 Choudhury, A. D., Banerjee, R., Kimbahune, S., & Pal, A. (2022). *New Frontiers of Cardiovascular Screening Using Unobtrusive Sensors, AI, and IoT*. Academic Press. Cambridge, MA.

33 Ponnada, S., Tak, T. K., Kshirsagar, P. R., Rao, P. S., & Dayal, A. (2024). Expanding applications of TinyML in versatile assistive devices: *From Navigation Assistance to Health Monitoring System Using Optimised NASNET-XGBOOST Transfer Learning*. IEEE Access.

11

Advancing Sustainable Intelligence Through a Unified Framework at the Edge by Utilizing TinyML for Environmental Monitoring

Krithikha Sanju Saravanan

Department of Information Technology, Sri Sivasubramaniya Nadar College of Engineering, Chennai, India

11.1 Introduction

Human-induced environmental consequences have become exponentially more severe and extensive. With urbanization and industrialization being expanded worldwide at an unprecedented rate, ecosystems are sustaining devastation. Global environmental issues such as deforestation, air/water pollution, and climate changes are being witnessed at new, expanding capacities. Deforestation destroys habitats, drives species extinct, and severely impacts the atmosphere by removing trees that remove carbon dioxide (a greenhouse gas) from the atmosphere. At the same time, industrial emissions and human waste continue to contaminate the air and water, harming the atmosphere and subsequently humans. This two-pronged environmental crisis is manifesting itself in the form of global temperature rises, increasing occurrences of extreme weather, and the collapse of biodiversity [1].

Keeping track of these environmental changes is essential for informed decision-making, policy development, and initiating action at a timely pace. Unfortunately, conventional approaches to environmental monitoring remain centralized and utilize models in which raw, unprocessed sensor data is sent to servers located in the cloud for processing and analysis. Although this model will work adequately well in urban and well-connected areas and for certain types of collected environmental data, it has several disadvantages of applying this model to remote, rural, or under-resourced areas. These disadvantages include high operational costs, a reliance on internet connectivity and latency, a significant amount of energy consumed, and a processing lag. Most often, these limitations are entirely enough to disallow the development and use of real-time, scalable monitoring systems where they are most needed. This is where Tiny Machine Learning (TinyML) makes its entry. TinyML is an emerging and quickly evolving branch of machine learning (ML) that focuses directly on the creation and application of ML models on ultra-low-power microcontrollers and edge devices found in sensors [2, 3]. These devices can be small enough to fit in your palm, operate and consume energy in the milliwatt range, and can run for months or years with a battery or energy-harvesting input. Data can be processed locally on the device, generating real-time outputs while eliminating larger data transfer to the cloud.

TinyML will have significant implications for how to approach environmental monitoring. It enables distributed intelligence at the edge and allows us to develop monitoring systems that are not just inexpensive, environmentally friendly, and useful but also scalable and adaptable to diverse environments [4, 5]. This opportunity means that it can deploy networks of smart sensors in forests, oceans, agriculture, industrial, and urban areas, and these would continuously monitor many parameters such as temperature, humidity, air quality, water quality, or even noise levels. These sensors would run lightweight ML models that would detect anomalies, trends, and do classification on environmental sounds or visuals without hosting in could processing.

One of the most significant advantages of using TinyML for environmental monitoring (and many other applications) is autonomy in resource-constrained environments. Consider a rural village with air quality monitoring devices. But many villages do not have reliable or even nonexistent connectivity. Using a sensible TinyML solution, an air quality monitoring sensor can onboard all the data to determine whether pollutants, such as PM2.5 or volatile organic compounds (VOCs) are present. If the threshold is crossed, the sensor will send the user alerts and record occasional events relative to the sensor data so they can be collected later. Similarly, acoustic sensors that monitor endangered species or illegal logging can relatively easily provide log function using TinyML acoustic recognition or classification models, and this become relevant to the work of rangers in conservation monitoring, if they are sent in real time.

Another major advantage is the decreased energy footprint of these systems. Traditional sensor networks based on constant cloud computation and data transfer typically drain power resources quickly and require battery changes every few weeks or a grid-powered infrastructure with robust power management strategies [6, 7]. TinyML-based systems minimize energy consumption by storing data locally and only transmitting results back to a cloud server when there is actionable and relevant data. This allows turbulent growth potential in the deployment of multifaceted, capable environmental models in remote and off-grid locations, such as deep forests, mountains, and marine contexts. TinyML could also contribute to the build of more resilient monitoring systems. Each node in a TinyML-enabled network can operate independently, so if one node fails or has a short-term network failure, it will not take down the entire network or contribute to data loss in the network. This decentralized system design enables robustness and flexibility, especially in dynamic or unpredictable environments. Further, the growth of open-source tools and accessible community-driven platforms that grow in the TinyML ecosystem allows researchers, students, and citizen scientists the opportunity to contribute to environmental monitoring work.

The application of TinyML in terms of environmental monitoring aligns with but also embraces a wider and slightly different global narrative around sustainable development and smart technology. It certainly fits into project efforts aligned with United Nations Sustainable Development Goals (SDGs), especially if they were to address climate action, clean water, and life on land [8]. Governments, not for profits and industry, are increasingly realizing the potentials of edge AI and TinyML, to advance their efforts to develop smarter cities and greener ecosystems. The rapid advancement of platforms (e.g. Arduino Nano 33 BLE Sense, Raspberry Pi Pico, and Google Coral) and software stack (e.g. TensorFlow Lite for Microcontrollers) have made deploying smart monitoring systems practically viable as never before.

TinyML will not be without challenges and include tackling the additional challenge of being able to create accurate, efficient ML models that will run on microcontrollers, as they have very small memory and processing power. Not to mention deploying a system accurately under real-world conditions (sensor noise, environmental light or weather changes, broken bits, etc.). In addition, integration to larger data infrastructure for long-term storage and analysis and decision support is an ongoing work stream. However, there are still ongoing practical improvements in model compression, hardware acceleration, and federated learning that are collectively addressing many of the current limitations. This chapter is created in response to the theme of sustainable intelligence. An edge-centered artificial intelligence (AI) framework will provide minimal energy consumption, low bandwidth usage, and little to no cloud dependency and enables data to be collected in real time for environmental monitoring. The target audience of this chapter includes researchers in TinyML, edge AI developers, Internet of Things (IoT) systems designers, environmental technologists, and graduate-level students studying sustainable AI systems.

The objective of this chapter is to provide a broad, unified framework for implementing TinyML-based intelligence at edge devices focused on environmental monitoring. The intent is to create an integrated architecture that combines sensing, edge inference, federated learning, and cloud aggregation into a single cohesive system. This chapter also provides a performance evaluation model for energy consumption, latency, and scalability of the system. The main goal is to demonstrate the feasibility of deploying ML models on microcontrollers that have limited resources, while also promoting a sustainable AI paradigm for low-power edge ecosystems.

The work presented in this chapter makes several significant contributions to advancing the field. It develops a comprehensive four-layer Unified TinyML Framework composed of the Sensing, Edge, Federated, and Cloud layers with an explicit architectural perspective. It establishes a unified analytical model to evaluate energy efficiency and latency in a combined manner for tasks performed at the edge. In addition, it proposes a lightweight federated aggregation strategy that is specifically optimized for resource-constrained microcontroller devices. Finally, the chapter develops a deployment-oriented model that allows for evaluating sustainability and establishes a practical end-to-end workflow for developing an environmental monitoring solution based on TinyML technologies.

11.2 TinyML Applications in Environmental Monitoring

The application of TinyML for environmental monitoring is broadly classified into four, as shown in Figure 11.1.

11.2.1 Air Quality Monitoring

Air pollution is one of the most urgent environmental threats that is currently facing, especially in urban and industrialized areas that are often highly populated. Having the ability to monitor air quality and health hazards in real time allows governments or the community to make an informed and proactive response to exposures from pollution sources. TinyML devices range in size but are essential

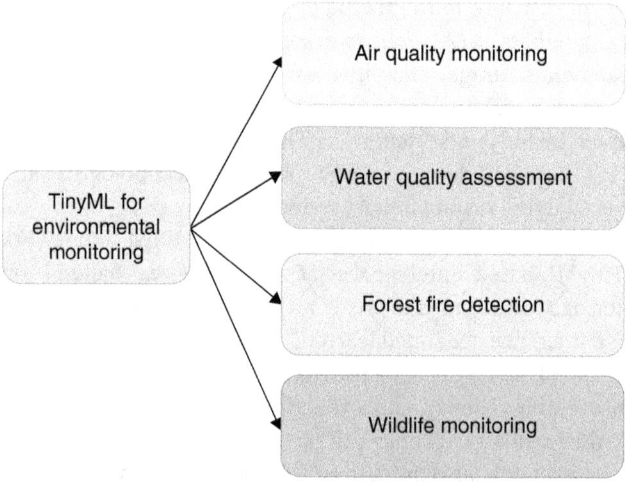

Figure 11.1 Application of TinyML in environmental monitoring.

in this scenario as they provide constant and localized air quality monitoring with little power consumption [9, 10]. Typical configurations include various sensors, including the MQ135 air quality sensor for CO_2 and NOx, the DHT22 temperature and humidity sensor, and the PMS5003 sensor to quantify particulate matter (PM) PM2.5 and PM10.

To allow for operation on limited hardware, model optimization techniques are necessary. For example, the technique of pruning is to reduce redundancy in the form of redundant neurons or connections in the neural network to reduce cost in memory and computation, without significant reduction in inference accuracy. Quantization can compress the model even further. This technique assigns lower precision (K usually 8-bit integers) to 32-bit floating-point weights and activations, typically making the compressed model smaller and lower power. In many practical applications, the data from multiple sensors may be fused into one vector called (Z), and this increased dimensionality can assist the model in the modeling of more complex patterns or anomalies. For example, assuming the fused sensor input vector called Z, the core computation during inference in a quantized neural network is as follows:

$$Y = Fq(Wq \times Zq + Bq) \tag{11.1}$$

where W_q and B_q are the quantized weights and biases, respectively, and F_q is the activation function, which may include ReLU or sigmoid and is applied in quantized space. The model can function in real time to provide classification or regression of pollutant levels subject to limits on memory usage and power consumption.

11.2.2 Water Quality Assessment

Access to clean and safe water is fundamental to health and ecosystem resilience. Continuous surface or groundwater monitoring across rivers, lakes, and reservoirs is necessary for detecting contaminations early and controlling runoff with pollutants. TinyML-based systems with analog pH probes, turbidity sensors, and dissolved oxygen analyzers can continuously and affordably record chemical and physical properties of water [11, 12]. For simple detection, typically use basic threshold logic and, for instance, if a pH or turbidity safety limit exceeds, then it is possible to identify a potential contamination incident. For more sophisticated detection, we can use knowledge distillation where a large, complex model trained on a complex dataset can teach a smaller model to approximate its behaviors. This creates compact and powerful models that can run on microcontrollers. Another innovation here is utilizing federated learning so each edge device can train models locally using their idiosyncratic data as training data, while still contributing to a global model, without sharing the raw data. This produces models that are more generalizable overall and more adaptable to various water bodies. The most common algorithm is Federated Averaging (FedAvg), which is defined as follows mathematically:

$$W(t+1) = \sum_{j=1}^{M} \left(\frac{Nj}{N}\right) \times Wj(t) \tag{11.2}$$

where $W(t+1)$ represents the new global weights after aggregation, M is the number of devices, Nj is the number of data points on client j, and $N = \sum_{j=1}^{M} Nj$. Local model weights $Wj(t)$ are generalized and trained independently, ensuring privacy, cybersecurity, and robustness.

11.2.3 Forest Fire Detection

Whether it is preventing increased damage to ecosystems from large-scale forest fires, or the loss of human life, early detection of forest fires is crucial. Remote areas are typically disconnected from the power grid and do not have a wired connection, making TinyML forest fire detection particularly useful. The system utilizes sensors including CO detectors, flame detectors, and other sensors like a temperature/humidity module to detect indicators of early fire behavior, which is an indication of fire signature [13, 14]. Temporal patterns such as increasing CO levels or an increase in temperature could be modeled using a lightweight recurrent neural network (RNN). Tiny RNNs are the optimized class of RNNs for low-power devices and can model the time-dependent environmental signals. The RNN updates the basic cell as follows:

$$Ht = \sigma(Wh \times H(t-1) + Wx \times Xt + b) \tag{11.3}$$

where Ht is the hidden state at time t, Xt is the input vector (e.g. sensor readings), σ is a nonlinear activation like $tanh$, and Wh and Wx are the weight matrices. These models are frequently trained on historical fire datasets and then distilled into explicit smaller versions when then placed in operation. Simpler but equally effective anomaly detection algorithms are also employed using moving averages. The anomaly score At is calculated as follows:

$$At = |Xt - \mu t| \tag{11.4}$$

where Xt is the current reading and μt is the moving average on previous readings. If At is above a threshold, an alert is raised. This is a useful supplement to the neural inference, providing a low-cost, real-time second layer of protection.

11.2.4 Wildlife Monitoring and Biodiversity Studies

Understanding wildlife behavior and species distribution is critical for conservation and ecological research. TinyML powered devices using passive infrared (PIR) sensors, microphones, and low-power audio classification chips allow for noninvasive, automated tracking of animal presence through motion and sound analysis [15, 16]. For audio-based detection, Tiny convolutional neural networks (Tiny CNNs) are used to classify environmental sounds or animal calls in real time [17]. These CNNs consist of a few layers to extract local patterns from spectrograms generated from audio data. The convolution operation for a single feature map is described by

$$Y(i,j) = \sum_m \sum_n x(i + m, j + n) \times k(m, n) \tag{11.5}$$

where $x(i,j)$ is the input matrix (e.g. spectrogram pixel) and $k(m, n)$ is the convolution kernel, with summation performed over the spatial window. The output $Y(i,j)$ is a feature that characterizes local acoustic patterns associated with the occurrence of some particular animal species or environmental event. To classify a final class, the model can apply a softmax activation function to obtain probabilities over the output classes:

$$P(Y \cdot i) = e^{zi} \Big/ \left(\sum_j e^{zj} \right) \tag{11.6}$$

where zi is the raw output (logit) for class i and the denominator normalizes the outputs into a probability distribution. This formalizes a high degree of confidence for detection of taxa such as birds, frogs, or large mammals. The pruning techniques for model optimization are vital for resource efficiency, while federated learning localizes models for specific habitats capturing regional patterns of biodiversity and making it possible for conservation groups to work collaboratively without needing to centralize sensitive datasets.

11.3 System Design and Methodology for Unified Environmental Monitoring Using TinyML

To unite various environmental monitoring applications into one, cohesive system requires a modular, scalable, and low-power architecture. The proposed system uses TinyML to provide on-device intelligence and real-time decision-making among distributed sensor nodes that are autonomous yet collaborative, to monitor air, water, forest, and biodiversity across a wide range of geographical localities. The architecture that defines the structure of the system has five layers, namely, Sensing Layer, Edge Intelligence Layer, Communication Layer, Aggregation & Storage Layer, and Cloud and Visualization Layer with Deployment Strategy and Power Management as shown in Figure 11.2.

The unified environmental monitoring application has an integrated workflow that accommodates the requirements for intelligent and automated, as well as different ecological and, therefore, system implications. The workflow starts with the Sensing Layer, where different distributed nodes collect specific to domain

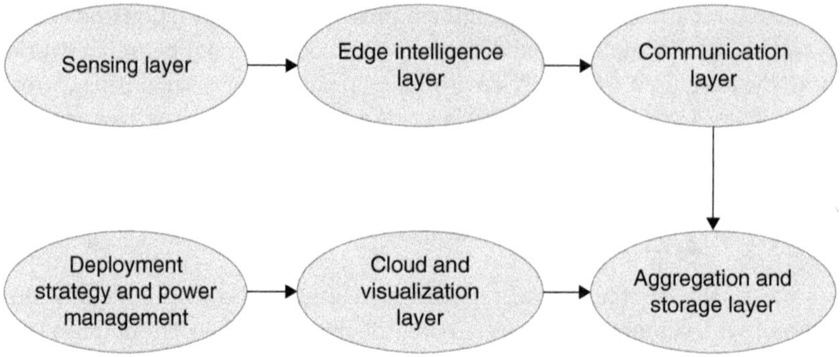

Figure 11.2 Five layers involved in the proposed unified framework.

environmental data such as air pollutants, water quality indicators, fire indicators, and wildlife behaviors through specific sensors integrated with low-power microcontrollers. In the Inference Stage, TinyML models that were optimized for edge solutions perform localized processing and detect anomalies and significant events autonomously, and in real-time, without cloud check. These outputs are then passed to the Communication Layer using a hybrid transmission modality of LoRaWAN (Long Range Wide Area Network), Wi-Fi, cellular, or Bluetooth Mesh that is dependent upon the specific deployment context. The data will then be sent to gateway devices in the Aggregation Layer. Data will be filtered, buffered, and stored locally in low footprint databases, such as SQLite, to allow for regional analysis and limit total network dependence. The Cloud Integration Layer represents a layer where aggregate telemetry data is sent to cloud servers to offer long-term storage, more complex visualizations in the form of dashboards, cross-domain analytics to identify broader environmental patterns, and the prospect for alerts and notifications using SMS, e-mail, and apps. Finally, a Feedback Loop is used, offering continual improvement of the system by retrained or refined models, which were developed using the cloud-stored historical data and federated learning methodologies, are sent back to the edge devices using over-the-air (OTA) updates, further enhancing the system in terms of accuracy, adaptability, and resilience over time [18, 19].

11.3.1 Sensing Layer

The Sensing Layer is a fundamental component of any environmental monitoring system as it provides the means to connect the real side of the environment with the computational intelligences. In a TinyML-based framework, the Sensing Layer is tasked with collecting raw environmental data and ensuring that the data is compatible with low energy, edge-based processing. The Sensing Layer is made up of a network of embedded sensor nodes as collections of low-power microcontrollers and domain-specific sensors. The sensor nodes are deployed in the setting according to the interest of the application (urban, rural, forest, aquatic, conservation zone, etc.) and types of observations (air monitoring, water monitoring, fire monitoring, wildlife monitoring, etc.). Each sensing node is oriented around consideration of three major elements, namely sensor type with its accuracy, microcontroller complexity, and energy efficiency.

11.3.1.1 Air Quality Monitoring Nodes

Air quality monitoring is essential in urban areas, industrial facilities, and impacts of wildfire and specific automobiles. Air monitory sensing devise typically include multiple sensors designed to measure gaseous pollutants and particulate load. MQ135 gas sensor has become a standard for measuring air for gases including, but not limited to, carbon dioxide (CO_2), nitrogen oxides (NOx), ammonia reducers, alcohol, and smoke. The MQ135 gas sensor operates under a chemical sensing mechanism with resistance fluctuations in response to the concentration of gaseous chemicals in the environment. MQ135 is not as precise as commercial equipment; however, due to its relatively low cost, it is a suitable choice for large-scale applications. PMS5003 PM sensor uses laser scattering methods to estimate the quantity of PM1.0, PM2.5, and PM10 particles in the air. This sampling information for respiratory health, pollution trends, and traffic levels are relevant to the highways, factories, and urban areas. Air quality measurements can be affected by temperature and humidity. DHT22 is a digital sensor that provides accurate measures of the ambient temperature and the relative humidity, both of which are provided as auxiliary input to the ML model, which adds context to the pollutant readings. DHT22 sensors typically connect to microcontrollers such as ESP32, which is a dual core computing device with a built-in Wi-Fi/Bluetooth module. ESP32 can run TinyML frameworks, such as TensorFlow Lite for Microcontrollers [20, 21], which means that the devices are capable of measuring real-time values, reflecting temperature and humidity to determine pollution spikes or unusual anomalies, which can be reported through to gateway devices or cloud services.

11.3.1.2 Water Quality Monitoring Nodes

Water quality is one of the most significant parameters for both environmental sustainability and human health perspectives. For monitoring water bodies such as rivers, lakes, and reservoirs, there is a need for sensors that can assess chemical, physical, and biological indicators. The normal voltage for the implementation of a water quality monitoring system consists of the following components: pH sensors measure water's acidity or alkalinity level. Oftentimes, abnormally high or low pH levels may indicate pollution from elements such as industrial waste, agricultural runoff, or acid rain. The cost-effective analog pH sensors measure the pH and are sufficiently accurate for continuous deployment in the field. Turbidity is the muddiness found in water caused by suspended particles. Turbidity sensors are typical photometric sensors in that they acquire photos and normal photodiodes use infrared light and measure clarity of water. An increase in water turbidity may indicate such elements are erosion, effluent discharge, or algal blooms. Dissolved oxygen (DO) meters measure how much oxygen is dissolved in water and is a key metric for assessing the health of aquatic life forms. An observed low Do reading could indicate contamination or biological decay was taking place. With appropriate water-based systems in mind, microcontrollers are widely used, and incremental size, power consumption, and built-in environmental sensors such as Arduino Nano 33 BLE Sense are used. In addition, nodes are usually deployed in waterproof on minimal buoyant floating casings with solar panels to enable long-term deployments in water systems.

11.3.1.3 Forest Fire Detection Nodes

Identifying forest fires early on can significantly shorten response times and prevent destruction to ecosystems. Forest fire monitoring nodes are intended to recognize early indicators such as gas emissions, thermal detections, and the presence of flames. The forest fire monitoring nodes typically consist of the following devices/technology: carbon monoxide (CO) sensors detect the incomplete combustion of fuels. In forest fire scenarios, CO sensors provide early warning alerts on the combustion process which often light the visible flames late in the combustion process. Flame sensors detect infrared or ultraviolet radiation emitted from flames. The flame sensors are directional in nature and essentially attempt to confirm the presence of fire (flames) in the immediate area/region. The risk of forest fires is increased by high temperatures and low humidity. Accordingly, temperature sensors and humidity sensors (e.g. DS18B20 sensor for temperature and DHT22 for humidity) are useful for predictive modeling of fire scenarios. The microcontroller(s) used in forest fire monitoring systems are generally STM32 series MCUs because they offer great computational performance and ultra-low active and sleep modes. Given the outdoor usage of these systems and the potential placement of these nodes in remote forested regions, power consumption becomes a primary consideration in the item design process. Many of the monitoring nodes are battery powered, in combination with solar energy harvesting modules, often in a sleep-activated state.

11.3.1.4 Wildlife Monitoring Nodes

Wildlife monitoring will usually use noninvasive, passive sensing techniques wherever possible to avoid disturbing the animal behaviors. PIR sensors measure motion by detecting changes in infrared radiation emitted from animals or humans. This is a great way to monitor mammals or birds near trail cameras, nests, or dens. Microphones and acoustic sensors capture real-world sounds. Models based on TinyML have been developed to classify the calls of the species and detect unusual activity in the acoustic environment such as poaching. These nodes are typically housed in environmental enclosures that are weatherproof and allow for camouflaging. They typically use an ESP32 or Nordic nRF52 microcontroller and have low-energy wireless communication with real-time capabilities. When combined with existing monitoring nodes for air, water, and fire each with domain-specific sensors, this single measurement system can provide continuous real-time data collection, energy efficient, covering a wide variety of ecosystems, and contribute to the comprehensive real-time environmental monitoring of ecosystems.

The information collected from the four paths, including pollutants, water quality conditions, fire risks, and the movement of wildlife, is processed locally at the edge with TinyML frameworks. Localization can detect anomalies, pollution variances, or fire risks, allowing an intelligent response with minimal energy. Sensor nodes independently detect insights and send to any gateway device or cloud platform. Real-time integration of these diverse sensing nodes allows for continuous environmental monitoring, and the integrated application provides the next step, the Intelligence Layer for the edge, which applies ML models that will process the data, provide statistical predictive analysis, can produce actionable insights to inform decisions about when to intervene, and help ensure timely response to environmental issues.

11.3.2 Edge Intelligence Layer

The Edge Intelligence Layer is the brain of a TinyML based environmental monitoring system, where the sensing nodes collect the data and that data is analyzed immediately on the sensor node. In this layer, the TinyML models are deployed directly on microcontrollers in the sensor nodes, which inherently minimizes the need for data to be shared across a network much of the time and enables decisions to be made while on the spot. The aim is to minimize broad, data sharing across networks to save energy and bandwidth, while also providing fast, reliable, and accurate information of the local environmental conditions from sensing nodes. The Edge Intelligence Layer is, therefore, important to converting raw environmental data into intelligence that allows timely actions to be launched. When considering an integrated environmental monitoring system, the Edge Intelligence Layer thus contains a suite of innovative methods to take into account performance optimization, limiting resource use as often as is reasonable, and rapidly responding to the many dynamic changes in environmental data. In this layer, the advanced methods include pruning, quantization, sensor data fusion, temporal modeling, audio classification, and federated learning, each suited to a specific task and challenges of an environmental monitoring context.

11.3.2.1 Pruning and Quantization

ML models deployed on microcontrollers often suffer from a lack of processing resources, such as memory, storage, and compute resources. To overcome these challenges, TinyML models are first optimized using pruning and quantization techniques that reduced model size and memory use but keeps accuracy within an acceptable range. Pruning is a technique that removes unused neurons or weights to reduce network complexity and size (in other words, it makes the network more efficient) without losing significant performance. By removing the redundancies in the model, pruning will reduce the overall memory usage and computational load on the hardware, and now it can run on the microcontroller that has limited resources. Similar to pruning, quantization reduces value ranges on the models numerical values (weights and activations, etc.) from 32-bit floating-point values to lower bit ranges (8-bit integers). Doing so decreases memory usage and computing requirements and, therefore, reduces the time it takes to perform inference while maintaining a relatively fixed accuracy. Together, pruning and quantization allow the running of TinyML models on edge devices and far from cloud environments with minuscule resources.

11.3.2.2 Sensor Fusion for Robust Environmental Pattern Recognition

The main purpose of the Edge Intelligence Layer is to process data using multiple sensors and make some inference from that processing. In a simple environmental monitoring system context, sensor fusion is key to merging various types of sensor data, such as air quality to water quality or fire detection to wildlife data, to understand the environment as a whole. One of the most important benefits of combining data streams from multiple sensor sources is the potential to spot complex patterns and relationships that might not be seen with any one of the sensor measures alone. Being to integrate different data streams enables better environmental pattern recognition, which can lead to being able to predict environmental events, such as spikes in pollution, contamination of water, or early-stage forest fires. This data processing can be done on the edge, so sensor data can be processed as it comes in, and not require remitting or streaming sensor data to centralized cloud servers.

11.3.2.3 Temporal Modeling with Tiny RNNs

Environmental data often contains seasons of data with also time patterns, which can include temperature patterns for air quality or water quality that shift over time, or temperature patterns over time. To capture dynamic temporal changes in the data, an RNN could be employed. RNNs are a unique kind of input–output system, or learning system that is particularly useful in the context of sequences of data because RNNs are able to keep track of previous inputs in the sequence. They could be used to build a model of forest fire risk based purely on sequential data of temperature and humidity. For example, it is well known in the environmental domain that temperature and humidity affect forest fire risk. Tiny RNNs that exist in the context of TinyML are designed for low-power computational devices, and they do a good job of employing computational resources and thus allow for many types of temporal relationships to be modeled in the data [22, 23]. This provides a better chance of making use of models to detect early attempts to describe an event like recognizing a fire has broken out, detecting changes in pollution levels, or changes in migratory movements of wildlife, where early detection can help enable timely response.

11.3.2.4 Audio Classification with Tiny CNNs

Sound is vital in wildlife monitoring, including detecting animal presence, their behaviors, and potential threats, like poaching. Thus, audio signals can be classified from acoustic microphones or sensors using CNN. There are tiny CNN that can classify audio signals, such as bird calls or animal movement or sounds to indicate potential human interaction for deployment on low-power microcontrollers. Tiny CNNs are good at recognizing patterns in spectrograms of audio signals. So, their models could classify the sounds to species, track migration, or even log unusual sounds, suggesting illegal activities. The classification power of tiny CNNs allows us to run them on edge devices that can classify audio in real time and greatly reduce having to send audio back to a server while still recognizing key metrics regarding the state of wildlife and wildlife habitats.

11.3.2.5 Federated Learning for Privacy by Preserving Knowledge Sharing

Federated learning is another important element of the Edge Intelligence Layer. This allows multiple devices or areas to collectively machine learn and data secrecy. In terms of environmental monitoring, it allows every edge device to learn from its own local data and send updates back to the central server without sending all raw data. This means that all environmental observations can be learned and the individual model created can ultimately be updated to the global model using secure communication methods. This is particularly useful in areas where data secrecy and data privacy are impacted, the sensitive areas of conservation or landowners who are kindly sharing their private space. Instead of uploading thousands of data from each sensor to a cloud platform, each device continually trains its own model from its own local observations. The result is continual improvement in the ability to detect while learning much about the data collected in all areas of interest.

11.3.2.6 Energy Efficiency and Data Minimization

The core idea of the Edge Intelligence Layer is based on the premise of performance and data energy consumption. This is especially important for environmental monitoring systems, since they are often deployed in remote locations that may be off-grid, where it is important to reduce both energy consumption and data transmitted. Locally processing data as close to the source on edge devices means that the system does not send vast amounts of raw data directly to a central server or cloud-based application, but rather only sends relevant insights like alerts or summaries, which in turn saves both bandwidth and energy. Additionally, edge devices continuously monitor events or parameter values in conjunction with predefined thresholds, which further minimizes the amount of data transmitted, since important events, such as pollution peaks, fire threats, or rogue animal movements, will be identified and transmitted. Improving the efficiency of existing communication infrastructure allows the monitoring systems to be deployed in demanding and resource-constrained operational environments.

11.3.3 Communication Layer

The Communication Layer is important for efficient and reliable data transmission between distributed nodes used for environmental monitoring. In cases where the nodes are deployed in remote areas that may be under connected, for example, forests, rural locations, conservation areas, or areas of water, a hybrid communication approach is utilized to account for varying power availability and the challenges of intermittent coverage.

11.3.3.1 LoRaWAN for Long-Range, Low-Power Communication

In the deployment of environmental monitoring systems in large, low populated areas like forests and conservation zones, LoRaWAN is a viable communication option. LoRaWAN operates in unlicensed radio bands and also has the advantage of very low-power consumption while obtaining long-range communications, which is ideal for scenarios with sensor nodes dispersed over long and remote distances, absent of reliable, high-bandwidth cell, or Wi-Fi network capability.

LoRaWAN provides for small data packets with transmission ranges in open areas of several kilometers to a few hundred meters in an obstructed environment. It utilizes low data rates and low-power needs for energy-efficient operation, particularly using solar or battery power, and is designed to optimize capture of data when deployed in a location that may not provide good coverage or power. With LoRaWAN gateways deployed across the monitoring area, multiple nodes can transmit data to the gateways, allowing for transmission to central aggregation points or into cloud-based platforms for analysis and for continuous environmental monitoring without frequent high-power transmission. In addition,

LoRaWAN provides low-cost, scalable networks, particularly beneficial in larger-scale deployments, for example, monitoring air quality across large urban or rural areas or environmental factors in conservation areas with sensitive ecosystems.

11.3.3.2 Wi-Fi or Cellular for Semi-Urban or Water Body Regions

In areas with improved connectivity, such as semi-rural areas, as well as on and in the water where access to Wi-Fi or cellular networks is provided, and communication infrastructures need to be deployed, Wi-Fi or cellular communication can be used with much higher data throughput and the ability to transmit data more frequently than low-power technologies, such as LoRaWAN. Unfortunately, at the current time, real-time measurements by water quality sensors, either in urban lakes, rivers, or on coastal water, can only be sent and made available in streaming or live format; this will enable immediate novation and immediacy of use and action. Wi-Fi provides high-bandwidth communications for relatively short distances; therefore, it is ideally suited for local use when power is not an issue. Wi-Fi has fast upload speed; therefore, it will and can facilitate data density/upload frequency as it integrates with infrastructure with ease, such as in projects associated with smart cities where various IoT enabled environmental monitoring systems for air pollution, water quality, and environmental parameters.

Alternatively, cellular communication is a viable option for places with no Wi-Fi available but adequate mobile coverage. Cellular networks can provide larger coverage areas, making them helpful in situations of a more distributed deployment. For example, monitoring remote bodies of water or industrial areas. Both Wi-Fi and cellular will be more energy intensive than LoRaWAN; therefore, they are typically implemented in locations of stable power supplies with higher demands for data transfer.

11.3.3.3 Bluetooth Mesh for Short-Range Node-to-Node Communication

If communications are required in a localized area between nodes and especially if there are multiple sensor devices close together, Bluetooth Mesh can be a good option. Bluetooth Mesh will allow for short-range node-to-node communication and will improve the scalability of the solution by allowing several devices to create a mesh network. Because a node can act as a receiver and a transmitter, several devices can work collaboratively without all devices communicating directly with the base station.

This mesh network offers redundancy, allowing for data transfer even if communication nodes or paths fail. In wildlife monitoring, for example, a series of sensor nodes in the forest can communicate with each other, using Bluetooth Mesh, to pass information about the presence or movement of animals or environmental parameters. When a key event occurs like an unusual sound, or movement, the network can notify other neighboring nodes immediately, allowing them to relay the information to a gateway with reduced sensed time, when the event occurs. Additionally, Bluetooth Mesh networks are energy efficient so they can be used in situations where there is continuous monitoring and limited power capabilities. Furthermore, they provide redundancy or fault tolerance that is essential to knowing that the communication network will perform reliably and consistently as the network could be deployed in perilous or remote conditions.

11.3.3.4 Event Triggered and Periodic Data Transmission

The system is structured to communicate data based on fixed frequency or event-based communications for events such as a spike in pollution, detections of animals, or an anomaly in the environment. Event-triggered communication allows the sensor node to transmit whenever it has novel information to report, such as a sensor reading of significant new environmental conditions, so the frequency of transmissions with the bandwidth can be optimized and the energy consumed in communications can also be minimized.

For example, an air quality monitoring node will send current values only when the new incoming pollution-level transmissions exceed a planned threshold such as high nitrogen oxides or PM levels. A wildlife monitoring node will transmit current data only when animal movement or animal sounds are detected. Using event-driven communications, reduce the frequency of transmissions, and only use fixed-frequency communications when require and, unsurprisingly, reduce the energy required to communicate, and build in underlying considerations that don't require continuous communication. In general, the indicating reliability of the Communication Layer field will ensure that individual systems fulfilling environmental monitoring are advised to communicate in a reliable way that consumes less power, and then doing so as timely as can and through human action, turn to idealization of decision/action based on observed data.

11.3.4 Aggregation and Storage Layer

The Aggregation and Storage Layer serves as the core component of the environmental monitoring system. This is a layer where the data from multiple sensor nodes are aggregated, stored, cached, and aggregated again and then sent to higher layer system processing and decision-making systems. The layer is primarily important as it mitigates network congestion, reduces power consumption by the sensor nodes, and allows for local decision-making.

11.3.4.1 Gateway Devices for Data Collection and Preprocessing

The Aggregation and Storage Layer consists of the gateway devices that serve as collection points for the processed outputs from many different distributed sensor nodes. The gateways can be arranged in a hub and spoke model where several sensor nodes connect to a single gateway that aggregates data from the many nodes within an area. The gateways function as the interface between the sensor network and the aggregated storage or cloud applications. Gateways are the point where data that the sensor nodes have processed using their TinyML models, converges, which, for example, can include aggregation of data from different types of sensors to provide a comprehensive representation of the assessed area including data from air quality, water quality, forest fire detection, and wildlife monitoring. Many gateway devices have the additional feature of buffering incoming data. This is important to temporarily store the data that comes from the sensor nodes at the gateway in case there is no connectivity to the cloud. The gateway can temporarily buffer that data, which means under short scenarios of network outages, data is not lost and can be sent along with the gateway data once the connectivity is restored.

11.3.4.2 Local Data Aggregation and Lightweight Storage

To also increase the efficiency of the system, gateways are equipped with inexpensive data storage solutions, so they have SQLite capability, a lightweight, fast, and no managing server database engine. This means the gateways can maintain local databases for the aggregated data from the sensor nodes, tracking historical measurements of air quality, water quality, or animal activity. The gateway can effectively manage small- to medium-sized databases using SQLite, as opposed to costly large database solutions, especially for resource-limited edge devices. The gateways can not only collect raw data but also aggregate data from multiple sensor nodes, collecting readings from a number of sources into a single, integrated product. In a monitoring system that collects air and water quality, the gateway would aggregate the two sensor readings into a single initial entry, thus retaining data of environmental interest holistically.

11.3.4.3 Cloud Synchronization for Remote Access and Advanced Analytics

Local data aggregation and storage are useful for real-time decision-making; cloud synchronization also has value in that traditional cloud storage can make aggregated data from the environmental sensors accessible and available for advanced analytics and long-term trend analysis. Once connectivity is restored, the impacted gateways store the aggregated data locally and use the cloud to synchronize and upload the data until the aggregated data can be synchronized, ensuring that organizations using the centralized system have the latest environmental data for whatever processing can be recommended. Subsequent to cloud synchronization, the sensor data analyzed at the gateway and cloud can be analyzed together regionally, where data from multiple sensor nodes could be captured, aggregated, and made available at the regional site/location.

For example, a region could then trigger alerts that can be shared with other local authorities such as state officials and local governments, conservation organizations, or those stakeholders for alerts and subsequent potential response and response time to the environmental hazard/threat. Storage at the cloud also protects historical data so it can be analyzed for trends and made available for long-term forecasting.

11.3.4.4 Regional Decision-Making and Alerts

A crucial benefit of edge aggregation is local decision-making that derives from near real-time data from co-located sensors. For example, a forest fire monitoring node detects a temperature spike, the gateway pushes an alert to local stakeholders, forest rangers, or local offices, in their predefined language immediately. This enhances local awareness while decreasing reliance on central cloud systems and minimizes a human's response time, particularly in remote locations where cloud systems may not have consistent connectivity.

Hence, the Aggregation and Storage Layer is vital for buffering, aggregating, and storing data from a multitude of dispersed environmental sensors. It positively contributes to the system by buffering and aggregating local information, which enhances network congestion, and provides localized decision-making, with cloud synchronization capabilities for greater data sharing and historical learning.

11.3.5 Cloud and Visualization Layer

The Cloud and Visualization Layer is the last step in the environmental monitoring system. It provides a layer that holds centralized data analysis, storage for the data over time, and visualization tools. It functions as the centralized layer for managing, interpreting, and visualizing the data collected by the edge devices in each environment, including urban, rural, forest, water, and conservation areas. Cloud servers in this layer host the heavy ML models and datasets, and visualization dashboards that allow stakeholders to monitor, analyze, and act on the data from environmental monitoring nodes. Another part of this layer is the availability of feedback loops to allow model improvements and updates in the cloud to be pushed back to the edge devices, allowing for continual refinements of the systems to enhance its adaptability and efficiency over time.

11.3.5.1 Centralized Data Analysis and Cross-Domain Analytics

One of the main purposes of the Cloud and Visualization Layer is for centralized data analysis of real-time sensor data collected from several sensor nodes conducting monitoring over multiple sites. Accumulate large volumes of data in real-time across numerous domains, from air quality to water assessments, forest fire detection, and wildlife detection and monitoring. Compiling these data sets into cloud infrastructure means that they can then use cross-domain analytics to synthesize the data and, more importantly, identify associations and trends that cannot be determined in data silos.

For example, air quality monitoring nodes detect increased PM, the cloud system can determine the temperature or humidity levels of forest fire detection nodes in the area and, therefore, ascertain whether there might be correlated data to show that poor air quality regions have some level of fire risk. Automatically sharing this type of analytics is an important jump forward, especially when associations can be used for predictive analytics for early warning signals, when making environmental management and disaster prevention analysis-based decisions.

Additionally, ML models that come with cloud services can continue to model changes to the environment using historical and real-time data. These changes may correspond with a change in the environment, new hazards, and, ultimately, anomalies. For instance, if nodes collecting water quality data show a discrepancy in terms of water oxygen levels, ML and other debasement strategies can cross-reference this with other driver's new pollution in the last month, low oxygen levels, and therefore measure and improve response times of active management.

11.3.5.2 Visualization of Environmental Parameters with Heatmaps and Timelines

Visualization is one of the keys to the Cloud and Visualization Layer, as it will provide the user with insights derived from vast amounts of data in an intuitive and actionable manner (e.g. dashboards). Cloud-based dashboards will provide the user with a set of visual representations of the environmental data, such as heatmaps, timelines, or trend charts that represent real time, and historical data to visualize the state of the environment over a multitude of geographical features.

Heatmaps are useful for visualizing spatial data [24, 25]. Examples of this could be modeling pollutant concentration, water turbidity, or water temperature spikes. A heatmap of air pollution modeling can show a city's geographical distribution of air pollution. Such heatmaps could assist authorities in identifying areas with higher pollution than an established threshold for intervention faster. Using a heatmap also visualizes a multitude of water quality parameters to depict those higher than the established thresholds, such as pH levels and turbidity, so areas that their remediation requires immediate attention can also be identified.

Timelines are another visualization method to visualize how environmental indicators change over time [26, 27]. For example, the cloud dashboard could be used to display how air quality measured with PM and gases like CO_2 that changes during the day or week, providing users information and a better knowledge of pollution trends and the effectiveness of policies and interventions. For forest incipient fire detection, timelines can serve to rapidly show temperature excursions and excursions of CO sensor levels, thereby showing evidence of how an incipient fire may be developing over time. Overall, timelines support the users in evaluating long-term trends, seasonal changes, or unusual events in the data. Both approach, heatmaps and timelines are updated dynamically, which supports the decisions that stakeholders need to undertake in a timely manner with updated information. These analysis and decision support visualizations almost always are coupled with geographical mapping systems like GIS, allowing users to drill down to the area or monitoring zones of concern to gather more detail of what may be happening.

11.3.5.3 Alerting and Notifications by Ensuring Timely Responses

Through the Cloud and Visualization Layer, the system allows near real-time alerts and notifications to all stakeholders via SMS, e-mail, or mobile applications when critical environmental events are detected or predicted. As an example, forest rangers receive alerts as soon as they detect early fire conditions such as a rise in CO or temperature. Public health notifications are created when air quality nodes report hazardous concentrations of particulates that may impact vulnerable sections of the population. The notifications are prioritized based on the event selected, which creates a differential in how quickly stakeholders are engaged or alerted. Early notification is intended to help keep minor events (e.g. anomalies) from evolving into major issues (e.g. hazards) whereby initiating early notification can keep, in this case, the population safer and more resilient to environmental stressors and hazards through data informed, timely intervention.

11.3.5.4 OTA Model Updates with Continuous Improvement and Adaptability

One of the biggest benefits of edge-based TinyML systems is local inference, lessening the demand for bandwidth and power. The Cloud and Visualization Layer plays a complementary role to this since it allows for efficient OTA updates, so the devices will never miss new model improvements, nor will users need to be present to manually update the devices. The retrained master models, based on historical data trends and real-time data trends, are then distilled into smaller versions and deployed to the edge. This ensures that the proposed system could be constantly evolving with changing conditions, helping to improve predictive power and ability to detect events. For instance, if a new contaminant or species of wildlife appears in the data, the models can be pushed to the devices so it is ensuring that the system is still accurate, relevant, and effective to monitor an environment over time.

11.3.5.5 Model Retraining and Cloud to Edge Knowledge Sharing

Federated learning is facilitated through the use of cloud-based systems, enabling edge or terminal devices to work together to build improved models without the explicit sharing of their raw data. Each device can perform training on its own set of local data and transmit only the updated model parameters to the cloud. The cloud can receive updates from individual local devices and aggregate those to create a global model that is then sent back to every edge device using OTA updates. This provides the additional layer of data privacy while still allowing the model to become even more localized, with features that are trained to adapt for unique conditions in each of the different regions. Because edges are taking part in and benefiting from a collective knowledge contribution, the models become increasingly localized, dynamic, and adaptive, providing the necessary framework by which data-driven and reliable, responsible, and efficient environmental monitoring can continue to be conducted, as changes in ecological patterns.

11.3.6 Deployment Strategy and Power Management

The proper deployment of a TinyML-based environmental monitoring system is determined primarily by how coverage, duration, and dependability can be maximized, especially in remote areas. Each node uses sources of energy that includes solar panels and energy harvesting modules as well as rechargeable battery sources in areas of sporadic sunlight. Duty cycling minimizes both power use and sensor activations, as sensors would use energy only when triggered by an event (a temperature spike, pollution breach, etc.). The deployment circuits are arranged in environmental clusters of Air, Water, Fire, Wildlife, allowing for any overlaps of technology in some boundary regions. Redundant nodes and failover nodes ensure that critical regions do not lose the operational capacity. This deployment approach priority is to guarantee that the deployment has been thoroughly thought out in terms of environmental sustainability, resilience, and continuous operational ability in uncertain and, at times, unpredictable conditions.

11.4 Performance Measures

The performance metrics presented are derived from a prototype-based analytical evaluation based on ESP32 hardware. Performance evaluation of a single TinyML-based environmental monitoring system comprises model-level metrics and system-level metrics to provide reliable, effective, and resilient behavior in a variety of environments with different conditions of use. At the model level, accuracy, precision, recall, and F1 will measure the model's ability to capture an environmental event such as a sudden increase in concentrations of a pollutant or an opening of wildlife during a forest fire, while minimizing false-positive and false-negative detections. With real-time systems in particular, inference time/latency is also important as it gives the amount of time elapsed between the acquisition of environmental data and an actionable outcome, which, in this case, can be the time taken to provide an alert. A small model size/memory footprint is also important, as edge devices have limited storage/memory and design techniques of reducing the model size include pruning and quantization, which achieve this while creating a model with comparable performance. Energy consumption per inference is particularly important when the node was powered by battery or solar to operate those in remote ways; the objective is to minimize energy consumption for a specific inference task and prolong the existence of those nodes. As well as measuring the performance of a model in ideal situations and conditions, the performance of it can be also evaluated using multiple datasets across studies.

In the system level, the effectiveness of a monitoring system is dependent on data transmission. Efficient data transmissions typically reduce the communication overhead by reducing alert or summary to limit communications, which will limit the network loads and energy consumption. Network latency, node uptime, and availability indicate the stability of the monitoring system and the promptness of data delivery, which matter in time-sensitive applications like forest fire detection. Coverage ratio indicates whether the monitoring system is surveilling the intended environment correctly. Power consumption and energy autonomy identify whether nodes are using energy efficiently. OTA update success rate indicates whether, to what extent, remote model and firmware updates can be relied upon. At the minimal acceptable level, a monitoring system should maintain low false alarm rates to maintain the systems credibility and create unnecessary intervention. Lastly, at the cloud and visualization level, alert delivery times, number of data aggregations that were complete, and reactivity of visualization confirm that the end user has timely and actionable insights. Overall, these indicate that the monitoring system should be efficient, reliable, and adaptable. Table 11.1 shows the mathematical expressions with explanation of the performance metrics for evaluating the proposed unified framework.

11.5 Case Study: Air Quality Monitoring

To show how TinyML can practically be implemented, the air quality monitor use case provides an example of a prototype. The air quality monitor is an embedded system composed of an ESP32 microcontroller that has 520 KB SRAM (static random access memory) and 4 MB of flash memory (which is used to store programs/data), connected to an MQ-135 air quality sensor and powered by a 2,000 mAh lithium-ion battery. The ML model that is implemented takes six input environmental parameters from the MQ-135 air quality sensor and performs calculations using a simple neural network architecture that includes a dense layer with 32 ReLU (rectified linear unit) activated neurons, followed

Table 11.1 Mathematical expressions with explanation of the evaluation metrics.

Metric	Equation	Explanation
Accuracy	Accuracy = (TP + TN)/(TP + TN + FP + FN)	TP = True positives (correct event detections), TN True negatives (correct nonevent detections), FP = False positives (false alerts), FN = False negatives (missed detections). Measures overall correctness in identifying environmental events.
Precision	Precision = TP/(TP + FP)	Proportion of correctly detected positive events (e.g. pollutant spikes) out of all detected positives. High precision minimizes false alerts.
Recall (Sensitivity)	Recall = TP/(TP + FN)	Proportion of true events correctly detected out of all actual events. High recall ensures no critical incidents (like forest fires) are missed.
F1-Score	F1 = 2 × (Precision × Recall)/(Precision + Recall)	Harmonic mean balancing Precision and Recall critical when both false positives and false negatives have serious consequences (e.g. early fire detection).
Inference Time (Te)	Te = toutput – tinput	tinput = time of sensor data capture, toutput = time actionable result is produced. Measures delay for edge devices to process sensor data and generate alerts.
Model Size Constraint (Sm)	Sm ≤ M_available	Sm = deployed model's memory size, M_available = available memory on microcontroller. Ensures models fit within edge device constraints.
Energy per Inference (Ee)	Ee = V × I × Te	V = operating voltage, I = current draw during inference, Te = inference duration. Tracks power consumed per inference essential for battery/solar nodes.
Data Transmission Efficiency (ηt)	ηt = D_processed/D_collected	D_processed = data actually sent (e.g. summaries, anomalies), D_collected = total raw data collected. High efficiency conserves bandwidth and power.

Table 11.1 (Continued)

Metric	Equation	Explanation
Network Latency (Ln)	Ln = t_cloud – t_event	t_event = time event occurs at sensor node, t_cloud = time data or alert reaches the cloud. Low latency is crucial for rapid response (e.g. fire alerts).
Node Uptime (Un)	Un = (T_active/T_total) × 100	T_active = duration node operates without failure, T_total = total monitoring period. High uptime reflects reliable continuous operation in harsh conditions.
Coverage Ratio (Cr)	Cr = (A_monitored/A_target) × 100	A_monitored = area covered by deployed sensors, A_target = total designated monitoring area. Ensures no blind spots in environmental surveillance.
OTA Update Success Rate (So)	So = (N_successful/N_attempted) × 100	N_successful = number of successful OTA model/firmware updates, N_attempted = total updates attempted. Tracks effectiveness of remote model improvements.
False Alarm Rate (Fa)	Fa = FP/(FP + TP)	Proportion of false alerts out of all detected positive events. Critical to avoid unnecessary interventions and maintain system trust.
Alert Delivery Time (At)	At = t_alert – t_event	t_event = time event detected, t_alert = time alert reaches user. Measures responsiveness of the system's notification pipeline.
Data Aggregation Completeness (Da)	Da = (D_received/D_expected) × 100	D_received = data received at cloud/gateway, D_expected = expected data based on node schedules. Ensures no data loss during transmission.
Visualization Responsiveness (Vr)	Vr = tdisplay – talert	talert = time alert generated, tdisplay = time dashboard updates. Measures how quickly visualizations reflect new data for decision-makers.

by a dense layer with 16 ReLU activated neurons and a softmax output layer that classifies the air quality in three classes (Good, Moderate, Poor). This ML model contains 1,248 parameters and has a total model size of 9.8 KB in float32 (32-bit floating-type numbers) format, which is reduced to 2.6 KB in int8 (8-bit integer) format after quantization; the latter size makes it possible to deploy the ML model onto a microcontroller. The system uses approximately 18 KB of RAM during operation (which is used to run the application's beacons) and has an inference time of approximately 22 ms; therefore, the air quality monitor has very low-energy usage per inference. The total energy consumed per inference equals $E = P \times t$, where P is power (in watts = 0.24 W) and t is time in seconds (0.022 s), so the total energy consumed per inference will be approximately 0.00528 J, clearly demonstrating that TinyML is a suitable solution for low-power edge devices.

The efficiency of TinyML as compared to Cloud Processing becomes clear when comparing the two processing methods. For example, with Cloud Processing, the amount of time to process data and send a response back would be approximately 1.2 seconds; however, using TinyML on-device, this time can be reduced to 22 ms. Additionally, in Cloud, an estimated 120 KB of bandwidth is required to send data between the device and the Cloud; however, when processed on-device using TinyML, only 2 KB would be needed. Finally, with regard to power consumption, Cloud would use approximately 0.8 J to process what TinyML would use 0.005 J. This results in a comparable energy efficiency of nearly 150× greater than cloud computing, therefore making TinyML ideal for real-time, low-power (battery-operated) edge applications.

11.6 Conclusion

The integrated TinyML-based environmental monitoring application provides a new and improved approach to ecological management with a sustainability focus. This is done so via sensing, edge intelligence, communication, aggregation, cloud processing, and deployment, thus allowing for real-time monitoring and localized detection and trust-based decision-making. The use of low-power microcontrollers for sensing capabilities, energy harvesting for low-powered, and internet communication through hybrid low-cost channels makes it a strong candidate for environmental monitoring in isolated areas. Likewise, in on-device TinyML inference, the application utilized minimizes detection latency. Furthermore, its modular architecture allows for domain-specific customizations to be found, such as accounting for multisensory ISO 14001 monitoring traceability and displays govern by other regulatory aspects. Will make continued improvements, including, but not limited to, OTA updates by integrating the federated learning process provided integration with on-board sensors, which has not been widely discussed. The model theories embodied within the concept of integrated embedded microcontrollers and the vision of environmental stewardship logistically empower environmental advocates, stakeholders, and societies with knowledge necessary to this process enhance ecosystem protection by having timely knowledge of eco-monitored developments of environmental, social, or economical details. Future work will be to broaden the system's scalability for a wider range of environmental domains and improve the integration of IoT devices to achieve a greater range for monitoring coverage purposes. Furthermore, an exploration of advanced ML methods could be used within a comments domain in order to optimize model data adaptation and to support decision-making in a robust with dynamic environmental monitoring.

References

1 Raihan A, Paul A, Rahman MS, Islam S, Paul P, Karmakar S. Artificial intelligence (AI) for environmental sustainability: A concise review of technology innovations in energy, transportation, biodiversity, and water management. *J. Technol. Innov. Energy* 2024;3(2):64–73.

2 Tsoukas V, Gkogkidis A, Boumpa E, Kakarountas A. A review on the emerging technology of TinyML. *ACM Comput. Surv.* 2024;56(10):1–37.

3 Elhanashi A, Dini P, Saponara S, Zheng Q. Advancements in TinyML: Applications, limitations, and impact on IoT devices. *Electronics* 2024;13(17):3562.

4 S. Kulkarni, S. Bhudhwale, "Real-time environmental monitoring in smart agriculture using TinyML and machine learning," in *2024 Int. Conf. Intell. Syst. Adv. Appl. (ICISAA)*, 2024, pp. 1–6, IEEE.

5 Hayajneh AM, Hafeez M, Zaidi SA, McLernon D. Tinyml empowered transfer learning on the edge. *IEEE Open J. Commun. Soc.* 2024 5;5:1656–72.

6 O Boiko, A Komin, V Shendryk, R Malekian, P Davidsson, "TinyML on mobile devices for hybrid energy management systems," in *2024 IEEE Int. Conf. Internet of Things (iThings) IEEE Green Comput. Commun. (GreenCom) IEEE Cyber, Phys. Soc. Comput. (CPSCom) IEEE Smart Data (SmartData) IEEE Cong. Cybermat.*, 2024, pp. 200–207, IEEE.

7 J.M. Ping, K.J. Nixon, "Simulating Battery-Powered TinyML Systems Optimised using Reinforcement Learning in Image-Based Anomaly Detection," 2024, *arXiv preprint arXiv:2403.05106*.

8 Leonidou LC, Theodosiou M, Nilssen F, Eteokleous P, Voskou A. Evaluating MNEs' role in implementing the UN sustainable development goals: The importance of innovative partnerships. *Int. Bus. Rev.* 2024;33(3):102259.

9 A Datta, A Pal, R Marandi, N Chattaraj, S Nandi, S Saha, "Real-time air quality predictions for smart cities using TinyML," in *Proc. 25th Int. Conf. Distrib. Comput. Netw.*, 2024, pp. 246–247.

10 A Datta, J Chakraborty, P Majhi, A Mondal, S Roy, S Nandi, *et al.*, "PolluSenseCheck: Cost effective TinyML-based air quality monitoring system with in-built sensor fault detection," in *2025 17th Int. Conf. COMmun. Syst. NETw. (COMSNETS)*, 2025, pp. 623–631, IEEE.

11 Pereira EA, da Silva Santos JF, de Andrade Barboza E. An energy efficient TinyML model for a water potability classification problem. *Sustain. Compu. Inf. Syst.* 2024 1;43:101010.

12 Tang X. Design of Li river water quality dynamic monitoring system based on raspberry Pi and TinyML. *J. Comput. Commun.* 2023;11(8):121–33.

13 VK Pandey, S Jain, SK Saritha, "Advanced IoT-based fire and smoke detection system leveraging deep learning and TinyML," in *2023 14th Int. Conf. Comput. Commun. Netw. Technol. (ICCCNT)*, 2023, pp. 1–10. IEEE.

14 Abdusalomov AB, Islam BM, Nasimov R, Mukhiddinov M, Whangbo TK. An improved forest fire detection method based on the detectron2 model and a deep learning approach. *Sensors* 2023;23(3):1512.

15 V Viswanatha, AC Ramachandra, PT Hegde, V Hegde, V Sabhahit, "TinyML-based human and animal movement detection in agriculture fields in India," in *Int. Conf. Emerg. Res. Comput. Inf. Commun. Appl.*, 2023, pp. 49–65, Singapore, Springer Nature Singapore.

16 U Goswami, A Saxena, "Bird Song Classification Using TinyML and Edge Impulse Tools," in *2024 IEEE Silchar Subsect. Conf. (SILCON 2024)*, 2024, pp. 1–9, IEEE.

17 KQ Nguyen, HC Nguyen, TN Le, VB Thai, BP Tran, LT Le, *et al.*, "Tiny-CNN: Structuring convolutional neural networks for accurate classification of rice leaf diseases in resource-constrained environments," in *Proc. 2024 9th Int. Conf. Intellig. Inf. Technol.*, 2024, pp. 171–178.

18 El Jaouhari S, Bouvet E. Secure firmware Over-The-Air updates for IoT: Survey, challenges, and discussions. *Internet Things* 2022 1;18:100508.

19 Syaputra N, Ade AS, Taqwa AT. Designing air quality detection systems with over-the-air firmware update methods for performance enhancement. *Tech-E* 2024;8(1):46–60.

20 Manor E, Greenberg S. Custom hardware inference accelerator for tensorflow lite for microcontrollers. *IEEE Access* 2022 11;10:73484–93.

21 Immonen R, Hämäläinen T. Tiny machine learning for resource-constrained microcontrollers. *J Sens* 2022;2022(1):7437023.

22 Qiang Y, Kumar ST, Brocanelli M, Zhu D, "Tiny RNN model with certified robustness for text classification," in *2022 Int. Joint Conf. Neural Netw. (IJCNN)*, 2022, pp. 1–8, IEEE.

23 Y Chang, R Thompson, C Hixenbaugh, "Tiny long-short term memory model for resource-constrained prediction of battery cycle life," in *Int. Conf. Mach. Learn. Optimiz. Data Sci.* 2024, pp. 131–144, Cham, Springer Nature Switzerland.

24 Gu Z. Complex heatmap visualization. *iMeta* 2022;1(3):e43.

25 Ning W, Wei Y, Gao L, Han C, Gou Y, Fu S, et al.. HemI 2.0: An online service for heatmap illustration. *Nucleic Acids Res.* 2022;50(W1):W405–11.

26 Chen Q, Cao S, Wang J, Cao N. How does automation shape the process of narrative visualization: A survey of tools. *IEEE Trans. Vis. Comput. Graph.* 2023. 30(8):4429–4448

27 Zhu E, Qi Q, Sha M. Identify the effects of urbanization on carbon emissions (EUCE): A global scientometric visualization analysis from 1992 to 2018. *Environ. Sci. Pollut. Res.* 2021;28:31358–69.

12

TinyML for Industrial Automation Predictive Maintenance

Shalini Kumari, Chander Prabha, and Nabanita Roy

Chitkara University Institute of Engineering and Technology, Chitkara University, Punjab, India

12.1 Introduction

Tiny Machine Learning (TinyML) is designed to run machine learning (ML) models on microcontrollers and other edge devices. They are often limited in memory, compute, and power [1]. TinyML addresses these limitations and enables ML algorithms to run on small, low-power devices. But the trick is to offer real-time inference while working under these constraints, making it a great fit for technologies such as industrial automation. These devices, which are often part of a network of Industrial Internet of Things (IIoT) devices, can gather and analyze data and perform tasks locally, without requiring continuous connectivity to a cloud server. This enables quicker reaction times, reduced latency, and improved data privacy, as data does not have to be transferred to a central cloud computing location [2]. The typical TinyML process is illustrated in Figure 12.1. The process starts with data collection from an IoT device, followed by preprocessing to clean and prepare the data. The ML platform is used to train the model, which is then converted to a suitable form for low-power devices [3]. The model is converted and deployed on the IoT device, which performs inference by predicting new data. This process demonstrates how TinyML enables ML on low-resource platforms. TinyML enables ML models to execute on teeny microcontrollers. There are all sorts of devices, from Raspberry Pi to ESP32. These are great devices, but even the smallest Pi draws hundreds of milliwatts, similar to the primary CPU. It takes a battery, not a smartphone, to power one through even a few days, making untethered experiences challenging. Because TinyML consumes less than one milliwatt of power, one must look to embedded devices for our hardware platforms.

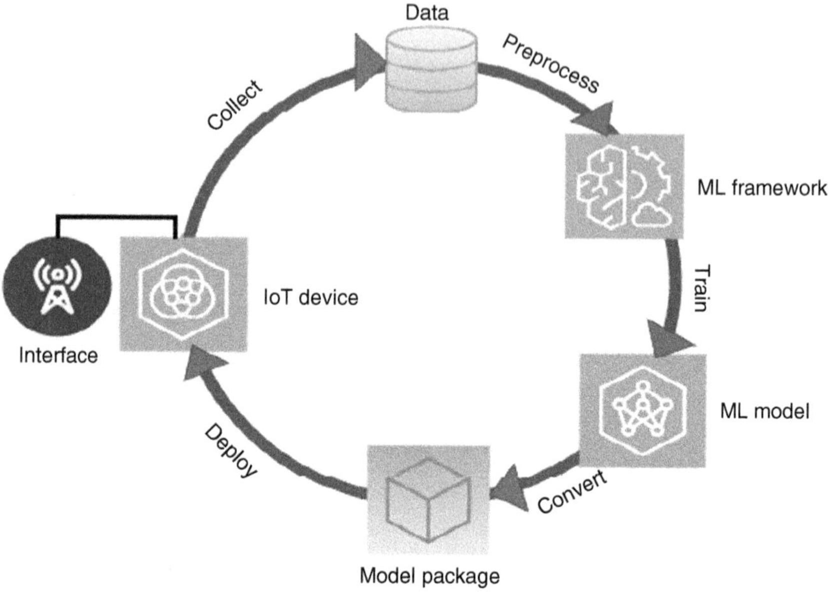

Figure 12.1 A typical workflow for developing a TinyML model.

TinyML uses extremely little power and can execute ML algorithms that will be run on such devices. TinyML is distinguished by:

- Its compact and low-cost devices (microcontrollers)
- Extremely low-power consumption
- Limited memory capacity
- Low lag time (nearly instantaneous) built-in ML algorithms analysis

Figure 12.2 uses data from machinery and other equipment to predict, based on actual usage, when repairs should be performed to prevent system failure [4]. That is not the case with preventive maintenance, which relies on set time intervals, and reactive maintenance, which occurs after a failure. Using appropriate sensors and ML algorithms, maintenance can predict the health of aviation equipment. It also employs big data analytics to predict the optimal time for repair by detecting equipment wear and tear or imminent failure. Less downtime, it is done before the devices have an opportunity to fail; greater operational efficiency, because maintenance is performed only if and when required, as opposed to on an arbitrary basis; and finally, savings – both in terms of repair costs afterward and loss of operating time. In addition, by catching problems before they happen, predictive maintenance helps create a more effective work process over time and improves safety.

The primary objectives of this chapter are as follows: (i) fundamentals of TinyML for industrial predictive maintenance: resource-constrained design and

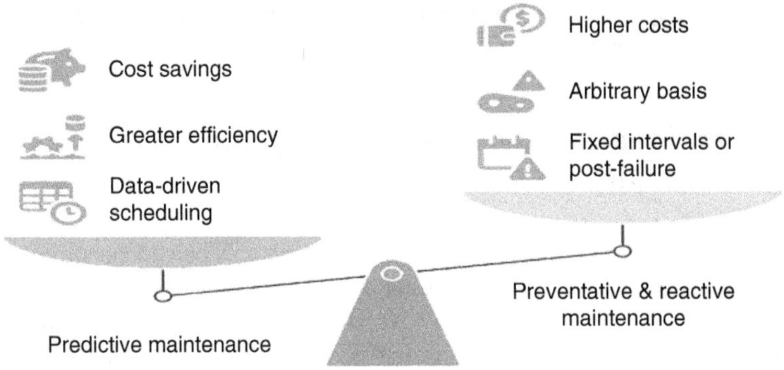

Figure 12.2 Predictive maintenance offers efficiency and cost benefits over traditional methods.

hardware software co-design. (ii) Compare ML and deep learning frameworks suitable for deployment on constrained edge devices, focusing on memory and speed metrics. (iii) Demonstrate various methods that can be used to reduce the model size: quantization, pruning, transfer learning, and knowledge distillation. Demonstrate their effect on inference. Examine three case studies of how practical TinyML applications have benefited from increased detection rate, decreased downtime, and cost savings. The research shows that an uncertainty model is critical for IIoT with edge computing architecture. Critical research questions include domain and concept drift, model management, and federated learning.

12.1.1 Motivation for Using TinyML in Industrial Predictive Maintenance

In industrial predictive maintenance, TinyML brings multiple benefits. The main driver is the potential for real-time monitoring and edge-based anomaly detection.

Using TinyML eliminates this dependency. The industrial sensor streams contain proprietary process parameters, production rates, and equipment configurations [2], which constitute competitive intelligence. By processing data locally, there is no risk of exposure to external [5] networks while also meeting data sovereignty requirements for sectors such as defense manufacturing and critical infrastructure. The transport of unrefined sensor data to the cloud from thousands of IIoT nodes incurs material bandwidth and cloud compute costs due to its scalability. Instead of raw time-series data, TinyML facilitates in-situ character extraction and anomaly scoring, transmitting alert flags or compressed summaries. As a result of these four drivers, along with the rapid evolution of model compression techniques and TinyML-bolstered frameworks like TensorFlow Lite for Microcontrollers and Edge Impulse, TinyML is becoming an increasingly popular and feasible architecture for industrial predictive maintenance deployments.

12.2 ML for Predictive Maintenance: Algorithms and Edge Suitability

The challenge of predictive maintenance is to achieve a balanced set of goals with ML models: predictive accuracy sufficient to detect failures before they happen, computational efficiency consistent with edge hardware constraints, and robustness to the conditions found in industrial environments. This section provides the main ML categories relevant to predictive maintenance based on TinyML and lists the algorithms' suitability for device deployment.

12.2.1 ML for Predictive Maintenance

TinyML can be leveraged for predictive maintenance (Figure 12.3). ML [5] involves training a model to learn patterns and make predictions based on data.

The most widespread form of ML in predictive maintenance is supervised learning: here, trainers label data, which they can then use in predictive maintenance applications such as regression and classification. The technique to apply when the objects to be predicted are continuous (nondiscrete), e.g. the leftover useful life (RUL) of a machine given sensor readings, and classification to assess whether equipment is in good or bad condition. By way of contrast, unsupervised learning is a method in which marked data is input to the machine, and the machine identifies [6] scales in the data distortions. Sorting into similar states with operations such as clustering can help, and finding anomalies is a key component of responding to abnormal behavior and potential failures, especially in edge products with TinyML. Deep learning, as a branch of ML, uses multilayer neural networks, and currently popular types of deep learning models used to analyze data include convolutional neural networks (CNNs) (also called convolutional neural networks) and recurrent neural networks (RNNs) (also called recurrent neural networks). However, due to the resource-constrained

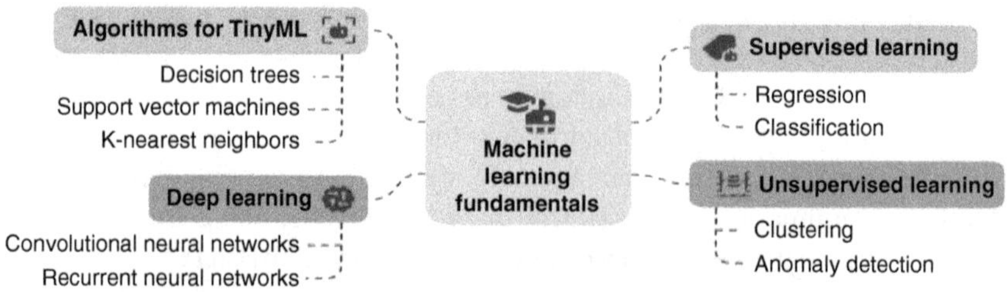

Figure 12.3 Machine learning techniques for predictive maintenance.

nature of deep learning, TinyML [7] apps must use smaller algorithms that can be executed on machines with fewer resources. They additionally deal with decision trees: to classify equipment, although with a smaller data set; support vector machine (SVM): to classify in rules: SVM classification; and K-nearest neighbors (K-NNs): to classify by likeness with earlier dataset points [3]. Usually, these lightweight algorithms work efficiently in predictive maintenance systems based on TinyML because they can be trained near real time, and anomalies can be identified on low-power side machines with small computing processors [8].

For instance, the predictive maintenance, industrial automation of machine sensor data, and vibration and temperature data are continuously recorded by the machine sensor unit. Raw signals are processed and converted into information-rich features, which are then introduced to a small ML model that can be executed on a microcontroller. TinyML guarantees low-energy consumption, low latency, and intelligence deployed on the device, making it well suited for edge devices in industry, as shown in the below formal representation:

Step	Stage	Pseudocode	Description
1	Data Collection	Initialize sensors (vibration, temperature) → Read values continuously → Store data	Collect real-time sensor data from machines
2	Data Preprocessing	Load dataset → Remove noise → Normalize values → Split into train/test	Prepare data for model training
3	Model Training	Initialize weights & bias → Loop over epochs → Compute prediction using sigmoid → Update weights using error	Train lightweight model (Logistic Regression)
4	Model Evaluation	Predict on test data → Apply threshold (0.5) → Compare with actual → Calculate accuracy	Check model performance
5	Model Conversion	Convert model → .tflite format → Apply quantization	Make model suitable for TinyML devices
6	Deployment	Load model into device → Initialize interpreter → Allocate memory	Prepare microcontroller for inference
7	Real-Time Inference	Read sensor → Normalize input → Run model → If output > 0.5 → Fault else Normal	Detect faults in real time
8	Alert System	If fault detected → Trigger LED / buzzer / send signal	Notify system or user
9	Anomaly Detection (Optional)	Compute mean (μ) & std (σ) → Calculate z-score → If z > threshold → anomaly	Lightweight alternative without ML

The system leaves a digital imprint of machine conditions using an efficient algorithm, such as logistic regression or small neural networks, to determine whether machines are in normal or damaging conditions. When the system detects anomalies or signs of failure, it sends warning messages, enabling early action and minimizing downtime.

12.2.2 Comparative Analysis of Algorithms for TinyML Deployment

Table 12.1 compares algorithm decisions for the deployment of predictive maintenance on TinyML. Evaluation was done across five dimensions essential for industrial edge systems. The memory consumption figures are indicative of the memory requirements of commonly trained binary fault classification models.

Table 12.1 Comparative analysis of ML algorithms for TinyML predictive maintenance deployment.

Algorithm	Flash Memory (KB)	Inference Latency (ms)*	Labeled Data Required	Handles Time-Series	Recommended TinyML Use
Decision Tree	2–10	<1	Yes	Limited	Binary fault classification, fast threshold decisions
Support Vector Machine (SVM)	10–50	1–5	Yes	No (feature-based)	Small dataset fault detection with feature engineering
k-Nearest Neighbors (k-NNs)	50–200 (data-dependent)	10–50	Yes	No	Low-frequency inference only; unsuitable for real time
Random Forest	20–100	2–10	Yes	Limited	Multi-class fault classification with moderate resources
CNN (1D, quantized INT8)	50–500	5–30	Yes	Yes (spectral/temporal)	Vibration spectrum analysis, bearing fault detection
LSTM (quantized INT8)	100–800	20–100	Yes	Yes (sequential)	RUL estimation, multivariate time-series anomaly detection
Autoencoder (quantized)	50–400	10–50	No (normal data only)	Yes	Unsupervised anomaly detection when fault labels unavailable

SVMs and decision trees are effective for basic binary classification problems that have very tight resource budgets (<20 KB). The preferred architecture for spectral pattern recognition in vibration-based fault detection is quantized 1D-CNNs, which achieve strong accuracy at 50–200 KB. The LSTM and GRU models, although powerful for RUL estimation, could be memory-intensive and may exceed the memory limits of many microcontrollers. As a result, careful layer reduction and quantization will be required to fit them into microcontroller memory. Generally, k-NN is not suitable for real-time TinyML inference because its memory footprint scales with the data and its search latency is linear.

12.2.3 Edge Computing and IIoT

Edge computing is a fundamental element of TinyML applications for predictive maintenance in current industrial settings [9]. The analysis covered in Figure 12.4 demonstrates how edge computing operates by running device-based operations on devices located at the information source rather than transferring data to cloud servers. The need for speed and low latency makes real-time predictive maintenance applications require this approach.

12.2.3.1 Role of Edge Computing in Industrial Settings

Industries using edge computing rely less on cloud computing, enabling faster, more timely applications. Local operations [10] on edge devices enable issues or anomalies to be detected without relying on a cloud network, eliminating lag. Edge computing is internet-agnostic, reducing data sent to the cloud and resulting in cost and bandwidth savings.

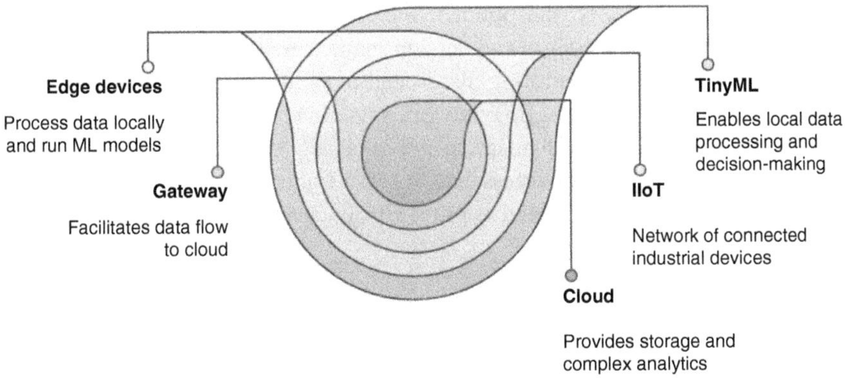

Figure 12.4 Edge computing and IoT architecture.

12.2.3.2 IIoT and Its Connection to TinyML

The IIoT connects TinyML with the technology that links physical devices and sensors to machines by communicating operational data. IIoT devices comprise sensors that track real-time data from motors, pumps, and turbines in industrial plants [11]. TinyML makes IIoT possible by providing on-device analytics for factory devices, enabling prognostics for machines and real-time decision-making without a heavy reliance on the cloud. On-site analytics are built into sensors, controllers, and embedded systems for IIoT devices. Devices can perform tasks like anomaly detection, failure prognostics, and monitoring without relying on the cloud. TinyML is useful for systems that require [12] fast processing in the face of unreliable connections or high latency. TinyML models are used by IIoT devices to do predictive maintenance as they monitor equipment in operation.

12.2.4 Architecture of a Typical IIoT System with Edge Devices

The system uses physical sensors and computing devices, optionally with a cloud, for real-time equipment monitoring [13]. The health status of equipment can be determined by edge devices running TinyML models directly on the device, for minimal latency and data communication costs.

The process begins with installing sensors on equipment to measure operating conditions, such as temperature, vibration, pressure, and other performance metrics related to machine health. The data is then processed on edge devices, which perform in-situ computations using TinyML models to identify anomalies and perform classification and regression. These devices use efficient data processing techniques to quickly analyze sensor data and trigger maintenance actions in real time, despite their limited processing capabilities. The data is then transmitted through a gateway, a device that sits between the edge devices and the cloud, which compresses the data and transmits it to the cloud. While data is processed locally, the optional inclusion of the cloud enables central storage, additional processing, and version management of ML models, thereby enabling a system for monitoring distributed machines. Finally, a management system is used to manage the IIoT network, enabling monitoring of device status, model deployment, and visualization and analysis of data from edge devices, thereby helping industries harness data to better understand processes and make decisions, reduce downtime, and improve efficiency and predictive maintenance.

12.3 TinyML for Sensor Data Processing

TinyML is an ideal solution for analyzing sensor data in industry because real-time, low-power ML operations on edge devices are feasible [14].

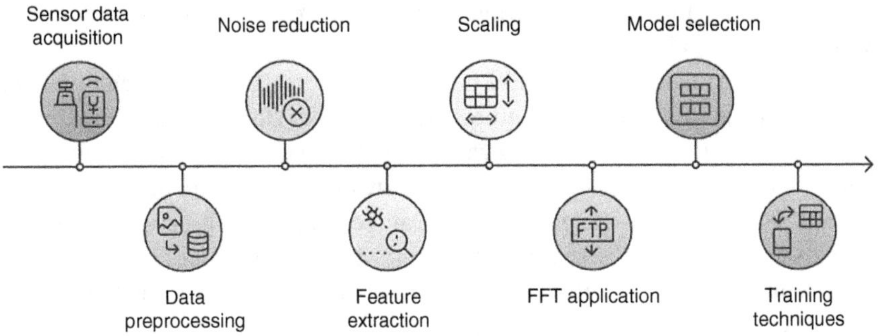

Figure 12.5 TinyML for sensor data processing.

As Figure 12.5 reveals, predictive maintenance requires efficient preprocessing and the deployment of lightweight models. Noise reduction techniques, suitable feature selection methods, and model optimization in a limited hardware platform are the three key impediments to this work.

12.3.1 Sensor Data Acquisition and Preprocessing

Predictive maintenance is based on sensor data acquisition, which industrial facilities rely on to achieve it. The present method of data collection is based on sensors providing essential monitoring data on the variables of health and performance of the machine [15]. Several types of sensors are applied to industrial plants to keep a control on the equipment condition and guarantee its efficiency. Implementation/temperature sensors are the most prevalent and are used to monitor equipment operation and identify issues with excessive heat on components such as bearings and motors. Vibration sensors measure the vibration frequency of machinery; high vibration frequency can signal problems such as misalignment, imbalance, or wear and tear. They are commonly used with high-speed rotating machinery, e.g. motors, pumps, and turbines. The pressure sensors observe the pressure levels in the hydraulic or pneumatic systems and are able to notice a leakage, problems with the valves, or blockages. Besides, current sensors can be used to measure electrical current in machines, allowing identification of issues such as overloading of a motor, short circuit, and other electrical failures. Together, these sensors provide invaluable information for proper maintenance and hassle-free operations.

Importance of Data Preprocessing: Data preprocessing is essential because ML models require data that has been filtered for noise and missing values and properly formatted [16]. Data preparation impacts predictive maintenance performance. There is noise from environmental (and hardware) limits and electrical noise in the sensor data. Common techniques such as low-pass filtering and moving-average filtering are applied to remove data noise and thus avoid incorrect analysis.

Raw sensor data used in predictive maintenance must be transformed to extract meaningful patterns. Statistical features extracted from vibration and temperature signals, such as mean, variance, skewness, and kurtosis, can help detect warning signs of failure. Peak-to-peak measurements are one type of time-domain characteristic that engineers use to detect faults. Data scaling is a preprocessing step that normalizes the sensor value range; therefore, features with large ranges (such as current and pressure) remain comparable to features with smaller ranges (such as vibration).

12.3.2 Techniques for Advanced Preprocessing

Fast Fourier Transform (FFT): An FFT is a mathematical tool that transforms time-domain signals (such as vibration data) into frequency-domain representations. Specific frequencies associated with bearing defects or unbalanced machinery can be identified using this method. Frequency spectrum analysis enables TinyML models to focus on the most significant signal characteristics.

Time-Series Analysis: The analysis of industrial sensor data, which mostly consists of time-series data, must include temporal pattern assessments. Autocorrelation, along with windowing techniques, enables the detection [17] of pattern types, periodic behavior, and abnormal events that remain undetectable in the original data. Departments that monitor industrial [18] equipment need time-series analysis to identify the natural evolution of machine operations driven by regular wear and tear.

Training strategies, along with optimizations, are key to small-capacity edge devices. The models require high accuracy and high speed, as well as low memory footprint, for optimal performance on edge devices [19]. The device's power must match the model's mathematical complexity. ML applications for real-time predictive maintenance can be accelerated using TPU or FPGA chips, along with enhanced algorithms, to achieve targets using fewer layers in the neural network [20]. Training strategies can also help improve training on smaller labeled datasets that are commonly limited to industrial applications. Better performance can be achieved with semi-supervised learning, which uses unlabeled data and active learning, in which the model requests data points.

12.4 Case Studies of TinyML in Industrial Predictive Maintenance

This section showcases two to three interesting examples of the use of TinyML in industrial predictive maintenance. TinyML enables industry applications to detect early signs of equipment failure, thereby reducing maintenance time, enhancing safety, and lowering maintenance costs, as shown in Table 12.2.

Table 12.2 TinyML case studies and applications.

Case Study	Application of TinyML	How It Works	Outcome	Illustration
Predicting Bearing Failures in Rotating Machinery	TinyML models, such as decision trees or lightweight neural networks, are deployed on edge devices (vibration sensors) to monitor the vibration patterns of machinery in real time.	Bearings receive constant vibration data from their mounted sensors. The system processes data stored within edge devices through TinyML models to identify abnormal vibration signals that generate warning alerts.	The approach reduces downtime by enabling early detection of bearing failures, facilitates proactive maintenance, and minimizes repair costs by preventing catastrophic damage to machinery.	Vibration data analysis for predicting bearing failure.
Detecting Anomalies in Manufacturing Processes	TinyML to monitor sensor data such as temperature, pressure, and flow rate to detect anomalies that could affect production efficiency.	The system constantly checks sensor data to discover abnormal events that exceed predefined threshold levels. The system raises an alert when it detects abnormal patterns that require operator action.	The system enhances operational efficiency, reduces material waste, and prevents production defects by enabling real-time corrective actions.	Real-time anomaly detection in manufacturing processes using TinyML.
Predicting Equipment Degradation in Wind Turbines	Wind turbines use TinyML models for parameter measurement of vibration, temperature, and wind speed across their components to forecast component degradation.	The system acquires wind turbine sensor information, which is analyzed using TinyML processing algorithms to detect component deterioration. The system creates a maintenance alert when degradation prediction occurs.	This predictive maintenance system minimizes downtime by enabling timely repairs, reduces emergency repair costs, and extends the operational lifespan of turbine components.	TinyML used for predicting equipment degradation in wind turbines.

Table 12.2 summarizes TinyML implementation across various industrial applications for predictive maintenance.

12.4.1 Case Study 2: Anomaly Detection in Manufacturing Process Monitoring

Continuous manufacturing processes, such as chemical reactors, injection molding lines, or precision machining cells, depend on maintaining [21] tight windows for process parameters. The temperature, pressure, and flow rate deviations indicate a process problem that has created equipment damage and out-of-spec product.

Multisensor fusion refers to the integration of temperature (RTD), pressure (piezoresistive), flow rate (ultrasonic), and electrical power measurements at sampling rates of 1–100 Hz. Due to low sampling rates and the multivariate nature of the process, monitoring using statistical features is preferred to deep learning of raw time series.

Model Architecture: To train an anomaly detection model based on autoencoders *using only* normal operational data. It reconstructs the sensor feature vector and flags anomaly cases when the reconstruction error exceeds the adaptively determined threshold. The encoder with $32 \rightarrow 16 \rightarrow 8$ neurons and the decoder with $8 \rightarrow 16 \rightarrow 32$ neurons use ReLU activations and INT8 quantization, occupying 35 KB of flash on the ESP32-S3 platform. The model uses 180 mW at all times and runs inference at 4 Hz.

12.4.2 Potential Benefits and Challenges

Table 12.3 presents the advantages of TinyML for predictive maintenance. These are attractive [22], but implementing them in industrial settings poses several challenges that require careful consideration.

12.4.3 Challenges in Implementing TinyML in Industrial Environments

Although Table 12.3 states that TinyML has several benefits [23], certain issues must be addressed when using it in an industrial environment. These are presented in Table 12.4.

12.5 Future Directions

The domain of TinyML for industrial predictive maintenance continues to advance rapidly through numerous opportunities to enhance system efficiency

Table 12.3 Potential benefits of using TinyML in industrial predictive maintenance.

Benefits	Description
Improved Reliability	TinyML models' ability to detect real-time anomalies leads to enhanced equipment reliability as they identify problems early on before their occurrence.
Reduced Maintenance Costs	Companies can schedule preventive maintenance activities proactively instead of performing time-based maintenance or responding to equipment breakdowns through accurate failure prediction. Maintenance expenses decrease because the elimination of unneeded inspections prevents catastrophic equipment repairs.
Increased Productivity	Predictive maintenance allows industries to keep equipment running efficiently, minimizing disruptions in production. With real-time predictions and early alerts, businesses can optimize their workflow and reduce idle times.
Energy Efficiency	By avoiding unnecessary downtime and ensuring machines run at peak efficiency, companies can reduce energy consumption. This is especially beneficial in large-scale industrial operations, where energy costs can be significant.
Enhanced Safety	TinyML models can help detect anomalies that could pose safety risks, such as overheating or mechanical failure. By preventing catastrophic equipment failures, safety risks to workers are minimized.

and scalability while ensuring security. Research in the next period will explain how to maximize model performance and implement enhanced privacy and advanced AI techniques for edge computing [25]. Three significant areas to focus on are lightweight model structures, federated learning algorithms, and adaptive systems designed to operate in changing industrial settings [26]. TinyML for industrial predictive maintenance is actively developing, as researchers explore diverse approaches to improve the effectiveness, scalability, and efficiency of the technology. This section outlines potential future research directions that will guide TinyML adoption in industrial environments.

12.5.1 Advances in Efficient Model Architectures for Industrial TinyML

At present, TinyML model validation is primarily performed after they are created on general-purpose hardware. The emphasis of future research is likely to shift toward hardware-native architecture design – the design of model topologies

Table 12.4 Challenges of using TinyML in industrial environments.

Challenge	Description
Data Scarcity	A high standard of labeled data serves as a necessary training component for machine learning model development. The availability of both data and high-quality labels is limited in most industrial applications. Few available high-quality labels limit model accuracy during training because strategies such as transfer learning and active learning may help address these difficulties.
Model Deployment and Updates	High-quality labeled data is essential for training machine learning models. In many industrial settings [24], data might be scarce or not available in large quantities. This can make training accurate models difficult, and strategies such as transfer learning or active learning may be needed to overcome this limitation.
Security and Privacy Concerns	IoT and edge devices' security remains at high risk from cyber-attacks. Industrial environments need robust protection systems for data security and model tampering prevention to incorporate TinyML. Privacy issues emerge during the processing of sensitive operational data on-site systems.
Limited Computational Resources	The designed TinyML models operate on low-power devices, but these systems also have processing and memory restrictions. Resource limits of devices establish an operational boundary that affects how complex models can be while still providing accurate predictions. It is essential to use efficient model optimization techniques such as quantization and pruning because they enable models to run without sacrificing performance during deployment.
Integration with Legacy Systems	The majority of industrial systems maintain outdated systems that fail to operate with contemporary IoT devices and machine learning models. The integration of TinyML models into legacy systems needs resolution of technical challenges to link historical equipment with contemporary sensors.

whose operations inherently match the computational primitives available on microcontroller hardware.

Hardware-Aware Neural Architecture Search (HW-NAS): Designs such as MCUNet optimize memory scheduling and neural architecture to address the resource constraints of microcontroller SRAM. Future upgrades will include multiobjective optimization across accuracy, power, and inference frequency. Also, an industrial-specific evaluation dataset is targeted, with industrial fault-detection performance as the optimization objective.

Spiking neural networks (SNNs) are a type of artificial neural network that uses a spiking representation to encode data and operate via sparse spiking events that occur only during information processing. This represents a stark [27] contrast to other artificial neural networks that operate using continuous activation values. Theoretically, SNNs could consume one to two orders of magnitude less energy than conventional deep neural networks (DNNs).

Research conducted in the early days demonstrated that SNNs could be used for time-series anomaly detection. However, industrial-level applications would require the development of training algorithms that consistently converge even in the presence of noise in sensor data.

Mixture-of-Expert (MoE) architecture employs a network of "experts," simply put. Depending on the expert's relevance to the condition, one activates. Thus, a single monolithic model is avoided to conserve computational power and improve efficiency [28]. In the case of industrial equipment with different fault modes and operating regimes, MoE architectures may achieve improved accuracy at lower average computational cost than single colossal models [29].

12.6 Conclusion

The groundbreaking TinyML system speeds up predictive maintenance in automation systems, while significantly enhancing efficiency, reliability, and sustainability. In this chapter, exploring the principles of TinyML and its applications in predictive maintenance, illustrated with use cases demonstrating TinyML's effectiveness. The system detects potential equipment failures, thereby avoiding downtime and maintenance expenses. Data security and privacy are enhanced when models are deployed on devices, eliminating the need to transmit sensitive data over long distances. There are several key challenges in using TinyML in industrial predictive maintenance processes. There are critical steps needed to implement these technologies, such as overcoming data limitations and designing system deployment and security protocols. Research in TinyML focuses on three principal objectives: developing efficient models, improving intelligent methods, and advancing distributed learning techniques within federated learning frameworks. TinyML has extraordinary potential for future industrial predictive maintenance applications. The future development of TinyML technologies will establish progressive pathways to optimize industrial processes, extend sustainability measures, and minimize operational expenses. The general acceptance of TinyML will transform equipment management across industries through advanced monitoring techniques, enabling more innovative industrial systems with enhanced reliability. Technological innovation in TinyML enables a fundamental, predictive-maintenance revolution, bringing substantial industrial improvements across diverse sectors.

References

1 T. Hafeez, L. Xu, and G. Mcardle, "Edge intelligence for data handling and predictive maintenance in IIOT," *IEEE Access*, 9, 49355–49371, 2021.

2 M. W. Hoffmann *et al.*, "Integration of novel sensors and machine learning for predictive maintenance in medium voltage switchgear to enable the energy and mobility revolutions" *Sensors*, 20, 7, 2020.

3 R. Kallimani, K. Pai, P. Raghuwanshi, S. Iyer, and O. L. A. López, "TinyML: Tools, applications, challenges, and future research directions," *Multimed. Tools Appl.*, 83, 10, 29015–29045, 2023.

4 D. L. Dutta and S. Bharali, "TinyML meets IoT: A comprehensive survey," *Internet Things (Amst.)*, 16, 100461, 100461, 2021.

5 Y. Cui, R. Butler, Z. Liu, T. Jaremko, and S. Hinds, "The future of predictive maintenance for variable frequency drives based on AI/ML" *IEEE Trans. Ind. Appl.*, 1–9, 2025.

6 Y. Bouabdallaoui, Z. Lafhaj, P. Yim, L. Ducoulombier, and B. Bennadji, "Predictive maintenance in building facilities: A machine learning-based approach" *Sensors*, 21, 4, 2021.

7 L. Capogrosso, F. Cunico, D. S. Cheng, F. Fummi, and M. Cristani, "A machine learning-oriented survey on Tiny Machine Learning," 2023, *arXiv [cs.LG]*.

8 A. Moin, M. Challenger, A. Badii, and S. Günnemann, "Supporting AI engineering on the IoT edge through model-driven TinyML," 2021, *arXiv [cs.SE]*.

9 M. Molęda, B. Małysiak-Mrozek, W. Ding, V. Sunderam, and D. Mrozek, "From corrective to predictive maintenance-A review of maintenance approaches for the power industry" *Sensors*, 23, 13, 2023.

10 E. Njor, M. A. Hasanpour, J. Madsen, and X. Fafoutis, "A holistic review of the TinyML stack for predictive maintenance," *IEEE Access*, 12, 184861–184882, 2024.

11 F. Arena, M. Collotta, L. Luca, M. Ruggieri, and F. G. Termine, "Predictive maintenance in the automotive sector: A literature review" *Math. Comput. Appl.*, 27, 1, 2, 2021.

12 A. Albanese and D. Brunelli, "Industrial visual inspection with TinyML for high-performance quality control," *IEEE Instrum. Meas. Mag.*, 26, 8, 17–22, 2023.

13 S. Pookkuttath, M. Rajesh Elara, V. Sivanantham, and B. Ramalingam, "AI-enabled predictive maintenance framework for autonomous mobile cleaning robots," *Sensors (Basel)*, 22, 1, 13, 2021.

14 M. M. Saeed, R. A. Saeed, and Z. E. Ahmed, “TinyML for 5G networks,” *TinyML for Edge Intelligence in IoT and LPWAN Networks*, Elsevier, 2024, 167–229.

15 O. Serradilla, E. Zugasti, J. Rodriguez, and U. Zurutuza, “Deep learning models for predictive maintenance: A survey, comparison, challenges and prospects,” *Appl. Intell.*, 52, 10, 10934–10964, 2022.

16 P. Strauss, M. Schmitz, R. Wostmann, and J. Deuse, “Enabling of predictive maintenance in the brownfield through low-cost sensors, an IIoT-architecture and machine learning,” in *2018 IEEE Int. Conf. Big Data (Big Data)*, 2018, IEEE

17 J. P. Usuga-Cadavid, S. Lamouri, B. Grabot, and A. Fortin, “Using deep learning to value free-form text data for predictive maintenance,” *Int. J. Prod. Res.*, 60, 14, 4548–4575, 2022.

18 R. Welte, M. Estler, and D. Lucke, “A method for implementation of machine learning solutions for predictive maintenance in small and medium sized enterprises,” *Procedia CIRP*, 93, 909–914, 2020.

19 A. Karpatne *et al.*, “Theory-guided data science: A new paradigm for scientific discovery from data,” *IEEE Trans. Knowl. Data Eng.*, 29, 10, 2318–2331, 2017.

20 T. Zhu, Y. Ran, X. Zhou, and Y. Wen, “A survey of Predictive Maintenance: Systems, purposes and approaches,” 2024, *arXiv [eess.SP]*.

21 M. Bevilacqua and M. Braglia, “The analytic hierarchy process applied to maintenance strategy selection,” *Reliab. Eng. Syst. Saf.*, 70, 1, 71–83, 2000.

22 E. Njor, J. Madsen, and X. Fafoutis, “A primer for tinyML predictive maintenance: Input and model optimisation,” *IFIP Advances in Information and Communication Technology*, Cham: Springer International Publishing, 2022, 67–78.

23 R. Sanchez-Iborra and A. F. Skarmeta, “TinyML-enabled frugal smart objects: Challenges and opportunities,” *IEEE Circuits Syst. Mag.*, 20, 3, 4–18, 2020.

24 P. P. Ray, “A review on TinyML: State-of-the-art and prospects,” *J. King Saud Univ. - Comput. Inf. Sci.*, 34, 4, 1595–1623, 2022.

25 S. Kumari and C. Prabha, “A comprehensive review on anomaly detection in images: Challenges and future research directions,” in *2023 IEEE North Karnataka Subsection Flagship Int. Conf. (NKCon)*, 2023, IEEE

26 C. Prabha, M. Malik, S. Kumari, N. Sharma, A. Sharma, and M. S. Khan, “A review on sensors and technologies in smart farming using AI and IoT perspective and their challenges,” in *2023 IEEE 2nd Int. Conf. Ind. Electr. Dev. Appl. (ICIDeA)*, 2023, pp. 322–327, IEEE

27 C. Prabha, P. Srivastava, H. Dixit, G. Singla, S. Kumari, and G. Kaur, “Machine learning for smart healthcare industry: A succinct review,” in *2024 Int. Conf. Sustain. Commun. Netw. Appl. (ICSCNA)*, 2024, pp. 1144–1149, IEEE

28 S. Kumari and C. Prabha, "A comprehensive review of deep anomaly detection techniques- an analysis," in *2024 IEEE 9th Int. Conf. Converg. Technol. (I2CT)*, 2024, IEEE

29 V. Tsoukas, E. Boumpa, G. Giannakas, and A. Kakarountas, "A review of machine learning and TinyML in healthcare," in *25th Pan-Hellenic Conf. Inf.*, 2021, Association for Computing Machinery (ACM)

13

TinyML for Computer Vision and Image Processing

Shalini Kumari and Chander Prabha

Chitkara University Institute of Engineering and Technology, Chitkara University, Punjab, India

13.1 Introduction

Automated defect detection is an important part of contemporary manufacturing systems with the advent of Industry 4.0. The traditional inspection schemes involve either manual inspection or machine vision processes with rule-based techniques [1], which are often low accuracy and inefficiently spatialized for complex working environments. The latest innovations in deep learning (DL) have greatly enhanced computer vision (CV) systems. These models, however, tend to be computationally memory- and cloud-intensive and, as such, may not be able to be deployed on embedded systems and edge devices. It enables real-time processing, minimizes latency, enhances privacy, and reduces energy consumption. The proposed framework in this chapter is a Tiny Machine Learning (TinyML)-based multi-class defect detection system. The system is designed to categorize nine defect types using a lightweight convolutional neural network (CNN) based on a truncated ResNet50. Transfer learning enhances feature extraction, whereas optimization methods such as quantization and pruning make the model edge deployable.

Existing cloud-hosted inference pipelines, which send raw data from intelligent sensors to a remote server for inference, are increasingly constrained by bandwidth costs and latency, potential privacy concerns, and the unavailability of server services in offline or low connectivity environments. TinyML, by bringing machine learning (ML) [1] inference engines to the resource-limited device footprint of microcontrollers and embedded CPUs, tackles these challenges head-on. TinyML for CV is an exciting and promising application domain. But vision sensors are increasingly common in embedded devices ranging from farm drones and factory [2] inspection robots to medical devices and smart home appliances.

The challenge that TinyML CV aims to address is how to close the gap between the computational demands of today's CNNs and the limited hardware available on microcontroller units (MCUs). The traditional CV system is entirely premised on cloud computing, which poses the risks of latency, privacy concerns, and dependence on the internet. These challenges can be overcome with TinyML, which enables on-chip processing, speeding up systems, increasing security, and reducing energy consumption.

While conventional CV models such as ResNet, EfficientNet, or YOLO are designed to maximize accuracy with little regard for computational efficiency, TinyML vision models prioritize operational efficiency while maintaining acceptable accuracy levels [3]. The new Internet of Things (IoT) paradigm encourages bringing intelligence to the edge layer: artificial intelligence (AI). Edge AI was coined to address the constraints of cloud-based AI, which do not suit real-time applications and devices with limited processing power and bandwidth [4]. As IoT and connected devices have become more widespread, the term has emerged as a requirement for real-time decision-making and low latency. This work has made the following contributions:

- Creating a lightweight multi-class defect detector based on DL.
- Edge deployment optimization with TinyML.
- Execution of real-time inference on resource-constrained devices.
- In-depth analysis in regard to accuracy, latency, and memory consumption.

13.2 Literature Review

Neural Networks and TinyML: A neural net is a ML model that mimics the human brain. A neural network has a single input layer, a single (or multiple) hidden layer, and an output layer. Processing the input data and making the network's final decision are handled by the input and output layers. As shown in Figure 13.1, the network's decision is defined by multiple layers of nodes with weights. A CNN has convolutional layers that extract features from images as straight lines, which can then be used to make better decisions. Due to this property of feature extraction, CNNs can be applied to image classification, such as the model we are going to use in this project. The weakness of CNNs and neural networks, generally speaking, is their size and complexity, and some neural networks, such as Resnet50, have more than 23.5 million parameters [5].

Besides, TinyML focuses on neural networks that can be deployed on-site and are not affected by communication latency. That is being served out of a server. TensorFlow Lite is one of the most popular TinyML platforms. The platforms on which we will be deploying TinyML are Google, PyTorch, and Meta's TinyML platform.

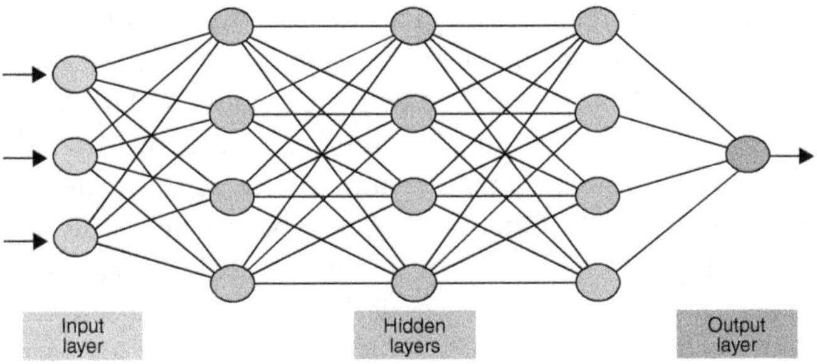

Figure 13.1 Neural network.

13.2.1 Lightweight CNN Architectures for Embedded Vision

MobileNet Family: The MobileNet family of CNN architectures is a milestone contribution. MobileNet [6] uses depthwise separable convolutions, separating each convolution into a depthwise spatial filter and a pointwise 1×1 projection, achieving a computational savings of 8–9× (depending on the kernel size; 9× for the commonly used 3×3 kernel) compared to standard convolutions while maintaining representational power. MobileNetV2 [7] used inverted residual blocks with linear bottleneck layers and achieved 71.8% ImageNet top-1 accuracy with a model size of just 3.4 MB when running on STM32H7 MCUs. The depthwise separable architecture enables extreme width-multiplier (α) and resolution-multiplier (ρ) scaling to get better efficiency. MobileNetV2 at $\alpha = 0.1$ and 96×96 input size, when deployed on STM32 targets, achieves 88% accuracy, with 220 ms inference time on a visual wake words (VWW) application [8]. MobileNetV3 [9], further leveraging hardware-aware neural architecture search (NAS) and the squeeze-and-excitation (SE) architecture, improved the desirable accuracy-efficiency trade-off [9]. The V3-Small model is particularly well suited to MCU-sized targets, with high accuracy at memory sizes under 1 MB.

Co-design and MCUNet: MCUNet [10] is a step toward co-design of neural architecture and inference engine for MCUs, rather than a model retraining approach that tends to adapt cloud-scale models to the edge. MCUNet includes two parts: TinyNAS, an NAS algorithm that optimizes for an optimal design under memory and latency constraints, and TinyEngine, an inference engine that avoids memory overhead through in-place depth-first scheduling. MCUNet achieves 70.0% top-1 accuracy on ImageNet, a level of accuracy previously considered impossible on MCUs using the STM32H743 with 1 MB SRAM and 2 MB Flash [10]. This work shows that system-algorithm co-design is critical to achieve high performance in the constrained environment of embedded vision devices.

SqueezeNet and EfficientNet-Lite: SqueezeNet [11] uses 1×1 "fire modules" (squeeze and expand layers) to implement AlexNet-scale accuracy with 50 times fewer parameters than the original AlexNet. Its small footprint (4.8 MB, precompression) makes it a natural benchmark for TinyML vision applications, but its performance is usually trumped by MCUNet and MobileNetV2. EfficientNet [12] pioneered compound scaling (uniformly scaling network width, depth, and resolution by a constant factor), resulting in a series of models ranging from EfficientNet-B0 to B7. EfficientNet-Lite models remove SE and adopt ReLU6 activation functions for better quantization and MCU compatibility, offering another promising alternative for devices with a little more capacity and resources than the extremely constrained MCUs. ML is changing the IoT scene by allowing more intelligent, automated systems [13]. Fundamentally, ML uses statistical models and algorithms to analyze data, identify trends, and generate predictions or judgments without clear programming guidance. The demand to incorporate intelligence into many previously impracticable applications, driven by the significant power and processing requirements [14] of conventional ML models, has propelled TinyML technologies.

Autonomous microvehicles are used across innovative sectors, smart environments, smart surveillance systems, and many more. TinyML makes them more efficient by enabling them to acquire complex behaviors with minimal energy consumption. The study [4] focuses on improving the performance of running DL on low-power autonomous driving cars (actions/s /s, performance, etc.) using modeled complex tasks. So, the machine could detect and classify objects under noisy conditions with limited resources [15]. The authors presented a computer vision algorithm (CVA) that replaces a CNN trained with the LeNet-5 model and only predicts under constant lighting. The comparison of the models is presented in Table 13.1.

Table 13.1 ResNet50 vs. MobileNet vs. EfficientNet comparison.

Feature	MobileNet	EfficientNet	Proposed (ResNet50)
Architecture Type	Depthwise Separable CNN	Compound Scaling CNN	Residual Network
Model Size	Very Small	Medium	Medium (optimized to small)
Accuracy	Moderate–High	High	High (after fine-tuning)
Speed	Very Fast	Moderate	Fast (after optimization)
TinyML Suitability	Excellent	Limited (needs reduction)	Good (after pruning + quantization)
Memory Usage	Low	Medium–High	Low (after optimization)
Best Use Case	Edge/mobile apps	High-accuracy systems	Balanced defect detection

It has been compared to MobileNet, which is better optimized for edge environments due to its depthwise separable CNN architecture, is very fast, requires low memory, and is highly suitable for TinyML applications, albeit with greatly reduced accuracy. EfficientNet is more accurate due to compound scaling, but it requires more computational resources and is less applicable to TinyML networks with limited optimization. The proposed ResNet-50, a residual network architecture, offers a middle ground: high accuracy post-fine-tuning, low memory consumption, and high speed post-pruning and quantization, and is, therefore, appropriate in areas such as defect detection where both speed and accuracy are important.

13.3 Algorithms Used for TinyML

Image segmentation separates an image into its parts, which are usually determined by color, intensity, or texture, as in the case of pixels [16]. One of the key stages in image segmentation is identifying object boundaries, which is the process of determining where different objects are by detecting variations in pixel values [17].

Object detection is the second fundamental step in CV, in which objects are recognized, and their locations (bounding box coordinates) are identified in a photograph or video. Hence, traditional methods (Haar feature classifiers and Histograms of Oriented Gradients [HOG] with support vector machines [SVMs]) have proven to be well-known approaches. In contrast, DL, particularly the architecture of CNN, has emerged as the most widely used approach for object detection tasks [18]. R-CNN (region-based CNN) is one of them, YOLO (You Only Look Once) is another, and SSD (Single Shot Multi-Box Detector) is the last one. YOLO reformulates the detection problem as a single regression problem, where we pass an image to a neural network that simultaneously predicts multiple bounding boxes and (somewhat spoiling the surprise) class probabilities. The core concept of YOLO is to split the image into a grid, with each cell predicting bounding boxes and Class probabilities, enabling real-time object detection at large scales.

It does so by comparing features measured in two images/video frames and finds matches. Any of the corners, edges, or any other salient points in a picture can be termed as a feature point. Feature matching is used in applications such as Visual SLAM (Simultaneous Localization and Mapping), 3D reconstruction, and image stitching. Feature matching algorithms can be separated into many categories such as SIFT (Scale-Invariant Feature Transform) and SURF (Speeded-Up Robust Features) [19]. More specifically, SIFT is invariant to scaling and rotation, which is why it works well with other image processing. Because of these dynamic scenarios, object tracking algorithms infer object locations across successive video images [11]. CVAs depend on extraction and representation, as well as on matching relevant image information. DL approaches have yielded research breakthroughs, enabling high-performance CVAs for real-world applications [19], including object detection, image segmentation, and object tracking, that approach human performance.

13.4 Dataset Description and Methodology

The CAD-SD [20] consists of normal images of the product and a screw on one side of which is a hex nut. The dataset anomalies and abnormal images are roughly categorized into local region anomalies and co-occurrence relation anomalies. The local area abnormalities are Scratch, where a part of the product has a scratch, and Paint, where a part of the product has paint attached to it. The deficiencies of the co-occurrence relation are over-coupling, where hex nuts are coupled along the screw rod, and lacking, where hex nuts are not coupled to both sides of the screw rod. The connection to the CAD-SD data can be viewed at https://drive.google.com/drive/folders/1yeampzTiB4uoTmmqIZkeCdMIXGujl3cU. The data is partitioned as follows: training: 70, validation: 15, and testing: 15.

The data consists of labeled images of various classes applicable to the field of application. The dataset is robust to changes in lighting, orientation, and background. All images are downsampled to a constant resolution to reduce computational complexity. Normalization of pixel values enhances convergence during training. To improve generalization and avoid overfitting, augmentation techniques are used. Figure 13.2 shows the augmentation techniques, and Figure 13.3 presents a sample of images from the CAD-SD dataset.

Below is the workflow for defect detection in a CV TinyML model. It begins with an image dataset, followed by preprocessing steps such as

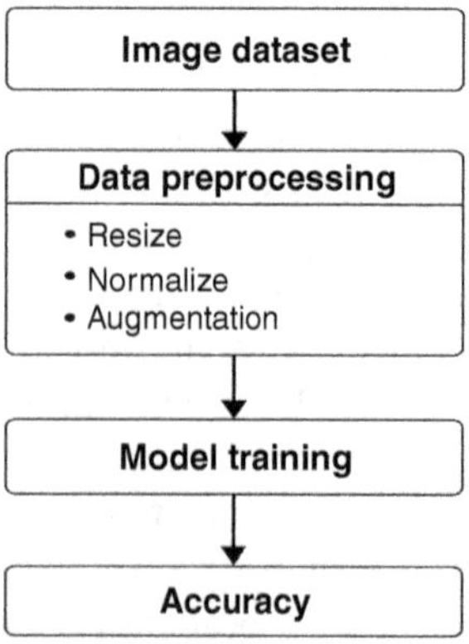

Figure 13.2 Methodology steps.

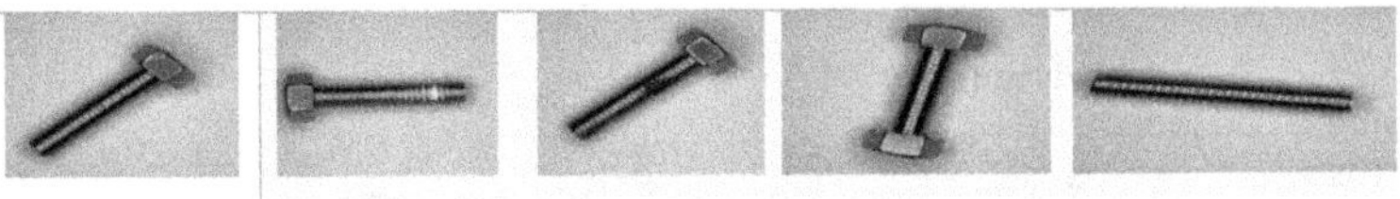

Figure 13.3 Samples of images of the dataset.

Table 13.2 Model architecture and training configuration.

Section	Details
Model Type	ResNet50
Feature Extraction	Pretrained layers used as feature extractor
Pooling Layer	Global average pooling
Classifier	Fully connected layer
Optimizer	Adam
Learning Rate	0.001
Batch Size	32
Epochs	30
Evaluation Metrics	Accuracy, loss

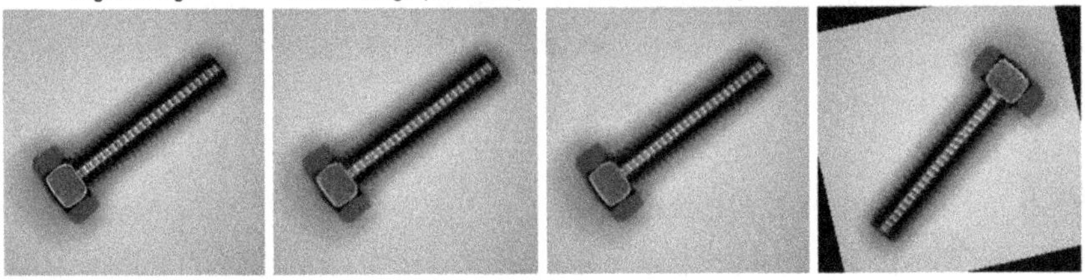

Figure 13.4 Preprocessing steps.

resizing, normalization, and data augmentation. The processed data is then used to test the trained model, and its final performance is based on accuracy. Table 13.2 presents model architecture and training configuration. Figures 13.3 and 13.4 present the sample of images and the preprocessing steps, respectively.

The model was architecture based on ResNet50, with the resultant feature layers pretrained; a global average pooling layer was then used, followed by a fully connected classifier. It is trained with Adam optimizer, a learning rate of 0.001, batch size of 32, and 30 epochs. Accuracy and loss measures assess the model's performance in achieving effective learning and generalization.

Table 13.3 Quantitative metrics.

Metric	Value (%)
Accuracy	94.85
Precision	92.20
Recall	91
F1-score	93

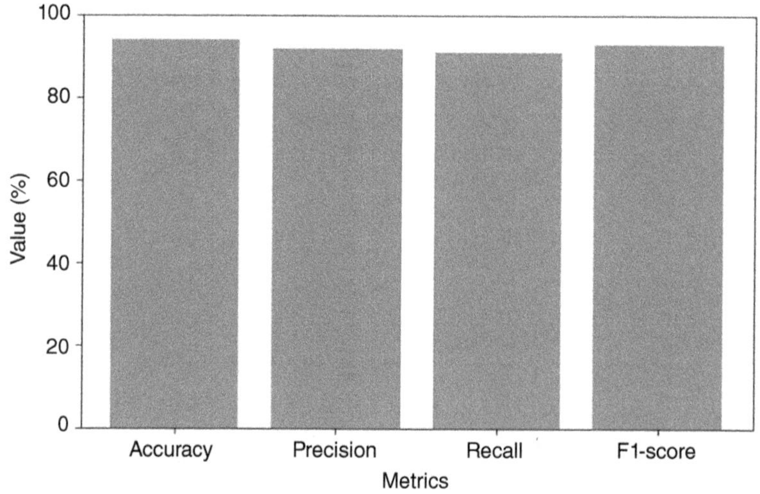

Figure 13.5 Model performance metrics.

13.5 Results and Discussion

Table 13.3 presents the accuracy, precision, recall, and F1-score; Figure 13.5 presents the graph; and Figure 13.6 presents the visualization of training and validation performance: (left) accuracy curves showing model convergence and (right) loss curves demonstrating stable learning and minimal overfitting over 30 epochs.

The model has high overall performance, with an accuracy of 94% and an F1-score of nearly 93%. The precision (92%) and recall (91%) are also strong, indicating that it can classify evenly. Overall, the results suggest that the model is reliable and generalizes well across metrics presented in Figure 13.6(a,b).

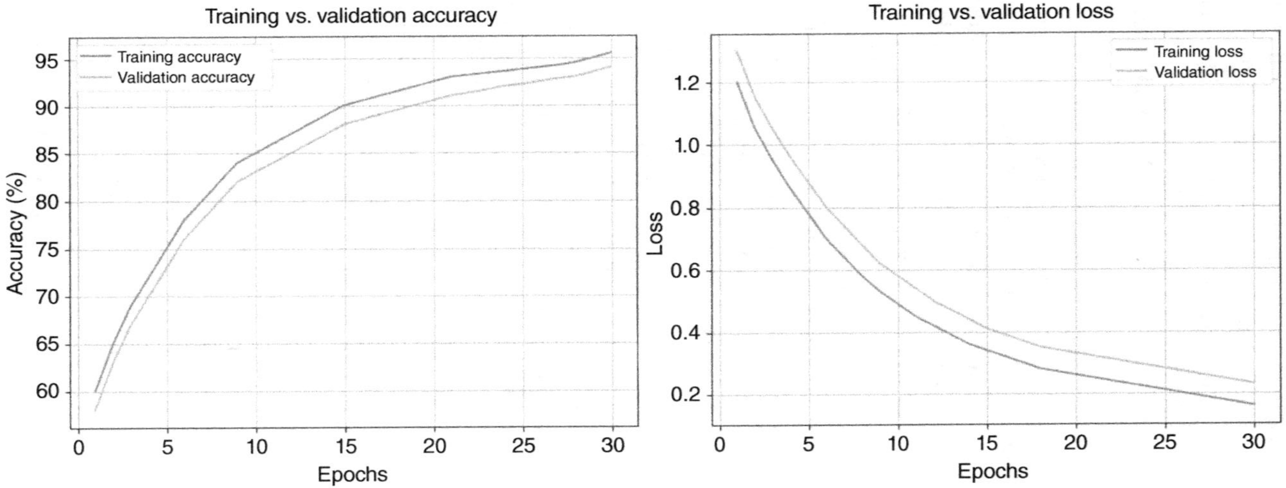

Figure 13.6 (a) Training and validation accuracy and (b) training and validation loss curves.

The results of the experiment show that the proposed TinyML-based system of defect detection provides a high classification accuracy on all of the nine defect types with an overall accuracy of 94%. The great accuracy (92%) and the recall (91%), as well as the F1-score of 93%, provide the opportunity to have a balanced trade-off between the false positives and false negatives, which is paramount in any industrial quality control when both the false alarms and missed defects will be costly.

The choice of ResNet50 as a backbone, adjusted through transfer learning and truncation, was effective at balancing representational strength and computational cost. Unlike MobileNet versions based on depthwise separable convolutions or EfficientNet based on a compound scaling, the truncated WideResNet50 has wider residual connections to preserve feature richness at lower depth.

The proposed model, as required in Table 13.1, is highly accurate compared to EfficientNet but retains the same TinyML suitability as MobileNet does after pruning and quantization. Figure 13.4 shows that the training and validation curves converge after 30 epochs, with minimal overfitting, which can be attributed to the data augmentation approaches used during preprocessing: rotation, horizontal flipping, and brightness adjustment. The fact that a 70/15/15 train-validation-test split is used also ensures that the reported metrics are good indicators of generalization performance, rather than a result of the training distribution. The post-training optimization strategies that were found to be critical were quantization and pruning. Quantizing these model weights to 8-bit integers with 32-bit floating-point accuracy reduced model size and enabled arithmetic operations to complete faster on MCUs. Additional pruning removed parameters that contributed only a small amount to the overall model, resulting in a sparse model more suitable for an embedded system. On-machine inference eliminates the privacy and latency cost of on-cloud pipelines. The property is highly useful in real-world industries where fast decision-making is required, and data sensitivity can make it impossible to transmit the necessary information over public networks. The architecture is consistent with the larger philosophy of TinyML presented in recent literature, particularly by adhering to co-design principles and by integrating model complexity and hardware constraints, as seen in MCUNet and its TinyEngine/TinyEngine pairing of TinyML and hardware. Although the data collection was balanced (nine classes), it was conducted under controlled laboratory conditions. The real industrial environment is more dynamic, with variations in ambient light, vibrations, and occlusions, which can significantly affect model robustness. In addition, the current system has been tested on only a single hardware platform; it has not been fully tested for portability to other MCU families with alternative memory architectures.

13.6 Conclusion and Future Scope

An end-to-end TinyML pipeline for multi-class industrial defect detection, including dataset preparation, model design, optimization, and edge deployment. Using a transfer-learned truncated ResNet50 architecture, the proposed framework achieved 94% accuracy across nine types of surface defects, demonstrating that high-performing CV models can be implemented on resource-limited microcontrollers. The combination of post-training optimization methods, including quantization and pruning, reduced the model's memory and computational footprints to the extent that embedded hardware accelerated its classification performance, as evidenced by high accuracy, recall, and F1-score values. Data augmentation and transfer learning also helped to guarantee that this model generalized well, even though the defect taxonomy has nine classes. In a broader sense, this article highlights the potential of TinyML to revolutionize industrial automation. It supports real-time, autonomous, and intelligent decision-making at the edge to overcome basic constraints of the cloud-dependent architectures, such as latency, bandwidth usage, and information privacy. The combination of lightweight neural network design, efficient inference frameworks, and edge hardware has provided an interesting avenue to deploy AI to manufacturing settings that used to be closed to solutions based on ML. Overall, the chapter confirms that TinyML is not only a trade-off between accuracy and efficiency but also a potent and useful paradigm for CV in real-world applications with constrained environments when appropriately designed.

Although the presented framework shows good performance and is highly viable in practice, several potential directions for future exploration exist.

Hardware-Aware NAS: Future directions for this work might include adding NAS that is subject to given MCU memory and latency constraints, such as the TinyNAS subset of MCUNet. This would enable the model architecture, per se, to be co-optimized with the target hardware and may result in better accuracy-efficiency trade-offs than can be attained by hand truncation and fine-tuning.

Federated Learning on Edge Intelligence: Federated learning protocols would allow multiple edge devices across multiple factory floors to collaborate in order to enhance a common model without centralizing sensitive production data. It would increase the model's robustness across various manufacturing settings while retaining data sovereignty.

Anomaly Detection and Continual Learning: It would also be possible to extend the system to detect anomalies unsupervised or semi-supervised, thereby decreasing reliance on large labeled datasets. Also, the implemented model could be enhanced with continuous or incremental learning mechanisms that would enable the deployed model to adapt to new types of defects that arise in production over time, without necessarily requiring retraining.

Multi-Sensor Fusion: Visual data can be combined with other sensor types, such as thermal imaging, acoustic emission, or vibration signals, to greatly improve defect characterization, especially for defects that cannot be readily identified visually. Multimodal sensor-fusion TinyML frameworks are a promising edge to consider.

Deployment over Heterogeneous Hardware Platforms: A set of benchmarking deployments of the optimized model on a series of microcontroller platforms, such as ARM Cortex-M series (or RISC-V-based MCUs), or dedicated AI accelerators, such as the Arduino Nicla Vision or Sony Supersense, would give us a comprehensive view of the model in terms of portability and scalability.

Real-World Industry Tests: Future efforts should test the system under real factory conditions, including environmental variability, full-speed conveyor imaging, and interoperability with programmable logic controllers (PLCs) or industrial communication protocols such as MQTT and OPC-UA. This would be an important milestone to commercial deployment.

Explainability and Trust: TinyML systems are increasingly being incorporated into safety-critical manufacturing processes; it would be beneficial to add an explainability mechanism, e.g. gradient-weighted class activation maps (Grad-CAM), to embedded inference operations to improve trust and enable regulatory compliance.

All of these research directions lead to a future in which TinyML systems will no longer be passive classifiers but active, adaptable, and explainable parts of intelligent industrial ecosystems, which perfectly aligns with the vision of Industry 4.0 and the new paradigm of Industry 5.0.

References

1. Chaoyi Tan, Xiangtian Li, Xiaobo Wang, Zhen Qi, and Ao Xiang, "Real-time video target tracking algorithm utilizing convolutional neural networks (CNN)," in *2024 4th Int. Conf. Electr. Inf. Eng. Comput. (EIECT)*, 2024, pp. 847–851, IEEE.
2. Z. Wu, "Deep learning with improved metaheuristic optimization for traffic flow prediction," *J. Comput. Sci. Technol. Stud.*, vol. 6, no. 4, pp. 47–53, 2024.
3. A. Khan and S. Islam, "Machine learning in computer vision," *Procedia Comput. Sci.*, vol. 167, pp. 1444–1451, 2020.
4. H. Ziang, J. Zhang, and L. Li, "Framework for lung CT image segmentation based on UNet++," 2025, *arXiv [eess.IV]*.

5 T. Wang, X. Cai, and Q. Xu, "Energy market price forecasting and financial technology risk management based on generative AI," *Appl. Comput. Eng.*, vol. 116, no. 1, pp. 29–34, 2024.

6 X. Wu, X. Liu, and J. H. Yin, *Multi-class classification of breast cancer gene expression using PCA and XGBoost*. MDPI AG, 2024.

7 V. Sze, Y.-H. Chen, T.-J. Yang, and J. S. Emer, "Efficient processing of deep neural networks: A tutorial and survey," *Proc. IEEE Inst. Electr. Electron. Eng.*, vol. 105, no. 12, pp. 2295–2329, 2017.

8 Haosen Wang, *et al.* "Rpf-eld: Regional prior fusion using early and late distillation for breast cancer recognition in ultrasound images," in *2024 IEEE Int. Conf. Bioinf. Biomed. (BIBM)*, 2024, pp. 2605–2612, IEEE.

9 Kangtong Mo, *et al.* "DRAL: Deep reinforcement adaptive learning for multi-UAVs navigation in unknown indoor environment," in *2024 7th Int. Conf. Mechatr. Comput. Technol. Eng. (MCTE)*, 2024, pp. 859–863, IEEE.

10 Xiangtian Li, Han Cao, Zhaoyang Zhang, Jiacheng Hu, Yuhui Jin, and Zihao Zhao, "Artistic neural style transfer algorithms with activation smoothing," in *Proc. 2025 2nd Int. Conf. Inf. Educat. Comput. Technol. Appl.*, 2025, pp. 1–6, IEEE.

11 Haocheng Guo, Yaqiong Zhang, Lieyang Chen, and Arfat Ahmad Khan, "Research on vehicle detection based on improved YOLOv8 network," 2024, *arXiv preprint arXiv:2501.00300*.

12 Xirui Tang, Zeyu Wang, Xiaowei Cai, Honghua Su, and Changsong Wei, "Research on heterogeneous computation resource allocation based on data-driven method," in *2024 6th Int. Conf. Data-Driven Optimiz. Complex Systems (DOCS)*, 2024, pp. 916–919, IEEE.

13 Chaoyi Tan, Wenqing Zhang, Zhen Qi, Kowei Shih, Xinshi Li, and Ao Xiang, "Generating multimodal images with GAN: Integrating text, image, and style," in *Proc. 2025 2nd Int. Conf. Comput. Multimed. Technol.*, 2025, pp. 16–21, Association for Computing Machinery (ACM).

14 K. Shih, Y. Han, and L. Tan, "Recommendation system in advertising and streaming media: Unsupervised data enhancement sequence suggestions," *Appl. Comput. Eng.*, vol. 145, no. 1, pp. 158–163, 2025.

15 B. Huang, Q. Lu, S. Huang, X.-S. Wang, and H. Yang, "Multi-modal clothing recommendation model based on large model and VAE enhancement," 2024, *arXiv [cs.IR]*.

16 M. Afif, Y. Said, and M. Atri, "Computer vision algorithms acceleration using graphic processors NVIDIA CUDA," *Clust. Comput.*, vol. 23, no. 4, pp. 3335–3347, 2020.

17 X. Shi, Y. Tao, and S.-C. Lin, "Deep neural network-based prediction of B-cell epitopes for SARS-CoV and SARS-CoV-2: Enhancing vaccine design through machine learning," 2024, *arXiv [cs.LG]*.

18 S. Kumari and C. Prabha, "A comprehensive review on anomaly detection in images: Challenges and future research directions," in *2023 IEEE North Karnataka Subsection Flagship Int. Conf. (NKCon)*, 2023, IEEE.

19 S. Kumari, C. Prabha, A. Karim, M. M. Hassan, and S. Azam, "A comprehensive investigation of anomaly detection methods in deep learning and machine learning: 2019–2023," *IET Inf. Secur.*, vol. 1, p. 2024, 2024.

20 K. Ishida, Y. Takena, Y. Nota, R. Mochizuki, I. Matsumura, and G. Ohashi, "SA-PatchCore: Anomaly detection in dataset with co-occurrence relationships using self-attention," *IEEE Access*, vol. 11, pp. 3232–3240, 2023.

14

Impact of Tiny Machine Learning on Embedded Systems for Advanced Image Processing

P. Priya[1], G. Lingeswaran[2], M. Prakash[3], G. Vijayakumari[3], Rajaram Venkatesan[4], and R. Saranya[5]

[1]Department of CSE, M.Kumarasamy College of Engineering, Karur, India
[2]Department of ECE, Velalar College of Engineering and Technology, Erode, India
[3]Department of ECE, Kangeyam Institute of Technology, Tiruppur, India
[4]Department of AI&DS, Kangeyam Institute of Technology, Tiruppur, India
[5]Department of EEE, Kangeyam Institute of Technology, Tiruppur, India

14.1 Introduction

Tiny Machine Learning (TinyML) is a new field that deals with the implementation of machine learning (ML) on embedded systems. In general, an embedded system is a resource-constrained device that exhibits limited processing power, memory, and power consumption. For a long period, these factors were obstacles in deploying sophisticated ML models on these devices. Only recently has there been any significant progress in compressing models and optimizing their performance to enable the efficient deployment of neural networks on microcontrollers (MCUs) and related ultra-low-power platforms. TinyML is a disruptive development for ML, allowing the deployment of intelligent algorithms on resource-constrained devices such as MCUs and embedded systems. Traditionally, ML models have needed significant computational resources, high-performance servers, or cloud-based infrastructure. The rapid growth of Internet of Things (IoT) technology and the increasing need to make decisions in real time at the edge of the network have emphasized the need for lean and energy-efficient ML solutions, as illustrated in Figure 14.1.

The primary driving force behind the development of TinyML technology is the potential for computation to be carried out close to the source of the data, thus lowering latency, improving data privacy, and allowing the functionality to be achieved in battery-powered devices. Real-time processing of data is a very essential requirement in various applications, especially in the IoT domain, such as

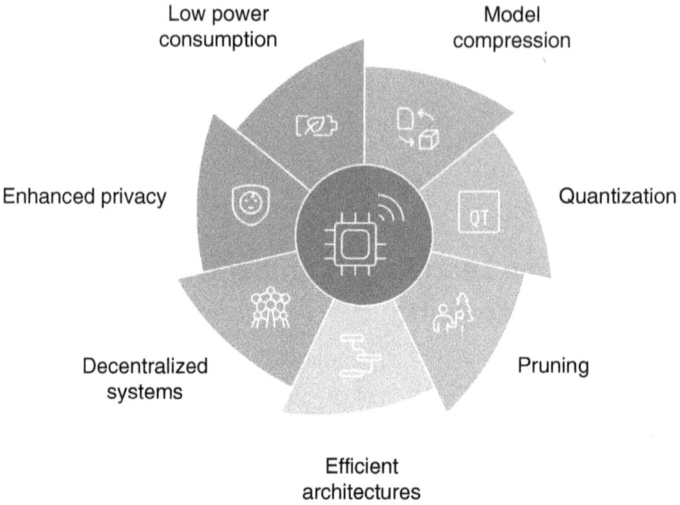

Figure 14.1 TinyML's impact on embedded systems.

healthcare, environmental sensing, industrial control, and intelligent surveillance. The implementations in these areas face several issues. Computation of data at the local level using TinyML overcomes most of these challenges and offers an environmentally friendly platform that can be used continuously with low-power consumption [1]. Notably, the combination of TinyML and image processing is particularly important for real-time visual inspection and decision-making at the low-power device level.

14.1.1 Importance of TinyML in Image Processing

Image processing is a critical task in a variety of applications, such as object detection, image classification, anomaly detection, and visual monitoring. Performing these tasks on embedded systems is a challenge in itself because of the limited computational capabilities. The usual approach to image processing in various applications is cloud-based image processing, which involves latency, high bandwidth requirements, and a variety of concerns related to data privacy. TinyML seeks to change this paradigm by performing image processing on the device itself, thus avoiding the need to continuously transmit data to the cloud. CNNs on MCUs introduce new optimization strategies that need to be implemented, which balance model complexity with power consumption [2]. For example, log-gradient input representation has proven useful in maintaining CNN accuracy while reducing quantization bit-width substantially, which in turn results in energy efficiency. Adaptive processing units like FP5A enable

CNN model execution with very negligible computational overhead and thus are suitable for battery-run IoT devices.

Image processing applications under TinyML are abundant and diverse. One use case in industrial automation involves vision-based sensors being implemented within automatic gauge reading systems running TinyML models to continuously verify visual data from machines to cut down reliance on human confirmation. Vision-based sensors allow monitoring of the environment and detect variations in an ecosystem with low energy over cost. Facial recognition and anomaly detection – on-device in intelligent surveillance – enhance data privacy by local computational knowledge of sensitive data.

14.1.2 Objectives and Scope

In this study, researchers developed a comprehensive research design that included experimental stimuli and used functional magnetic resonance imaging to measure the neural activity of participants while they were in normal wakefulness and under hypnosis. The focus of this chapter is to provide an in-depth review on the integration of TinyML and image processing on embedded systems. This chapter focuses on the basic ideas, technological advancements, and practical applications of TinyML in real-time image processing. It also reviews the methodologies like log-gradient input image optimization, which improves the performance of the convolutional neural network (CNN) in energy-restricted hardware, and adaptive processing elements like FP5A, which improve the performance of deep learning models without affecting energy efficiency. It also illustrates the difficulties related to TinyML deployment for image processing, which concern retaining the best performance with a reduction in power consumption, guaranteeing real-time processing, as well as reducing hardware limitations. The chapter discusses advanced solutions and emerging research trends in this domain, targeting both the practical knowledge and theoretical foundation for the design of appropriate TinyML-based image processing solutions in embedded systems.

The rest of the chapter is organized as follows. Section 14.2 presents an overview of the essential concepts related to TinyML, its characteristics, advantages, and challenges in relation to embedded image processing systems. Section 14.3 presents the architectural model of implementing the TinyML in embedded systems, including the different layers of the implementation from the acquisition of the sensor data to the final decision-making process. Section 4 discusses the different techniques of the TinyML that can be effectively utilized in the image processing systems. These techniques include CNNs, log-gradient input representation, quantization, and pruning techniques. Lastly, Section 14.5 discusses the applications of the image processing systems that utilize the TinyML technology in different fields of application. The final part of the chapter discusses the emerging trends in the field of TinyML and the prospective opportunities that can be achieved by incorporating the technology in the development of intelligent edge devices in the future.

14.1.3 Key Contributions

In this chapter, we provide a structured and comprehensive overview of TinyML in the context of image processing systems, particularly with respect to how ML systems are deployed in such systems. Unlike other survey papers, which focus primarily on ML algorithms, we provide a systems-oriented overview of TinyML by incorporating architectural design, lightweight neural networks, and optimization techniques for efficient ML systems in MCU environments. We also provide an overview of the layered architecture framework for efficient image processing systems using TinyML, efficient CNN architectures and feature representations such as log-gradient images, and key optimization techniques such as quantization, pruning, and adaptive processing elements for efficient image processing systems in MCU environments [3]. Additionally, we also provide some of the key applications of TinyML in image processing systems, as well as some of the key challenges in efficient ML systems in MCU environments.

14.2 Architecture Model for TinyML in Embedded Systems for Computer Vision

Although TinyML holds a lot of potential, it is not straightforward to execute image processing on TinyML on embedded devices. The big challenge is balancing the trade-off between model accuracy and resource efficiency. MCUs are equipment's while processing image based computationally expensive tasks, specifically in computer vision (CV) domain, are the ultimate source of burden due to their shortcomings in serving the extremely evaluated computational power and often quite limited by on-chip memory.

The major problems include efficient model optimization of wild CNNs on edge devices. This makes CNNs very powerful for tasks like image classification, object recognition, and face detection, but at the cost of being computationally expensive. Common frameworks used in converting and optimizing models to battle the challenge of large models like model quantization (lowering the number of bits used to represent weights and activations), model pruning (removal of less relevant network connections), and knowledge distillation (downstream transfer of knowledge from a more massive neural network to a smaller one).

A second challenge is data acquisition and preprocessing. TinyML devices do not have the processing capabilities to perform complicated image transformations or other data augmentation, as they are different from conventional systems. Therefore, preprocessing must be either very lightweight or embedded into the model itself, as demonstrated using log-gradient input images that preserve correctness during changing illumination while executing on lower computational loads [3, 4]. Additionally, real-time performance is crucial for many applications (e.g. surveillance or industrial monitoring). They may then experience latency issues, so they need to implement a low latency detector that provides computational architecture like MobileNet or Tiny-YOLO for constrained hardware.

14.2.1 Sensor Layer (Data Acquisition)

The sensor layer is the most important part of the TinyML model used in embedded systems, as it is the connection point where the raw data from the environment are collected. This layer consists of devices such as cameras, microphones, accelerometers, temperature sensors, and other devices that are connected to the IoT. These devices are designed to operate in low-power modes, and the data collected is usually precise enough for further processing. The data collected can include images from cameras, sound, temperature, motion, and other environmental variables. Cameras are used to take pictures, while motion sensors are used to detect events. The major problem associated with this layer is achieving low-power consumption while allowing for continuous data acquisition. For this reason, many sensors are in low-power mode or configured to record data only on an event trigger. Upon events-of-interest – for instance, movement or significant changes in environmental conditions – the feature of data collection is turned on. This further helps in prolonging battery life without compromising nonevent detection by the system. Also, there is the possibility of some simple filtering and noise suppression at the sensor level, being an initial preprocessing step to clean the data and prepare it for its subsequent processing. In summary, the components described earlier form the very basic building blocks necessary to efficiently process and manage the data each level needs for functionality.

14.2.2 Preprocessing Layer

This section considers the preprocessing layer of TinyML; this converts raw sensor data into formats that are usable by the model. Given the strict memory and compute budgets of these embedded devices, any such preprocessing should utilize minimum power and memory. The primary goals of preprocessing are noise reduction, removal of irrelevant information, and data quality improvement. In image processing alone, this could involve normalizing the intensities of pixels into the range [0, 1] or performing edge detection functions, such as Sobel filtering.

14.2.3 Model Layer (Inference Engine)

It contains both efficient models running well on small hardware, including CNNs for images, recurrent neural networks (RNNs) for time-series data, and decision trees for simple choices. MCUs represent very constrained platforms in terms of power and memory, so these models are optimized carefully. The pruning helps eliminate unnecessary connections, hence shrinking the model at no significant cost to accuracy. Adaptive compression helps shrink the size further while retaining real-time performance.

14.2.4 Execution Layer (Hardware Abstraction)

This layer is concerned with the mapping of the general ML model to the hardware and the management of hardware resources, which include the central processing unit (CPU), memory, and specialized processors such as digital signal processors (DSPs) and neural processing units (NPUs). For example, ARM Cortex-M MCUs often use CMSIS-NN libraries to improve the performance of neural networks on hardware. The execution layer is also responsible for the control of power consumption to increase battery life. The model is optimized for the hardware to run with low-power consumption. Efficient execution in this layer is critical for fast results, which is important in real-time applications like anomaly detection and environmental sensing.

14.2.5 Communication Layer (Edge-to-Cloud Connectivity)

It facilitates the transfer of data from the embedded system to other systems, such as cloud computing and other edge devices. The communication protocols that can be supported include MQTT, HTTP, Bluetooth, and LoRaWAN, depending on the best fit for the application. This layer offers relevant data to the cloud server for processing in case the data cannot be processed at the edge device level. The cloud can also provide potential upgrades or new configurations to the device. Data transfer efficiency helps in power saving when there are a few connections at a remote location. Data encryption helps in the prevention of leakage of sensitive data in the communication layer. Additionally, edge aggregation can be used, where data from several devices is transferred to a local gateway, which then sends the data to the cloud. This helps in conserving bandwidth.

14.2.6 Output and Decision-Making Layer

The last tier is the decision and output layer. It converts what the system detects into action or warnings. After the system has been able to interpret an input based on predefined rules or thresholds, it then determines an ensuing course of action. For example, a smart security system can automatically turn on the alarm when it detects a breach. In industrial automation, such a layer can produce a maintenance notification when equipment activity goes beyond the norm. This level of the system usually communicates with actuators, displays, or external devices. It also stores the result for future analysis. The key point is that this layer enables quick responses, which are essential for safety. Good control systems make people decide more effectively, reduce delays to a minimum, and still deliver accurate and reliable results.

14.3 TinyML Techniques for Image Processing

TinyML image processing techniques in embedded systems are designed to deploy small ML models on low-power devices. This is to perform real-time visual analysis where data is gathered. These techniques are of utmost significance in smart surveillance, industrial automation, healthcare monitoring, and environmental sensing. In all these uses, data privacy, rapid response, and continuous operation are of utmost significance. One of the fundamental methods is model quantization, where the accuracy of weights and activations (e.g. from 32-bit floating point to 8-bit integer) is lowered, reducing significantly memory usage and computational load without loss of accuracy. Pruning techniques reduce the model's performance by eliminating the redundant connections between the neurons in neural networks. It decreases the model size with no loss in performance. In image processing applications, CNNs are preferred, but their traditional implementations are computationally too expensive to be used in embedded systems. To assist in solving this, TinyML applies depthwise separable convolutions such as those from efficient networks like MobileNet that reduce parameters without reducing performance. Hardware acceleration techniques like the application of DSPs and NPUs also significantly enhance the efficiency of the processing, so computationally complex image processing procedures like facial detection and anomaly identification can be implemented on small, embedded devices. Such TinyML methods bridge the gaps of memory constraint, real-time processing needs, and power consumption and make advanced image processing possible to run by embedded systems without the need to rely on cloud infrastructure and thus make them viable for decentralized, smart IoT applications [5].

14.3.1 CNNs for Image Processing

CNNs provide the core architecture for modern image processing tasks because they can automatically learn spatial hierarchies of features. Unlike traditional ML paradigms, which are based on hand-designed feature extraction, CNNs can directly process raw pixel values and, as a result, detect meaningful patterns like

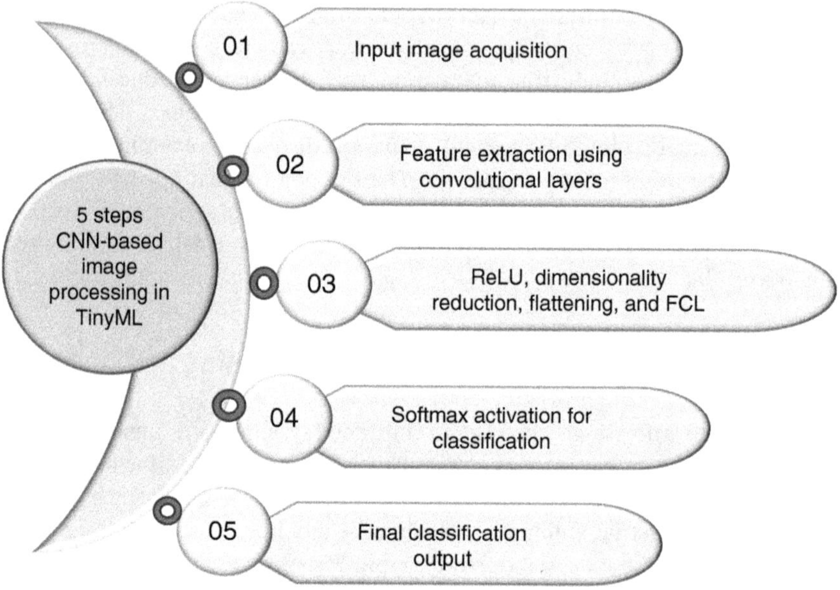

Figure 14.2 Steps involved in CNN-based image processing in TinyML.

edges, textures, and the structural components of objects. The basic building blocks of CNNs include convolutional layers, pooling layers, activation functions, and fully connected layers are shown in Figure 14.2. For uses of TinyML with computational as well as memory limitations, CNN architectures must be optimized. Deep CNNs like VGGNet or ResNet are computationally intensive to deploy in embedded devices, and therefore, lightweight models like MobileNet, SqueezeNet, and EfficientNet are suitable.

These models use techniques like depthwise separable convolutions to reduce the parameters and the computations without compromising accuracy. TinyML-based CNNs have extensive applications across the board from real-time object detection to face recognition, medical imaging, and smart surveillance. For example, CNNs deployed in edge devices can detect and classify objects in intelligent cameras to allow for automatic security surveillance without cloud processing. Edge TPU and AI accelerators also optimize CNN performance in embedded devices by relocating computation from the MCU. Quantized CNN models with weights kept in lower precision modes like INT8 rather than FP32 optimize power usage and improve inference rate, hence making CNNs a power-friendly tool for TinyML-centric image processing applications [6, 7].

$$Y(i,j) = \sum_{m=0}^{M-1}\sum_{n=0}^{N-1} X(i+m, j+n)\,K(m,n) \tag{14.1}$$

where

$Y(i, j)$ = Output feature map value at position (i,j)
$X(i+m, j+n)$ = Input image pixel at shifted position
$K(m, n)$ = Kernel (filter) weight at position (m,n)
M, N = Height and width of the convolutional kernel

14.3.1.1 Flowchart: CNN-Based Image Processing in TinyML

The CNN-based image processing pipeline in TinyML follows a structured sequence of steps from data acquisition to final classification. The following is the logical **flow of operations** in CNN-based image processing for embedded systems:

1) **Input Image Acquisition**
   - o Capture image from an embedded camera or IoT sensor.
   - o Preprocess the image (resize, normalize, grayscale conversion if needed).
2) **Feature Extraction Using Convolutional Layers**
   - o Apply multiple convolutional layers to detect edges, textures, and patterns.
   - o Use kernels (filters) to extract important features from the image.
3) **Nonlinearity Activation (ReLU)**
   - o Apply **Rectified Linear Unit (ReLU)** activation function to introduce nonlinearity and enhance model learning.
4) **Dimensionality Reduction via Pooling Layers**
   - o Apply **Max Pooling or Average Pooling** to reduce the size of feature maps and retain essential features.
5) **Flattening & Fully Connected Layers**
   - o Convert 2D feature maps into a 1D vector.
   - o Pass through fully connected layers to learn complex patterns.
6) **Softmax Activation for Classification**
   - o Apply the **Softmax function** to predict the probability of different classes (e.g. object categories).
7) **Model Optimization (Quantization & Pruning)**
   - o Optimize model weights using **quantization** (FP32 → INT8) to reduce size.
   - o **Prune unnecessary neurons** to improve efficiency on embedded devices.
8) **Final Output (Object Detection or Classification Result)**
   - o Output the final class label or bounding box (for object detection).
   - o Send results to the MCU or display unit for further processing.

14.3.2 Log-Gradient Input Images for Enhanced Efficiency

Log-gradient input image processing is a new technique that maximizes the efficiency of image analysis particularly suited for use in TinyML applications by prioritizing important features and removing redundant or less important information. Unlike raw pixel intensity, log-gradient transformation generates edges, contrast, and gradient changes in an image, thereby enabling ML models to assign significance to meaningful visual information while restricting the influence of spurious background information. This approach is particularly helpful in power- and memory-constrained environments because it allows for compression of input data before it is consumed by the model. Instead of looking at the full-resolution image, gradient changes and intensity changes in log scale are retained only. The advantages of this approach are:

Reduced Computational Complexity – Since the model operates on a smaller and narrower dataset, it requires fewer processing cycles.

Lighting Robustness – Log-gradient input renders models efficient even in changing lighting conditions, and hence, it is suitable for autonomous vehicles, smart surveillance, and biomedical imaging.

More Rapid Inference Times – The modified image requires less computation on the convolutional layers, with CNN-based TinyML applications subsequently being a lot more efficient.

$$G(x,y) = \log\left(1 + \left|\frac{dI(x,y)}{dx}\right| + \left|\frac{dI(x,y)}{dy}\right|\right) \tag{14.2}$$

where

$G(x, y)$ = Log-gradient value at pixel (x,y)

$I(x, y)$ = Input image intensity at (x,y)

$\frac{dI(x,y)}{dx}$ = Gradient in the x-direction

$\frac{dI(x,y)}{dy}$ = Gradient in the y-direction

log = Natural logarithm function

A practical example of this technique is the gesture recognition system used on low-power embedded platforms, processing only the gradients of the hand movement, rather than the entire image.

14.3.3 Quantization and Pruning Techniques

Quantization:

Quantization decreases model parameter precision (activations and weights) from high-precision floating point (FP32) to lower-bit representations, such as INT8 or even INT4. This achieves 4× or higher model size reduction and significantly reduces computational load.

Post-training Quantization

Applied to the model after training, quantizing the 32-bit floating-point values to reduced-bit representations.

Quantization-Aware Training

Quantization effects are maintained in consideration during training and thus accuracy loss during switching to lower-bit computation is reduced.

Quantization is especially useful in TinyML applications like real-time face detection, object tracking, and industrial automatic quality inspection.

Pruning:

Pruning is another form of optimization that removes redundant or comparatively less significant connections in a neural network, thus reducing the size of the model but maintaining it as precise as it was previously.

$$\text{Sparsity} = \frac{\text{Number of Pruned Parameters}}{\text{Total Parameters}} \times 100\% \tag{14.3}$$

Weight Pruning:

It eliminates weights from the network with less impact on the output.

Neuron pruning is the removal of whole neurons or channels that do not greatly affect the final decision-making process.

Regularized Pruning:

Removes specific convolutional filters or layers to decrease the network structure.

Pruned and quantized models are especially well suited for low-power IoT devices, mobile robots, and wearable sensors where computational and storage resources are extremely constrained.

14.3.4 Adaptive Processing Elements (e.g. FP5A) for Efficient Computation

Adaptive processing elements such as FP5A are critical to the optimization of computational efficiency for image processing tasks in TinyML systems. Hardware acceleration through such elements is performed with the goal of adapting processing resources based on the input data complexity, thus optimizing for energy efficiency and computational resource utilization.

Adaptive Processing Works

1) **Dynamic Precision Adjustment:** FP5A types of architectures vary on the precision of computation based on the relative importance of different segments of an image. For example, high-detail areas (like edges in a face recognition application) use higher precision, while background areas use lower precision, thus reducing computational load.
2) **Parallel and Asynchronous Processing:** In contrast to most MCUs that perform operations serially, APEs perform parallel computations, with a massive latency reduction.

14.4 Image Processing Applications of TinyML

14.4.1 Real-Time Image Classification on MCUs

Image classification is, of course, one of the most common applications of TinyML to small devices. The goal here is the sorting of visual data from cameras or sensors. TinyML is capable of real-time image classification using small CNNs on MCUs, such as the ESP32 or ARM Cortex-M series, without any cloud interactions. Applications requiring fast decisions – such as quality control of products, animal monitoring in the wild, or gesture recognition in wearables – rely heavily on image classification. The greatest challenge is to run complex neural network tasks on resource-constrained devices. This challenge is pursued by techniques such as model quantization and pruning and using depthwise separable convolutions, such as in MobileNet. Additionally, techniques like log-gradient input images enhance the performance of the model when illumination conditions change, hence improving the consistency of classification.

14.4.2 Vision-Based Environmental Monitoring

TinyML has become very important in environmental monitoring to enable vision-based field analysis of data on embedded platforms. These applications involve the cameras capturing photographs or videos of the natural conditions in an area and executing TinyML models to detect changes or deviations, such as those in plant health, indicators of pollution, or animal activity. A very important example of this is the use of TinyML for vegetation health based on color and leaf morphology analyses that can indicate drought stress or disease. The efficiency of such monitoring naturally depends on battery life and data processing speed, particularly when the location is isolated or inaccessible. By shrinking model sizes through techniques like quantization and pruning, TinyML enables such monitoring tasks under limited battery life with reduced power consumption [8].

14.4.3 Smart Surveillance Systems with On-Device Facial Recognition

TinyML enables face and anomaly detection in real time directly on edge devices within the domain of intelligent surveillance. Traditional architectures for surveillance send video streams to a central server where processing is performed, which becomes bandwidth-intensive and prone to latency. In contrast, TinyML supports local processing through the execution of CNN-based face detection models on MCUs themselves. So, it guarantees data privacy because facial data would not need to be sent to the cloud, thus protecting privacy-sensitive information. Systems generally make use of lightweight CNN architectures, such as MobileNet or SqueezeNet, optimized for low-power hardware. For example, ESP32-CAM modules integrated with TinyML models can verify whether personnel are authorized or to detect intruders and thus easily alert when suspicious activity is identified. In this configuration, the most valuable advantage is the minimum response time allowed by on-device processing, which removes cloud latency. Additionally, energy efficiency by TinyML allows for the continued running of surveillance devices without interruption, making this well suited for security applications in residential, commercial, and industrial areas.

14.4.4 Case Study: Image Regression on ESP32

One of the applications of TinyML in real-world embedded systems is the application of image regression models to MCUs such as the ESP32, enabling real-time data processing. Image regression is the estimation of a continuous variable from visual input, such as measurements of object distance or temperature inferred from thermal imagery. One of the case studies demonstrated how CNNs can be employed to estimate temperature from factory images. Thermal images were taken using a low-resolution ESP32 camera, and the images were analyzed using a basic CNN model that was trained to estimate temperature change. Log-gradient input images increased the model's resilience to varying lighting conditions, and quantization techniques reduced the model size to facilitate efficient processing on the MCU.

The largest challenge was to trade-off inference speed and accuracy, and this was addressed by model design optimization and computation reduction. Hence, the system enabled low latency accurate temperature monitoring, demonstrating the capability of TinyML to enable complex image-based forecasting on low-cost and low-power hardware.

TinyML has revolutionized the application of embedded systems to image processing by bringing real-time intelligence to the edge. Applications of TinyML that are built to provide real-time classification, auto gauge reading, environmental monitoring, and smart surveillance, among others have been proven feasible as well as reliable alternatives with enhanced data processing and model deployment efficiency. The capability of executing such complex image processing operations locally independent of any cloud servers reduces latency and improves both data privacy as well as power efficiency [9].

14.5 Optimization Strategies for Image Processing on TinyML

14.5.1 Reducing Computational Load and Power Consumption

Quantization of the model is a popular approach to reduce computational complexity, which involves decreasing the precision of weights and activations from

32-bit floating-point to 8-bit integers. The effect of this approach is the reduction of memory and computational requirements, making it easier to deploy models on MCUs. Pruning is another major approach, which involves the removal of weights or neurons that have less influence on the output of the model. The removal of less important connections results in a compact and fast model with a slight loss of accuracy [10]. Depthwise separable convolutions are especially useful in CNN-based image processing applications, which involve the splitting of convolution operations into pointwise and depthwise operations, resulting in a drastic reduction in multiplications. By employing specialized libraries such as CMSIS-NN, operations on ARM Cortex-M processors are optimized for better performance while maintaining power consumption at the lowest level possible.

$$E_{\text{total}} = N_{\text{MAC}} . E_{\text{MAC}} + E_{\text{memory}} \tag{14.4}$$

where

E_{total} = Total energy consumed by the model
N_{MAC} = Number of multiply accumulate (MAC) operations
E_{MAC} = Energy consumed per MAC operation
E_{memory} = Total energy consumed for memory access

Object identification in real time on low-power IoT devices can achieve its requirements without sacrificing energy efficiency or performance, by leveraging several techniques including quantization, pruning, depthwise convolution, and hardware acceleration with onboard circuitry.

14.5.2 Enhancing Real-Time Processing Capabilities

Real-time image processing is part of applications that require fast responses to visual input, such as monitoring and anomaly detection. Real-time processing on TinyML hardware can be achieved only by deploying several optimization strategies together. A very popular strategy is model compression, the goal of which is to eliminate unimportant neurons and layers from the network with minimum degradation in accuracy, and it comes with extra benefits in terms of speed of inference and memory utilization. Knowledge distillation involves a large, complex teacher model transferring information to a much smaller student model; the latter learns to mimic the output generated by its teacher yet remaining compact enough for real-time deployment. Architecture models based on parallel processing allow multicore MCUs to perform data acquisition and model inference in parallel, even further enhancing real-time performance. All these different techniques combined achieve fast, low-power image processing that can support edge deployments.

14.5.3 Balancing Accuracy and Efficiency

One of the most serious challenges that exist in image processing, but particularly regarding TinyML, is that of obtaining an acceptable trade-off between precision of models and optimal utilization of computational capabilities. It is possible to obtain high precision without maintaining devices' capabilities utilized at a low level through models such as dynamic model selection. With this technique, the system could switch models of varying complexity depending on the number of resources present or the necessity of the operation. For instance, at low power, one can utilize a less complex model and a higher complexity and accurate model when the resources are available. One of the strongest methods used is adaptive quantization, in which the accuracy of model weights is adjusted according to the complexity of the input data. For instance, high-contrast images can tolerate higher quantization without loss of accuracy [11].

14.5.4 Implementing Efficient Data Handling and Memory Management

Data pipelining is obtained through the creation of a continuous processing cycle wherein data acquisition, preprocessing, and inference are processed in parallel without the creation of bottlenecks. Using dense data representations such as Flat Buffers over compressed data saves memory space and speeds up data serialization. Adequate memory allocation techniques such as dynamic memory allocation and fixed-size memory pools avoid fragmentation and allow the model to use resources efficiently. These data processing and memory management techniques become even more critical while handling high-resolution images, where inefficiencies as small as a fraction of a percent can result in drastic slow-down or power consumption.

14.6 Challenges and Future Directions

14.6.1 Challenges in TinyML-Based Image Processing

TinyML has introduced new methods of applying ML models on extremely low-power embedded devices, but applying it to image processing has certain drawbacks. The drawbacks arise from hardware constraints, model optimization, real-time processing of data, conserving energy, and security issues. Here are several points of view the TinyML faces while implementing in picture preparing applications as shown in Figure 14.3.

14.6.1.1 Hardware Limitations and Computational Constraints

TinyML models run on memory-, compute-, and power-constrained MCUs and edge devices. Unlike their cloud AI counterparts that run on GPUs and TPUs,

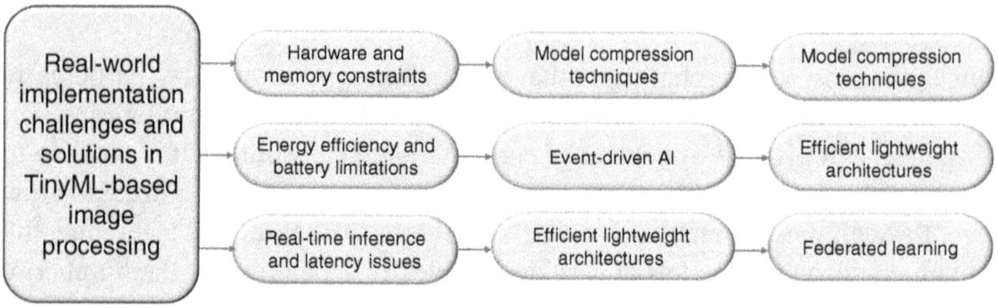

Figure 14.3 Challenges in TinyML-based image processing.

embedded devices process with a few megabytes of RAM and lightweight processors.Training deep learning models such as CNNs and Transformers consume lots of processing and memory. It is difficult to accomplish complex image processing for TinyML hardware [12, 13].

Recommended Solution: Leverage miniature model sizes (e.g. MobileNet and EfficientNet) and hardware acceleration techniques (e.g. Edge TPU and ARM Cortex-M processors).

14.6.1.2 Model Compression Trade-Offs

To deploy large AI models onto TinyML hardware, we use methods like knowledge distillation, pruning, and quantization. Such methods can lead to decreased accuracy, deteriorated feature extraction, and higher errors in results.

Challenge: There is usually a trade-off for model size vs. model accuracy, especially working with high-resolution images.

Potential Solution: Adaptive quantization methods, mixed-precision, and hybrid models with trade-offs between performance and efficiency.

14.6.1.3 Energy Efficiency and Power Consumption

TinyML applications find their typical use in battery-operated IoT devices, wearables, and security cameras, where power efficiency is critical. Continuous image processing depletes the battery life, restricting the use of vision-based applications in real time [14].

Challenge: Ongoing operation of a CNN model on an embedded platform results in overheating and rapid battery depletion.

Potential Solution: Employ edge-triggered or event-driven AI, such that image processing occurs only when certain conditions are satisfied (e.g. motion detection prior to image classification).

14.6.1.4 Real-Time Processing and Latency Issues

The majority of TinyML applications, such as autonomous vehicles, security surveillance, and factory automation, require real-time decision-making. But executing AI models on low-power MCUs results in latency, and real-time processing is therefore challenging.

Challenge: TinyML is not fast enough to handle real-time processing for time-critical image classification applications.

Potential Solution: Using dedicated co-processors (e.g. Edge TPUs, NPUs) and asynchronous computation methodologies to reduce latency.

14.6.1.5 Data Privacy and Security Concerns

TinyML enables on-device inference, which reduces confidentiality with a lower amount of cloud data transfers. The threat of security vulnerabilities, including adversarial attacks, model tampering, and side-channel attacks, still exists.

Challenge: The challenge here is that TinyML models can be reverse-engineered or even cracked, raising the security concerns.

Potential Solution: Edge lightweight encryption, hardware security extensions, and federated learning-based edge secure AI inference.

14.6.2 Limitations of Current TinyML Approaches

Despite the wide possibilities offered by TinyML in providing intelligent capabilities to constrained resources, there are some limitations to be addressed in the real-world deployment scenario. One of the issues is the accuracy, energy consumption, and memory usage trade-off, where deep neural networks that provide high accuracy are associated with high memory requirements and computational resources, which is not possible for MCUs and other low-power devices. Even though different optimization techniques are available to reduce memory consumption and energy requirements of deep neural networks, it may also impact the accuracy and number of features that can be learned from the data. Another challenge that is posed is the scalability and deployment issues, as the deployment and management of TinyML models across many distributed IoT devices can be challenging due to issues such as device heterogeneity and the management and maintenance of the system. In the real-world deployment scenario, some issues that can be posed include the lack of training capabilities, latency constraints, unreliable network connectivity, and hardware incompatibility, which can affect the performance of the system in dynamic environments. In addition, security and robustness issues can be posed, as embedded devices can be prone to security attacks such as model extraction, adversarial attacks, and data tampering.

14.6.3 Future Directions in TinyML-Based Image Processing

To address such challenges, recent research directions/future perspectives to improve TinyML-based image processing have concentrated on innovative strategies. Some promising directions are shown in Figure 14.4.

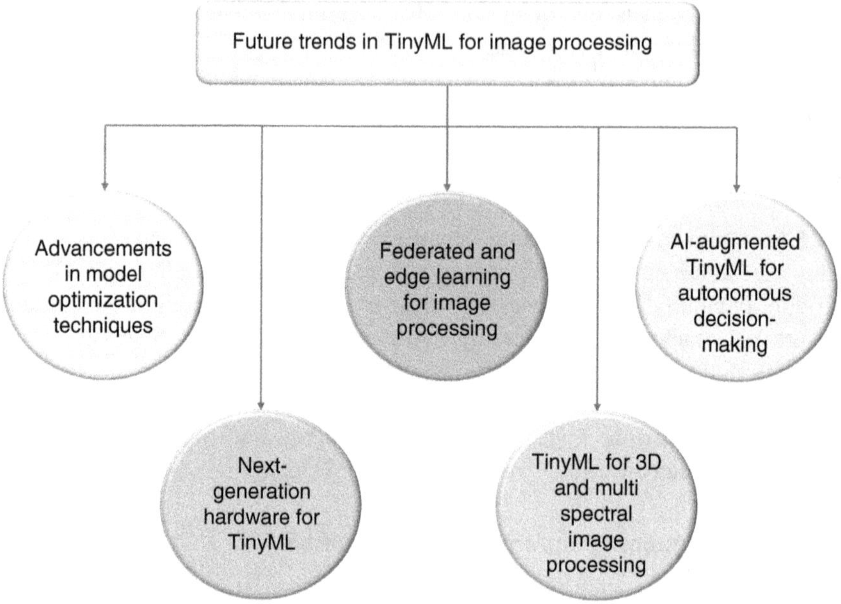

Figure 14.4 Future trends in TinyML for image processing.

14.6.3.1 Advancements in Model Optimization Techniques

Dynamic Model Compression: Scientists experiment on dynamic pruning and quantization for when the lapse of a model varies based upon resources that can be allocated during computing.

Sparse CNN Architectures: Instead of using dense CNN models, sparsity-based networks reduce computations while maintaining accuracy.

Hybrid Models for TinyML: Joining forces between deep learning and classical CV techniques will result in enanced performance optimized for constrained hardware.

14.6.3.2 Next-Generation Hardware for TinyML

TinyML hardware is evolving with innovations in dedicated AI silicon, neuromorphic processing, and low-power accelerators [15, 16]. Those developments include the following:

- RISC-V-based TinyML processors that are optimized for embedded AI workloads.
- NPUs designed for accelerating edge AI computations.
- Energy-efficient memory technologies (e.g. ReRAM, MRAM) to reduce power consumption.

14.6.3.3 Federated and Edge Learning for Image Processing

Instead of sending raw images to the cloud, federated learning enables AI models to train on-device, ensuring data privacy. Future advancements include:

Edge-to-Edge AI Training: Devices communicate with each other to learn collaboratively.

14.6.3.4 TinyML for 3D and Multispectral Image Processing

The present and future research trends are shifting from the classification of 2D images to the development of capabilities that can be used for the analysis of 3D images, LiDAR images, and hyperspectral images.

14.6.3.5 AI-Powered Autonomous Decision-Making with TinyML

The upcoming TinyML technologies are expected to be combined with reinforcement learning and self-tuning AI models to provide autonomous decision-making capabilities for intelligent robots, autonomous drones, and intelligent traffic control systems [17]. TinyML is increasingly being used for low-power on-device AI applications in different industries for real-world image processing tasks in the healthcare, security, agriculture, and automation industries. Despite the challenges posed by hardware limitations, latency, and security issues, the current advancements in model optimization, hardware, federated learning, and adaptive AI are expected to make the development of high-performance TinyML systems easier in the short term. Thus, TinyML is expected to unlock new avenues for ultra-low-power embedded intelligence, thereby redefining AI vision applications for the next decade.

14.7 Conclusion

TinyML has recently come into its own as a revolutionary paradigm for the realization of intelligent image processing at the edge on low-power embedded systems. By extending ML to edge devices, TinyML tackles fundamental issues related to latency, data privacy, and energy efficiency. This paper focuses on the complementarity between TinyML and the latest advances in image processing based on lean architectures such as CNNs, optimization methods such as quantization and pruning, and hardware–software co-design. Real-time image classification, intelligent surveillance, and environmental monitoring are just a few examples of the applicability of TinyML to various application domains. The current state of the art is challenged by computational constraints, energy efficiency, and the trade-off between accuracy and efficiency.

References

1 P. P. Ray, "A review on TinyML: State-of-the-art and prospects," *J. King Saud Univ.-Comput. Inf. Sci.*, vol. 34, no. 4, pp. 1595–1623, 2022.

2 J. Paul, L. Schmid, M. Klaiber, and M. Rössle, "Extraction of measurement device information on an ESP32 microcontroller: TinyML for image processing," *Procedia Comput. Sci.*, vol. 246, pp. 2002–2011, 2024.

3 Lu, Qianyun and Boris Murmann, "Improving the energy efficiency and robustness of TinyML computer vision using log-gradient input images," 2022, *arXiv preprint arXiv:2203.02571.*

4 Haoyu Ren, Darko Anicic, and Thomas A. Runkler, "TinyReptile: TinyML with federated meta-learning," in *2023 Int. Joint Conf. Neural Netw. (IJCNN)*, 2023, pp. 1–9, IEEE.

5 Lutfi Eren Erdogan, *et al.* "TinyAgent: Function calling at the edge," 2024, *arXiv e-prints*: arXiv-2409.

6 Y. Abadade, A. Temouden, H. Bamoumen, N. Benamar, Y. Chtouki, and A. S. Hafid, "A comprehensive survey on TinyML," *IEEE Access*, vol. 11, pp. 96892–96922, 2023.

7 L. Capogrosso, F. Cunico, D. S. Cheng, F. Fummi, and M. Cristani, "A machine learning-oriented survey on tiny machine learning," *IEEE Access*, vol. 12, pp. 23406–23426, 2024.

8 Minh Tri Lê, Pierre Wolinski, and Julyan Arbel, "Efficient neural networks for tiny machine learning: A comprehensive review," 2023, *arXiv preprint arXiv:2311.11883.*

9 A. Elhanashi, P. Dini, S. Saponara, and Q. Zheng, "Advancements in TinyML: Applications, limitations, and impact on IoT devices," *Electronics*, vol. 13, no. 17, p. 3562, 2024.

10 R. Kallimani, K. Pai, P. Raghuwanshi, S. Iyer, and O. L. A. López, "TinyML: Tools, applications, challenges, and future research directions," *Multimed. Tools Appl.*, vol. 83, no. 10, pp. 29015–29045, 2024.

11 N. N. Alajlan and D. M. Ibrahim, "TinyML: Enabling of inference deep learning models on ultra-low-power IoT edge devices for AI applications," *Micromachines*, vol. 13, no. 6, p. 851, 2022.

12 Riya Samanta, Bidyut Saha, Soumya K. Ghosh, and Ram Babu Roy, "Optimizing TinyML: The impact of reduced data acquisition rates for time series classification on microcontrollers," 2024, *arXiv preprint arXiv:2409.10942.*

13 V. Kumar, G. Vijayakumari, M. Prakash, T. Velmurugan, and C. Alakesan, "Optimized brain tumor classification using artificial BEE colony-enhanced convolutional neural networks," in *2025 10th Int. Conf. Commun. Electr. Syst. (ICCES)*, Oct. 2025, pp. 1808–1814, IEEE.

14 E. Kim, J. Kim, J. Park, H. Ko, and Y. Kyung, "TinyML-based classification in an ECG monitoring embedded system," *Comput. Mater. Continua*, vol. 75, no. 1, pp. 1751–1764, 2023.

15 F. Dehrouyeh, L. Yang, F. B. Ajaei, and A. Shami, "On TinyML and cyber-security: Electric vehicle charging infrastructure use case," *IEEE Access*, 2024.

16 G. Vijayakumari, V. Kumar, M. Prakash, D. Baskaran, S. Jayabratha, and G. Lingeswaran, "Lung tumor classification in medical imaging using HHO-enhanced convolutional neural networks," in *2025 4th Int. Conf. Innov. Mech. Ind. Appl. (ICIMIA)*, Sep. 2025, pp. 1901–1908, IEEE.

17 F. Oliveira, D. G. Costa, F. Assis, and I. Silva, "Internet of Intelligent Things: A convergence of embedded systems, edge computing and machine learning," *Internet Things*, vol. 26, p. 101153, 2024.

15

TinyML-Based Audio and Speech Signal Processing

Tina Babu[1], Rekha R Nair[1], and Balamurugan Balusamy[2]

[1] *Department of Computer Science and Engineering, Alliance School of Advanced Computing, Alliance University, Bengaluru, India*
[2] *School of Engineering and IT, Manipal Academy of Higher Education, Dubai, UAE*

15.1 Introduction to Audio Processing on Edge Devices

Audio processing has been implemented by cloud environment known to exist because of the computational demands of complex algorithms. Audio processing is now available on edge devices with extremely small resources due to the emergence of Tiny Machine Learning (TinyML). The shifting paradigm has numerous advantages, but the technical issues that accompany its implementation require particular solutions with the help of particular approaches [1]. This evolution is actually a manner of transforming our thinking in regard to audio application, taking this feature off the cloud, and placing it at the edge [2]. Edge computing brings the computation nearer to the data source and eliminates the need to have permanent access to the internet, thereby making it redundant in many instances of small machine learning (ML) applications and models to implement in the real-time settings and scenarios like smart meters and smart refrigerators [3]. The most significant characteristics, which differ cloud audio processing and edge-based audio processing, are illustrated in Table 15.1. Edge-based audio processing is particularly valuable for applications requiring immediate responses such as wake-word detection, where latency directly impacts user experience [4, 5].

Typical microcontroller (MCU) units that are implemented in practical edge devices operate in much harsher environments than cloud infrastructures [6]. As shown in Figure 15.1, this is a common resource constraint when using MCUs in audio TinyML applications. Such resource constraints impose direct restrictions on audio processing. For instance, let us consider a standard audio sample with a sampling frequency of 16 kHz and a bit rate of 16 bits.

Table 15.2 summarizes the MFCC feature extraction steps along with their computational complexity and memory requirements.

Table 15.1 Comparison of cloud vs. edge audio processing.

Parameter	Cloud Processing	Edge Processing
Latency (ms)	100–1,000	10–100
Privacy	Data transmitted to remote servers	Data remains on device
Connectivity	Requires internet connection	Functions offline

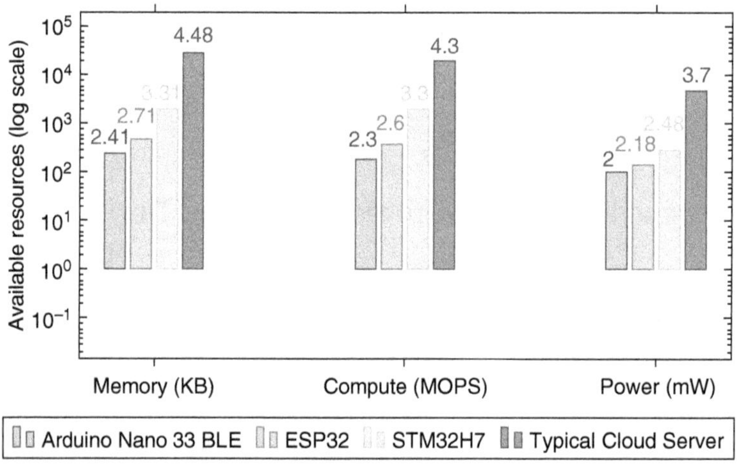

Figure 15.1 Resource constraints in typical audio TinyML devices compared to cloud computing resources. Note the logarithmic scale highlighting the orders-of-magnitude difference in available resources.

Table 15.2 MFCC feature extraction steps: computational complexity and memory requirements.

Step	Operation	Computational Complexity	Memory Requirements
1	Frame the signal	O(N)	O(M)
2	Apply window function	O(M)	O(M)
3	Compute FFT	O(M log M)	O(M)
4	Apply Mel filter bank	O(M · B)	O(B)
5	Take logarithm	O(B)	O(B)
6	Apply DCT	O(B · C)	O(C)

It will take: memory rate = 16,000 * 2 = 32 KB/s. With only 256 KB of SRAM available, the system can store eight seconds of audio data. It needs efficient feature extraction and streaming architectures. Time of processing is another important constraint. If we refer to the time required to process an audio frame as T_n and the length of the audio frame as T^{ϕ}, then real-time processing will require $T_n > T^{\phi}$. This results in buffer overflows and data losses [7].

Despite these challenges, on-device audio processing offers several compelling advantages:

1) **Privacy Preservation:** The fact that such sensitive data is locally processed significantly improves user privacy. It is impossible to eavesdrop on the process and steal sensitive data. This is extremely important in the context of using voice assistants whose operation involves capturing audio data [8], [9].
2) **Reduced Latency:** Latency problems could occur, and the overall latency of the system can be represented as

$$T_{\{total\}} = T_{\{capture\}} + T_{\{proc\}} + T_{\{comm\}} + T_{\{resp\}} \tag{15.1}$$

Edge computing basically eliminates T_{comm}, which, depending on the network conditions, may constitute hundreds of milliseconds [10]. It is crucial to consider this aspect for interactive services because latency negatively impacts the quality of the user experience.
3) **Enhanced Reliability:** Processing on the device will ensure that the process will function even without the need to access the internet. The measure of reliability is given by the system availability, and this can be measured through Pavailability = P(device working) × P(network available). Edge processing eliminates the need to consider P(network available), improving reliability significantly.
4) **Energy Efficiency:** Wireless transfer of information generally consumes more energy than computations performed locally to perform audio operations. The energy ratio is, therefore, defined as follows: $\eta = E_{transmission}/E_{computation}$. In case of audio systems, $\eta > 10$, and this is why local computations are preferred [11].

In this chapter, the author elaborates on the design and the implementation of TinyML methods of audio and speech processing on edge devices with resource constraints. In contrast to the conventional methods of speech processing, which are based on the idea of cloud-based computation, TinyML allows to perform inference in real time and directly on MCUs with limited computing capabilities.

The key contributions of this chapter include:

- Overview of the TinyML audio processing pipeline.
- Analysis of lightweight neural architectures suitable for speech processing.
- Discussion of model optimization techniques such as quantization and pruning.
- Insights into deploying audio inference systems on MCU-based devices.

The rest of the chapter is structured as follows. Section 15.2 discusses methods of audio feature extraction used in TinyML systems. Section 15.3 discusses neural network designs for audio tasks. Section 15.4 gives model optimization plans. Section 15.5 demonstrates the real-life uses of TinyML in audio. Lastly, future research directions and problems are addressed.

Although some of the surveys address speech processing and ML algorithms, the chapter is concerned specifically with the opportunities and challenges related to the deployment of audio intelligence on edge devices with extremely limited resources.

The main contributions of this chapter are as follows. The presentation of a unified theory behind the feature extraction algorithms and the neural network architecture that has been adapted to MCUs for TinyML applications. Trade-off analysis of the interrelationships among the accuracy, memory, computation complexity, and power efficiency of embedding the ML inference process within an embedded audio system. A comparative look at the popular architectures used, including convolutional neural networks (CNNs), recurrent neural networks (RNNs), and transformers.

TinyML Audio Processing Pipeline: A typical TinyML audio processing pipeline consists of several stages optimized for resource efficiency:

- **Audio Acquisition:** Capturing raw audio through a microphone with appropriate sampling frequency
- **Preprocessing:** Filtering, normalization, and noise reduction
- **Feature Extraction:** Transformation of raw audio into compact, information-rich representations
- **Inference:** Running optimized neural networks on the extracted features
- **Postprocessing:** Applying decision logic to inference outputs

Each stage should be meticulously crafted to function under the limitations of the device and still deliver acceptable performance levels.

Key Performance Metrics: When designing TinyML audio systems, several key metrics must be balanced:

- **Accuracy:** Measured using task-specific metrics such as classification accuracy, F1-score, or word error rate (WER)
- **Latency:** End-to-end processing time from audio capture to result
- **Memory Usage:** Peak memory consumption during processing
- **Energy Efficiency:** Battery life impact, often measured in μJ per inference
- **Throughput:** Number of inferences possible per second

The objectives do frequently stand in contradiction with one another; the performance of one is oftentimes detrimental to the performance of the other. The optimization of various TinyML audio implementations requires a canny equilibrium of these parameters, biased toward the specification requirements of the specific applications [12].

15.2 Audio Feature Extraction for Resource-Constrained Devices

The TinyML model cannot be represented in small sizes that are rich in data and can be processed using the neural network algorithm, audio feature extraction, which is the critical stage in the entire process. This attribute could prove highly useful in implementing the requirements with regard to the inference under constraints with respect to memory and computation demands.

15.2.1 Time-Domain vs. Frequency-Domain Features

Raw audio data in time domain give a direct measure of amplitude change over time which is frequently too high dimensional to be processed on MCUs efficiently. Transforming these signals to the frequency domain by means of transforms such as Fast Fourier Transform (FFT) produce more compact and meaningful representations as exhibited in Figure 15.2. Specialized libraries like the CMSIS-DSP have high performance FFT functions on ARM Cortex-M processors to allow real-time spectral processing with minimal computational overhead and memory consumption.

Time-domain representations maintain the raw signal information, but since they are very dimensional, their use is not feasible in MCUs. Therefore, frequency-domain transformations are the basis of most TinyML audio pipelines, which allows providing a more compact and discriminative representation.

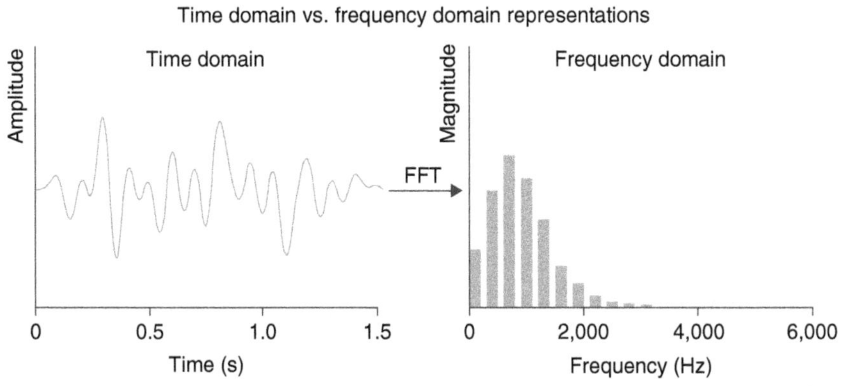

Figure 15.2 Time- vs. frequency-domain representations of audio signals.

15.2.2 Mel-Frequency Cepstral Coefficients

Mel-frequency cepstral coefficients (MFCCs) are popular speech and audio recognition characteristics since they encode the spectral content of audio signals into a sparse form that is similar to human acoustic perception. They have the best applications in ML models that apply to speech recognition and sound classification. MFCC features are popular in TinyML applications, as they offer informative audio features and have relatively low computational complexity. Optimized embedded libraries can be used to create efficient MFCC extraction pipelines, for which feature extraction may be performed on MCU-based edge devices.

Where N is the length of the input signal, M is the frame length (number of samples per frame), B is the number of Mel filter banks used in the filter bank, and C is the number of cepstral coefficients retained after applying the discrete cosine transform (DCT). These stages of processing comprise the heart of the audio feature extraction pipeline of numerous speech and sound recognition TinyML-based systems.

MFCC features can be used to classify audio signals with precision by converting the raw audio signals into smaller spectral representations. In the case of TinyML, the optimization of the standard MFCC extraction algorithm may be carried out by:

- Reducing the number of Mel filters (typically from 26–40 to 8–20)
- Computing fewer coefficients (often 8–13 instead of 13–20)
- Using fixed-point arithmetic instead of floating-point
- Precomputing the Mel filterbank and Discrete Cosine Transform (DCT) matrices

These optimizations are able to cut 60–80% of the memory usage with little effect on recognition accuracy. In the context of frequency-domain representations, MFCCs offer a set of perceptually inspired features, providing a fair trade-off between recognition and computational complexity.

15.2.3 Log-Mel Spectrograms and Filterbank Energies

Log-Mel filterbank energies are a less complex form of MFCCs that do not include the DCT stage. This representation retains the frequency information of perceptual relevance, and fewer calculations are done. The mathematical expression of the Log-Mel filterbank energies is

$$S[m] = \log\left([\![sum_{(k=0)}]\!]^{([\![N/2]\!]^2)} [\![|X[k]|]\!]^2 \cdot w_{(m[k])} \right) \tag{15.2}$$

where *X[k]* represents the fast Fourier transform (FFT) of the input signal frame at frequency bin k, $H_m[k]$ denotes the response of the m-th Mel filter at frequency bin k, and M is the total number of Mel filters in the filter bank. Table 15.3 compares

Table 15.3 Resource requirements for audio feature extraction (16 kHz, 30 ms frames).

Feature Type	Computation Time (ms)	RAM Usage (KB)	Flash Usage (KB)	Accuracy (%)
Raw Waveform	0.1	30.0	1.0	76.5
Log-Mel (20 filters)	3.1	2.8	8.4	91.8
MFCCs (13 coefficients)	3.8	1.6	9.2	92.7

the resource requirements and performance of different audio features on a typical Cortex-M4F MCU running at 80 MHz with 256 KB of RAM.

15.2.4 Lightweight Feature Extraction

For extremely constrained devices, even simpler features may be necessary. Zero-crossing rate (ZCR), energy, and spectral centroid (SC) provide lightweight alternatives that can be computed with minimal resources:

$$\mathrm{ZCR} = \frac{1}{2(N-1)} \sum_{(n=1)} [\![N-1]\!] \mid sgn(x[n]) - sgn(x[n-1]) \mid \tag{15.3}$$

$$SC = \frac{\sum_{([\![k=0]\!]^{(N/2)})} |Z[k]|k}{\sum_{([\![k=0]\!]^{(N/2)})} |Z[k]|} \tag{15.4}$$

Recent work by Zhang *et al.* has shown that combining these lightweight features with simple neural architectures can achieve 83–87% accuracy on keyword spotting tasks while requiring less than 1 KB of RAM for feature extraction.

15.3 Neural Network Architectures for Audio TinyML

This section discusses optimized neural network architectures specifically designed to process audio in TinyML settings, where memory and computational resources are extremely limited. The summary of different architectures of TinyML is presented in Table 15.4.

15.3.1 Efficient and Compact Neural Architectures for Audio TinyML

Audio TinyML neural network designs should find the balance between expressiveness and an extremely resource-efficient design. Small convolutional models like depthwise separable CNNs are much smaller in terms of the number of parameters, and they maintain a high level of classification performance [13].

Table 15.4 Comparison of audio TinyML architectures.

Architecture	Parameters (K)	Accuracy (%)	Latency (ms)	Memory Usage (KB)
DS-CNN	24	94.5	15	42
TC-ResNet	66	96.2	23	135
MicroNet	18	92.7	12	38
LSTM-FC	38	93.8	28	82

Lightweight recurrent models and temporal convolutional networks also make the sequential modeling of audio patterns easier. These architectures are typically run together with optimized feature representations with MFCCs to provide real-time MCU inference.

The foundation of audio TinyML is efficient feature extraction. MFCCs remain popular due to their compact representation:

$$\mathrm{MFCC}_i = \sum_{([\![k=0]\!]^k)} log(S_k) \cdot cos\left(\frac{i(k-1/2)\pi}{K}\right) \tag{15.5}$$

where S_k represents the energy in the k-th mel filter bank. DSC-CNN (Depthwise Separable Convolutional Neural Networks) significantly reduce parameters while maintaining accuracy:

$$\mathrm{DS(X) = PW - Conv(DW - Conv(X))} \tag{15.6}$$

Temporal convolutional networks provide efficient sequential processing:

$$h_t = \sigma(W_d * [h_{(dt-d)}, \cdots, h_{(tt-1)}] + b) \tag{15.7}$$

The weights are mapped to low-bit representations through quantization:

$$w_q = \mathrm{round}\left(\frac{w_f - w_{(min)}}{w_{(max)} - w_{(min)}}(2^b - 1)\right) \tag{15.8}$$

where b is the bit-width of quantization.

15.4 Model Compression and Optimization for TinyML

Optimization of the model is important in allowing ML models to execute on embedded devices with limited resources. Some of the smallest TinyML applications can run on a few hundred kilobytes of memory and even less processing power on MCUs. Thus, there is a need to make the neural network models smaller and less complex and still attain decent accuracy [14].

15.4.1 Weight- and Precision-Level Optimization

Weight-/precision-level optimization methods strive to minimize neural network model memory and computational power. A common method is quantization, where the weights and activations of neural networks have lower-precision representations (e.g. 8-bit integers rather than 32-bit floating-point numbers). This drastically saves memory as well as enhances the speed of inference on embedded hardware platforms.

$$Q(r) = \text{round}\left(\frac{r}{\Delta}\right) \times \Delta \tag{15.9}$$

Post-training quantization (PTQ) applies quantization when training is done, while quantization-aware training (QAT) considers the effects of quantization while training and leads to better accuracy in most cases. An eight-bit QAT can typically retain performance within 1–2% of that attained for floating-point keyword spotting models, while PTQ typically results in 3–5% degradation.

Besides quantization, parameter pruning is often used to remove redundant weights and filters to reduce the memory footprint and computation complexities. The structured pruning techniques give way to MCU-based pruning because they do not impair hardware efficacy while allowing high model compressibility. Together, precision reduction and pruning form the first layer of optimization for TinyML deployment in the audio domain.

15.4.2 Architecture- and Knowledge-Level Optimization

In addition to compression on a weight level, TinyML optimization can go to architecture- and knowledge-level strategies. Knowledge distillation provides small student models to inherit behavioral traits of larger teacher networks, and neural architecture search (NAS) can automatically discover resource-efficient designs subject to hardware constraints. Complementary methods like layer fusion also ensure a reduced amount of memory access overhead since several operations are combined into single execution units.

Knowledge distillation transfers knowledge from larger "teacher" models to compact "student" models using soft targets:

$$L_{KD} = \lambda L_C E(y, \sigma(z_s)) + (1 - \lambda)T^2 L_{(KL)}\left(\sigma\frac{z_t}{T}, \sigma\frac{z_s}{T}\right) \tag{15.10}$$

where T is temperature parameter used to soften the output probability distribution, α is the weighting factor that balances the contribution of the hard-label classification loss and the soft-label distillation loss during training, and z_t and z_s represent the teacher and student logits, respectively. NAS techniques like

Table 15.5 Comparison of model optimization techniques.

Optimization Technique	Memory Reduction (%)	Compute Reduction (%)	Typical Accuracy Impact (%)
8-bit Quantization	75	60–70	1–5
Pruning (50% sparse)	50	35–45	2–6
Knowledge Distillation	70–90	75–95	1–4
Neural Architecture Search	Variable	Variable	Often improved

ProxylessNAS and MicroNets automatically discover efficient architectures tailored to resource constraints by optimizing:

$$min_{(\sigma,w)}L_{val}(w,\sigma)s.t.Cost(\sigma) < Target \tag{15.11}$$

The fusion of a series of operations is referred to as layer fusion, which helps to reduce the number of memory transfers, and is especially important in fusing convolution, batch normalization, and activation functions. Table 15.5 contains many of the optimization methods that have been used in audio TinyML and their advantages and disadvantages in terms of memory saving, computational saving, and accuracy loss.

Deployment Frameworks for TinyML Audio Systems: To run ML models on edge devices with MCUs, special frameworks are needed to enable efficient inference with little memory and computation needs. TensorFlow Lite for Microcontrollers (TFLM) is one of the most popular frameworks that allow ML models to execute directly on embedded systems without the need of a full operating system. CMSIS-NN is another popular library that provides optimized neural network functions including convolution, activation functions, and pooling on ARM Cortex-M processors. These frameworks can be vital in allowing real-time audio and speech recognition systems to run directly on the edge devices.

15.5 Case Studies and Real-World Applications

We provide some of the common real-life applications of TinyML-based audio systems on resource-limited machines. All the case studies are organized to cover the application context, design decisions for features and models, and performance monitored at the deployment level. This allows direct comparison, illustrating trade-offs of accuracy, latency, consumption, and energy efficiency in real life.

15.5.1 Keyword Spotting Systems for Wake-Word Detection

One of the applications of TinyML audio that is commercially successful is keyword spotting system (KWS) used to identify keywords in audio content

Table 15.6 Performance metrics for keyword spotting systems across different microcontrollers.

Device	Model Size (KB)	Accuracy	Power (mW)	Latency (ms)
Arduino Nano 33 BLE	80	92.4	10.5	120
ESP32	180	94.7	15.2	90
STM32F746	250	96.2	22.8	45

in searches by users of search engines like Google and YouTube [15]. Modern wake-word systems must have a very high level of accuracy, with very low-power usage. The designing issue is high recognition accuracy but ultra-low consumption of power and latency on MCUs that have extremely small memory resources.

The system can be mathematically represented as

$$f(X) = \text{softmax}(W_{(fc)} \cdot pool(\sigma(W_{(conv)} *)X + b_{(conv)}) + b_{(fc)}) \tag{15.12}$$

where W_{conv}, W_{fc}, b_{conv}, and b_{fc} represent the learned parameters. Zhang *et al.* [16] demonstrated that quantized eight-bit models can achieve accuracy within 2% of full-precision models while reducing power consumption by 4.3×.

Practically, the small convolutional structure and hard quantization permit the inference to be evoked on the fly on stringent energy allowances. Table 15.6 shows deployment results demonstrating that as model capacity increases, accuracy improves, though power consumption and latency also increase, which explicitly points out the trade-offs in embedded wake-word systems.

15.5.2 Audio Anomaly Detection for Industrial Equipment

Acoustic patterns that are abnormal due to degradation or failure in industry applications can be detected through TinyML-based anomaly detection at an early stage. Such systems need to be robust to work under highly varying noisy conditions while being computationally lightweight. Autoencoders are preferred for this job since they are capable of learning compact representations of regular audio data and can detect anomalies through reconstruction errors. Reconstruction error E is a good indicator of abnormality:

$$E = \sum (X - \hat{X})^2 \tag{15.13}$$

When deployed on factory-floor MCUs, such TinyML-based systems have demonstrated tangible operational benefits, including reduced unplanned downtime and improved preventive maintenance efficiency [17].

15.5.3 Environmental Sound Classification

The classification of environmental sounds is crucial in several smart city and urban monitoring applications, such as traffic monitoring, human safety, and noise pollution levels. Such models that run on edge devices perform continuous monitoring without the help of cloud services. Smart city applications utilize TinyML for environmental monitoring with traffic analysis in security systems [18]. The mathematical model uses spectral feature extraction via Mel filter banks:

$$S_{\{mel\}} = \mathrm{M} \cdot [\![|STFT(x)|]\!]^2 \tag{15.14}$$

where M refers to the Mel filter bank matrix, while STFT(x) denotes the short-time Fourier transform of audio signal x. The TinyML models help in achieving high accuracy in classification with limited memory and power constraints, thereby making them very suitable for distributed sensing applications.

15.5.4 Challenges and Limitations of TinyML Audio Systems

Even with all the opportunities for TinyML in audio and speech processing applications, there are several issues related to the deployment of the system on low-resource hardware. MCUs have limited memory, computing power, and energy; therefore, they cannot support complex ML models. Another problem is environmental noise. Recorded audio in practical environments is accompanied by various sources of interference such as reverberations, environmental noise, and others, potentially impacting the efficiency of speech recognition and sound classification systems. Multilingual speech recognition is another challenge to implement, as multilingual models consume more energy and memory, exceeding the limits of MCUs. Voice-based TinyML devices will also be vulnerable to security concerns such as adversarial attacks and spoofing. Therefore, developing efficient and secure audio models is of high importance.

15.6 Conclusion and Future Research Directions

TinyML has revolutionized the domain of edge intelligence by empowering ML models to perform their tasks directly within resource-restricted embedded devices. This chapter has outlined some of the methods that can be used in TinyML for audio and speech processing. It has been discussed that methods such as feature extraction using MFCC, quantization, pruning, and other deployment frameworks have made it feasible for intelligent audio processing systems to operate on MCUs. A number of applications, which include keyword spotting, environmental sound classification, and audio anomaly detection in the industry sector, show how TinyML has helped achieve real-time edge intelligence. However, there are certain challenges associated with TinyML, such as its ability to operate in a noisy environment, multilingual speech recognition, and potential security threats, such as audio adversarial attacks. Future work in TinyML audio systems will likely be concerned with designing efficient transformer architectures, enhancing on-device learning algorithms, and incorporating federated learning techniques that enable edge devices to learn from each other in a distributed manner while ensuring data privacy. This will continue to enhance the utility of TinyML-powered audio intelligence in many practical settings.

References

1 R. R. Nair, T. Babu, S. Kishore, J. Poornima, M. Sambasivudu, and M. Bhargavi, "Webcam-based OCR system with text-to-speech conversion," in *2024 Int. Conf. Sustain. Commun. Netw. Appl. (ICSCNA)*, 2024, pp. 692–698, IEEE.

2 M. D. De Assuncao, da A. Silva Veith, and R. Buyya, "Distributed data stream processing and edge computing: A survey on resource elasticity and future directions," *J. Netw. Comput. Appl.*, vol. 103, pp. 1–17, 2018.

3 P. Warden and D. Situnayake, *TinyML: Machine Learning with TensorFlow Lite on Arduino and Ultra-Low-Power Microcontrollers*. O'Reilly Media, 2019.

4 R. Krishnamoorthi, "Quantizing deep convolutional networks for efficient inference: A whitepaper," 2018, *arXiv preprint arXiv:1806.08342*.

5 J. Nayana, S. Bhat, R. R. Nair, and T. Babu, "Audio to sign language conversion using natural language processing," in *2022 3rd Int. Conf. Commun. Comput. Ind. 4.0 (C2I4)*, 2022, pp. 1–6, IEEE.

6 M. Capra, R. Peloso, G. Masera, M. Ruo Roch, and M. Martina, "Edge computing: A survey on the hardware requirements in the internet of things world," *Future Internet*, vol. 11, no. 4, p. 100, 2019.

7 L. Lai, N. Suda, and V. Chandra, "CMSIS-NN: Efficient neural network kernels for ARM Cortex-M CPUs," *J. Mach. Learn. Res.*, vol. 23, no. 1, pp. 1–3, 2022.

8 S. Balasubramanian, K. Mittal, and P.-H. Tseng, "Private speech recognition with TinyML: Challenges and opportunities," in *IEEE Int. Conf. Acoust., Speech, Signal Process. (ICASSP)*, 2021, pp. 8163–8167.

9 F. McKee and D. Noever, "Safeguarding voice privacy: Harnessing near-ultrasonic interference to protect against unauthorized audio recording," 2024, *arXiv preprint arXiv:2404.04769*.

10 Y. Zhang, K. Qian, Z. Qin, R. Pang, B. Wang, and Y. Ni, "SoundCLR: Contrastive learning of representations for audio signals," *IEEE/ACM Trans. Audio Speech Lang. Process.*, vol. 31, pp. 2278–2291, 2023.

11 Y. Vaizman, N. Tucker, and A. Jalota, "Energy-aware TinyML: A review of energy-efficient approaches at the edge," in *Int. Conf. Mach. Learn. Optimiz. (MLOps)*, 2020, IEEE.

12 C. R. Banbury *et al.*, "MLPerf Tiny benchmark," in *Neural Information Processing Systems (NeurIPS) Workshop on Machine Learning Performance*. PMLR (Proceedings of Machine Learning Research), 2021.

13 S. Myer and S. Tomar, "Optimized MFCC feature extraction for low-resource devices," in *Proc. Int. Conf. Audio Anal. Process.*, 2022, pp. 324–331, IEEE.

14 M. Hussein, Y. S. Mohammed, A. I. Galal, E. Abd-Elrahman, and M. Zorkany, "Smart cognitive IoT devices using multi-layer perception neural network on limited microcontroller," *Sensors*, vol. 22, MDPI, p. 5106, 2022.

15 S. Garai and S. Samui, "Exploring TinyML frameworks for small-footprint keyword spotting: A concise overview," in *2024 Int. Conf. Signal Process. Commun. (SPCOM)*, 2024, pp. 1–5, IEEE.

16 Y. Zhang, N. Suda, L. Lai, and V. Chandra, "Hello edge: Keyword spotting on microcontrollers," *IEEE Internet Things J.*, vol. 10, no. 3, pp. 2784–2797, 2023.

17 Y. Koizumi, S. Saito, H. Uematsu, and N. Harada, "TinyML for industrial audio anomaly detection: Design and implementation," in *Proc. 2022 Workshop Audio Signal Process.* IEEE, 2022, pp. 45–52.

18 Z. E. Ahmed, A. A. Hashim, R. A. Saeed, and M. M. Saeed, "TinyML network applications for smart cities," in *TinyML for Edge Intelligence in IoT and LPWAN Networks*. Elsevier, 2024, pp. 423–451.

Part V

Advanced Topics in TinyML

16

Mitigation Strategies for Enhancing Security and Privacy in TinyML Systems

Nitin Rakesh, Monali Gulhane, and Pawan Kumar Verma

Symbiosis Institute of Technology, Symbiosis International (Deemed University), Pune, India

16.1 Introduction

Tiny Machine Learning (TinyML) has become a paradigm shift in edge intelligence by enabling machine learning (ML) models to be executed on low-resource devices (microcontrollers, wearable sensors, embedded Internet of Things (IoT) platforms, etc.). In contrast to traditional artificial intelligence (AI) systems, which are often relying on cloud infrastructure and high-performance computing resources to be operational, TinyML is able to support real-time inference, low latency, low bandwidth consumption, and energy-efficient network endpoint implementation [1–3]. This ability has enhanced its deployment in a broad spectrum of application areas, such as healthcare surveillance, smart agriculture, industrial predictive maintenance, environmental sensing, autonomous systems, and smart buildings [4,5–12, 25]. Accelerated progress in model compression, quantization, lightweight deployment systems, and dedicated edge hardware implementations have contributed to the fast development of TinyML. Efforts in benchmarking, e.g. MLPerf Tiny, have continued to standardize the performance measurement of low-power ML systems, and studies of FPGA accelerators, custom hardware architecture, and energy-efficient edge AI have been made to further reinforce the viability of deploying intelligent models on highly constrained devices [1, 4, 13–15]. Meanwhile, the combination of TinyML and Edge AI has provided fresh possibilities to decentralized intelligence, when devices can handle sensitive data on their own and make independent decisions without ongoing cloud reliance [2, 7, 12, 25].

Although these benefits exist, there are major challenges that are presented by the implementation of TinyML in security- and privacy-sensitive applications. The edge devices usually have a small memory, limited processing power, and low-power limits, which makes it challenging to apply standard security measures, including heavyweight encryption, sophisticated intrusion detection models, and complete-scale secure execution infrastructures [2, 15, 16]. Also, TinyML systems are often deployed in physically unprotected or untrusted systems, which makes them more susceptible to model tampering, data leakage, adversarial attacks, communications interception, and unauthorized access [16–19]. Such risks are even more critical when they are applied in areas like healthcare, automation of industry, and intelligent transportation, where ineffective inference or disclosed personal information have severe safety, privacy, and operational impacts [5, 17, 20, 25].

The solution to these issues is to devote the current research to security- and privacy-conscious TinyML frameworks. Intel SGX, AMD SEV-SNP, Arm TrustZone, and RISC-V physical memory protection have been considered as trusted hardware to enhance isolation, integrity, and trusted execution on the device or platform level [18, 21–23]. On the same note, privacy-friendly designs, including federated learning, local differential privacy (DP), secure aggregation, anonymization, and lightweight cryptographic protocols, are under investigation to safeguard user data when training and when conducting inference [19, 20]. These strategies are especially relevant in edge computing, whereby personal and operational data are constantly being sensed, processed, and exchanged in distributed nodes [17, 19, 20].

In this regard, this chapter reviews the key security and privacy issues in TinyML deployments and explains mitigation strategies in resource-constrained edge resources. The chapter sets out to give a systematic knowledge of vulnerabilities in TinyML systems, such as threats to data integrity, model inference, communication security, and personal data privacy, as well as to identify the contribution of privacy-preserving learning, trusted execution, communication security protocols, and lightweight protection systems toward a trustworthy TinyML system [2, 7, 9, 16, 17, 20]. The chapter is a contribution to the growing body of knowledge required to guarantee the safe, reliable, and responsible application of TinyML to the real-world setting by synthesizing recent advances in the field of TinyML, Edge AI, hardware-assisted security, and distributed privacy protection [7, 9, 12, 25]. Figure 16.1 presents some approaches of TinyML applications to enhance security and privacy.

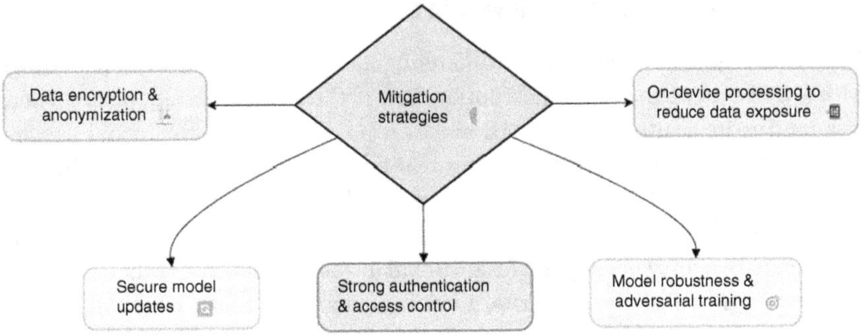

Figure 16.1 Illustrating mitigation strategies for security and privacy in TinyML.

16.2 Background

16.2.1 Concept and Evolution of TinyML

TinyML is the process of using ML models on devices with few resources, such as microcontrollers, sensors, and embedded systems. These devices are designed to operate right on the edge of the network. With relatively little power, storage, and computational capability, they allow real-time data processing occur. Like GPUs or cloud servers, traditional ML consumes a lot of processing capability. Conversely, TinyML allows you to execute intricate AI models straight on low-power tiny devices. Thanks to power and internet problems, this fresh concept has made smart systems feasible in many areas where they were not previously conceivable. TinyML has evolved and expanded under changes in technology, software, and ML methods [22]. AI applications first had to employ centralized cloud systems as their capacity was restricted by the need for a lot of computational capability. ML has been able to reach the edge as microprocessors and sensors have been quicker and better in conserving electricity. Large advances ahead in chip design, such as the development of low-power devices like Google's Edge TPU and NVIDIA's Jetson Nano [18], have driven this trend. ML models can operate on devices with limited memory or processing capability thanks to software tools as TensorFlow Lite for Microcontrollers, and model reduction techniques include quantization and trimming. Because of this, TinyML was created, which enables AI working on the device itself, which cuts down on delay, boosts efficiency, and ensures real-time operation.

16.2.2 Key applications of TinyML in Edge AI

TinyML has a lot of uses in many different areas because it can work in settings with few resources and little interruption. One of the most important places where it is used is in healthcare. TinyML makes it possible to make personal gadgets that can check on a patient's health in real time and find problems like high or low blood sugar [23]. These devices don't need to rely on an online service to decide when to tell users or healthcare providers. This cuts down on delay and makes sure that answers happen faster. Small ultrasound machines that are developed by TinyML also allow a doctor to view data around them, which makes the healthcare delivery more effective, particularly in those places that are difficult to access or lack a sufficient number of doctors. Another significant field of the use of TinyML is Smart agriculture. IoT devices based on TinyML can measure soil moisture, temperature, and humidity to guarantee that food management, pest control, and watering are done in the most efficient way they can be. Rejecting cloud-based systems and consuming less energy, the devices will be able to process data closer to homes and make fast decisions like turning on watering systems or informing farmers that help is required [13]. The automotive industry is incorporating TinyML into self-driving cars to give them real-time enhanced decision-making. ML devices locate objects, identify lanes, and monitor vehicle health, among other tasks. By managing data from cameras, LiDAR sensors, and other locally available sources, autonomous automobiles can rapidly make significant decisions. They are thereby much more efficient and safer. Smart home systems also extensively rely on TinyML. Voice agents, security cameras, smart thermostats all handle sensor, audio, and video data locally using TinyML [14].

16.2.3 Security and Privacy Concerns in TinyML Deployments

Although TinyML has numerous applications, it also generates a lot of security and privacy concerns that must be addressed to guarantee dependability of operations. The possibility of hacking on TinyML devices is one of the main concerns. Standard security techniques such as firewalls, attack detection systems, or strong encryption are difficult to use on these devices because of their limited computational capability [15]. TinyML devices, therefore, be less valuable and endanger the data they handle if they are subject to threats like denial-of-service (DoS), illegal access, and data stealing. Many TinyML applications that rely on gathering and managing personal data about individuals also create significant privacy concerns. In the healthcare sector, for instance, TinyML devices might gather health-related data that, if stolen or misused, would lead to significant invasions of privacy. Also, because TinyML devices often work in spread settings, it is very important to make sure that the data sent between edge devices and centralized platforms is kept private and correct [24]. TinyML devices can be attacked by man-in-the-middle (MITM) attacks, spying, and data capture because they don't have private communication routes. This means that secret information could be leaked. Model theft and inversion attacks are also more likely to happen when TinyML models are used on edge devices [1]. Background work has been summarized in Table 16.1, with applications, related work, future trends, challenges, and scope. The model already used by a criminal to receive training data privately, user preferences, or secret formula could be reverse-engineered by a criminal.

16.3 Security Risks in TinyML

16.3.1 Threats to Data Integrity

The security of the data is a key aspect of any ML system, and TinyML is not an exception. The TinyML devices tend to handle and operate directly with data, and thus, it is more probable that information will be modified or lost. The loss of data security can occur in many ways since most of these gadgets operate in environments where dynamic cannot be secure. Another potential vulnerability to TinyML data security is that it might be altered during transmission between edge devices and central computers. Unless there is appropriate security and secure routes, attackers are able to steal and manipulate data during its transmission. This leads to the system getting false or corrupted data [3]. TinyML machines do not possess much computing power, so it is difficult to create error detection and error repair systems that can perform well. This exposes them to such hacks. Another factor that can jeopardize the security of the data is to physically interfere with the devices. Locating edge devices in remote or visible locations is the reason they are frequently installed in such places they not be guarded against direct access.

16.3.2 Vulnerabilities in Model Inference and Training

Model reasoning and training can frequently be performed on edge devices with not many resources in TinyML. This exposes the system to several shortcomings. A major concern is the inference process, i.e. when the device makes predictions using the learnt model and is safe. Inversion of models attacks are some of the attacks that attackers attempt to invert the model in order to obtain confidential information such as the training data or intimate techniques when you lack adequate defense [20]. During such attacks, the attacker poses the model various questions as well as examines the responses to determine more about the structure of the model and the data that it has been trained on [5]. This poses a great risk on privacy and more so when personal information such as health or financial data is involved. Another weakness of TinyML is the possibility of adversarial attack

Table 16.1 Summary of background work.

Application	Finding	Future Trend	Challenges	Scope
Secure Model Training	Lightweight encryption techniques for model updates	Optimization of lightweight encryption for TinyML devices	Ensuring encryption doesn't hinder performance or power usage	Applies to all TinyML systems with secure model training
Federated Learning [4]	Minimizing data exposure during training	Wider adoption of federated learning for privacy preservation	Achieving model convergence while maintaining privacy	Ideal for privacy-sensitive applications like healthcare
Differential Privacy	Preventing reidentification of sensitive data	Enhancing methods for balancing data utility and privacy	Maintaining data utility while adding noise for privacy	Enhances privacy in machine learning systems
Homomorphic Encryption	Performing computations on encrypted data	More efficient homomorphic encryption schemes for TinyML	Balancing overhead with security guarantees	Essential for confidential computing in sensitive sectors
Data Anonymization	Anonymizing datasets to ensure individual privacy	Improving anonymization techniques for data utility	Ensuring anonymization doesn't degrade data quality	Vital for maintaining data privacy while ensuring utility
Edge Device Authentication [19]	Verifying device identity in edge networks	Stronger authentication protocols using biometrics	Verifying device identity and mitigating spoofing attacks	Important for distributed edge AI systems needing device trust

Secure Communication	TLS, DTLS, and ECC for secure communication between devices	Advancements in lightweight communication security protocols	Securing communication without adding significant latency	Covers communication between IoT devices and cloud platforms
Hardware-Based Security	Using TEEs like Intel SGX for secure execution	Developing TEEs with lower energy consumption	Overcoming hardware limitations on TinyML devices	Key for sensitive operations or data in TinyML
Secure Boot	Ensuring trusted software runs on devices	Secure boot tailored for TinyML platforms	Ensuring secure boot doesn't delay device startup	Ensures integrity and trustworthiness of embedded devices
Adversarial Training [2]	Training models to recognize and defend against adversarial inputs	Refining adversarial training to be more robust	Effectively detecting adversarial inputs without increasing false positives	Critical for high-stakes applications in edge AI
Model Inversion Attacks	Preventing the extraction of training data from models	More effective methods to protect against model inversion	Preventing information leakage through model updates	Ensures confidentiality of training datasets in TinyML
Data Poisoning	Identifying malicious data in federated learning	Developing techniques to mitigate data poisoning	Detecting malicious data contributions in federated learning	Relevant for federated learning models
Regulatory Compliance	Adherence to GDPR and other privacy laws	Evolving regulations for TinyML deployments	Complying with varying global privacy laws	Ensures compliance with privacy laws in edge AI systems

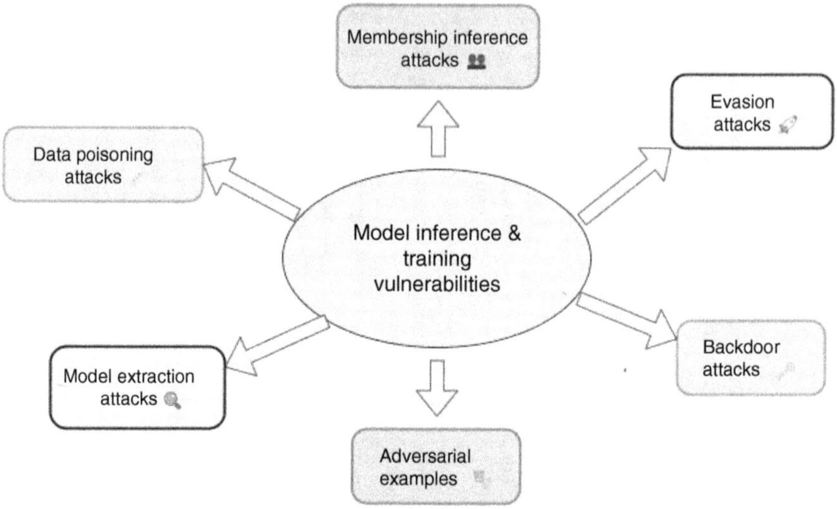

Figure 16.2 Illustrating vulnerabilities in model inference and training.

when reasoning about a model. In adversarial attacks, the attackers manipulate the input data in illicit ways to deceive the model to make incorrect guesses or decisions. As an example, a hacker alters a photo or a sensor image to the point of causing a face recognition or object detection system to identify another object, which would be very disastrous. It is particularly hazardous that adversarial cases be used in edge AI, where devices are exposed to numerous untrusted inputs and cannot rely on the cloud-based correction or validation. Aside from the problems that can happen during inference, TinyML models [6–8] can also have problems during training. Figure 16.2 shows the flaws that can happen during model reasoning and training, which shows the possible security risks. Federated learning lets teaching happen in different places, but it also comes with its own problems.

The nature of federated learning is decentralized, making it difficult to ensure that any training data and model modification are accurate and realistic. In collaborative learning, bad actors have the ability to introduce malicious data or modify model updates, and this leads to a model that is not functioning correctly [6]. Since TinyML gadgets lack much computing power, they cannot afford more robust model validation algorithms such as DP. This complicates the process of ensuring the safety of the model during the training process.

16.3.3 Data Privacy Risks in Edge Devices

Among the most significant concerns regarding TinyML-based deployment is data privacy, as these devices frequently handle personal information and in the location where the privacy not be assured regularly. One of the greatest threats to data privacy is the possibility that one can access any confidential information stored on the device without authorization. Many TinyML applications such as fitness gadgets and health tracking apps collect personal data such as blood pressure, heart rates, and sleep patterns. Unless these gadgets are properly configured in terms of security and access parameters, there is a likelihood that attackers can have access to this data, and this would constitute an infringement on privacy. Sending data from edge devices to the centralized computers or cloud platforms has privacy concerns [11, 12], in addition to the problems with data local storage. On TinyML systems, edge devices are frequently connected to cloud-based infrastructure to additional work, receive updates on models, or maintain a view of things at a distance. But sending private or important data over unprotected lines of communication can result in data capture, spying, or MITM attacks, in which hackers get to private data while it's being sent. Even when encryption is used, it's hard to be sure that data will stay private while it's being sent because of the chance that cryptography methods or keys will not work properly. Also, a lot of TinyML apps depend on ML models that are taught with private user data, which adds to privacy issues. Some of these risks can be reduced by federated learning because data stays on local devices. However, data privacy must still be carefully managed because model changes could accidentally reveal data about the local dataset. Model inversion attacks can also be used to get private data from a learnt model, which is another way that users' privacy is at risk. DP, homomorphic encryption, and safe multiparty computing are some of the methods that can be used to protect private data while it is being stored or sent. Also, privacy-protecting shared learning methods can keep user data from getting out while still letting models get better.

16.4 Privacy Risks in TinyML

16.4.1 Personal Data Exposure in IoT Devices

The increase in the number of TinyML-driven IoT devices has raised numerous concerns with regard to privacy, particularly in regard to sharing of personal data. Examples of IoT devices that continuously collect and process vast quantities of sensitive and personal information include smart home appliances, activity trackers, and outdoor sensors. By adding TinyML to these devices, the processing of data can occur on the device, which reduces the processing of data in the cloud and allows decisions to be made in real time. However, this local data processing and retention is what also increases the probability of personal data being stolen as long as the devices are not locked down accordingly. In many cases, TinyML collected data are quite confidential. This includes health precautions, whereabouts, or even individual preferences. A wearable device monitoring your heart rate, sleeping patterns, and exercise, e.g. holding large amount of information on your personal health status. Attackers could get to this private info if these devices are broken into, which would be a major breach of privacy. This exposure could be done on purpose, like when data is stolen, or by chance, like when data is sent or saved incorrectly or without enough protection. Also, IoT devices in edge computing settings are often put in places that are weak or open to the public, which makes them more likely to be physically tampered with or accessed by people who aren't supposed to. For example, a hacker could get into a device and take out private data, or they could put malware on it and change the data that is being recorded. Algorithm 16.1 explains the Edge AI and TinyML approaches, which can preserve the privacy.

Algorithm 16.1

```
# Step 1: Secure Data Collection & Storage
def secure_data_collection(D):
   for data in D:
      data = anonymize_data(data) # Remove PII
      data = encrypt_data(data, E_M) # Encrypt using chosen encryption method
   return D
# Step 2: Secure Model Training Using Federated Learning
def federated_training(M, E, R):
   round = 0
   while round < R: # Repeat for R training rounds
       selected_devices = select_devices(E) # Select edge devices for training
       model_updates = []
          for device in selected_devices:
          local_model = M # Copy model for local training
          local_model = train_local_model(local_model, device) # Train on edge
          device
          local_model = apply_differential_privacy(local_model, P_M) #
          Privacy-preserving training
          model_updates.append(local_model)
          M = aggregate_models(model_updates) # Federated aggregation
   round += 1
  return M
# Step 3: Secure Communication Between Edge Devices
def secure_communication(E):
   for device in E:
```

```
        establish_tls_connection(device) # Use TLS/DTLS for encryption
        authenticate_device(device) # Verify identity of the edge device
    return True
# Step 4: Secure Model Inference & Defense Against Attacks
# Step 5: Secure Model Deployment & Continuous Monitoring
```

16.4.2 Privacy Issues in Federated Learning for TinyML

Using federated learning to train device mastering models without sending nonpublic records to a far-flung server is a potential way to protect privateers. Federated learning is very helpful in TinyML as it shall, we models, be built properly on edge devices such as smartphones, wearable techniques, and sensors, while making sure that personal facts in no way leave the tool. By retaining person information nearby and proscribing the publicity of personal information, this decentralized schooling method offers huge privateers benefits. However, although it has benefits, shared learning in TinyML systems additionally comes with its own privateer's problems. One of the principal concerns is that version inversion assaults would possibly happen. In this type of attack, the bad man can look at the adjustments that a tool sends at some point of federated learning to figure out personal statistics about the local dataset. As an example, an attacker wants to use the modifications that a device sends to discover about someone's health or personal behavior. In shared learning, version updates only percentage a version's parameters or gradients. This means that there's still a massive chance of statistics leaking at some stage in these updates. There is also the risk of information poisoning to take into account. Numerous aspect devices work collectively in cooperative gaining knowledge of to assist educate the version. If an attacker takes over a tool that is a part of the gaining knowledge, they could upload horrific facts that could exchange the version and make it much less reliable. It is viable for this form of assault to decrease the first rate of the version or make it act in a damaging manner, all while making it look like real information inputs. To fix those privateers problems, shared studying systems need to use high-tech safety methods like DP, which hides personal facts via adding noise to model adjustments. Secured methods for collecting updates can also assist in ensuring that modifications cannot be linked to precise customer. Strong identification and anomaly detection systems also can help discover and prevent humans from being evil inside the shared learning manner.

16.4.3 GDPR and Other Regulatory Concerns in Edge Computing

TinyML finds increasing use in edge computing environments. Following privacy guidelines such as the General Data Protection Regulation (GDPR), is therefore,

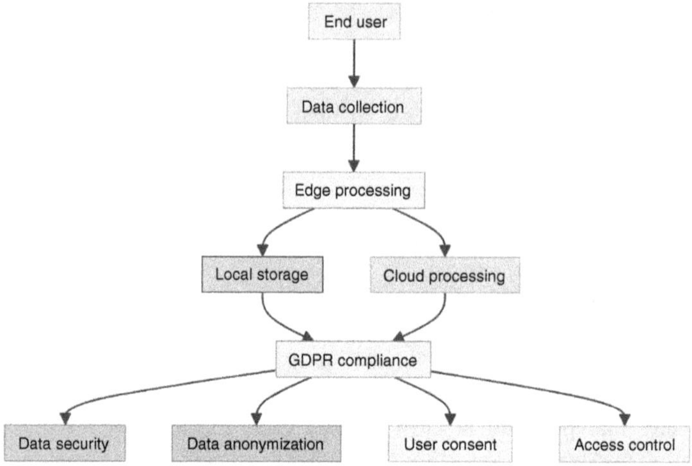

Figure 16.3 GDPR and other regulatory concerns in edge computing.

quite crucial. Designed by the European Union, the GDPR seeks to safeguard personal data and ensure that companies manage it in a transparent, safe, and ethical manner. The legislation lays rigid guidelines for the acquisition, storage, handling, and distribution of personal data. People also have rights to see, alter, or delete their own data. TinyML systems placed on edge devices find it difficult to comply with GDPR since these devices are not centralized. Figure 16.3, which centers on data protection problems, shows concerns regarding GDPR and policies in edge computing.

16.5 Mitigation Strategies for Security in TinyML

16.5.1 Secure Model Training and Inference Techniques

Using SMPC, many users collaborate to train a model without exchanging their personal data. In shared learning environments, where many computers train together without sharing their raw data, SMPC performs efficiently. Using homomorphic encryption, which maintains the data private throughout the transaction, executes computations on protected data. During model inference, small-scale ML devices are sometimes easily attacked adversely. Small variations in the input data might cause the model to veers in these attacks.

16.5.2 Secure Communication Protocols for Edge Devices

One of the most crucial security concerns for TinyML systems is ensuring that edge devices securely interact with central computers or other connected devices.

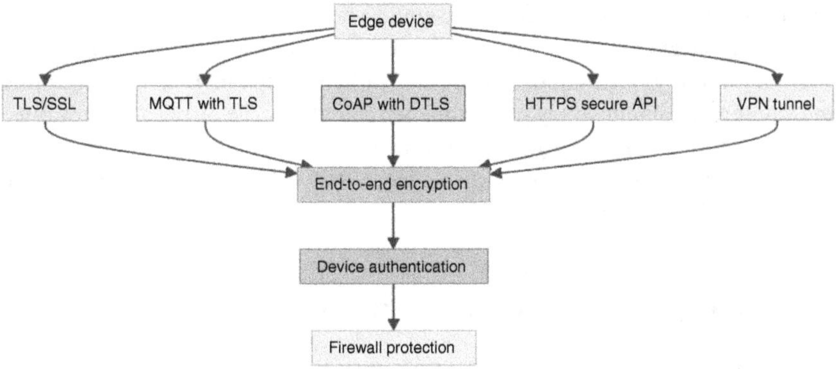

Figure 16.4 Illustrating secure communication protocols for edge devices.

TinyML devices commonly operate in locations where they need to transmit and receive data from outside systems, for example, to update models, exchange data, or make decisions in real time; therefore, it is rather crucial that these channels of communication be secure to prevent data breaches, interception, or manipulation. Safe communication techniques must be implemented in TinyML systems to handle these problems. One of the most often used methods to guarantee data security is TLS, or transport layer security. TLS codes data during transmission; therefore, those who are not meant to cannot view or listen in. By looking to determine if the data was altered during transit, it also guards its security. Figure 16.4 offers secure communication techniques for edge devices, safeguarding data confidentiality and privacy, as shown in equation (16.1).

$$\text{SecurePacket} = (EKe(D), HKm(D)) \tag{16.1}$$

where

$$EKe(D): EncrypteddatausingencryptionkeyKeK_eKe$$

$$HKm(D): MessageAuthenticationCode(MAC)computedusingkeyKmK_mKm$$

SecurePacket: The final transmitted message that ensures confidentiality and integrity

TLS addition to TinyML devices helps to protect data sent between edge devices and centralized computers or cloud-based systems against hacking. Another excellent communication approach is datagram transport layer security (DTLS), a variant of TLS evolved for connectionless conversation. Often visible in IoT structures with restrained assets is it. Though with much less additional attempt, DTLS affords the identical degree of safety as TLS. For TinyML devices that do not have reminiscence or processing capability, DTLS guarantees that even low-energy devices might also securely transmit and acquire facts without slowing down. Safe channels of conversation should offer greater than actually TLS and DTLS. They need to also have method to ensure that best allowed devices connect to the community. Techniques like mutual authentication in which the customer and the server validate every other's names can also assist or prevent unwanted access. Also matching to TinyML structures are elliptic curve cryptography (ECC) and other lightweight encryption plans, since they offer too much security with minimal additional effort to computers.

16.6 Mitigation Strategies for Privacy in TinyML

16.6.1 Privacy-Preserving Techniques (DP, Homomorphic Encryption)

Privacy protection tactics are crucial to reduce privacy risks in TinyML systems, primarily when handling private intimate truths. The first-rate ways of privacy protection in TinyML include DP and holomorphic encryption. They both help preserve the data of protect persons and, at the same time, allow evaluation and model training to occur. Differential privateers are a method for hiding unique record factors in datasets or version modifications through adding noise to them. The overall usefulness of the facts isn't always affected. If an attacker gets access to the model or its effects, this approach makes positive that they can't tell if everyone's records are inside the dataset. DP can be used in TinyML during version training, in which noise is added to the version's slopes or adjustments before they're shared or put together. This makes sure that private statistics like fitness records or private behavior remains nonpublic. Attackers have a tougher time getting particular facts when noise is delivered, which protects user privacy.

DP is very useful in decentralized structures like federated mastering, where data stays on character devices and only updates that have been accumulated are shared. With holomorphic encryption, however, calculations be finished on protected records without having to decode it first. In different words, private records can be treated safely even in places with few computer resources, such as on TinyML gadgets. When used in healthcare, homomorphic encryption lets TinyML models use protected medical data to make choices or predictions without ever showing the raw data. The privacy preserving equation for TinyML can be explained as shown in equation (16.2).

$$\text{Enc}(f(x + N(0, \sigma 2))) = f(\text{Enc}(x)) + \varepsilon \tag{16.2}$$

where

x: Sensitive input data (e.g. health, behavioral data)
$N(0, \sigma 2)$: Gaussian noise for DP, with variance $\sigma 2$
$\text{Enc}(\cdot)$: Encryption of Homomorphic Function
ε: DP for budget

16.6.2 Federated Learning for Distributed Privacy

Federated learning is a way to train ML models without sending raw data from edge devices to central computers. This method works especially well for TinyML because it lets devices learn and get better without putting the privacy of the data they create at risk. With federated learning, private personal data is trained directly on the device instead of being sent to the cloud to be processed. Only model changes or gradients are sent to a central server. These changes are then put together by the server to make a more accurate global model. This model is then sent back to the edge devices to be trained again. This spread method is much better for privacy. There are very low chances of theft of data transferred, i.e. because the raw data does not go outside the local machine. To make the model changes even more secure, federated learning could be applied together with other privacy-enhancing techniques, such as the DP. In federated learning, updates are shared with noise added to them to ensure that the privacy of individual data points is preserved even in case an attacker receives the changes. Due to this fact, the idea of shared learning is an excellent one since it helps preserve privacy in spheres of life such as healthcare, banking, and tracking of personal devices, where a personal user data is customarily processed. The federated learning also assists in reducing the dangers of having all of your information in one aspect.

In a regular ML format, a lot of personal information is stored in centralized files. This renders them easy to hack and other individuals who do not deserve to see them. Federated learning reduces the volume of the private information that should be stored at a single location. This hazards user information away. Nevertheless, it remains difficult to ensure the correctness and honesty of the model updates since the malicious players endeavor to introduce erroneous data or modify the updates. To maintain safety and privacy of shared learning systems, techniques such as secure aggregation, anomaly detection, and strong identification are required.

16.6.3 Data Anonymization and De-Identification Approaches

Anonymization and de-identification of the information represent essential privacy considerations that can be made to ensure the confidentiality of personal data and, at the same time, allow TinyML systems to process data and model ML. These methods are quite handy in areas of healthcare, finance, and social media where files are commonly full of personal information that must be secured to comply with protection policies such as GDPR. Anonymizing data refers to the process of discarding or transforming personally identifiable information (PII) in a collection of data in such a manner that it cannot be directly or indirectly identified with a person. Anonymization typically refers to the process of discarding the things that could be used to identify someone such as names, addresses, or social security numbers and replacing them with pseudonymous names or general statements. To give an example, medical information in healthcare applications, where TinyML is applied, anonymized by removing patient names and other direct identifiers. The valuable medical data that should be used as training models would not be lost. A privacy protection method that works well is anonymization, although, in some cases, it renders the data less helpful, particularly when precise personal data is required to train the models. While de-identification is similar to anonymization, it usually only involves changing or removing certain pieces of information that can be used to identify someone. The process of de-identification keeps some data traits that could still be useful for research while making it impossible to quickly identify the person. Some methods that change the characteristics of data while keeping its general structure and links are data hiding, tokenization, and modification.

16.7 Challenges and Open Issues

16.7.1 Scalability of Security and Privacy Strategies

Ensuring the functionality of security and privacy in TinyML systems is also difficult since it must be capable of scaling to the necessary degree. TinyML is becoming increasingly used in more and more businesses, including in healthcare and smart cities. This implies that a vast amount of edge devices will be to be secured. To date, most of the security and privatization techniques that we possess are designed to work with centralized systems that have greater storing and processing capabilities, thus a huge issue. When devices become millions or even billions, it can be difficult to get these techniques to work with the devices that are not known to have many resources. As an example, due to the limited memory capacity and processing power of TinyML devices, failure of the encryption and identification systems relying on complex algorithms. Similarly, the system becomes difficult to manage and implement security rules on masses of devices as it expands.

16.7.2 Balancing Performance and Security in Resource-Constrained Devices

Data protection is provided by using advanced cryptographic methods to ensure that the information can be safe during transmission or storage, e.g. it makes the device harder to operate, consequently increasing its energy consumption and the frequency of early breakdowns. Likewise, intricate security mechanisms like federated learning or safe model training models require significant computational power, meaning that TinyML devices will struggle to respond with latency or operate information as rapidly as possible. Any slowing in the workplace could be quite counterproductive due to situations such as autonomous vehicles or healthcare where decisions should be made immediately. Trading security as high performance, conversely, expose the system to hackers or data leakages or privacy intrusion [10].

16.8 Conclusion

TinyML has become an enabling technology of next-generation edge intelligence as it enables ML models to run on highly resource-constrained devices. Its capability to facilitate low-latency, energy-efficient, and real-time decision-making has rendered it very useful in safety-critical and privacy-sensitive areas including healthcare, environmental monitoring, smart infrastructure, industrial automation, and autonomous systems. Nonetheless, the same factors, which render TinyML appealing when used in edge deployments, such as limited memory, lower computing power, irregular connectivity, and openness of hardware, also contribute to its special susceptibility to security attacks and privacy invasion.

This chapter pointed out that the need to provide trustworthiness in TinyML systems goes beyond the customization of traditional cloud-based safeguards. Adversarial manipulation, model tampering, unauthorized access, insecure communication, inference leakage, and privacy exposure at training or deployment are some of the threats that require lightweight, edge-aware, and hardware-conscious defenses. In that regard, privacy-preserving learning algorithms, secure aggregation, local DP, homomorphic encryption, trusted execution environments, hardware-assisted isolation, and lightweight authentication protocols are some of the promising research directions toward creating secure and resilient TinyML ecosystems.

Simultaneously, there are a number of unaddressed open issues. One of the outstanding issues is how to strike a balance between the strength of security, privacy assurance, energy consumption, and inference on limited equipment. Scalability is also a significant issue, especially when TinyML becomes more embedded into large-scale distributed IoT and edge AI systems. In addition, practical regulatory frameworks will be necessary to address regulatory compliance and responsible deployment of AI, including data minimization, transparency, auditability, and safe model update processes in practical deployment.

All in all, the future of TinyML will require the implementation of the integrated security and privacy architectures that should not only be lightweight and efficient but also robust, scalable, and flexible to the emerging threats. It will be necessary to advance such reliable TinyML frameworks to facilitate the use of edge intelligence securely in critical areas of application.

References

1 Xu, K., Zhang, H., Li, Y., Zhang, Y., Lai, R., and Liu, Y. An ultra-low power TinyML system for real-time visual processing at edge *IEEE Trans Circuits Syst II Express Briefs* 2023, 70, 2640–2644.

2 H. Han and J. Siebert, “TinyML: A systematic review and synthesis of existing research,” in *Proc. Int. Conf. Artif. Intellig. Inf. Commun. (ICAIIC)*, Jeju Island, Republic of Korea, 2022, pp. 269–274, IEEE.

3 Bao, G., and Guo, P. Federated learning in cloud-edge collaborative architecture: Key technologies, applications and challenges. *J. Cloud Comput.* 2022, 11, 94.

4 Bi, M., Wang, Y., Cai, Z., and Tong, X. A privacy-preserving mechanism based on local differential privacy in edge computing. *China Commun.* 2020, 17, 50–65.

5 Malche, T., Maheshwary, P., Tiwari, P.K., Alkhayyat, A.H., Bansal, A., and Kumar, R. Efficient solid waste inspection through drone-based aerial imagery and TinyML vision model. *Trans. Emerg. Telecommun. Technol.* 2023, e4878.

6 Kallimani, Rakhee, Krishna Pai, Prasoon Raghuwanshi, Sridhar Iyer, and Onel LA López. TinyML: Tools, applications, challenges, and future research directions. *Multimed. Tools Appl.* 83, 10 (2024): 29015–29045.

7 Ooko, S. O., and Karume, S. M. (2024). Application of tiny machine learning in predicative maintenance in industries. *J. Comput. Theor. Appl.*, 2(1), 131–150.

8 Tsoukas, V., Gkogkidis, A., Boumpa, E., and Kakarountas, A. (2024). A review on the emerging technology of TinyML. *ACM Comput. Surv.*, 56(10), 1–37.

9 Njor, Emil, Mohammad Amin Hasanpour, Jan Madsen, and Xenofon Fafoutis. A holistic review of the TinyML stack for predictive maintenance. *IEEE Access* (2024). 12:184861–184882.

10 Paolone, G., Paesani, R., Pilotti, F., Camplone, J., Piazza, A. and Di Felice, P., 2025. Smart lighting systems: State-of-the-Art in the adoption of the EdgeML computing paradigm. *Future Internet*, 17(2), 1–50.

11 Grzesik, P. and Mrozek, D., 2024. Combining machine learning and edge computing: Opportunities, challenges, platforms, frameworks, and use cases. *Electronics*, 13(3), 640.

12 Letaief, K.B., Shi, Y., Lu, J. and Lu, J., 2021. Edge artificial intelligence for 6G: Vision, enabling technologies, and applications. *IEEE J Sel Areas Commun*, 40(1), 5–36.

13 C. Banbury, *et al.* “MLPerf tiny benchmark,” 2021, *arXiv preprint arXiv:2106.07597*.

14 Wu, X., Wang, M., Lin, J., and Wang, Z. Amoeba: An efficient and flexible FPGA-based accelerator for Arbitrary-Kernel CNNs. *IEEE Trans. Very Large Scale Integr. (VLSI) Syst.* 2024, 32, 1086–1099.

15 Zaman, K.S., Reaz, M.B.I., Ali, S.H.M., Bakar, A.A.A., and Chowdhury, M.E.H. Custom hardware architectures for deep learning on portable devices: A review. *IEEE Trans. Neural Netw. Learn. Syst.* 2021, 33, 6068–6088.

16 J. Huckelberry, Y. Zhang, A. Sansone, J. Mickens, P. A. Beerel, and V. J. Reddi, "TinyML security: Exploring vulnerabilities in resource-constrained machine learning systems," 2024, *arXiv, arXiv:2411.07114.*

17 Segers, L., Talebi, B., da Silva, B., Touhafi, A., and Braeken, A. Trustworthy environmental monitoring using hardware-assisted security mechanisms. *Sensors* 2024, 24, 4720.

18 Pinto, S., and Santos, N. Demystifying arm trustzone: A comprehensive survey. *ACM Comput. Surv. (CSUR)* 2019, 51, 1–36.

19 Immonen, R., and Hämäläinen, T. Tiny machine learning for resource-constrained microcontrollers. *J Sens* 2022, 2022, 7437023.

20 Atanane, O., Mourhir, A., Benamar, N., and Zennaro, M. Smart buildings: Water leakage detection using TinyML. *Sensors* 2023, 23, 9210.

21 Costan, V. Intel SGX explained. *IACR Cryptol EPrint Arch. Paper* 2016/086, 1–118.

22 Sev-Snp, A.M.D. (2020). Strengthening VM isolation with integrity protection and more, *White Paper*, 53(2020), 1450–1465.

23 K. Cheang, C. Rasmussen, D. Lee, D. W. Kohlbrenner, K. Asanović, and S. A. Seshia, "Verifying RISC-V physical memory protection," 2022, *arXiv arXiv:2211.02179.*

24 Kumar, M., Zhang, X., Liu, L., Wang, Y., and Shi, W. Energy-efficient machine learning on the edges. In *Proc. 2020 IEEE Int. Parallel Distribut. Process. Symp. Workshops (IPDPSW)*, New Orleans, LA, USA, 2020. IEEE

17

Compliance, Data Security, Law and Ethical AI Regulation in Decentralized Approached Using TinyML

Monali Gulhane

Symbiosis Institute of Technology, Symbiosis International (Deemed University), Pune, India

17.1 Introduction

Edge computing is the use of machine learning (ML) models directly on devices with limited resources, like sensors, wearable tech, smartphones, and embedded systems. This is made possible by the fast growth of ML methods. This way of thinking, called Tiny Machine Learning (TinyML), lets you handle and make decisions about data in real time at the point of gathering, so you don't need a lot of centralized storing and computing power. Because TinyML might be used in many various fields including healthcare, gardening, transportation, smart homes, and environmental tracking, many people are intrigued in it. When data security, latency, and bandwidth are very critical, its capacity to manage data discreetly and on its own appeals much. But as TinyML technologies have gained favor, they have raised further moral and legal questions. These include data privacy, rule adherence, and running artificial intelligence (AI) systems. TinyML devices are used by many individuals as they can store and handle private and delicate data. This causes great concern among individuals on the way data is managed, distributed, and maintained secure. Decentralized TinyML exacerbates these issues as data typically resides on the device rather than being sent to centralized services. This makes ensuring that regulations and laws pertaining to data security are more difficult. Data safety is among the most critical considerations when building TinyML systems. Maintaining privacy and safety is especially crucial as many TinyML applications gather data about people's health, location, and activity. Existing regulations such as the California Consumer Privacy Act (CCPA) in the United States and the General Data Protection Regulation (GDPR) in the European Union (EU) provide a clear pathway for how personal data should be obtained, stored, processed, and shared. These guidelines stress

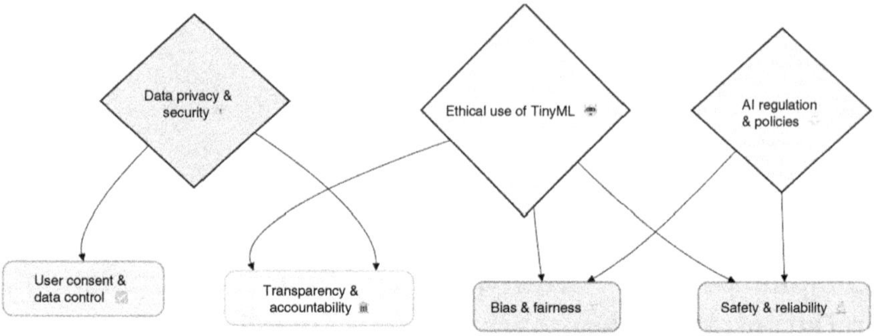

Figure 17.1 Law and ethics in TinyML: addressing compliance, data privacy, and AI regulation.

the importance of personal consent, transparency, visibility, and the right to delete personal data. However, TinyML devices make it harder to adhere to the guidelines. Existing compliance frameworks relying on centralized data storage are not applicable to TinyML devices as data are stored in a distributed manner and often independently.

Also, regulating AI has become very important as ML models, like the ones used in TinyML, start to make choices that have effects that last a long time. More and more regulatory bodies around the world are realizing that they need to set rules for the creation, adoption, and use of AI technologies to make sure that everything is fair, clear, and accountable [1]. For example, the planned Artificial Intelligence Act (AI Act) for the EU divides AI systems into groups based on how dangerous they are. Higher risk AI applications need for more rigorous oversight. TinyML might be regarded as a high-risk AI system as it is often utilized for safety-critical activities such health monitoring and self-driving automobiles. This means that practical applications of the technology necessarily have significant societal impacts. Figure 17.1 illustrates the intersection of TinyML with legal, ethical, compliance, data privacy, and AI regulation. Beyond legal and ethical issues, there are social concerns. The most notable ethical concern in AI models is bias.

For instance, biased facts can lead to incorrect outcomes in medical applications and exclude certain groups of humans from fair access to care. In addition, one of the key issues to deal with today is the lack of transparency in decision-making of AI systems [2]. TinyML systems are, by definition, "black boxes," so it cannot be apparent how a determination is reached. This in turn makes it more challenging to account for AI systems and build trust in them. TinyML also has social consequences. The widespread use of AI-powered structures in our everyday lives raises a number of issues about human rights, using AI for decision-making. As TinyML-pushed structures automate extra jobs, as an instance, concerns regarding activity loss and the effects of recent technologies on society must be addressed. Specifically, while TinyML devices proliferate in each public and personal environments, one ought to additionally consider how AI is utilized for espionage or control [3]. These issues make it critical to develop techniques for the improvement, use, and monitoring of TinyML technologies including moral requirements as well as criminal ones. Together with adherence to statistical privateness guidelines and AI suggestions, TinyML structures need to encompass fairness, duty, and transparency.

17.2 Related Work

Writings on legal systems, compliance, and data security abound as well. Conversely, because TinyML is still relatively new, there is in fact little research on it. Still, several research on related subjects have provided insightful analysis of the moral and legal concerns TinyML must address. Several studies have discussed the issues that the decentralised systems create with data privacy and rule adherence [4]. Edge computing and the Internet of Things (IoT) particularly clearly exhibit these issues. Raza *et al.* have, for instance, examined the privacy concerns raised by IoT devices and highlighted the risks associated with data breaches and unapproved access. TinyML addresses private data including health and sensor data via edge devices; hence, issues are the same for it. Numerous studies have examined how laws as the CCPA and the GDPR affect the IoT and AI. De Franceschi and Scaglione, as an example, discuss the issue, making sure policies are observed while information processing happens at the brink as opposed to happening in an imperative cloud, especially difficult for TinyML packages running on devices with restricted assets, ensuring that users provide permission, that facts is kept secure, and that things are clear [5]. Numerous studies have produced approaches for controlling AI that would guarantee moral development and use of AI structures.

Lots of writing has been written about the ECU synthetic AI Act, which changed into advised via the ECU Commission in 2021. Researchers like Floridi *et al.* stress on how important its miles for AI-driven structures to be accountable, open, and honest, particularly in excessive risk areas such as healthcare and self-using vehicles, which might be a number of the primary regions in which TinyML is making a distinction. These rules were made for AI structures that had been more complex at the beginning, but using them on TinyML makes me wonder what form of monitoring is proper for decentralized devices with few assets. Neves *et al.*'s research showed how critical it's far too just accept governing requirements that balance new thoughts with ethical worries. Worries about ethics in TinyML, like synthetic bias and how clear the decision-making manner is, are also getting greater attention [6]. A number of studies, just like the one with the aid of Mehrabi *et al.*, has seemed into the ethical troubles that AI can purpose, especially the chance that AI structures will discriminate without which means to Table 17.1 summarizes key findings, limitations, and impact of related

Table 17.1 Summary of related work.

Key Findings	Limitations	Impact
Identified privacy risks in IoT devices, highlighting vulnerabilities in data transmission.	Focused primarily on IoT devices, not specifically on TinyML or edge-based AI systems.	Raised awareness of the privacy risks in connected devices, relevant for TinyML in healthcare and IoT.
Discussed difficulties in ensuring GDPR compliance with decentralized data processing systems [7].	Did not focus on TinyML specifically; concentrated more on general IoT security concerns.	Highlighted the challenges TinyML faces in data privacy compliance under regulations like GDPR.
Explored the ethical implications of edge-based AI systems, emphasizing accountability.	Did not specifically address the constraints of TinyML devices.	Provided a framework for implementing ethical AI principles in decentralized AI applications.
Advocated for AI regulations that ensure transparency, fairness, and accountability.	Focused more on large-scale AI systems, not TinyML specifically.	Influenced global discussions on AI regulations, including the need for transparency in TinyML.
Identified risks of bias in AI systems, and how they can lead to discriminatory outcomes [8].	General focus on large-scale AI models rather than TinyML.	Emphasized the importance of fairness and bias mitigation, which is critical for TinyML applications in sensitive areas like healthcare.
Proposed a framework for managing data privacy in IoT, applicable to edge-based computing.	The IoT framework was not tailored to TinyML's computational limitations.	Paved the way for more privacy-aware IoT and TinyML solutions, focusing on decentralizing data processing.
Introduced the AI Act, which classifies AI systems by risk and establishes governance guidelines.	The AI Act is still under development and does not directly address TinyML's unique challenges.	Set the foundation for regulating AI, influencing future legislation for TinyML.
Examined fairness in AI and proposed ethical guidelines for AI-driven systems [9].	Limited focus on TinyML's unique challenges regarding fairness and transparency.	Influenced best practices for fairness in AI systems, essential for TinyML applications in healthcare and safety.
Discussed federated learning as a privacy-preserving technique applicable to TinyML.	Federated learning techniques are computationally intensive and difficult to implement in resource-constrained TinyML devices.	Advanced TinyML privacy by providing privacy-preserving techniques, improving regulatory compliance.

Table 17.1 (Continued)

Key Findings	Limitations	Impact
Analyzed regulatory compliance challenges in AI, particularly in edge computing systems.	Focused more on general AI and edge computing rather than TinyML specifically.	Provided insights into compliance challenges, especially relevant for TinyML in global deployments.
Explored the use of differential privacy in edge computing and TinyML applications.	Challenges in balancing privacy with model performance, particularly in low-resource environments.	Enhanced TinyML privacy by introducing differential privacy techniques, helping mitigate data privacy concerns.
Investigated the implementation of explainability in AI models, promoting transparency [10].	Focused mainly on large-scale AI models, not on the edge-based nature of TinyML.	Influenced the development of transparent and explainable TinyML systems, improving trust and accountability.
Identified bias in AI and proposed methods for mitigating bias in AI training datasets.	Did not specifically focus on TinyML's resource limitations in addressing biases.	Contributed to the development of ethical frameworks to reduce algorithmic bias, crucial for TinyML applications in sensitive areas.

work in the field. There is a lot of work on large-scale AI models, but these issues are also important for TinyML because biased data can spread through devices with limited resources that can't fix or lessen biases in real time.

17.3 Compliance Challenges in TinyML

17.3.1 Regulatory Landscape for AI and ML

As regulators and organizations grapple with the ethical, legal, and societal implications of AI and ML, the regulations governing these technologies are evolving rapidly. Basically, the rules for AI and ML are designed to ensure these technologies are developed and deployed in a safe, transparent, accountable, and equitable way. AI regulation is still in its infancy, and different jurisdictions are taking different approaches to cope with the increasing influence of AI in society. One example is the EU's proposed AI Act. This categorizes AI systems according to their risks and then provides rules by which they should be regulated.

More risky AI applications, such as medical care or autonomous vehicles, are subject to more regulation, while less risky applications are not [11]. Like the AI Act, other laws like the CCPA in the United States and the GDPR in EU are very important to the legal environment, especially when it comes to user agreement and data protection.

17.3.2 Step 1: Define Compliance Variables

Let C be a compliance variable that represents the degree to which an AI system meets regulatory standards, as shown in equation (17.1).

$$C = \text{Compliance level of AI system} \tag{17.1}$$

17.3.3 Step 2: Define Ethical and Legal Factors, as Shown in Equation (17.2)

Let E represent ethical considerations, and L represent legal constraints.
E = Ethical guidelines

$$L = \text{Legal constraints or regulations } (e.g., \text{GDPR, CCPA}) \tag{17.2}$$

17.3.4 Step 3: Measure AI System Risk

Let R be the risk level associated with the deployment of the AI system (e.g. high risk for healthcare or autonomous systems); this can be explained in equation (17.3).

$$R = \text{Risk level of AI system (categorized by application area)} \tag{17.3}$$

17.3.5 Step 4: Define Regulations Applied to the System

Let R_{AI} represent the regulatory guidelines specific to AI, as shown in equation (17.4).

$$R_{\{AI\}} = \text{Regulatory framework for AI systems (e.g.European AI Act)} \tag{17.4}$$

17.3.6 Step 5: Compliance with Risk and Regulation

The degree of compliance C can be modeled as a function of risk R and applicable regulations R_{AI}, and ethical/legal factors E and L, as shown in equation (17.5).

$$C = f(R, R_{\{AI\}}, E, L) \tag{17.5}$$

where f represents the functional dependency of compliance on these factors. The higher the risk, the stricter the regulatory requirements.

17.3.7 Step 6: Final Compliance Equation

The final compliance level of an AI system is determined by the combination of these factors, as shown in equation (17.6).

$$C = k_1 * R + k_2 * R_{\{AI\}} + k_3 * E + k_4 * L \tag{17.6}$$

where

k_1, k_2, k_3, k_4 are constant coefficients that determine the relative importance of each factor in ensuring compliance.

C is the final compliance value (a high value indicates high compliance, while low values indicate low compliance).

17.3.8 Compliance Requirements for TinyML in Various Sectors

TinyML applications that deal with nonpublic health information must adhere to stringent privacy regulations within the healthcare enterprise. Those encompass the Health Insurance Portability and Accountability Act (HIPAA) inside the United States and the GDPR within the EU. These methods and rules require informed consent of the individuals prior to gathering, retention, or utilization of their data, which contributes to protection of sensitive medical data. Besides, the devices of TinyML used in the medical sector must comply with strict protection guidelines to protect victims and guarantee the efficiency and reliability of the epoch regarding real-time diagnosis and treatment. The GDPR and CCPA regulations that are applied in the IoT domain put greater importance on facts protection, cyber security, and protection. These principles mandate the use of devices that store, collect, or work on personal facts or belong within a critical framework to be compliant to defend user facts and give them control over their information. The fact that the computing capability of TinyML devices is limited exposes them to safety concerns. Such a challenge makes it difficult to implement powerful safety measures like encryption, authentication, and access manipulate. Small ML is faced with the difficulty of ensuring compliance with regulations in terms of security, responsibility, and risk minimization in projects like self-driving cars and drones. Overcoming the challenges, developers and producers will be able to see that TinyML generation is not only in line with the requirements of the regulatory bodies but also provides safe and reliable solutions in healthcare and IoT implementations.

17.3.9 International Variations in Compliance Standards

One of the largest issues with TinyML compliance lies in the fact that the rules differ depending on the country and region. Each country has various laws and regulations that address issues such as data security, AI ethics, and ML usage. This can be a challenge to companies that operate in more than a single country. But in places like the United States, data privacy laws aren't all the same. For example, California has its own rules (CCPA), but other states don't have any complete data protection laws at the government level. Different approaches are also taken to regulate AI. People who buy things or use AI systems do not have as many legal rights in places where AI regulations are not well developed, like many in the Global South.

17.4 Data Privacy in TinyML

17.4.1 Data Collection, Storage, and Processing in TinyML Systems

Statistical series, recording, and processing in TinyML systems normally show up on edge devices, which are commonly microcontrollers or sensors that don't have lots of sources. These devices are allowed to collect and assess facts domestically so that they don't have to send everything to the cloud or vital computer systems. TinyML technology performs an important function in decreasing latency, improving actual time decision-making, and safeguarding records privateness. TinyML systems can gather a range of records, together with outside inputs such as temperature and humidity, and personal records such as pulse or rate, human movement, and behavior. Security is a critical consideration of statistical control, given the commonplace use of such gadgets in private areas such as health, smart domestic, and private assistive devices. These devices typically have constrained storage capacity, leading to the adoption of strategies such as statistical compression or intermittent facts transfer to cloud-based totally storage for effective statistical control. Neighborhood processing often stores best relevant facts and eliminates intermediate results to save reminiscence. TinyML processing relies on ultra-light and optimized device learning fashions for duties together with facts classification, anomaly detection, and trend popularity. Distributed processing presents advantages in preserving privacy by means of mitigating the threat of statistical breach through network transmission, but it's far difficult to comply with privacy regulations and norms. Ensuring statistical security and integrity is the largest challenge in TinyML. Data processing across multiple allotted devices complicates security protocol compliance and increases the danger of statistical breaches and unauthorized get admission. To enhance TinyML security and statistical privateness, it's important to strike the balance between native processing strengths and compliance and confidentiality protocols. Using technology and best practices can enhance the efficient and stable deployment of TinyML devices across industries. Privacy and personal facts need to be protected through the groups that create the gadgets and those developing the gadgets. Software developers must ensure their models are protected and comply with privacy regulations.

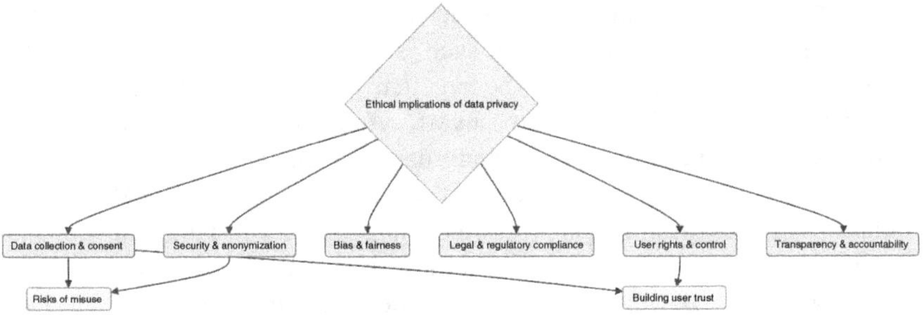

Figure 17.2 Ethical implications of data privacy in TinyML.

17.4.2 Ethical Implications of Data Privacy in TinyML

Data privacy is a big moral issue in TinyML because the technology deals with many sensitive pieces of information, such as in smart homes, medical devices, and wearables. As TinyML is increasingly used in applications where people's health information, behaviors, and movements are monitored, there is a high risk that these data will be exploited. The moral issue arises when you consider the data privacy and how much control a user has over their data and if they are aware of what data is being collected and how it will be used. Data privacy is a huge social issue when it comes to TinyML systems because many of those devices are autonomous and collect data without consent. For example, smartwatches and fitness bands track people's health data and users don't always know how much data is being collected. The ethical consequences of concerns about data privacy in TinyML programs and solutions are represented in Figure 17.2.

For ethical reasons, it is important users are fully informed about how their data is being used and can provide or withdraw consent at any point. Ethical concerns also exist with the transparency and accountability of AI algorithms in TinyML. There is a risk of unintentional bias and discrimination, as these are often "black boxes" and users cannot see how data is processed and decisions are made.

17.4.3 Legal Frameworks Governing Data Privacy (GDPR, CCPA, etc.)

The legal guidelines that defend statistical privateness have grown in significance as greater and greater TinyML units take care of personal and touchy data. In the United States and the EU, CCPA and GDPR are two of the most essential privateness laws. The purpose of these policies is to shield people's privateness by outlining how nonpublic data ought to be gathered, saved, handled, and shared. This way, customers will have manage over their very own data. The GDPR, which grew to be regulation in May 2018, is one of the strictest regulations in the world for defending nonpublic records. It says that people whose data is being taken must be fully told about what that data is being used for and how long it will be kept. It also gives people a number of rights, such as the right to see their data, the right to be forgotten (also called "right to be forgotten"), and the right to be able to take their data with them. Making sure TinyML systems follow GDPR rules can be hard, especially since many devices handle data on their own and privately. GDPR rules on accessing and deleting data might not always work with TinyML's decentralized structure, since data is processed and thrown away without any central control. The CCPA, which went into force in 2020, also gives people in California the right to know what personal information companies are collecting about them and to ask that this information be removed. People can also choose not to have their personal information sold. Like GDPR, CCPA makes companies very responsible for being open, responsible, and getting permission from users before collecting and handling their data. To be in line with the CCPA for TinyML systems, gadget makers and service providers must make sure that the rights of users' data are respected.

17.5 AI Regulation and Ethical Considerations

17.5.1 Overview of AI Regulations and Guidelines

As artificial talent (AI) and machine studying (ML) technologies develop, regulations and laws have been made to make certain they are evolved and utilized in an accountable way. Global rules are intended to defend people's rights, maintain everybody secure, and encourage the moral use of AI. The EU deliberate AI Act is one of the biggest ones. It classifies AI apps depending on how dangerous they are. Excessive risk AI structures, like those utilized in healthcare or self-riding automobiles, want strict policies about duty, openness, and performance promises. Lower-Risk AI systems, however, don't observe as many rules. The AI Act stresses the significance of openness, equality, and tracking in AI systems. This makes certain that AI structures work in methods that humans can recognize and trust. There are fewer regulations that adjust AI in the America. For instance, California has passed the CCPA to address a number of the privacy problems that come with AI technology. On the international stage, consortia such as the OECD and the International Telecommunication Union (ITU) have released ethical tips for the development of AI. These recommend ethical AI that is nonpublic, obvious, and honest. The recommendations are extra complex with the arrival of TinyML. TinyML employs system mastering models that run on gadgets with constrained sources, making it more difficult to manipulate and monitor. TinyML structures are designed to stand on my own and run locally on edge devices. This causes humans to consider responsibility, transparency, and how to make certain AI structures comply with regulations.

For this reason, TinyML authors need to take into account how to ensure that their structures conform to next applicable laws and take into account the social implications of AI on the sting.

17.5.2 Addressing Algorithm Bias in TinyML Systems

One of the challenges of AI is biased algorithm, which is obtained during the course of device; acquiring knowledge of models provides erroneous outcomes due to biases in the education facts or in the design of the program itself. Algorithm bias is particularly crucial to keep an eye on TinyML structures since these versions are frequently deployed in areas like health, protection, and social services, where biased results might be detrimental. There are numerous pathways to bias being introduced in TinyML systems: biased education records that fail to recreate the real world, bad facts series algorithms, or even a bias in the algorithms that govern the records. For example, a TinyML model used for fitness tracking might only paint properly with facts from a sure institution of people and no longer so nicely with data from different groups. This can mean that people from below-represented organizations get wrong or destructive advice. To forestall laptop bias, programmers need to make certain that the training data is varied and ordinary of the human beings the model will assist. This indicates getting records from a whole lot of exceptional corporations of humans and thinking of things like age, gender, race, and monetary role. Equity measures can also be utilized by writers to peer how well their models work for exceptional agencies and make changes to ensure all people receive equal consequences. One more way to deal with bias in TinyML systems is to use methods that reduce bias while training the models. Some methods that can help make TinyML models less biased are reweighting the training data, using hostile debiasing methods, or putting fairness limits on the optimization process. Figure 17.3 shows the problem of algorithmic bias in TinyML systems and some possible answers.

17.6 Challenges and Future Directions

17.6.1 Balancing Innovation with Ethical and Legal Constraints

One of the hardest components of creating the usage of TinyML is locating the right balance among the fast pace of technical development and the want to observe the law and morals. This makes it a powerful tool for making matters easier and quicker. On the other hand, as TinyML structures grow to be greater commonplace, they address extra personal facts, like health measurements, private behaviors, and data about the environment. These are numerous ethical and legal dilemmas, most of which revolve around privacy of facts,

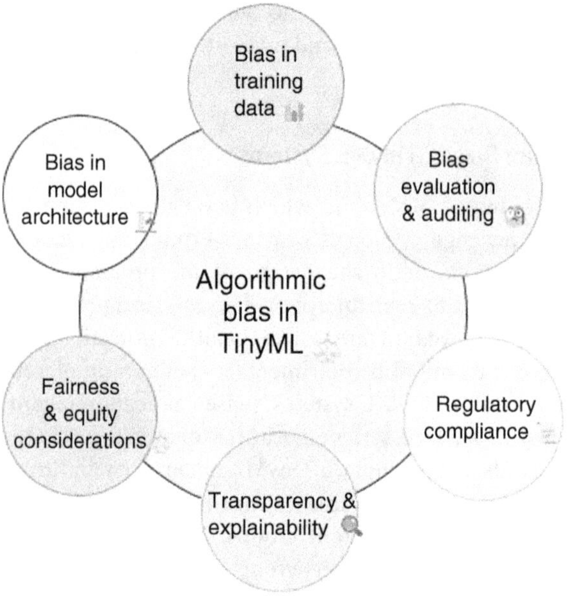

Figure 17.3 Addressing algorithmic bias in TinyML systems.

consent, and algorithm ethics. TinyML devices must be innovative, but they must be designed so that they do not break the law (such as the GDPR and CCPA). With the guidelines about the privacy and protection of data, the programmers are compelled to think about how they obtain, purchase, and utilize the data. Ensuring that AI fashions are honest and explainable is even more difficult, because TinyML devices should be understandable and explainable, and it is more difficult than making it clear and concise in terms of how they work, especially in high-stakes eventualities like healthcare or autonomous vehicles. We desire regulation, ethics, and technology experts to find the correct balance between the advantages of the new, edge-based totally AI and the threat to human privateness and security. The challenge is to come up with some regulations that would not only encourage new innovations but also protect the rights of people and hold onto the populace of belief so that TinyML technology can be made to remain within the most appropriate societal confines. This is a significant aspect of ensuring that TinyML has a sustainable future that would be ethical to everyone and meet the regulation and ethics.

17.6.2 Emerging Trends in TinyML Regulation

Because TinyML is growing and being utilized in increasingly fields, the policies that govern its use are converting. One new trend is that humans are paying extra interest to AI hazard evaluation and system control at the edge. Regulatory organizations are beginning to investigate the problems that can happen while

AI models are used on devices with few assets. One step toward a prison framework that directly handles the unique functions of TinyML is the EU's AI Act, which classifies AI systems into companies based totally on how dangerous they are. Any other new fashion is the flow toward strategies that shield privacy, like federated studying and differential privateness. This led machine to gain knowledge of fashions research from facts without sending nonpublic facts to central computers. Those strategies are intended to make the facts processed by means of TinyML systems more secure and more private. They do this by making sure that records safety legal guidelines are accompanied and keeping the AI models useful. Federated mastering, for example, maintains the statistics at the tool at the same time as nearby fashions are taught, combined, and up to date in a decentralized method. These principles underscore the fact that AI must be transparent, responsible, and honest. They demand that developers be able to construct verifiable, explainable, and bias-free models. This is increasingly receiving attention since individuals are worried that AI could be abused in other ways like espionage and biased judgment. Guidelines also must be developed to deal with the risks of edge autonomous decisions in TinyML.

17.6.3 Future Research and Development Needed in Compliance and Ethics

To ensure that these technologies are created on a sustainable basis, the future of research and development on TinyML compliance and ethics should be centered on two issues. To start with, it should be global compliance rules. Because TinyML devices could work all over the world, developers must take into account the way they can comply with the numerous complicated regulations being region-specific. Global data privacy standards, AI, and device safety would aid the compliance, and it would also enable many individuals to apply TinyML in a manner that is compliant with the local laws and morals [12–17].

17.7 Conclusion

TinyML is currently redefining the application of ML to resources with limited capabilities; therefore, there is a growing need to tackle the legal, ethical, and regulatory issues that follow. Small ML systems processing information on edge devices have convenient advantages such as privacy, real-time, and latency processing. However, they also pose serious threats in areas such as data protection, compliance, and ethical implementation of AI in areas such as consumer electronics, autonomous vehicles, and healthcare. The role of privacy protection depends on the regulations and guidelines extensively: CCPA and GDPR. TinyML is spread, making it more difficult to do compliance because the existing data privacy legislation was not designed with the edge computers in mind. TinyML systems need new methods to comply including collective learning and differential privacy, which keep private data secure and help the models to work through privacy-protecting techniques.

References

1 Prakash, S., Balaji, J.N., Joshi, A., Surapaneni, K.M. Ethical conundrums in the application of Artificial Intelligence (AI) in healthcare—a scoping review of reviews. *J. Pers. Med.* 2022, 12, 1914.

2 Wang, C., Zhang, J., Lassi, N., Zhang, X. Privacy protection in using artificial intelligence for healthcare: chinese regulation in comparative perspective. *Healthcare* 2022, 10, 1878.

3 Panagopoulos, A., Minssen, T., Sideri, K., Yu, H., Compagnucci, M.C. Incentivizing the sharing of healthcare data in the AI era. *Comput. Law Secur. Rev.* 2022, 45, 105670.

4 Khalid, N., Qayyum, A., Qayyum, A., Al-Fuqaha, A., Qadir, J. Privacy-preserving artificial intelligence in healthcare: Techniques and applications. *Comput. Biol. Med.* 2023, 158, 106848.

5 Richardson, J.W., Smith, C., Curtis, S., Watson, S.E., Zhu, X., Barry, B.A., et al. Patient apprehensions about the use of artificial intelligence in healthcare. *Npj Digit. Med.* 2021, 4, 140.

6 Pereira, T., Morgado, J., Silva, F., Pelter, M.M., Dias, V., De Cássia Nogueira Barros, et al. Sharing biomedical data: Strengthening AI development in healthcare. *Healthcare* 2021, 9, 827.

7 Rahman, A., Hossain, M.S., Muhammad, G., Kundu, D., Debnath, T., Rahman, M.S., et al. Federated learning-based AI approaches in smart healthcare: Concepts, taxonomies, challenges and open issues, *Clust. Comput.* 2022, 26, 2271–2311.

8 Elhoseny, M., Haseeb, K., Shah, A.A., Ahmad, I., Jan, Z., Alghamdi, M.I. IoT solution for AI-enabled PRIVACY-PREServing with big data transferring: An application for healthcare using blockchain. *Energies* 2021, 14, 5364.

9 Madan, Bhagyashree S., Neha J. Zade, Neha P. Lanke, Shabana S. Pathan, Samir N. Ajani, and Prashant Khobragade. "Self-supervised transformer networks: Unlocking new possibilities for label-free data" *Panam. Math. J.*, vol. 34, no. 4, 2024, pp. 194-210. 10.52783/pmj.v34.i4.1878.

10 Ali, S., Abdullah, Armand, T.P.T., Athar, A., Hussain, A., Ali, M., et al. Metaverse in healthcare integrated with explainable AI and blockchain: Enabling immersiveness, ensuring trust, and providing patient data security. *Sensors* 2023, 23, 565.

11 Angerschmid, A., Zhou, J., Theuermann, K., Chen, F., Holzinger, A. Fairness and explanation in AI-informed decision making. *Mach. Learn. Knowl. Extr.* 2022, 4, 556–579.

12 Shinde, R., Patil, S., Kotecha, K., Ruikar, K. Blockchain for securing AI applications and open innovations. *J. Open Innov.: Technol. Mark. Complex.* 2021, 7, 189.

13 Tagde, P., Tagde, S., Bhattacharya, T., Tagde, P., Chopra, H., Akter, R., et al. Blockchain and artificial intelligence technology in E-health. *Environ. Sci. Pollut. Res.* 2021, 28, 52810–52831.

14 Munjal, K., Bhatia, R. A systematic review of homomorphic encryption and its contributions in healthcare industry. *Complex Intell. Syst.* 2022, 9, 3759–3786.

15 Mosaiyebzadeh, F., Pouriyeh, S., Parizi, R.M., Sheng, Q.Z., Han, M., Zhao, L., et al. Privacy-enhancing technologies in federated learning for the internet of healthcare things: A survey. *Electronics* 2023, 12, 2703.

16 Keshta, I. AI-driven IoT for smart health care: Security and privacy issues. *Inform. Med. Unlocked* 2022, 30, 100903.

17 Olatunji, I.E., Rauch, J., Katzensteiner, M., Khosla, M. A review of anonymization for healthcare data. *Big Data* 2022.

Index

d

k

m

S

t

y

z

www.ingramcontent.com/pod-product-compliance
Lightning Source LLC
La Vergne TN
LVHW021048221026
850618LV00045B/29
* 9 7 8 1 3 9 4 3 5 1 3 7 4 *